KENNEDY VS. CARTER

KENNEDY VS. CARTER

The 1980 Battle for
the Democratic Party's Soul

Timothy Stanley

UNIVERSITY PRESS OF KANSAS

© 2010 by the University Press of Kansas
All rights reserved

Published by the University Press of Kansas (Lawrence, Kansas 66045), which was
organized by the Kansas Board of Regents and is operated and funded by Emporia
State University, Fort Hays State University, Kansas State University, Pittsburg State
University, the University of Kansas, and Wichita State University

Library of Congress Cataloging-in-Publication Data

Stanley, Timothy.
    Kennedy vs. Carter : the 1980 battle for the Democratic Party's soul / Timothy Stanley.
        p.   cm. .
    Includes bibliographical references and index.
    ISBN 978-0-7006-1702-9 (cloth : alk. paper)
        1. Presidents—United States—Election—1980. 2. Kennedy, Edward M. (Edward Moore),
1932–2009. 3. Carter, Jimmy, 1924– 4. Political campaigns—United States—History—
20th century. 5. Primaries—United States—History—20th century. 6. Democratic Party
(U.S.)—History—20th century. 7. Presidential candidates—United States—Biography.
8. Presidents—United States—Biography. 9. Legislators—United States—Biography.
10. United States. Congress. Senate—Biography. I. Title. II. Title: Kennedy versus Carter.
    E875.S74 2010
    324.973—dc22

British Library Cataloguing-in-Publication Data is available.

Printed in the United States of America

10 9 8 7 6 5 4 3 2 1

Dedicated to RW
Accipere quam facere praestat injuriam!

Contents

A photograph section follows page 56.

Preface

I began this project at a moment when the Democratic Party seemed to be in terminal decline. In 2004, they nominated a vacillating centrist, John Kerry, as their presidential candidate. Despite being a handsome, articulate senator, and despite running in the midst of a difficult war and a poor economic forecast, Kerry was defeated by incumbent Republican George W. Bush by 3 million votes. The European press was astonished, and liberals in the United States were despondent. Many were convinced that America was an innately conservative country, and this was confirmed by a general trend in historiography and political science of pessimism toward its capacity for social reform. Only a minority argued that Kerry's problem was that his centrist message had failed to energize a natural Democratic majority.

When I finished this project four years later, the world was a completely different place. Barack Obama was elected in a convincing victory, bringing a message of change that embraced many old-fashioned tenets of U.S. liberalism. He pledged to introduce universal (albeit voluntary) health insurance, spend the country's way out of a recession, and end the war in Iraq. Most importantly, his color and personal history represented a triumph of American meritocratic values over centuries of racism. Interestingly, the prominent role that Senator Edward Kennedy played at the party's nominating convention was not a vote loser (as it was so often claimed in the past) but an emotional, triumphant celebration of liberal values and ambitions. He reminded the country of his own presidential candidacy nearly thirty years earlier, declaring, "The work begins anew. The hope rises again. And the dream lives on."

Obama's election suggests that Americans can get elected on a relatively liberal platform, if the conditions are right. Of course there are many other reasons why he was elected too, and the purpose of this book is not to provide a blueprint for liberal electoral victory. But history cannot be separated from the context in which it is written, and I am somewhat smug that the argument I began making four years ago in articles and conference papers has been proved so prescient.

My simple ambition in writing this book was to explore a seminal moment in American political history and to turn it on its head. A vast volume of literature on American politics in the 1970s had appeared since the late 1990s, much of it scornful of liberal performance and potential. It argued that while President Jimmy Carter had been a moderate, decent man, his base had failed to appreciate the changing dynamics of the era. The American public rediscovered its innate conservatism in the 1970s, so the orthodoxy goes, and were in no mood to spend vast sums on new social programs, protect the civil rights of gays, or bail out blighted urban centers. The liberals railed against Jimmy Carter, and in an act of extreme and arrogant opportunism, Edward Kennedy agreed to lead them in an ill-considered, futile charge against the president. His defeat in the 1980 Democratic presidential primaries suggested that liberalism was on the decline even among Democrats. Carter's defeat in the fall (assisted by Kennedy's personal attacks) confirmed that America was a conservative country. The relative domination of the presidency by Republicans until 2008 was the outcome of the mistakes and blunders of the 1970s.

My original intention was to write a study of the 1980 Democratic primaries that confirmed this view. However, it quickly changed direction. My first glances at polling information, internal communications, and newspaper accounts revealed that far from being an outside hope in the 1980 battle, Kennedy was a very strong candidate indeed. He actually started the campaign season as the front-runner and consistently led Reagan in trial heats. Much of the Carter administration was convinced it would lose, and in 1979 at least, the GOP regarded Kennedy as the strongest possible candidate. I discovered that the reasons why the senator lost the election were complex and do not provide a damning indictment of liberalism's weaknesses—far from it. The American public in the 1970s was neither liberal nor conservative, but instead anxious, angry, and desperate for leadership from any direction.

The book evolved into a study of how Jimmy Carter alienated his own supporters, how and why Ted Kennedy ran against him, what the Kennedy campaign has to say about America in the 1970s, and, finally, whether or not the 1980 election really was a turning point in electoral history. I hope that it will be of interest to social and political historians; Kennedy's candidacy has never been the subject of such a study, and much of the literature on the 1980 campaign tells its story from the landslide backward. But I also hope that it will be of interest to political scientists and policy makers. The book explores how one liberal won the hearts and minds of the American public and built a remarkable, unique coalition out of urban and suburban voters of all stripes. It also examines how a president elected on a relatively liberal platform angered liberals, divided his party, and lost the nation. Both of these issues should fascinate Team Obama.

I thank my supervisor, Professor Tony Badger of Clare College, for his advice and assistance in completing this project. I am profusely grateful for the opportunities he has given me, in addition to his patience and good humor. Prof. Ed Berkowitz, Dr. Gareth Davies, Dr. Andrew Preston, Dr. Dominic Sandbrook, Prof. Bruce Schulman, Dr. Joshua Zeitz, and Prof. Julian Zelizer also gave me plenty of good counsel.

Trinity College provided the bulk of the funding toward this study, for which I am very thankful. I would also like to acknowledge support from the Sarah Norton Foundation and the Radcliffe Institute at Harvard, which provided me with a research fellowship to complete work on the National Organization for Women papers. They proved exceptional hosts, and I enjoyed presenting my findings to them very much. Also great hosts were Prof. Olson, Carl Ashley, and the monks of St. Anselm's, with whom I had many wonderful conversations about Niebuhr, Maritain, and the past and future of U.S. liberalism.

This research was made possible by the support of a number of archival institutions, the staffs of all of which were helpful and kind. Bruce Montgomery at the University of Boulder is especially deserving of mention.

I also have to thank all of those interviewed here, and their staffs for coordinating our meetings. I was struck by the gracious use of their time. Deserving of special thanks are Peter Mandler and Harold Meyerson, who put me in touch with all the socialist sources, and Adam Clymer, who gave me an introduction to most of the Democratic officials I interviewed. This work would not have been possible without Adam and his friendship. It was inspired by his biography of Kennedy and his incisive and brilliant journalism.

I must thank my mother, who has doted on me unhealthily all these years, and my good friends Dom. Alban, Alex, Chris, Daniel, Elizabeth, Hannah, Nick, Rupert, and Sarah. Fr. Ray made this last year of writing a joy. Dr. Madsen Pirie was encouraging and kind, and I will always value our friendship. I am grateful to anyone who helped talk me out of going on *The Apprentice* to complete this book instead.

KENNEDY VS. CARTER

Introduction

This is the story of the 1980 Democratic presidential primaries, when the liberal senator Edward M. Kennedy challenged the moderate incumbent President Jimmy Carter for their party's nomination. The historical importance of the contest cannot be overstated. Nineteen eighty was a bad year for Democrats and is widely regarded as marking the end of the party's postwar domination of U.S. electoral politics. The Kennedy-Carter clash tore the Democrats apart and contributed to Jimmy Carter's landslide defeat at the hands of Republican Ronald Reagan in the fall. Not until 2008 would a Democratic ticket ever again win a majority of the popular vote in a presidential election. The primaries took place against a backdrop of economic decline, cultural upheaval, and humiliation overseas. The Democratic Party was bitterly divided over how to respond to these challenges, and the cautious Jimmy Carter and the radical Edward Kennedy represented wildly different approaches to complex and seemingly intractable problems. In 1980, Democrats engaged in a devastatingly divisive public debate about the purpose of their party and the best way to advance social reform in contemporary America. Why this debate happened, how it was resolved, and what it had to say about the state of the nation on the eve of the "Reagan Revolution" are the subject of this study.

This book can be read not only as the story of a particular election, but as a revisionist history of the 1970s as a whole. The decade has often been portrayed as a conservative one, when religious reawakening, chronic inflation, and tax revolt revived the fortunes of the Republican Party and forged a new electoral majority that set the nation on a rightward path for the next thirty years. And yet Edward Kennedy's liberal insurgency offers an interesting challenge to many existing historical assumptions about the politics of the decade. Although he was ultimately unsuccessful, his crusade to rebuild the ailing New Deal coalition was energetic and popular enough to suggest that America was not quite as profoundly conservative a country in the 1970s as many historians and political scientists have hitherto suggested. Indeed, the narrative of the primaries offers a fresh and surprising alternative perspective of an overlooked and much misunderstood decade.[1]

Frustrated by three years of ineffectual government that had failed to control spiraling inflation and unemployment, Edward Kennedy entered the primaries in November 1979. The senator and the president championed two very different visions of liberalism. Kennedy argued that Democrats should offer voters a "choice, not an echo." His liberalism blended the social democratic economics of the New Deal with the social tolerance of the 1960s. Putting principle before opportunism and even consensus, he argued that working- and middle-class Americans would only vote Democrat if the party offered them a real alternative to Republican policies. In one of his finest speeches, Kennedy argued that "sometimes a party must sail against the wind. We cannot afford to drift or lie at anchor. We cannot heed the call of those who say it is time to furl the sail."[2] Although he always acknowledged that the political wind was blowing rightward in the 1970s, Kennedy nevertheless urged Democrats to let their consciences be their compass and bear left.[3]

In contrast, Jimmy Carter thought that the Democratic Party should not challenge its epoch but seek to better reflect it. He embraced a cautious, frugal kind of politics that emphasized efficiency and competence over activism and passion. He believed that government should be small, but do certain compassionate things well. Progress came incrementally through the creation of public consensus around specific policy points. Unlike Kennedy, the cultural revolution of the 1960s largely passed Jimmy Carter by. This was not to say that he was reactionary, rather that his values were steeped in the politics of the Deep South and the moral preoccupations of the small-town Baptist church. Indeed, their different approaches to government reflected the very different upbringings of Kennedy and Carter. The former was the brother of a president and a wealthy East Coast playboy. The latter was a humble small-business man from Georgia who remarked upon his inauguration that he desperately wanted to walk into the White House because he had "never seen inside."[4]

Democrats ultimately chose Carter's leadership over Kennedy's. Although the senator enjoyed a healthy lead over the president in early polls, his support crumbled throughout the winter of 1979. He was beaten 2–1 in the first-in-the-nation Iowa caucus of January 1980 and suffered an almost unbroken string of defeats through to March. He then picked up some spectacular comeback victories, starting with

New York and Connecticut, but it was too little, too late. Despite a widely supported move to hold an "open convention" in August, Carter secured the nomination for a second time on the first ballot. But his victory was a hollow one. The nation slipped further into recession throughout the primaries, rendering the president's reelection unlikely. In November 1980, conservative Republican Ronald Reagan was elected in a 51–41 percent landslide. The GOP also gained a majority in the Senate—the first time they controlled a house of Congress since 1954. It looked as though America had entered a new political era.

Democrats in Decline

Most historians put the blame for the humiliating defeats of 1980 squarely on the shoulders of liberals—particularly stalwart, uncompromising liberals like Edward Kennedy. Liberalism in the 1970s, they argue, was chronically disunited and increasingly unpopular. First, the Democrats were torn apart by the generational conflict between older New Deal liberals and the plethora of young social protest movements that emerged in the 1960s, referred to in this study as the New Politics. The New Politics campaigned for an immediate end to the Vietnam war, massively expanded welfare programs, personal liberation, and environmentalism, and against the domination of politics by so-called power elites. Many of the blue-collar (skilled and nonskilled manual workers) constituent groups attracted to the Democratic Party's position on bread-and-butter economic issues were nonetheless culturally conservative and therefore alienated by the Democrats' flirtation with the New Politics.[5] The presence of feminists, hippies, yippies, Black Power advocates, gays, lesbians, and overt socialists within the party left many working-class Americans feeling abandoned and marginalized by a movement that had once claimed to represent them. Yet no Democrat could hope to govern the party or the country without the support of both the New Politics and the New Dealers. This created a cultural barrier to effective and decisive leadership that historians have suggested no Democrat was able to overcome in the 1970s.[6]

Second, growing disunity within the ranks corresponded with (and often sped) declining popularity. Most political scientists argue that while the Democratic Party slipped to the left throughout the 1970s, American society swung to the right. Thus, 1980 was a realigning election within which a long-term trend toward conservatism was confirmed by a landslide victory for the GOP. Postwar socioeconomic change forced liberals to make choices that were principled but electorally disastrous. In the 1960s the Democratic Party's support for civil rights began the undoing of its natural majority by alienating the South. Its difficult alliance with the social protest and peace movements in the early 1970s further alienated ethnic white middle- and working-class support in the North. Inflation and the association of liberals with profligate spending laid the seeds of a final realignment in 1980. Reagan's victory was then a popular repudiation of liberalism and big government, and the beginning of an era of conservative political hegemony.[7] The Hollywood actor did for the Republicans in 1980 what Roosevelt had done for the Democrats in 1932: he established their status as the new majority party.

There was then a push-pull dynamic at work: Americans were repulsed by liberalism's failures and attracted to conservatism's potential.[8] Tired orthodox liberal remedies to recession, such as massive public spending projects, appeared to have fueled rather than alleviated recession. These had sparked stagflation, an odd combination of high inflation and high unemployment that defied economic orthodoxy: one is supposed to dampen the other.[9] The public registered discontent first in a series of statewide tax revolts and then by the election of a conservative administration. The middle class was beginning to "define its interests in terms of a rollback of government programs aimed at helping other groups." The Republican revolution thus reflected the wider will of the nation, and many Democrats have argued that their party still needs to learn the central lesson of the paradigmatic election of 1980: that America is a fundamentally conservative country.[10]

For many historians, the political significance of the 1970s therefore was the dramatic decline of liberalism—a decline predicated on its failure to realize that political and economic circumstances had changed dramatically. Jimmy Carter is often given credit for recognizing this state of affairs and attempting to endorse traditionally conservative positions to stymie Republican success.[11] Plagued by a divided and antiquated Democratic Party, inflation, and growing public antipathy toward liberal economics, his political options were severely restricted.[12] Nevertheless, he tried to govern outside of special interests, did not exclusively identify with orthodox Democratic politics, and prioritized "moral leadership" over sectional philosophies.[13] Carter has subsequently gained admirers for his attempt to construct a new electoral coalition around moderate fiscal and social policy, a strategy that arguably foreshadowed that of President Bill Clinton in the 1990s.[14]

In contrast, Kennedy's defiant call to "sail against the wind" was evidence that liberals failed to recognize that the coming revolution was inevitable and irreversible.[15] If they had perhaps modified their rhetoric and dropped some of their commitments in 1980, then they may have limited the damage that the realignment wrought.[16] Kennedy has been typically presented as the unenthusiastic puppet of interest groups, forced to run by a nepotistic political machine hubristically seeking to maintain political influence.[17] His candidacy was even faintly ridiculous, taking into consideration his involvement in the death of an intern in 1969 and his well-publicized marital breakdown.[18] "The fact that a . . . politician like Ted Kennedy could command more respect than Carter in 1979," opined one historian, "spoke volumes about the lack of rationality in the Democratic Party."[19] Liberals were more concerned with ideological purity than winning elections—they were "intellectually clueless and politically inept."[20] Kennedy's approach to economics was fiscally illiterate and politically insensitive. Some political scientists have argued that the national process of disillusion with liberalism was echoed within the Democrats and that Kennedy's ready identification with social libertarianism put him out of step even with his own party.[21] His defeat was inevitable, and his initial popularity was based solely on his family name rather than his own abilities.[22]

Kennedy vs. Carter Reconsidered

However, this interpretation of Kennedy's defeat belies the facts. Edward Kennedy was a surprisingly popular presidential candidate in 1978 and 1979. He was the overwhelming choice not only of the Democratic Party, but of the American public too, who consistently told pollsters that they preferred him to Ronald Reagan. Liberals endorsed the senator not out of pique, but because they thought he was very probably the next president of the United States. His defeat in the primaries was far from inevitable, and their outcome was influenced by a series of foreign crises that gave President Carter the opportunity to regain popularity. It is no exaggeration to say that the outcome of the 1980 Democratic nomination process hinged on happenings thousands of miles away, in Iran and Afghanistan. Carter manipulated public opinion on events within these countries with admirable acumen. He used patriotic support and the considerable political and financial clout of his office to engineer a series of early victories that directed momentum away from Kennedy. So pronounced were these factors of historical accident that, in her detailed account of the 1980 elections, journalist Elizabeth Drew concluded that "there are those who believe Kennedy's politics are all wrong for this period, but this hypothesis cannot be tested, given the clouds on the campaign."[23]

Kennedy then lost the early primaries, and lost them decisively. Historians often refer to these results when they criticize his campaign. However, in the later primaries, he won remarkable, deep victories in several states by welding together the ordinarily diffuse "Kennedy coalition" of voters that is traditionally associated with his brother Robert.[24] This coalition comprised ideological liberals, traditional Democratic constituencies (white, blue-collar workers), and newly enfranchised minorities (blacks, Mexican Americans, the very poorest).[25] In 1980 the coalition gave Edward Kennedy upset victories in ordinarily conservative states such as Arizona and South Dakota. It also allowed him to win industrial states such as New York, Michigan, and Pennsylvania. Importantly, Kennedy showed electoral strength among those groups that political scientists have argued were becoming more conservative on economic and social questions. He not only revived the New Deal coalition, but also expanded it to include urban and suburban conservatives.

The senator's popularity within his own party stretched across the ideological fractures that undoubtedly existed within the liberal family in the 1970s. He reached out to disparate groups whose competition for control of the Democratic Party had torn it apart in the late 1960s and early 1970s. One of the greatest challenges facing any liberal in the 1970s was finding a way to bring these different constituencies and their representatives together—to carve out a message that would unify a messy, incoherent, quarrelsome grass roots into a party fit for government. It is widely argued within political science that the Democratic Party is an awkward coalition and that keeping all of its constituent parts happy at once is difficult but crucial for victory at the ballot box.[26]

During the primaries, Edward Kennedy demonstrated a remarkable—if not unique—ability to do precisely this. Among his support could be counted labor; feminists; lesbian, gay, bisexual, and transgender groups; socialists; hawks; New Deal politicians; antiwar activists; and environmentalists. This was one of the key strengths of the Kennedy candidacy that historians have unfairly overlooked. But while personality and folk memory surrounding the Kennedy family played their part, the remarkable coalition of New Politics and New Deal factions that backed the senator was not attributable purely to him alone.

In 1980 Kennedy rode a momentum within the Democratic Party of increased alliance building, greater unity, and the legitimization of social and cultural liberalism that began in the mid-1970s.[27] This process was made possible by the emergence of universalist ideas, such as national health insurance and full employment legislation. Such proposals placed an emphasis on economic programs that elevated the poorest while benefiting the majority.[28] New coalitions were constructed in the mid-1970s to lobby for such proposals that brought together labor, the civil rights movement, liberal congressional representatives, religious groups (including most mainstream Protestant and Catholic churches), feminists, and even some on the fiscally conservative wing of the party. Therefore, the unity among liberals that Kennedy promised was accumulating long before his candidacy was declared. Similarly, Kennedy did not invent opposition to Jimmy Carter. He merely gave voice to a growing movement of rebels who began organizing dissent long before he declared his candidacy. The Kennedy candidacy was born out of a renaissance of coalitional activity among the American left that has been almost entirely overlooked by political historians.

The liberal bogeyman of U.S. politics, Edward Kennedy, was in fact quantifiably more popular than both Jimmy Carter and Ronald Reagan in 1980. Much of the evidence presented here for the senator's surprising electoral strength comes from public opinion and voter exit polls. The use of such information is inevitably controversial because interviewees can lie, questions can be selective, samples can be inappropriate, and data compilation can be inexact. However, polls remain the only practical method by which political scientists can determine what the American people are thinking at a given moment. Although exit poll data are far from perfect, they do provide historical snapshots of popular opinion and cannot fairly be dismissed out of hand. In this book, a wide range of polls has been used with the aim of producing as accurate a conclusion as possible, including interviews conducted by political campaigns and media outlets. Despite all the possible variables, throughout the 1980 campaign season, these various polls showed a consistent picture and rarely contradicted each other. They all confirmed that Edward Kennedy was denied the nomination by a series of historical accidents, and if these had not taken place, then it is conceivable that he could have defeated Jimmy Carter in the primaries and fought Ronald Reagan in the fall. Had he done so, it would have been on a platform that was supported by much of the American public—a platform of universal health care, massive federal job programs, and price/wage controls.

The implications of such a reading of the 1980 campaign are obvious. If it can be demonstrated that Kennedy was capable of erecting a
potentially popular movement of economic protest built around liberal
platforms and themes, then it would seem inappropriate to regard the
1970s as simply a period of encroaching conservatism. A better, more
nuanced political history is needed.

This book begins not in 1980 but in 1976, the year Jimmy Carter
surprised the world by winning his party's nomination. The story
starts here to show just how divided the Democratic Party was in the
1970s and to illustrate the kind of challenges that the new president
faced in governing an apparently ungovernable nation. But the wider
goal of this narrative is also to give liberal activists something many
historians have hitherto denied them: a voice in their own history.
Liberals from many different backgrounds and within very different
organizations (United Auto Workers, Americans for Democratic Action, National Organization for Women) demonstrated a remarkable
degree of self-discipline and unity in 1976, and this contributed significantly to Carter's election. What then happened from 1977 to 1979, as
the administration alienated its own base, is an excellent case study in
how *not* to govern as a Democrat—or, at the very least, in the dangers
of undervaluing the support of the party's grass roots. Many liberals
believed that Carter failed to exploit the Democratic domination of
electoral politics in the late 1970s. They charged him with betraying
the markedly liberal platform on which he had been elected in 1976.
In 1979 they felt confident enough to break from Carter and attack his
record because they regarded Kennedy's nomination and election as
almost inevitable. Kennedy's campaign was not his own, and to properly comprehend it, one has to understand why liberal Democrats felt
moved to draft him into the race.

In hindsight, the 1970s were a period of conservative growth and
liberal decline; militant liberals, unable to realize these facts, were responsible for many of their own defeats. But Kennedy's candidacy and
the support it enjoyed imply that from their vantage point, liberals
may not have been entirely unjustified in believing the potential for
liberal reform still existed. The degree to which they were correct is
the key concern of this study. We cannot totally rewrite history; the
1970s did witness a political backlash against big government and social license. But a case can be made for greater sensitivity toward liberal voices, a more nuanced understanding of the value of historical
accident in authoring political history, and a more generous appreciation for the enduring popularity of American liberalism.

1

Jimmy Carter Goes to Washington

Jimmy Carter was inaugurated president on 20 January 1977. Although many historians have treated Carter's presidency as the end of an era, at the time, it felt like the beginning of a new one. Carter and his wife, Rosalynn, pleasantly surprised the crowds that lined Pennsylvania Avenue by choosing not to drive to the White House in a limousine, but rather to stroll hand in hand as if they were on their way to a picnic. One observer reported, "As he walked along, with [his daughter] Amy prancing, jumping, and dancing along at his side, he was shattering recent Presidential practice and legend—the idea that a President must be remote and removed from the people." This had been the theme of his election campaign, and although some suspected that it was a mere trick of style, his words at the podium assured America that it promised a substantive change in policy too. "We have learned that more is not necessarily better," he told the crowd, "that even our great nation has its recognized limits, and that we can neither answer all questions nor solve all problems. We cannot afford to do everything, nor can we afford to lack boldness as we meet the future. So together, in a spirit of individual sacrifice, we must simply do our best." After the hubris of Vietnam, the greed of Watergate, and the disappointment of the Great Society, Carter offered America humility. His vision of government was one that was both compassionate and competent, active yet modest.[1] Although this vision seemed to many to be calculated to appeal to floating voters, those who new Jimmy Carter best appreciated that it represented an earnest and radical departure from the liberal tradition. Arguably, this was just what America was looking for.[2]

Why Jimmy Runs

Jimmy Carter was a genuine son of the South. He was born and raised in the tiny southwest Georgia hamlet of Plains near the larger town of Americus. The family had lived in Georgia for several generations, and his great-grandfather, Private L. B. Walker Carter, fought for the Confederacy. Jimmy's father was a prominent business owner in the community, and his mother was a registered nurse. The land that bred this future president was God-fearing, patriotic, humble, and populist in instinct. The impact of Franklin D. Roosevelt's New Deal was both personal and mixed.[3] "We learned to appreciate the stability of the agricultural programs brought in by federal government action," remembered Carter, "but my father never forgave President Franklin Roosevelt for requiring that hogs be slaughtered and cotton be plowed up when these production control programs first went into effect. He never again voted for Roosevelt."[4]

Jimmy Carter attended Georgia Southwestern College and then the Georgia Institute of Technology before being admitted to Annapolis. He graduated from the academy sixtieth in a class of 822 and went on to join the U.S. Navy as a seaman aboard an atomic-powered submarine. Carter trained in nuclear engineering and rose to the grade of senior lieutenant.[5] The death of his father cut his promising naval career short, and he returned home to tend to his family's peanut business. He was an ambitious man, and following his election to the state senate, he ran for governor in 1966. He was easily defeated but refused to give up. Carter remodeled his rhetoric and style to become more homely and populist, and after conducting a conservative campaign in 1970 (which was probably necessary to get elected), he was inaugurated governor in 1971.[6] In office Carter was branded one of the "new Southern governors," a group of Democratic moderates who eschewed racist appeals and who were pro-business and technocratic. He reorganized state government to make it more efficient, appointed blacks to official positions, hung Martin Luther King's portrait in the state capitol, and extended educational benefits. It should be noted, however, that he also resisted court-ordered busing to desegregate schools and fought the Supreme Court to retain the use of the death penalty at a state level.[7]

As the executive of a state rich in electoral votes, Jimmy Carter met many presidential aspirants and entertained several at the governor's mansion in Atlanta. His reaction to them was a revealing mixture of honesty and hubris. "We decided," said his wife Rosalynn, "that

Jimmy knew a lot more about a lot of things than did those men who were running for President."[8] Carter probably started thinking about a presidential run as early as 1971, and in 1972 two men who worked for him, Hamilton Jordan and Peter Bourne, suggested he draw up a plan of action. Jordan wrote Carter a memo in which he argued that America was unhappy with the reelection of Republican president Richard Nixon. The country had been forced to vote for the incumbent because the Democratic Party seemed radical, divided, and out of touch. Its presidential nominee, South Dakota senator George McGovern, was an anti–Vietnam war activist who had been tarred as a socialist and a libertine. His views on "acid, amnesty, and abortion," which were wildly exaggerated by the media, tagged him as a voice piece of cultural revolution, and President Nixon exploited his poorly thought-out welfare policies to suggest (erroneously) that he was a careless spender too.[9] His nomination had split the party, alienating older blue-collar supporters. Even the powerful AFL-CIO sat out the election in protest—the first time it had not endorsed a presidential nominee in forty years.[10] Jimmy Carter himself had been a part of a fledgling "Anyone But McGovern" movement that had tried to deny McGovern the nomination at the Miami convention.[11] McGovern went down to a 2–1 defeat in the fall, and its memory still haunts the Democratic Party today. For many, the South Dakotan became an emblem of the reckless, militant, self-indulgent liberalism of the 1970s.[12]

After the election, Hamilton Jordan detected "a general distrust of government and politicians at all levels" and suggested that an outsider candidate would stand a chance against a wide field of well-established but unloved hacks. Moreover, McGovern's candidacy had shown how a little-known politician with a loyal constituency of party irregulars could capture the nomination without much money or personnel. Before 1972, presidential nominees were selected at conventions by delegates, most of whom were appointed by political bosses. Primaries, in which registered Democrats voted for the candidate of their choice, could be used as an indicator of popularity and electability, but their result was not binding. In this manner, the party establishment, especially big labor, ensured the exclusion of antiestablishment radicals.[13] However, after rules changes came into effect in the late 1960s (written in part by McGovern himself), the system opened up.[14] The role of primaries and caucuses, wherein small groups of local Democrats gathered to vote for a nominee in a specific locale, was expanded, and quotas were introduced to ensure that the delegations represented their states' racial, gender, and generational makeup.[15] As a result, the power of labor and state parties over delegate selection declined, and more ethnic minorities, women, and young people were elected. These folks had loyalty to nothing but their own conscience.[16]

The nomination process was transformed. Presidential candidates now had to campaign for a year at a time to perform well enough in early primaries to build up a sizable number of delegates to take to the convention. They had to appeal to motivated special interest groups, not politicians or even necessarily the general public. The result was further issue militancy and polarization. But importantly, it also opened the process up to outsider candidates with little money or authority, but plenty of activist fervor. This was the system that made Jimmy Carter's nomination in 1976 possible.[17] Hamilton Jordan believed that if Carter started running now, built up a grassroots campaign, and stressed his outsider status, then he could pull off an early upset victory that would gain him national attention and momentum.[18] Enthralled by the proposition, Carter declared his candidacy.

The Carter Message

What was the character of this courageous would-be nominee? A technocratic problem solver, Governor Carter approached issues from a nonideological perspective. He wallowed in detail and purposefully chose staff members with contradictory philosophies in order to get different points of view.[19] He was a politician who saw the world not in black and white, but rather in various shades of gray. He loathed demagoguery and cheap appeals to the heart.[20] His speaking style was reserved, modest, and highly technical. This frustrated many commentators, who could not understand his ability to excite voters with his banal and complex answers to straightforward questions.[21] But lifelessness at rallies came across as reasonableness on TV. He also had a beautiful smile and an ability to project old-fashioned gentility. The flip side of his character was that he could be cold and a little mean. He despised ideologues and grifters, regarding himself as being above the mud and blood of everyday politics. He bore grudges, remembered slights, was impatient with fools, and was overly sensitive to criticism.[22] In 1988 a leading presidential contender flew to Plains to ask Carter for his advice. The trip was intended as a display of respect for an elder statesman. However, Carter probably interpreted it as a grubby effort to elicit his endorsement. The candidate and his wife were greeted politely but coolly and felt decidedly unwelcome. After a three-hour flight, they weren't even offered a cup of tea. "So much," reflected the wife to her husband, "for Southern hospitality." Any other politician would have welcomed the attention; Carter scorned it.[23]

But in 1976 the public knew barely anything at all about Jimmy Carter, and perversely, that was probably his greatest strength. In the antiestablishment atmosphere of the 1970s, enigma was a virtue. His national exposure was limited, and he lacked a power base in the party outside of Georgia—organizational weaknesses, yes, but proof that Jimmy was his own man.[24] He had served as the chairman of the 1974 Democratic congressional campaign committee, but he barely registered in the early polls. So hopeless did his cause seem that when he first told his mother that he planned to run for president, she replied, "President of what?"[25]

Yet Carter understood the depth of the anti-Washington mood and the palpable yearning among the general public for something new. In 1974, Richard Nixon was forced to quit office after being accused of involvement in a break-in at the Democratic Party's headquarters at the Watergate Hotel. A lengthy congressional inquiry revealed that the president bugged his staff, engaged in campaign smears, bribed, cajoled, and probably avoided taxes.[26] This was the imperial presidency at its worst—a system of executive privilege and power that seemed out of control and responsible to no one. Fear and paranoia gripped politics, and fed a profound distrust of elected officials. Nixon was pardoned by his successor, Gerald Ford, and many Americans thought that the establishment had helped the crooked president escape justice. After Watergate, new checks were placed on the presidency in an effort (not always successful) to limit its power. Although this rebalancing was necessary and healthy, it reduced the presidency's authority dramatically and increased antipathy toward the kind of big or activist government that Democrats often used to advance social reform. This would prove to be a problem when Jimmy Carter came to govern. But as an outsider candidate, popular antigovernment feeling played into his hands.[27]

Jimmy Carter confounded many political commentators because they could not understand his appeal.[28] What they missed was that it was his very vagueness that people latched on to—his speaking in terms of general themes and his desire to be a president that "feels your pain and shares your dreams and takes his strength and his wisdom and his courage from you."[29] When talking about both enduring love and the intangible nature of modern problems, he expressed better than anyone America's crisis of confidence in itself. To quote one journalist, "What national leaders and other candidates perceive as a political crisis is actually a spiritual crisis, and that more spiritual communication is the best way to reach Americans. . . . The barefoot boy with cheek is mixing politics with religion." Indeed, Carter's pronounced and open Christianity earned him the support of much of the evangelical Protestant community and allowed him to address America's sense of distress in a far more profound way than any of his opponents could. "Without embarrassment (to himself or his audience) Carter is able to softly preach love."[30] The more cynical (and more liberal) lead columnist of the *New Republic* wrote, "My impression is that audiences yearn to believe Jimmy Carter. They're looking for something."[31] The blank canvas of Carter's personality allowed people to project anything onto it that they wished.

Jimmy Carter's philosophy of good, small, efficient, humble government reflected wider suspicions that America was ungovernable.[32] America was paranoid, disillusioned, frightened, economically sick, and desperate for new hope and a return to old values. Crucially, it was fractured and divided too—between taxpayers and welfare recipients, pro-war and antiwar Americans, suburbs and city dwellers, the culturally hip and the culturally arcane. The 1960s were to blame. If the 1960s were a binge of reform, rebellion, protest, and permissiveness, then the 1970s were the painful morning after. The Vietnam war spawned an angry, ugly protest movement that many older Americas saw as naive and unpatriotic, engendering generational and cultural conflict.[33] Civil rights reform failed to end de facto segregation or violent unrest in Northern cities, and African Americans became progressively more militant in their demand for economic equality. Whites fled to the suburbs in retreat, leaving behind atrophy, crime, and underinvestment.[34] Social provision became a racialized issue. If the federal government was not giving away people's tax dollars to welfare queens, then they were redistributing jobs and degree programs through affirmative action. All of this made it much more difficult for liberals to sell welfare to American voters, and even more difficult to justify the kind of steps that were still desperately required to integrate the country.[35]

Established patterns of family life (often governed by patriarchy and repression) were collapsing. Feminism and gay liberation offered alternative lifestyles that liberated individuals from social conformity.[36] Violence on TV, sex education, long hair, public nudity, bed-ins, frequent use of pot, and free love were aesthetic rebellions that shocked the older generation.[37] But the organized forces of social change demanded more. The feminist movement campaigned for access to abortion, homemakers' rights, and an Equal Rights Amendment (ERA) that would enshrine equality within the constitution. They achieved a great deal: perhaps their greatest success was the Supreme Court's decision in *Roe v. Wade* (1973) that overturned many state laws against abortion.[38] Equally importantly, they gave a politicized space within which women might discover their own personhood. This was the identity revolution, whereby formerly marginalized groups began to organize, demand recognition, and fight for equal treatment.[39]

If the 1960s started a heady cultural revolution, the 1970s saw a counterrevolution, bolstered by religious revival. In an era of cultural flux, people sought certainty in traditional values and Christian faith. Evangelical congregations swelled and the televangelist was born—wealthy and powerful pastors who used television to send a message of redemption to an enormous home audience.[40] A coalition of conservative groups broadly known as the New Right perfected the art of protesting against social change and reversing it by courting or intimidating elected officials.[41] Organizations such as the antifeminist Eagle Forum, led by the brilliant Phyllis Schlafly, whipped up feverish opposition to liberal legislation.[42] For the women of the Eagle Forum, the ERA, with its provisions guaranteeing equal pay, access to divorce, no sexual discrimination, and, potentially, the right or duty to fight on the front line of any war, was not a liberating document but a threatening one. It undermined the social status of housewives, and it challenged traditional tenets of gender relations and responsibility. Thus many Americans who theoretically stood to gain from the cultural revolution rejected it and joined the swelling ranks of social conservatives.[43]

Vietnam, Watergate, and the cultural revolution had left America with an existential crisis. But America faced a real and physical one, too, in the form of economic decline. Precisely why the American economy suffered in the 1970s is a matter open to debate. It may well have been due to the military spending on the Vietnam war, the rising cost of labor, poor productivity, the inept application of price and wage controls during the Nixon administration, oil prices—or all of the above.[44] But we can be certain that the crisis began with the war between Israel and Egypt in 1973. The West supported Israel and was punished by the oil-producing Arab countries for its loyalty. They hiked up the price of oil, ending the era of cheap fuel and causing terrible shortages and growing public hysteria.[45] Higher oil prices sparked an inflationary spiral, and wages and prices rose and rose to keep up with each other. Inflation exaggerated imbalances and imperfections in the domestic economy, and rising costs led to closures and unemployment. The era of stagflation was born—a bizarre and fearful combination of high inflation and high unemployment.[46]

Stagflation was frightening because it defied traditional remedies of recession. Orthodoxy held that inflation and unemployment were symbiotically linked to each other and to the cyclical pressures of supply and demand. Most economists since the 1930s had accepted a trade-off between inflation and unemployment. In a period of recession, the government could risk spending more to alleviate unemployment. This in turn would cause inflation. However, when the economy improved, the government would cut spending to reduce inflation. This in turn would (probably) increase unemployment.[47] The problem with stagflation was that if an economy was experiencing both inflation and unemployment, then it was unclear precisely what to do.[48] Unemployment peaked at 8.5 percent in 1975, while inflation hovered at 10 percent. The worst-hit sectors were the traditional blue-collar industries regarded as the backbone of the American economy, especially car makers.[49]

Middle-class Americans were perhaps less keen than they had ever been before to bail out ailing sectors of the economy because inflation had already caused their taxes to spiral. As the cost of homes increased, so too did property taxes. As wages went up, people found themselves in new income tax brackets. Government spending, which had once been something that gave aid to middle-class Americans, became a drain on their personal finances.[50] The welfare queens were making money out of other people's misery. A new consensus emerged that saw big government as being not only authoritarian but inflationary too. No link between deficit spending and inflation has ever been proven, but politicians found one anyway. Policy makers argued that they faced a choice between raising and cutting spending, tackling unemployment and reducing inflation. The spending that was necessary to create job programs or raise welfare payments would cause the incomes of those in employment to decline. Politicians had to decide where the votes were—helping those out of work or those already in it.[51]

Jimmy Carter's message—that there were no simple solutions to the problems of America, that politicians were out of touch, and that the nation needed a spiritual renewal as much as a material one—suited his epoch perfectly. It provided few answers, although Carter would later show himself to be more conservative on economic matters than the average Democrat. But the message deflected criticism through avoiding specifics, while all the time suggesting to voters that Carter felt their pain in a way that politicians so far away in Washington did not.[52]

Liberalism Divided in the 1976 Democratic Primaries

America's paralysis was reflected in the troubled administration of President Gerald Ford. Conservative, but pragmatically so, Ford had to deal with both recession and collapsing confidence in government in the wake of Watergate.[53] Although the heavily Democratic Congress pressured him to pass into law new Social Security and health programs, as well as emergency funding for job creation schemes, Ford tried to reduce the budget deficit and cut taxes.[54] He fell back on an insistent use of the veto that led to gridlock on Capitol Hill. While the Democrats attacked the president for being mean, the Republicans attacked him for sapping America's defenses. Ford had entered negotiations to hand the Panama Canal back to the Panamanian government, as well as a further round of arms limitations talks with the USSR called SALT II. Combined with his (albeit qualified) support for the ERA and for *Roe v. Wade*, Ford seemed to lack conservative principles and philosophical backbone.[55] In 1976, Southern and Western Republican activists backed former California governor Ronald Reagan's attempt to take the party's presidential nomination away from him. Ford won renomination, but only just, and only after throwing sops to the radical right. The effort of disgruntled conservative activists to change their party's policies, foreshadowed liberals' own struggle within the Democratic Party four years later. The 1970s was a period of revival in ideological politics and grassroots mobilization. It energized both parties but sometimes alienated ordinary voters.[56]

The Democratic primary was no less divided, and the vast array of candidates (there were twelve—only a handful are discussed here) demonstrated just how splintered the party had become. Democrats were every bit as confused and fratricidal as their fellow countrymen. Their biggest controversy was Vietnam. In the 1968 Democratic primaries, incumbent president Lyndon Johnson was effectively forced out of the race by the antiwar candidacies of Minnesota senator Eugene McCarthy and New York senator Robert Kennedy. With his younger brother Edward serving as campaign manager, Kennedy won four out of five primaries that he entered in a frantic, frenetic contest that reflected the apocalyptic politics of the period. Shortly after winning the California primary, Robert was shot dead by a Palestinian American student called Sirhan Sirhan, shattering the dreams of the antiwar movement and depriving it of its most likely nominee.[57] The August nominating convention in Chicago was a violent disaster that saw peace campaigners clash with the police force of Mayor Richard Daley live on TV.[58]

In 1972 and 1976, the battles of 1968 were rehearsed over and over again in a succession of divisive presidential primaries. In 1976, the jingoistic, old-guard, New Deal wing of the party was represented by Senator Henry M. Jackson of Washington State. The New Dealers' view of government was shaped by their collective memory of the 1930s. Experience of mass unemployment convinced them that government had a responsibility to provide work and social support for needy Americans.[59] Compassion was a vote winner too. Franklin D. Roosevelt's New Deal fostered an alliance with powerful trade unions, a class-based politics, and the creation of a network of economic interest groups that gave the Democrats majority party status well into the 1960s.[60] Roosevelt's coalition combined the votes of the Solid South with those of the urban working class in the North: Catholics, Jews, large segments of the African American community, immigrants, blue-collar workers, and the ghetto poor.[61] The coalition's diverse elements, although ordinarily antagonistic (they fought for jobs, were culturally dissimilar, and often spoke different languages), could unite behind the New Deal because of the benefits it distributed to them. It provided jobs for the unemployed, higher prices for farmers, and cheap social housing, transforming the lives of an entire generation that experienced poverty and misery in the wake of the 1929 Wall Street crash.[62]

In the 1940s, under the shadow of McCarthyism, most New Deal liberals became virulent anticommunists, and they abandoned many of their shamelessly socialistic ambitions of the 1930s in favor of a rights-based liberalism that stressed issues related to quality of life and equality of opportunity.[63] The New Deal's values were well reflected in the Johnson administration, which balanced a commitment to eradicate poverty at home through its ambitious Great Society programs with a commitment to contain the spread of communism overseas.[64] Men like Henry Jackson, with his allies in the trade union movement, championed increased defense spending and a proto–social democratic response to stagflation. Jackson firmly believed that America could spend its way out of recession. He was also tough on law-and-order issues, skeptical of environmentalism, and opposed to the use of court-ordered busing to desegregate schools. When Jackson entered the presidential primaries of 1972 and 1976, he performed best among white blue-collar ethnics of European descent, Jewish voters (he was strongly pro-Israel), retirees, and self-proclaimed conservatives.[65]

At the beginning of the primaries, Jackson's major liberal opponent was Arizona congressman Mo Udall. A witty and laconic representative (Udall once suggested that the federal government might cure inflation by handing it over to the post office: "That'd sure slow it down"), he endorsed the traditional plethora of liberal programs (health care, federally funded education, and tax reform) and was socially tolerant. However, he was critical of military outlays, big business, and big labor, and he had once voted to support antiunion legislation in Congress.[66] Although middle-aged, Udall represented a younger generation of liberals known as the New Politics Democrats: liberals who had first cut their teeth in politics in the McCarthy and Kennedy campaigns of 1968. These liberals, drawn from the white-collar sectors of the new postwar economy, lacked their parents' partisanship, paranoia toward communism, and memories of mass poverty.[67] Rather, they were interested in causes that lay outside of class or party politics; indeed, they found politics-as-usual distasteful and anachronistic.[68] The alliance between liberal politicians such as Kennedy, McCarthy, and later McGovern, and these fresh young voters produced a New Politics and a vibrant challenge to the old political order.[69]

For the New Politics, Vietnam seemed to point to a wider sickness within American society and politics—a distasteful militarism and a pandering to bureaucratic authority.[70] More subtly, opposition to Vietnam highlighted the New Politics critique of New Deal economics.[71] The New Politics believed that President Johnson's promise of "guns and butter" (funding for both the Great Society and Vietnam) was fundamentally flawed. Not only had it self-evidently fueled inflation, but it had also demonstrated that federal policy was dictated by the needs of the "overgrown military-industrial complex."[72] The standard New Deal remedies for recession—"greater consumer purchasing power, more public works, and public employment"—were inadequate and even morally bankrupt.[73] Mo Udall argued that these typically amounted to pork-barrel economics, granting contracts or federal funds to politically powerful interest groups. Even the labor movement, which "intoxicated with success and seemingly unlimited profits and higher wages," had become "less productive" and thus inflationary.[74] Concern with the impact of excessive growth was reflected in the growing influence of the environmentalist and consumer movements, both of which prioritized the needs of consumers over producers.[75] This was reflected in Mo Udall's long-running campaign against open-cast mining.[76]

In the 1976 primaries, Udall performed best among young, better-educated voters employed in white-collar and public service jobs. The New Politics could be labeled a libertarian movement, one that rejected the materialism of the 1930s generation that placed an emphasis on productivity, growth, consumerism, industrial expansion, and personal advancement. The economics and philosophy of the New Politics wanted people to reevaluate their lives altogether, to live smaller, healthier existences that were possibly poorer but happier and free from the constraints of state or privately imposed power structures.[77] There was a kind of hip outrageousness to much of the New Politics. Running on a similar platform to Udall was former senator Fred Harris, who had also entered the 1972 contest under the controversial slogan "No More Bullshit."[78] In 1976 he performed poorly again, but he ran an innovative campaign that won plaudits from conservative commentators and even opponent Jimmy Carter.[79] Harris donned a cowboy hat and traversed the country in a beat-up pickup truck, sticking to populist, redistributive themes that stressed class interests over racial, gender, or regional identity.[80] It was a failed but laudable attempt to reclaim populism for the left and associate it with popular, antiestablishment imagery.

Incredibly, the man with the largest percentage of Democratic support at the beginning of the primaries was the neoracist governor of Alabama, George C. Wallace. He offered a populist platform that was mildly economically redistributive but socially conservative.[81] Wallace had run insurgent campaigns in 1968 and 1972 that had captured a great deal of blue-collar and rural support for its opposition to court-ordered busing and rising taxes. He enjoyed a natural bastion of support in the South that he expected to help maintain his front-runner status in the early primaries.[82]

Jimmy Carter ran against big names with natural, if diffuse, constituencies. Jackson enjoyed the (albeit tentative) support of a great number of unions, and Udall had environmentalists, peace activists, and consumer groups stumping for him.[83] But this did not deter Carter's unshakable self-belief. With little money and no media attention, he focused all of his effort on the Iowa caucus, the first in the nation. Other candidates invested their money in delegate-rich states like New York and California. But in rural Iowa, Carter pressed the flesh, stayed in people's homes, handed out flyers in the street, shook hands in supermarkets, and targeted churches.[84] On election day, he won just 28 percent and actually ran behind the uncommitted vote at 37 percent. But no matter how small or unrepresentative of typical Democratic voters, the Carter bloc gained him national attention and propelled him to the front of the race. Jimmy Carter's against-the-odds candidacy captured the popular imagination. The following week, he won the New Hampshire primary, and so began a string of victories that knocked out his main contenders and established his front-runner status: beating Wallace in Florida and North Carolina, Jackson in Pennsylvania, and Udall in Wisconsin.[85] In almost all cases, Carter won the rural areas but lost the cities.[86] In the South, he portrayed himself as a moderate alternative to Wallace, exploiting regional pride and a desire for integration into national politics after the trauma of the 1960s.[87] In the North, he cast himself as a conservative man of faith, building a firm bloc of support that, although nowhere near a majority of Democratic voters, held solidly throughout the primaries and delivered him winning pluralities. In this manner, a moderately conservative candidate probably out of touch with much of the Democratic polity was able to persistently beat a divided left.[88]

Liberals of every hue panicked. Galvanized by the possibility of losing the nomination to a conservative, many coalesced around an "Anybody but Carter" ticket, headed by young California governor Jerry Brown. Jerry Brown, like many New Politics people who entered mainstream politics in the 1970s, labeled himself as a neoliberal.[89] These neoliberals were elected en masse in typically marginal districts or states in the Democratic landslide of 1974, triggered by Watergate. With the winding down of Vietnam, they turned their attention to economic issues.[90] Although they were still committed to social liberalism, they were skeptical about the benefits of increased government spending.[91] They typically represented baby boomers entering middle age, living in the suburbs, and worrying about soaring prices and environmental degradation. Few were members of unions, and they expected their congressional representatives to put them, not their party, first.[92]

When he was elected governor of California in 1974, Jerry Brown exchanged his free "limousine for a modest Plymouth, and spurned an extravagant janitorial mansion 13 miles from the capitol for a mattress on the floor of a $250-a-month apartment across from his office."[93] Brown was a mercurial bachelor who practiced yoga and had spent some time in a seminary. Style reflected substance. Brown frequently characterized the 1970s as "an era of limits" that required a reduction in federal spending.[94] "Government," he argued, mixing fiscal discipline with environmentalism, "must lower its expectations in an age when not only government is limited in its responses, but the planet itself is losing resources capable of maintaining the high consumption of Americans."[95] Even the poor would have to reduce their standard of living in an era of limits. Welfare, suggested Brown, "was a charity, not a right."[96]

In the 1976 primaries, Brown entered late and campaigned for reductions in federal spending, military commitments overseas, and even public sector costs. But his pronounced social liberalism appealed to New Dealers and to New Politics people horrified by the thought of a little-known fundamentalist from the Deep South taking the Democratic nomination. In addition, Brown reached out to younger voters and he ran strongly in the West.[97] The governor won impressive victories, many of them on the back of write-in campaigns in New Jersey, Maryland, California, and Oregon.[98] The sudden power of the Anyone But Carter coalition implied that deep suspicions remained among liberals toward their new nominee. Nevertheless, the ABC movement proved to be too little, too late. By dominating the South and performing strongly in the Midwest, Carter secured enough delegates and easily won the nomination.[99]

Winning the Party Over

Carter inherited a party that was deeply suspicious of him. His solution to this problem was to endorse a series of policy positions that would lure liberals back.[100] To quote his chief domestic policy adviser and fellow Georgian, Stuart Eizenstat, "Carter was kind of on the fault line of the party. . . . He was fiscally conservative but racially liberal." Hence, while it was traditional for Democrats to run a liberal primary campaign but a moderate general one, "Carter broke that mold. We ran from the center in the primaries and then after we had secured that and we needed to get the organized activist liberal elements of the party behind us for the general election . . . we really moved to the left. By the appointment of Walter Mondale as the Vice Presidential nominee, who was a more traditional Democrat, by the adoption of a program for National Health Insurance I negotiated with the United Auto-Workers [UAW] and by endorsing a generally liberal Democratic platform in 1976."[101]

This bargaining process is crucial to understanding the rift between the Carter administration and the liberal organizations that had campaigned for it. To take Eizenstat's example, Carter equivocated throughout the primaries over health care, implying at first that he thought that the government should only supply a small number of health benefits to the very needy. But when he needed to shore up his labor support, he met with the influential UAW president and gave a public statement endorsing the union's national health insurance (NHI) plan. One UAW staffer explained that this support for NHI was a litmus test for Carter in the primaries. "All along, as you tend to do in politics, we had fooled ourselves that there was a greater gut commitment to healthcare than there probably was." Jimmy really fooled them and the UAW was "surprised" and "distressed" at the lack of commitment shown by the governor once he was elected.[102] In the weeks running up to the 1976 Democratic Convention, the nominee endorsed full employment legislation, tax reform, labor law reform, NHI, increased education funding, a pardon for draft dodgers, and the ERA. Given his propensity to endorse everything and anything yet commit himself to nothing and nobody, Carter earned a reputation as a political chameleon. "They wanted to put Carter on Mount Rushmore," mused comedian Pat Paulsen. "But they didn't have room for two more faces."[103]

The strategy worked, and the convention was perhaps the most unified for a generation. The keynote speech was by African American representative Barbara Jordan and was a successful attempt to bury more than a century of division over race.[104] Although the convention remained culturally more pluralistic than the Republican one, and although feminists and other special interest political action committees helped write much of the platform, it avoided protracted conflict, demonstrations, or a ballot fight.[105] This was largely because the Democratic Party was determined to win the election. But it was also because the losers counseled for support of the nominee. Carter in turn placated them through his selection of liberal Minnesotan Walter Mondale as his vice presidential candidate and his willingness to endorse a markedly liberal and ambitious platform.[106] The Democratic Party and labor reunited and the AFL-CIO happily endorsed Carter.[107] Carter's victory in the fall relied heavily on labor turnout, after it "put its most intensive political campaign in history" behind him.[108]

Carter tapped into American aspirations for spiritual renewal and a return to honest, open government. His "came from nowhere" victory showed that the American dream had not died: hard work could still succeed, and all that was required of a nominee was determination and honesty. In an era of shrinking prosperity and dashed hopes, this was an attractive message. Also, Carter's nomination seemed to reintegrate the South back into mainstream politics and offered the hope of burying its segregationist past forever; he thus enjoyed considerable "favorite son" status throughout the region. Yet despite his personal qualities, Ford's unpopularity, and America's poor economic performance, Carter ran a surprisingly poor fall campaign.[109] At the end of the convention, he had a commanding thirty-three-point lead over Ford. But in September, he gave a speech before the American Legion in which he stated he would pardon draft dodgers. This angered conservatives and triggered a two-month slide in his approval ratings.[110] Later that month, *Playboy* published an interview with Carter in which the governor admitted that he had sometimes felt "lust in my heart" for women other than his wife. The baffling, almost childish nature of his remarks was less damaging than the fact that he had agreed to be interviewed by *Playboy* in the first place.[111]

Ford's campaign replayed these mistakes while emphasizing their candidate's experience and gravitas. By Election Day, the two were even in the polls. Ford's momentum was hindered by a mistake he made in the presidential debates when he claimed that Eastern Europe was not under Soviet domination.[112] This slip, along with the controversial choice of conservative Robert Dole for the vice presidential ticket, possibly cost Ford a close election. When the vote finally came in after a long and tense election night, there were only two percentage points between the candidates. That Carter came near to losing demonstrated the risk that comes in putting a little-known candidate on a presidential ticket. Mystery can generate rebellious excitement, but it can also delay the inevitable discovery of past mistakes, expose a fundamentally ill-prepared candidate to a cynical press, and even eventually disappoint.

Dissecting 1976

Carter's personality and the way he interpreted the 1976 election are crucial to understanding the mistakes that he made over the next four years. He narrowly pulled off victory by dominating returns in his native South and performing moderately well in the industrial Northeast. Ford did considerably better in the West. The new president believed that his electoral appeal was unique and that he had won not because of but in spite of his party's support. Immediately after the election,

Carter's pollster, Patrick Caddell, wrote him a long memo notifying him that "the time is ripe for political realignment in America—for the construction of a political coalition based on a successful Carter administration." He warned that a Democratic administration could not rely on partisanship for the maintenance of its majority. "The number of Independents is growing because the number of young people in the voting population is growing. The parties are literally 'dying.'" In large part, Caddell blamed this situation on encroaching social conservatism among older voters and the registration of a younger class of voter, the majority of whom "do not become partisans. They are disenchanted with issues and ideology in American politics." Moreover, their "liberalism is somewhat different from the traditional definition. In fact, they tend to be more economic conservatives and social liberals." In contrast, the "blue-collar ethnics" who had been the bedrock of the New Deal economic coalition, while still attracted to the politics of "economic growth to provide a larger pie for everyone," were "no longer solely motivated by economic concerns. . . . They are now concerned with social issues, particularly those relating to change in society. This is one of the most vulnerable groups in the Democratic coalition." Thus, older and younger voters were polarized, and Carter faced the difficult task of both holding "the older parts of the party and [capturing] the growing segments of the overall electorate—the young and the middle class." To do this, Caddell suggested Carter create "a context that is neither traditionally liberal nor traditionally conservative, one that cuts across traditional ideology."

He also warned that growing internal party conflict reflected changes in the national issue agenda and growing socioeconomic conflict within the once-powerful New Deal coalition. Liberalism had splintered, largely over war and peace, but increasingly over tax and inflation too. By treading water between generations of liberals, Caddell warned Carter that he could be attacked by both the Republicans and the Democrats. In many regards, the latter "would be more dangerous" than the former. He would face opposition from both "the liberal establishment" and "the Young Turks" (neoliberals). The liberal establishment had "a different set of national priorities" than Carter, and its ringleader was Massachusetts senator Edward Kennedy. "Kennedy," reported Caddell, "senses problems with Governor Carter and that Carter is unnecessarily antagonistic to him. He and others may develop a mind-set that enables them to build up seemingly rational arguments for opposing the president's policies and even instigating political opposition." The recently elected generation of Young Turks could prove problematic despite being "against large governments, more strident against special interests and more concerned about a lot of the new issues." They had to be "handled properly" because they were "not wedded to political tradition or to political protocol. They are, on the whole, articulate and politically ambitious."

Caddell's analysis succinctly outlined many of the problems facing the Democratic coalition, particularly its generational divide over Vietnam and the recession. In many regards, the controversial memo was a bold and intelligent assessment of a volatile political situation. But there was an important tension in Caddell's analysis between asserting that the New Deal coalition was in decline and arguing that Carter had simply failed to energize it. Although Carter had taken 80 percent of registered Democrats, Caddell noted that "this margin was almost not enough. . . . We lost the rest of the Democrats to Ford while picking up the independent and moderate voters as final decisions were made. Had Carter been able to carry 85 percent of the Democratic vote, matching past Democratic performances, the result would have been a victory by several additional percentage points." Although he had swept voters self-defined as liberal, he did so by significantly smaller margins than Kennedy or Humphrey. "Some liberals, particularly younger ones, defected to Gerald Ford." He also "ran behind most recent Democrats in most of the urban Democratic centers and ran ahead of most recent Democratic candidates in other areas." Caddell appeared to concede that in "broadening" the Democratic majority, Carter had paradoxically narrowed it too.[113]

The overall conclusion of Caddell's memo flattered Carter's vanity. The president elect believed that politics as usual was over: people had voted for him because they were tired of partisan appeals, of politicians who chased votes with money, and of lazy, liberal largesse. They wanted efficiency, honesty, a smaller, more capable government, and a compassionate ear.[114] However, Caddell's analysis was wrong in two important regards. First, as we shall see in the next few chapters, the Democratic Party was considerably more united in the late 1970s than he gave it credit for. Many New Politics liberals had come of age and were now running for office. Although this undoubtedly put strains on the Democratic machinery as it tried to integrate them, it also meant that they had to make amends with old enemies to keep their electoral coalitions together and get things done.[115]

Both the New Deal and the New Politics mellowed in the 1970s. Even some old union bosses tempered their social views as they slowly accepted the cultural changes taking place around them.[116] For instance, relations between big labor and feminist organizations had always been strained. Yet in 1973, the AFL-CIO endorsed the ERA and would become one of its biggest champions.[117] This was accomplished by feminists organizing within trade unions, sharing ideas, and building points of common interest.[118] One activist described the deal thusly: "The political clout of big labor will be called in to play by endorsing and currying the favor of pro-ERA candidates in state houses and then keeping the 'yes' votes in line."[119] In return, "organized labor sees some advantage in its alliance with the women's movement since only one out of every nine working women in the United States belongs to a labor union."[120] Labor and feminists calculated that in the conservative mood of the 1970s, they needed each other. As another activist explained, "The entire labor movement will gain as women win equal rights. The employers' attempts to divide workers by sex will be curbed; women will play an increasing role in the labor movement, adding their numbers and power to roll back the employers' antiunion offensive; the greater unity in our ranks will increase the unions' ability to win better wages." To a certain extent, the new labor-feminist accord represented a return to class-based politics.[121] This produced a plethora of innovative coalitions at a state level that was often overlooked by the national media. In Kentucky, the Kentucky Labor Council, Catholics for ERA, and the Jewish War Veterans Auxiliary marshaled the state's ERA extension campaign.[122] In Virginia, the Labor for Equal Rights Now (LERN) council provided the effective leadership for the National Organization for Women's campaign.[123] LERN represented twenty-three major unions, from the Bicycle Messengers to the ordinarily conservative Teamsters.[124]

Most importantly, the shifting issue agenda of the mid-1970s brought Democrats back together and played to their traditional electoral strengths. Vietnam was over, and both Nixon and Ford had made negotiation with communists socially acceptable through arms negotiations with the USSR and goodwill trips to China. Abortion was legalized and the death penalty banned. Much of what the New Politics had campaigned for had become law—and under a Republican administration too. Concepts such as affirmative action, integrated schools, homemakers' rights, access to divorce, abortion, penal reform, and even basic rights for gays and lesbians had accumulated the air of orthodoxy by the late 1970s.[125] These changes corresponded with a gradual liberalizing of America's social and racial attitudes.[126] As white children were educated with black children, so their prejudices declined. Divorce soared, overall church attendance fell, racially mixed marriages increased, and gays and lesbians became a regular feature of popular culture.

It helped that Americans were distracted from awkward and divisive social issues by the sudden decline in the U.S. economy. Increases in the cost of living and the possibility of joblessness forced many registered Democrats to change their priorities.[127] The Democratic Party broadly benefited from this trend because it motivated its economic base to attend the polls.[128] Liberals could sit back, blame the Republicans for the recession, and gently remind the public that big spending had saved the world in the 1930s. The philosophical and fiscal differences between the New Politics and New Deal were defined by the economics of the 1960s, a period marked by growth and low unemployment. In an era of recession, liberals of either hue were forced to return to first principles and respond to the immediate needs of their core constituencies. Therefore, they began to push for measures to create employment and resolutely defended social spending against cuts designed to curb inflation.[129]

As in the case of the ERA, Democrats started to build dynamic new coalitions to promote certain programs and ideas. In 1976 the most powerful such program was probably the Humphrey-Hawkins Full Employment Act (H.R. 50), which would have mandated the federal government to find a job for anyone who wanted one.[130] Coauthored by Senator Hubert Humphrey and an African American representative, Augustus Hawkins, it enjoyed a remarkable breadth of appeal. New Dealers saw it as a way of managing the economy better, of introducing industrial policy by the back door.[131] Civil rights activists hoped it would create jobs for both black and white citizens, reducing the necessity of polarizing affirmative action initiatives.[132] In this regard, it was a piece of universalist legislation designed to "improve the life chances of groups such as the ghetto underclass by emphasizing programs . . . [to] which the more advantaged groups of all races can positively relate."[133] The endurance of Social Security and Medicare proves that giving the middle class a stake in welfare programs makes them politically secure.[134] Meanwhile, environmentalists hoped to use Humphrey-Hawkins to push green jobs. Feminists thought it would integrate women into the workforce. Even fiscal conservatives, like Senator Gary Hart (a man who spent his 1974 campaign reassuring Colorado audiences that the New Deal was dead and buried) endorsed it as a helping hand for people back home who could not find a job.[135]

The 1976 Democratic platform endorsed Humphrey-Hawkins in all but name. Indeed, it was one of the most radical platforms in the party's history, promising to implement tax and welfare reform, increase Social Security benefits, create green energy programs, and institute national health insurance.[136] This wide-ranging liberalism was key to the party's unity during the election: it gave practically every stakeholder group an investment in a future Carter administration. Therefore, the administration was wrong to assume that the Democrats were wholly fratricidal. In comparison with 1968 and 1972, they were remarkably harmonious and ready to get on with the job of governing.

But even if the party machine was starting to come back together, was the base not still splitting? Caddell argued that Carter's margin of victory was small and that it relied on voters that only he could have attracted. He therefore assumed, not unreasonably, that the victory was one for the new president, not his party. But he was wrong.

Jimmy Carter could and should have done better in 1976. After all, he headed the ticket of a very popular party. Democratic electoral performance was strong in the early to mid-1970s, and it arguably outperformed even Carter in 1976. Nixon's huge landslide reelection in 1972 did not translate into a Republican one, and he gained only 12 House seats and lost 2 in the Senate.[137] In the post-Watergate counter-landslide of 1974, Democrats captured 57.1 percent of the popular vote and gained 49 seats in the House.[138] Senate Democrats took 4 seats to enjoy a 61-to-38 seat advantage. In the 1974 and 1976 congressional races, the Democratic margins of victory were as deep as they were wide. In 1974, Democrats won 209 House seats with margins of over 60 percent of the total vote. The Republicans only took 52 seats with such margins. In 1976 the figures were 208 for the Democrats and just 89 for the Republicans.[139] Moreover, polling from the 1974 elections indicated that the results were influenced far more by economics than scandal: working- and middle-class Democrats were tired of recession and stagflation and were coming home.[140]

Where Carter did win, he did so by "welding together varying proportions of Roosevelt's New Deal coalition—the South, the industrial Northeast, organized labor, minorities, and the liberal community." Importantly, he did not win substantial majorities in all these factions; indeed, he performed less well in the industrial Northeast than Humphrey had done in 1968.[141] Carter benefited from a reverse-coattails effect and a heavy, pro-Democrat turnout by union members.[142] In Ohio, Democrat Howard Metzenbaum beat Senator Robert Taft Jr. by 118,000 votes, ten times Carter's margin over Ford. In eighteen states with a Senate or gubernatorial race, Carter was ahead only in five.[143]

Nationally, the Democratic Party held its vote (at 55.5 percent, considerably higher than Carter's) and gained one seat in the House. The balance was unchanged in the Senate. The Democrats continued to enjoy an extraordinary margin among governorships too. After the 1976 elections, it claimed 37 governorships to just 12 for the Republicans and 1 independent. The party's strength was not limited by region, and four states chose Ford over Carter but elected Democratic governors.[144] The importance of labor in the campaign, the liberal economic platform, and Carter's outperformance by other more established liberals suggested that the Democratic Party was in a stronger position than its new president.[145] In New York State, for instance, the new, economically liberal senator, Daniel Patrick Moynihan, was elected by "reviving the alliances and ambitions of the New Deal in the state where they were born." He ran far ahead of Carter.[146]

Inevitably, this created a situation in which many representatives thought that they did not owe their victory to the new president. Rather, he owed his to them.[147] This meant that they expected him to deliver on the programs he had promised them. When he did not, they were understandably angry.

The mid-1970s were a transformative moment in American politics, and the Democratic Party emerged from them arguably every bit as popular as it had been in the early 1960s. The winding down of the Vietnam war, the scandal of Watergate, and the misery of stagflation bolstered the opposition party and played to its advantage. Indeed, Democratic liberals in 1976 had good cause to be cautiously optimistic. Points of contention between Democratic traditions had weakened. As the New Politics activists matured, the New Deal establishment reconciled itself to social change. The party controlled both elected branches of government—in the case of the legislative branch, by a healthy majority. Jimmy Carter had been elected by a renewed liberal coalition committed to the passage of a number of ambitious programs. The Democratic National Committee's private postelection polling found that the public generally regarded Carter as an economic liberal on the basis of his party's platform. Yet 91 percent of Carter's voters told the Democratic National Committee that they voted for him because of economic issues.[148]

It was therefore logical for liberals to assume that Carter was bound by his word and electoral necessity to implement their platform. Moreover, despite the surprise success of the Georgian's remarkable campaign to win the nomination, liberals still thought that the Democratic Party basically belonged to them. After all, Carter had only won because he faced a divided left-wing field—a field populated by relatively unimpressive candidates—to become the nominee. The real titan of liberal politics had sat out the race. In his absence, Carter had borrowed, rather than convincingly won, the loyalty of ordinary Democrats. Liberals could be certain that he would reclaim the party the moment the peanut farmer threatened to lead it astray. The man waiting in the wings was Senator Edward Kennedy.[149]

2

The Man from Massachusetts

Edward Moore Kennedy, who was born in 1932, was the youngest and least ambitious of the four Kennedy brothers. Although his father, Joseph Kennedy, liked the idea that someday all of his sons might grow up to be president, Ted's age (he was seventeen years younger than Jack) meant that he was spared much of the immediate attention that his older brothers received. This suited Ted, who was more interested in sports and socializing than he was in politics. Indeed, throughout much of his life, he remained a party animal and found it difficult to adjust to the standards of sobriety and seriousness that a public life called for.[1] He was handsome and gregarious, could occasionally be an effective orator, and exuded considerable personal charm. Moreover, his life story framed that of many Americans in the 1960s. The triumphs and tragedies of his family defined the decade, and Ted would forever be associated with the ambitious, elegant, energetic Camelot of his brother Jack's presidential administration. If Jimmy Carter was characterized by his outsider status and his greatest asset was his distance from the Democratic Party, then Edward Kennedy might be called the insider's insider. The party was family, and it defined his career, his personal life, and even his personality. All its internal contradictions could be found within Ted—its magnificence and its flaws. It made him, just as his brothers Jack and Bobby had helped shape it in return.[2]

Despite being famous and clubbable, Kennedy was a distant and intensely private man too. As the family's attention focused on Jack's career, he found himself playing a supporting role in the great Kennedy family political pageant. This would explain his later unease at running for the presidency: it was a job that he was not psychologically prepared for.[3] Kennedy was the model of an English aristocratic statesman, the man who approaches politics as an act of public duty. Driven by noblesse oblige rather than raw ambition, he stumbled into the arena wide-eyed and not quite sure of what to do. Yet he was there because he had to be. It was expected of him. As is true of all great political families, Kennedy was not an individual but a brand. The Rockefellers are all charitable industrialists, the Churchills gung-ho war dogs, and the Clintons populist profiteers. The Kennedys were patrician champions of the little man—whether they liked it or not.[4] That was exemplified by Ted's performance on the stump. Kennedy enjoyed crowds and responded better to them than his brothers did, but that did not translate into a love for campaigning itself. Although he made it look easy, there was something mechanical about the way he pressed flesh and whipped up drama. "Kennedy seems to have a real passion for the issues," opined one critic, "and a mere tolerance, however energetic he is, for the process."[5]

Scandal is often a symptom of discomfort toward power. Anxiety and a desire to escape responsibility can breed carelessness. Kennedy's political career was awash with silly mistakes.[6] After schooling at Fessenden School and Milton Academy, Ted entered Harvard in 1950. Here he had his first brush with infamy: he was briefly expelled in 1951 after he was caught cheating on a Spanish exam.[7] He sought refuge in the army and then served as a diplomatic attaché in Paris before being readmitted to Harvard in 1953. Later he took a law degree at the University of Virginia and was welcomed into the Massachusetts bar.[8] As his brothers' political careers took off, Ted played a backroom role, managing Jack's 1958 election as a junior senator from Massachusetts. However, a political opening became apparent when Jack Kennedy was elected president in 1960. Joseph Kennedy was determined to have as many family members in the Senate as was politically possible, and he decided that Ted should take his brother's seat. It was a presumptive ambition: Ted was not yet thirty in 1960. Nevertheless, Joseph convinced the governor of Massachusetts to appoint a family friend as senator—a friend who pledged that he would not seek to be returned in the special election set by Massachusetts law for 1962. When the special election took place, Ted had come of age and was ready to run. He showed signs of doubt, however, and suggested to Robert that it might be better if he tried for Massachusetts attorney general instead. But run he did. He was opposed by the Cambridge intellectual establishment, who accused him, not unfairly, of being a carpetbagger. Before the big debate, Robert visited Ted in Hyannis Port to coach him on what to say. Ted wasn't even sure how to explain why he wanted to be a senator in the first place. This anxiety was alien to his elder brother. Robert said, "Tell them about public service. Tell them why

you don't want to be sitting on your ass in some office in New York."
In the event, the debate went well. Capitalizing on his brother's post–
Cuban missile crisis popularity and a well-organized campaign that
promised to "do more!" for Massachusetts, Ted was easily elected.[9] He
was then reelected in 1964 for a full term. As a senator, he was fairly
unremarkable. His liberalism was orthodox and attuned to the politics
of the era: pro–civil rights, pro–Great Society, and pro-Vietnam.[10]

Kennedy faced a bright but junior role within Camelot. He was a
point man for the family, a bubbly face in private negotiations, or a
watchful presence in the Senate.[11] But a series of tragedies catapulted
Kennedy into a leadership role within his family and the wider nation,
redefining him as a public and a private person. He was left of center
stage, but bruised, scarred, and unsure of his lines. Ted emerged from
the 1960s not a spokesman for the nation's hopes and dreams, as Jack
had been at the decade's beginning, but rather a reminder of its recent
nightmares.[12] Edward Kennedy was bonded to the American people by
a shared trauma.

The first such tragedy was Joseph Kennedy's stroke in 1961. This
left Jack as head of the family. Then when Jack was assassinated in
1963, Robert assumed that role, and Ted became his deputy.[13] In 1964
Ted was in a plane crash that killed the pilot and one of his aides.
He was pulled from the wreckage by Indiana senator Birch Bayh and
spent several weeks in the hospital recovering from a back injury and
internal bleeding.[14] The incident left Kennedy physically scarred. Despite the health implied by his large, impressive body, Kennedy's back
never fully recovered, and he had to learn to live with constant, sear-
ing pain. The accident left him unable to endure standing up for long
periods of time. In the 1980 campaign, admirers and activists were
surprised when they lined up to shake his hand that he could only remain standing with the aid of an assistant, who would hold the back of
a chair up against Kennedy's spine for him to rest on.[15]

Then there was 1968. Bobby Kennedy's campaign was a frenzied,
epic struggle for the nomination. Taking on the Democratic Party
machine, he tried to weld African Americans, poor whites, and blue-
collar conservatives together around an antiwar, compassionate, but
tough-minded candidacy. At campaign rallies, masses of ordinary people clutched and grabbed at Bobby as if trying to tear a piece of him
off to keep for themselves. Ted was his brother's campaign manager,
performing a similar role to the one that Bobby had played for Jack in
1960.[16]

Ted took Bobby's assassination hard. He had developed the kind of intense relationship that Bobby had once enjoyed with Jack, and the limited responsibility of being his brother's helper had given him a new, comfortable sense of status within the family.[17] Now he was alone and in charge. His first public duty was to deliver a moving eulogy at his brother's funeral that perfectly captured Bobby's spirit. "My brother need not be idealized, or enlarged in death beyond what he was in life," he said. Robert simply wanted to be remembered as "a good and decent man, who saw wrong and tried to right it, saw suffering and tried to heal it, saw war and tried to stop it."[18]

Robert Kennedy was radicalized by his run for the presidency. He came face-to-face with poverty and depravation, the scale of which he little imagined could have still existed in contemporary America.[19] The same process slowly happened to Ted, central to which was his comparatively late decision to renounce the war in Vietnam.[20] With Bobby's death, the torch was passed, and the youngest brother suddenly found himself at the helm of an enormous, awkward, raucous coalition of angry voters: steelworkers, grape pickers, college radicals, social workers, teachers, welfare queens, civil rights activists, and Catholics.[21] This new status was immediately apparent at the 1968 Chicago convention. As violence dominated the streets outside, inside, a movement quickly grew to put Ted on the ballot as a unity candidate. It was supported not only by antiwar protesters but also by machine politicians like Mayor Richard Daley. Kennedy turned down the offer. He was too young, and it was too soon. It would have been an act of unimaginable hubris to have accepted the honor. Moreover, Ted had barely had time to recover from the shock of his brother's death. The convention had asked too much.[22]

Yet the perception of Ted's potential as a president had been established, and it lingered for nearly twenty years. Crucially, it was rooted not in his own abilities (which were plentiful, if embryonic) but rather in the memory of his brothers' triumphs and tragedies. This identification with a myth cut across class, ideological, and racial barriers. *Time* magazine reported, "One former Kennedy aide recalls a Boston antiwar parade in which Kennedy, one of the marchers, came up to a group of hardhats waving Back Our Boys in Vietnam signs. 'The hardhats cheered Ted and waved at him, and after he'd passed by, they continued waving their signs.'" Crowds greeted Ted in just the same way that they had Robert: feverishly and fanatically. A senator accompanying Kennedy on a tour of a hospital recalled that the reaction he received "wasn't political. It was regal. People wanted to touch him—not just 21-year-old student nurses but 45-year-old orthopedic specialists.

It was astounding and a little frightening. I've never seen that reaction to anybody in my life, in politics or out. The closest thing I can remember was when I attended an Elvis Presley concert."[23]

The Kennedy myth might have been enough to propel Ted into the White House but for one terrible mistake. On the day that the Americans landed on the moon, the newspapers also reported that Edward Kennedy had been involved in an incident on Chappaquiddick Island in Martha's Vineyard, Massachusetts.[24] On the evening of 18 July 1969, Kennedy attended a small party to which had been invited a gaggle of interns from Bobby's campaign. He offered to give one of them, young Mary Jo Kopechne, a ride home. What happened next is a matter of some controversy, but (whether for innocent reasons or not) Kennedy drove off the main road, down a dimly lit track, and straight into a river. According to his testimony, Kennedy dived into the water several times to try to rescue the poor girl. But tired and in shock, he eventually gave up and wandered into town. Early the next morning, he reported the incident to the local police. Although some have argued that his delay in seeking help was a symptom of shock, others suspect that it was a symptom of political self-preservation. Many have hinted that his reasons for driving off the main road were adulterous. Kennedy was found guilty of leaving the scene of an accident; he was probably driving drunk.[25]

Whatever the motives for his moonlit drive or his actions after the incident, there can be little doubt that Chappaquiddick irrevocably damaged Kennedy's reputation.[26] It permanently tarred him with scandal. His least generous critics painted the senator as a lascivious, self-obsessed monster, and Chappaquiddick became a word that, like Watergate, instantly conjured up ideas of corruption, arrogance, and the abuse of power—the kind of traumas that people voted for Jimmy Carter to heal. One biographer wryly suggested that accusations that Kennedy "lacked character" were due to "a failure to cover up, as though the ability to hide one's past failings were a qualification for the Presidency that his brothers possessed but he did not."[27] Many commentators and friends predicted that Chappaquiddick had put the presidency beyond Kennedy's reach.[28] The first sign that it had done significant damage was when he lost reelection as majority whip in the Senate in 1971—to the conservative Robert C. Byrd of West Virginia.[29]

The problem was that while Edward Kennedy's mystique was rooted in the hopeful, trusting politics of the early 1960s, his career flowered in the paranoid, cynical atmosphere of the 1970s. Journalism had changed from a profession that largely reported what it was told into something more investigative, confrontational, and considerably less deferential. The public, now used to seeing abuses of American military power on color TV live from Vietnam, had largely lost its faith in the establishment and came to expect the worst of its leaders. Jack cheated on his wife and Bobby was accused of playing dirty tricks in elections, but the media ignored their worst excesses.[30] They were less kind to Ted—and there was plenty to report.[31] During her marriage to Ted, Joan Kennedy had two miscarriages and one of her children contracted cancer. This would have placed a great strain on any marriage, but both husband and wife were chronic drinkers, and Ted could barely conceal his infidelities.[32] Joan became an alcoholic in the mid-1960s and was arrested for drink driving in Virginia in 1974. By 1977 she was living separately from her husband, and they officially divorced in 1982.[33]

It was suspected during the 1980 campaign that his personal history might limit Kennedy's appeal to feminist groups. Moreover, the role of women in his campaign would have to be limited lest the press cast aspersion.[34] Chappaquiddick dented Kennedy's image and weakened him as a moral force. For instance, when he stated during the Watergate crisis that "if our country stands for anything it is that no man is above the law," Senator Barry Goldwater retorted, "There is still that little truism which says people who live in glass houses shouldn't throw stones."[35] This character issue was perceived to be problematic enough to derail a Kennedy candidacy.[36] In a collection of personal notes compiled at the beginning of the 1980 campaign, Kennedy loyalist Ted Sorensen wrote under a column titled "Negatives," "credibility . . . moral fitness . . . family unit." When picking a president, Americans often make an instinctive choice based on personality. Edward Kennedy's personality was one of the most scrutinized in American political history, and every consideration of it came back to the same terrible thing: Chappaquiddick.[37]

Yet what is so remarkable about Edward Kennedy's career is not just that it survived Chappaquiddick, but that it veritably flourished. Throughout the 1970s, he was not only a front-runner for the Democratic presidential nomination, but *the* front-runner. To be sure, the immediacy of the Chappaquiddick incident overshadowed the 1972 primaries, probably discouraging a Kennedy candidacy.[38] He was also influenced by personal affection for McGovern and the suspicion that Nixon was going to win big.[39] Nonetheless, polls suggested that Kennedy was the favorite among Democrats, even after the nomination was settled, and he was repeatedly urged by allies to step in.[40] Front-runners Hubert Humphrey and George McGovern publicly identified him as the man they would most like to share the ticket with.[41] While stumping in Massachusetts, McGovern told a crowd that he was approached by a group of excited young women who asked him if he knew Senator Kennedy personally. McGovern replied to them that he did, and they erupted into giggles. "Oh Senator McGovern," they said, "Please don't take this the wrong way. We like you very much but we can't wait for 1976."[42]

It was almost embarrassing. Wrote one journalist, "Sometimes it was difficult to tell who the Democratic presidential candidate was, George McGovern or Edward Kennedy. Whenever Kennedy appeared with McGovern, the crowd invariably doubled. Time and again, cheering spectators would brush past the nominee to gush over an embarrassed Ted. McGovern had trouble articulating bread-and-butter issues for man-in-the-street Democrats—a task that comes easy for Kennedy. While living with impending defeat this fall, Democrats dreamed of victory next time with Ted."[43] At the nominating convention, McGovern fought hard to put Kennedy on the ticket, but he resisted all appeals.[44] Nevertheless, the only state that McGovern took that year was Massachusetts, and it was probably thanks entirely to Kennedy's support.

A good indicator of the popularity of liberals in the early 1970s was how much Richard Nixon hated them. Kennedy was at the top of his enemies list. Nixon's dislike of Ted, like Carter's, was rooted in the politics of class envy. Nixon had worked hard all his life to attain office, whereas it seemed to be handed to Ted on a plate. Nixon regarded himself as a champion of modest Republican, Protestant values. Kennedy was the epitome of liberal East Coast decadence.[45] Nixon placed bugs in Ted's Senate office to try to figure out whether or not he would run in 1972. The Watergate tapes have revealed that he saw Kennedy as his strongest and likeliest opponent. Kennedy's was the only candidacy that was regarded as being able to win the support of both the remnants of the Daley Chicago machine and McGovern's activists, which would have undermined Nixon's centrist strategy.[46] The tapes have also unearthed the rather distasteful pleasure Nixon took in Chappaquiddick.[47] Not only did he thrill at the thought of Kennedy's career ending, but he also saw the accident as a validation of his anti-establishment paranoia. For Nixon, like many Americans, Chappaquiddick confirmed that the liberal patriarchs were essentially degenerate and morally contemptible.

In 1976, a Kennedy nomination appeared inevitable. With the economy in recession, both Ted and the party were ahead in the polls. Henry Jackson confidently predicted, "If he runs, he'll get the nomination. It's that simple."[48] Gallup gave him an edge over Ford of 50 percent to 43 percent, and he led his nearest Democratic opponent by 36 percent to 15 percent.[49] One report from a "Milwaukee for Jackson" event described "an almost palpable longing by many for Senator Edward M. Kennedy."[50] Again, considering that the election was defined in large part by Watergate and the corruption in American politics that it had revealed, it was remarkable that Ted was even considered a likely candidate. His strength lay in the excitement he generated, his ability to move people. Said *Time* magazine, "Democrats agree that Kennedy is most capable of unifying the various elements that can be rallied to the party's side—liberals, the labor unions, big-city ethnics, Catholics, blacks, the Spanish-speaking."[51]

Some have argued that 1976 was Ted's best chance to take the nomination. Again, his refusal to run was overwhelmingly personal: his son had been diagnosed with chondrosarcoma, a fast-growing cancer, in a leg, and Kennedy chose to spend time with his family. His son survived but lost the limb, and Kennedy took a sabbatical from campaigning to nurse him back to health.[52] Yet again, personal tragedy had interrupted or redirected his political career.

In both the 1972 and 1976 contests, Ted Kennedy was the specter at the feast, a highly popular choice with activists whose entry into the race could have dramatically altered its outcome.[53] He typically ran either closer to or further beyond the Republican rival.[54] Inevitably, Kennedy's popularity sparked jealousy among other Democrats. Chief among these was Jimmy Carter. After he had become a front-runner, Carter was asked by insiders whether or not he thought he could take on a Kennedy. The question was insulting. It implied that the party belonged to Ted and that Carter was simply borrowing it—that as soon as the Kennedy family asked for it back, he would have to hand it over. Any other politician would probably have responded to such questions with good grace, given the special role the Kennedys had in the party's history. Carter replied with competitive anger. He reportedly told journalists that he refused to "kiss his ass" for the nomination and welcomed Kennedy's entrance into the race.[55] Indeed, journalist Garry Wills argued persuasively that Carter actually sought a Kennedy challenge throughout his presidency. At various points from 1976 onward, he could have forestalled Kennedy's wrath by giving him a symbolic or literal role within the administration. Instead, he repeatedly insulted him and froze him out, starting with the 1976 election campaign, in which he was given barely anything to do.[56] In turn, Kennedy spent only one day at the nominating convention in New York and displayed for Carter in the general election "all the zeal of a zombie."[57] From the very beginning, the two were clear rivals for the affection of their party. Carter was jealous of Kennedy's mystique, and Kennedy was a little frustrated that it was Carter, and not him, on the party's ticket.

The Kennedy Coalition

Why was a man with such deep personal problems a front-runner for his party's nomination? The answer is partly personal. Handsome, charismatic, and (usually, but not always) an effective stump speaker, Kennedy was an impressive man to behold. He was bigger than his brothers, his features fat and purple, his hair windswept, his jaw impressively firm. While Jimmy Carter was a small, impish, wiry little man, Kennedy was like a football player slightly going to seed. He had inherited his brothers' coy shyness, boyish smile, and catlike sensuality. When he spoke to individuals one on one, it was as if they were the only people alive in the entire world. If crowds went wild at the sight of Edward Kennedy, the reason was at least in part because he had the kind of physical and personal charm that was worth going wild for.[58]

But Kennedy's allure undoubtedly largely lay in his family name. It conjured up warm, exciting images of the early 1960s when America was still growing, still young, still beating the communists, still advancing ever outward to the stars while bringing justice and economic opportunity to the folks down here on earth. The name accompanied a powerful, cross-class, cross-racial electoral coalition. It was composed of ethnic minorities, the poor, and blue-collar conservatives—those who had the most to benefit from competent, compassionate government. Edward Kennedy cemented his family's relationship with these people through activism within the Hispanic farmers' unions, big labor, and the civil rights movement. In essence, Edward Kennedy carried his brother's mantle and his devotion to controversial but worthy causes. But America in the 1970s was a more complicated country. In turn, Edward Kennedy was a more complex and flawed champion of the people than either of his brothers had been.[59]

Throughout the 1970s the "Kennedy coalition" of white-collar liberals, ethnic minorities, and blue-collar whites was straining at the seams. The question of whether Ted was capable of holding it together troubled liberals, and troubled Kennedy himself. Kennedy's own constituency of Boston was rocked by a violent battle to end the court-mandated busing of children to achieve racial balance in schools.[60] The courts argued that unofficial segregation remained in Boston so long as black and white children attended different schools. While many liberals and civil rights campaigners agreed, white working-class residents were horrified at the thought of their children being bused across town to attend a majority black school. They took to the streets to prevent the busing, clashing with police and turning many parts of South Boston into no-go areas. At the height of the conflict in September 1974, Kennedy attempted to address a crowd of protesting "Southies." He wanted to ask them to put aside their racial prejudices and obey the law. The crowd responded violently, and the senator was "struck with a tomato and punched and kicked."[61]

Kennedy's failure to defuse the Boston crisis confirmed to some critics that his coalition had long since been suffocated by the senator's embrace of "the aimless, indulgent libertarianism of the 1970s."[62] From the late 1970s South Boston became Republican at the state and national levels.[63] Kennedy had lost this crucial section of Massachusetts society partly because it had become more conservative, but also because his behavior and policies conflicted with many orthodox Catholic teachings.[64] Kennedy supported equal access to abortion, gay rights, and the heady rush of liturgical reforms that had transformed the Catholic Church since 1962. His name was increasingly associated with the cultural liberalism of the New Politics in an era when some suspected social license was unpopular.

But Kennedy's actions in Boston were also bold and daring, and they earned him many admirers.[65] They showed that far from being cocooned from rising social conservatism, Ted was a witness to racism within his own comparatively liberal state. Moreover, it demonstrated his figurehead status. Many Bostonians had urged him to confront protestors head-on because Kennedy was "the only person who can explain to people why they have to obey the law." Robert had done much the same within the black community after the assassination of Martin Luther King.[66] The incident built Ted credentials on the issue of civil rights and confirmed his role as a leader of unpopular causes. After all, Robert had certainly courted controversy too in 1968, when he spoke out against the Vietnam war. One campaigner, who worked with the senator on black people's health issues, recalled telling his friends after witnessing Kennedy's performance, "every black man has got to have a white man, and Teddy is mine."[67]

Moreover, Kennedy's liberalism was far more complex than his critics often gave him credit for. It was a kind of tough liberalism that reflected Jack's staunch anticommunism and Bobby's fights against organized crime. His record of voting on law enforcement issues was a disappointment to the liberal Americans for Democratic Action, and in 1977 he cosponsored a controversial wiretapping bill with Republican Strom Thurmond.[68] He fought for simplification of the criminal code, extending sentences, empowering judges, and reducing court times.[69] For this, civil rights groups often attacked him. He was favored by conservative senator Jim Eastland of Mississippi to replace him as head of the Judiciary Committee, which he did in 1979. Eastland's endorsement had little impact on the final choice, but it was remarkable nonetheless, considering the different political persuasions of the two men.[70] Also, Kennedy was a vigorous supporter of deregulation and a champion of free-market solutions to social problems.[71] His support for the deregulation of the trucking and air industries in the late 1970s brought him into conflict with sector unions and Senate liberals, including George McGovern.[72] Thus, while Kennedy's philosophy was a liberal one, it was nuanced and sensitive to the political climate of the 1970s. Although the Kennedy coalition was untried electorally, this did not mean it had ossified or that Ted's politics belonged entirely to the late 1960s.

Carter Goes to Work

Liberals like Edward Kennedy were not very comfortable with the new president. There were both philosophical and cultural differences to overcome. Liberals certainly disagreed with Carter over specific policy points, but much of this was realized through their visceral discomfort with the way he ran his administration. A good case in point was the awkward relationship between Carter and the Democratic Speaker of the House, Representative Tip O'Neill. O'Neill was almost a caricature of a New Deal liberal. A product of the powerful Tammany Hall political machine, he was steeped in the wheeler-dealer politics of urban Massachusetts. He led not by personality or press relations, but by power and influence. He once remarked that whenever he was at a state function with Senator Edward Kennedy, a hundred people would approach Kennedy and ask for his autograph while another hundred would approach O'Neill and ask for a job.[73] O'Neill had experienced the misery of the Great Depression and the miracle of the New Deal. For him, government was a legitimate tool in the War on Poverty.[74]

At his first breakfast meeting with the new president, the rotund O'Neill discovered to his horror that one of Carter's first economies was on White House catering. Instead of the bacon and eggs that Gerald Ford had given congressional leaders, O'Neill and Senate leader Robert C. Byrd were presented with a modest continental breakfast. O'Neill contained his shock for the duration of the meeting and immediately after cornered Mondale to lodge a formal complaint. "I did not get as big as I am," remarked O'Neill, "on croissants and orange juice."[75] The breakfast incident identified a bigger clash of philosophy and substance. O'Neill believed that the presidential election had been won by a return to party partisanship and public enthusiasm for the liberal Democratic platform.[76] Carter's modest first budget appeared to betray both. Unsatisfied by the pace of liberal reform, at another leadership breakfast meeting on 3 May 1977, O'Neil openly charged Carter with "neglecting social programs in order to balance the budget." For Carter, who took "strong exception to this charge," this was indicative of the economic illiteracy of liberals.[77] But for O'Neill it was a matter not only of principle, but also of political reality. Reminding Carter of the coalition that had elected him, O'Neill pleaded that "the basis of our party is liberal and you are going to have to appeal to them" once again in four years' time.[78] O'Neill's frustration with Carter's caution was influenced by the 1976 victory. He and many liberals did not see the need to delay the expansion of public services they had promised the electorate.[79] Thus, an apparently minor misunderstanding over the proper food to serve at breakfast gave a cultural dimension to conflict over philosophy and political strategy.

To be sure, Jimmy Carter's presidency actually began rather well. His decision to walk to his inauguration was a public relations triumph.[80] After the tainted glitz of the Nixon years and the sordid revelations of Watergate, Carter tapped into the American fetish of the common man. He was not blunt like Harry Truman or charmingly inarticulate like George Bush Jr., but rather exuded Protestant bourgeois standards of humility and simplicity. He forbade the playing of "Hail to the Chief," carried his own luggage everywhere, held frequent town hall meetings where people could address him directly, and wore a cardigan on national television.[81] The 1970s might be remembered primarily for its brashness, but it was also the age of the

Waltons, Superman, and *Happy Days.* Many Americans responded to the uncertainties of the decade by retreating into nostalgia. Carter's personal, though not necessarily personable, style suited this mood.[82]

He pulled off some early policy triumphs too. Carter ordered a pardon for draft dodgers that, although not entirely popular, drew a line under the rankling issue of Vietnam.[83] He reordered government, cutting bureaucracy, and, despite some false starts, eventually mastered foreign affairs.[84] However, within weeks of his inauguration, Carter began to make mistakes. A scandal that whiffed of Watergate caused the first substantial dip in Carter's popularity. Carter had appointed his old Georgian friend Bert Lance as head of the Office of Management and Budget within the administration. Within months, a story broke that implicated Lance in shady dealings, corruption, and larceny at the Georgian Calhoun National Bank.[85] Carter was forced to sack Lance. Not only did the Lance affair indicate that Jimmy was every bit as flawed and human as Richard Nixon or Gerald Ford, it illustrated significant problems in his attitude to staffing. Carter filled his administration with friends from Georgia rather than congressional insiders, an act of loyalty and anti-Washington principle, but shortsightedness too. It meant that some of his staff were unfamiliar with Washington and were regarded with contempt by members of Congress.[86] Others were perhaps unsuited to the discipline and rigor that government and the public eye demanded. At first Carter chose not to appoint a chief of staff at all (a key organizational mistake—it left his office in chaos), but the effective head of his office was the young Hamilton Jordan, who would later manage Carter's reelection campaign. Jordan gained a reputation for being frivolous, even decadent. He drank openly and perhaps excessively and was rumored to have used cocaine (he certainly smoked dope in his White House office). At a dinner party, he was supposed to have caused great offense when he took a hungry look at the opulent bosom of the Egyptian ambassador's wife and commented, "I've always wanted to see the pyramids." When he was accused of making a pass at a young lady in a Washington bar and then spitting Amaretto at her when she declined, the White House issued a thirty-three-page denial.[87]

These were not isolated accidents, and they pointed to a bigger problem of political style. Carter believed that the presidency should be above petty politicking, negotiation, and even compromise. His was a moral vision for the office, not a political one. He would set the context for government, and any legislative proposals he cared to make would be supported or considered on their ethical merits alone.[88] This approach to governance was highly naive. It was partly influenced by his governorship of Georgia, which enjoyed a significant degree of executive power and privilege.[89] Carter did not appreciate that the White House had a symbiotic relationship with Congress that had to be nurtured delicately. He reveled in his outsider status, erroneously believing that he was elected not because of his party label or the support of thousands of trade unionists, feminists, environmentalists, and other special interest activists, but because of his unique vision for the country. This hurt the Democratic officeholders who thought that they had helped elect him. They did not understand the new culture of the White House and found the president to be aloof and inconsiderate.[90]

Carter handled Congress just as badly. Upon taking office, he promised to deliver a $50 tax rebate to the voters. It was a typically mean-spirited example of federal "largesse," but the president had committed himself to it, and so O'Neill and his staff worked their hardest to push the rebate through Congress. No sooner had a majority in favor of the giveaway been achieved than Carter changed his mind. The economy had picked up, and he no longer saw the need for such a stimulus to consumer spending. Moreover, with a now-growing economy, inflation looked more threatening than unemployment. Carter did not discuss the reversal with the congressional leadership but presented it as a fait accompli, leaving Democrats angry and confused.[91]

Next Carter decided to veto a series of water projects that Congress had voted funding for. Many were in fact pork-barrel constructions, although some provided water to farmers and homeowners in areas of desperate shortages in the West.[92] Carter refused to negotiate with the congressmen affected by the veto, and his action triggered growing suspicions that he was unfriendly to the interests of the parched West.[93] This was the first occasion that opposition to Carter united congressional liberals ordinarily in conflict with one another. Western neoliberals like Colorado senator Gary Hart, who otherwise styled himself as an anti-pork-barrel fiscal conservative, lurched violently to the left when moneys to their own states were withdrawn.[94] Likewise, Hart joined liberals angry at the administration's apparent disinterest toward rising health care costs, labor law reform, or joblessness.[95] Carter eventually caved in to the Western lobby, which proved to be a humiliating admission of insensitivity. But the damage to his reputation was done.

The water projects and the tax rebate confirmed a degree of confusion and conflict within Carter's domestic policies that were the product of making policy in an economically uncertain era. Initially,

Carter's economic advisers prompted him to introduce a mild stimulus to the economy in the form of the $50 rebate and expanded funding for projects run under the umbrella of the 1973 Comprehensive Employment and Training Act. The package was not quite as bold as labor or liberals hoped, but it passed through Congress largely untouched.[96] However, while unemployment seemed to call for a limited expansion of the economy in 1977, in early 1978, inflation began to climb steeply. The price of food rose in the spring because of a hike in cattle field and fuel costs during the harsh winter.[97] Initially, Carter responded with jawboning—attempting to use the moral force of the presidency to encourage unions and companies to voluntarily lower prices and wages. Labor showed characteristic disdain; it opposed wage controls and thought that the government should tackle unemployment before trying to lessen the take-home pay of the luckily employed.[98] Carter's solutions to his economic problems were often complex and contradictory. While he took action to deregulate some industries (notably trucking and air travel), he extended it to others (particularly hospitals). When he asked employees to limit their wage increases to 7 percent, he offered them a difficult-to-calculate tax rebate as a reward.[99] Although he told the country in no uncertain terms that inflation was "our most serious domestic problem," he seemed to avoid a clear, precise course of action. This piecemeal approach suited Carter's technocratic, nondogmatic style of government. But it did not suit the epoch.[100]

Carter was right to place an emphasis on tackling inflation. Undoubtedly inflation stirred greater unemployment as it devalued money, savings, and investments. But it was also the issue that Americans most cared about. Unemployment was high in the late 1970s, but without a full-blown recession, it did not yet touch every area of society; rather, it was concentrated among traditionally Democratic constituencies like manufacturing workers and those at the low end of the pay scale.[101] More Americans were touched by the misery of rising prices than they were by joblessness, and therefore they tended to prioritize it as an economic issue in polling. This was compounded by a sharp hike in oil prices in 1979 by OPEC that led to long lines at the gas pump. The frustration of having to rise at six in the morning to wait for several hours for a tanker of overpriced gas was too much for some to bear. Reported one journalist, "In suburban Bethesda, Maryland, Texaco Station Owner Robert Cooke was tired of the hassle. He had watched fistfights in the lines and been offered bribes by motorists seeking short cuts. 'Women have offered to go in the back room with me. Once a guy cut in line and a woman went up and tried to pull him out of his car. Sometimes you wonder if the money you make is worth all this.'"[102]

In this context, Carter became convinced of the efficacy of a balanced budget and a restriction of the money supply. He believed that by cutting federal outlays, he could stem inflation and cut prices. Not only would he have to delay many of the programs that he had committed himself to in the general election of 1976, but he would also have to reject the New Deal and Great Society philosophy of using government spending to stimulate the economy.[103] Many politicians agreed with the president, and some began endorsing the idea of a "balanced budget convention" that would pass a constitutional amendment mandating the federal government to balance its books every fiscal year. Such ideas were potentially popular among conservatives and middle-class Americans frustrated with skyrocketing grocery bills. But liberals were horrified to hear them being expressed by the Democratic president that they had helped elect.[104]

The first two years of Carter's administration were certainly not an unqualified disaster. The economy operated reasonably well, and job creation was impressive.[105] Moreover, the president was given to flourishes of leadership that confounded his opponents and astonished his critics. He settled the question of the Panama Canal, signing a treaty in 1977 that transferred control of the American-built canal to the nation of Panama despite the strong opposition of much of the Republican Party and the general public.[106] Carter's greatest achievement by far was the Camp David accords. Peace in the Middle East had become a top diplomatic priority for the United States following the Yom Kippur War of 1973. Not only would peace guarantee a steady flow of oil, but it might better secure Israel's future, grant a homeland to the displaced Palestinian peoples, and allow Arab countries to focus on development rather than Soviet-fueled military adventurism. A renewed focus on the Middle East also highlighted the imaginative direction into which Carter was taking U.S. foreign policy. Rather than seeing everything through the prism of the cold war, east versus west, Carter was determined to heal the divides between rich and poor nations, north and south. His diplomacy was characterized by an admirable commitment to promoting human rights and economic development. Securing peace between Israel and Egypt offered the chance to bring stability to a region in desperate need of humanitarian assistance.[107]

On 5–17 September 1978, President Anwar el-Sadat of Egypt and

Prime Minister Menachem Begin of Israel met at Camp David for a
tense conference to decide the future of relations between their countries. Carter hoped that the two might become reconciled through the
use of personal diplomacy, that they might reach agreement on their
borders, that Egypt might recognize Israel, and that Israel might compromise on its territorial claims. The talks quickly reached a personal
and bitter impasse, and by the tenth day, both sides were threatening to withdraw. However, Carter's calm intervention and determination eventually won Sadat and Begin over. He gently brought them
together, minimized their differences, and maximized their common
fears, needs, and ambitions. On 17 September the three leaders emerged
from Camp David with a framework for peace, at the center of which
was Egypt's recognition of Israel and Israel's withdrawal from the occupied region of the Sinai.[108]

It is inconceivable that any other president could have achieved
such a remarkable pact without the overt or implicit threat of force.[109]
Carter's postpresidential work as an overseer of elections, diplomat,
and humanitarian confirm his commitment to peace and remarkable
personal abilities. The Camp David accords renewed America's faith
in the president and contributed to the Democratic Party's comparatively strong performance in the 1978 elections.[110] For the next two
years, the administration would remind the nation again and again of
the historic agreement, almost to the point of desperation. Indeed, its
prominent role in the 1980 election highlighted the fact that Carter
had little else to be proud about.[111]

The problem was that the president failed to project a clear sense
of leadership or ambition. The vagueness that had helped avoid controversy when running for the presidency proved crippling in office.[112] He seemed contrarian, hopelessly technocratic, and obstinately
modest. His attempts to tone down the presidency were initially welcomed, but what at first looked like humility quickly became feeble
and muddled. The achievement of Camp David was received by pundits not as evidence of Carter's ability, but rather an indictment of
potential wasted.[113] Why was he able so capably to bring together two
sworn enemies when he could not hold together his own party? Why
was he able to bring peace to the Middle East but not stability to the
dollar? How could he be so charming, so graceful on one occasion, yet
so stubborn and elliptical on others?[114]

No one experienced that disappointment more deeply than the
Democratic Party. As Carter's mistakes, failures, or inactivity on issues as wide-ranging as labor law reform, the Equal Rights Amendment,

and health and safety legislation mounted up, some began to suspect that he was simply deaf to their entreaties and scornful of their ambitions.[115] Paranoia grew. The White House, it was rumored, was not just uninterested in liberal reform; it was opposed to it. In some cases, the White House had dedicated itself to reversing reform altogether.

An instructive example was the Humphrey-Hawkins act, the full employment bill that everyone, including Carter, had endorsed in the primaries. Upon assuming office, Carter's staff sought to adapt the bill to suit their own priorities.[116] They understood its psychological importance to the Democratic Party, but they fundamentally rejected its philosophy and mechanisms. "What we tried to do," explained Stuart Eizenstat, "was to try to bring Humphrey-Hawkins into an orbit in which we could sign it because it would have been politically disastrous to try to defeat it, but to make it more sensible from an economic standpoint and more balanced in terms of the trade-off between inflation and unemployment. . . . We couldn't simply discard it; we had to work with it to make it livable." What was produced was a "much diluted measure from the kind of prescriptive mandates that the original 1975 bill had," and its major success for the administration was that it "avoided a major confrontation with the left."[117]

Carter's team constructed a new bill that they hoped would be more palatable to business and conservatives.[118] It removed the original's prime concepts of "Federal Government as Employer of Last Resort" and of setting a "Specific Employment Goal." Instead, it would provide nonbinding "goals and targets," reject an "open-ended job guarantee," incorporate a "commitment to achieve price stability," and publish a regular report on unemployment. Although the administration tried to retain "the spirit of the original Humphrey-Hawkins bill," it regarded reduction of unemployment and containment of inflation as unequivocally "conflicting objectives."[119] All of this took a decidedly long time to do because the administration was in no hurry to pass it. Carter only formally endorsed the bill in October 1977, "bowing at last to intense pressure from Blacks and organized labor."[120] The new bill prioritized efficient bookkeeping and inflation reduction over job creation.[121] Humphrey-Hawkins was so watered down that when Carter announced his endorsement at a press conference, one White House staffer wondered aloud to reporters "why the bill's supporters accepted it."[122]

Humphrey-Hawkins went through several revisions in the House that left it effectively gutted.[123] The compromise bill that finally faced the Senate on 13 October 1978 bore little resemblance to the original.

It retained a goal of 4 percent unemployment by 1983, but also included objective inflation rates of 3 percent by 1983 and zero by 1988.[124] Undoubtedly the conservative mood of the House and wider fears about growing price inflation contributed to HR 50's reordering of priorities.[125] But liberals were convinced that the biggest problem was an absence of leadership from Carter. He had endorsed the bill, they reasoned, so why didn't he push it through in its original form? If the president was capable of bringing peace to the Middle East, then he could surely get a liberal bill through a Democratic Congress.[126]

The administration never entirely rejected the bill because it understood the power of the liberal coalition behind it.[127] By October 1978 Carter's aides pressed him to support H.R. 50 as "one of the few bills in which we are clearly aligned with our major constituencies— labor and the minority community." They made these recommendations in the light of "the likelihood of future tight budgets," and one can infer that elements of Carter's staff hoped the bill might soften up the Democrats for a round of budget cuts.[128] A memo to Carter from his entire economic team concurred with this view, additionally arguing that "if we are not seen as doing everything we can criticism from the Black Caucus and others may escalate, and, we are afraid, *spill over into the Midterm Convention.*"[129] Carter bowed to this collective wisdom, and many activists judged Carter's renewed efforts to have been genuine and generous.[130] He swung behind the bill and it eventually passed through the Senate—but he had lost a significant amount of goodwill among the labor and African American communities, and the final bill was a hollow reminder of a noble ambition.[131]

Kennedy, Carter, and the Battle for Better Health Care

Ted Kennedy found it hard to sit by and silently watch the presidency being so poorly used.[132] For a man whose own myth was built on the memory of civil rights, the Great Society, the antiwar movement, and the youthful, charismatic presidency of Jack Kennedy, it was distressing (at best) to see Carter vacillate or (at worst) to see him clumsily unpick the many achievements of the postwar Democratic Party. Men like Carter saw tragedy and turmoil as moments that best suited reflection, modesty, and a sensible reconsideration of one's ambitions. Kennedy saw them as opportunities—challenges to be faced and overcome. Inflation and unemployment demanded not a return to conservative fiscalism and balanced budgets, but bold and active government.

Cultural, religious, and sexual backlash called not for a recommitment to traditional values, but rather confrontation and a war on prejudice. After all, Kennedy had not avoided the racial warfare on the streets in Boston; rather, he had met it on its own terms and attempted to shout it down. That, reasoned Kennedy, was true leadership.[133]

It is important to understand that Kennedy did not simply run against Carter because he disliked him personally or disapproved of his style of government. Rather, he came to believe that Carter actually posed a threat to liberal reform and that the many goals that Kennedy thought America should commit itself to would never be realized under his presidency.[134] Kennedy's decision to run was influenced by perhaps the most significant policy debate of the 1970s—significant in the sense that it rumbles on into the twenty-first century. The debate over this single issue defined the campaign of 1980 and, arguably, continues to divide moderates and radicals within the Democratic Party today. It is the issue of how best to provide health care in America.[135]

In the early 1970s Kennedy became a proponent and coauthor of comprehensive national health insurance legislation.[136] The dream of providing health care coverage to all Americans entered the Democratic lexicon as part of Harry Truman's Fair Deal platform in the 1940s, although the political problems of the next twenty years meant that it became sidelined.[137] However, in an inflationary era, the extension of cheap or even free health coverage gained added momentum. Improvements in medical technology combined with a general upsurge in prices to push health care further out of the reach of middle-class Americans. National health insurance (NHI) was therefore an example of how the economic crises of the 1970s, far from dampening the case for liberal reform, confirmed it in the eyes of many.[138]

The personal appeal to Kennedy of NHI was partly grounded in his deep commitment to social reform. But it went further than that. Improved health care coverage was an idea that was attractive to middle-class families as well as the urban poor because it could potentially cut household bills. It was essentially a civil right, but a civil right for *all* Americans and not simply fashionable minorities living in northeastern ghettos.[139] The extension of the language of "rights" into Middle America integrated traditional liberal concerns into the language and themes of the 1960s. It suddenly gave white middle-class voters a stake in the Great Society. Kennedy told audiences that health care was a right, "not a privilege for the few." Because it was a right, it should be implemented immediately and not at a time that economic circumstances might permit it. Denial or delay was tantamount to discrimination against ordinary people who just couldn't get the money together to pay for it. To tell health care consumers that their inability to pay was no cause for a refusal of treatment was a potentially powerful political ploy that forged an alliance between the urban poor and struggling suburbanites.[140]

Kennedy often compared the fight for health care to the fight for the freedom of blacks to vote, turning it into a moral issue rather than just a public policy one. He pointed out, "We are the only industrialized nation in the world outside South Africa that does not have universal, comprehensive health insurance. And here, as well as in South Africa, black people are sick twice as often; they receive less care; they die younger, and sooner."[141] NHI was then a way of keeping faith with Bobby's natural constituency. The influence of NHI continues to run like a thread through the modern Democratic Party. Defining the first term of Clinton's administration and Gore's 2000 presidential platform, it symbolizes the high intentions and perpetual frustrations of universalist liberal reform.[142]

Edward Kennedy submitted an NHI bill to Congress in 1973, with Representative Wilbur Mills in the House.[143] After Mills left Congress, California representative James C. Corman took up his cosponsorship. Kennedy's bill called for a single-payer, not-for-profit insurance scheme that would cover every American, regardless of wealth. It was coauthored and supported by the Committee for National Health Insurance (CNHI), a coalition between the ordinarily antagonistic AFL-CIO and UAW.[144] The coalition contained feminist; labor; lesbian, gay, bisexual, and transgender; civil rights; and traditional New Deal groups and was a perfect example of how universalist ideas could bring liberals together.[145] Most of the member organizations of the CNHI would campaign for Kennedy in 1980, and in many regards, it was an embryonic stage in his wider struggle to assume the party's leadership.

Facing the threat of a presidential veto, the Kennedy-Corman bill did not leave the health subcommittee.[146] Throughout 1974–1976 Kennedy negotiated with the Ford administration for compromise legislation.[147] The result was an administration-endorsed catastrophic health insurance bill, which Kennedy initially supported on the Senate floor.[148] What happened next illustrated the degree to which 1970s liberals were often the prisoners of activist forces beyond their control. The CNHI denounced Kennedy's support of the compromise Ford bill, and he quickly withdrew his endorsement. Even Edward Kennedy, brother of two liberal martyrs, was a hostage to his own constituency, and the incident demonstrates that he was every bit as much a product of his movement as its steward.[149]

To be fair to the CNHI, its actions were informed as much by electoral realism as they were by high principle. Its members thought that enough constituent groups were ready to campaign for its preferred bill by 1977 and that they could get a better deal with a larger congressional majority in 1976.[150] Ford's willingness to negotiate seemed to demonstrate the inherent popularity of NHI and that its political hour had come.[151] Inflation also increased the need for drastic and speedy enactment.[152] Although most union members enjoyed health coverage, inflation had driven up the cost of premiums, hampering businesses and leaving state government with large bills.[153] Thus, while the issue militancy of the late 1970s may in retrospect seem foolhardy, it was a reflection of the apparent inexorable leftward drift of the times.

Carter endorsed comprehensive NHI during the Democratic primaries, largely to woo the UAW and labor.[154] However, when he came into office, he delegated the formulation of legislation to former Lyndon Johnson staffer Joseph Califano.[155] Califano procrastinated and took over a year to produce his proposals.[156] He warned Carter that NHI "will be among the most complex and bedeviling policy initiatives of your administration." He predicted that NHI would face a well-financed opposition lobbying campaign and would require a sustained political effort "probably extending over several congressional sessions."[157] He also suspected that the administration was insufficiently attracted to NHI to sustain such an effort.[158] Califano's delay aggravated tensions with Kennedy and labor, who sensed they were losing both momentum and their opportunity to gain commitments of support from representatives facing reelection in 1978.[159] Their concern was informed by a fear that "Congress thinks the country is becoming more conservative and the new young Congressmen appear, for the most part, to be more concerned with being re-elected than with principles and issues."[160] Eventually Califano was sacked by Carter. After leaving office, he wrote a bitter memoir that claimed the president was fundamentally conservative and that it was he, not Califano, who had crippled health care reform.

Under pressure from Kennedy and the CNHI's membership, the Carter administration finally endorsed an NHI proposal in July 1978. This would phase in NHI in three incremental stages.[161] The first stage was the introduction of a hospital cost-containment program, an anti-inflationary measure that also hoped to reduce consumer health care prices.[162] The latter two stages were ill-defined and were predicted to take several years to come into effect. Although he welcomed the principle of cost containment, Kennedy argued that because "it does not deal with all segments of the system and because it is transitional, it is not likely to have long term effect unless it is followed in short order by comprehensive legislation."[163] Moreover, he believed that catastrophic coverage could potentially cause costs to rise because hospitals would inflate prices to cover their losses.[164] As with the concept of full employment, Carter evaded accusations of broken promises by redefining the language he had used earlier. Thus, "comprehensive" became not NHI, but a system that eventually covered all, regardless of means or universality/equality of provision.[165]

Carter had "imposed two difficult constraints: a significant role of the insurance companies and minimal impact upon the federal budget."[166] The CNHI was hostile to the involvement of private firms in any comprehensive health care plan, insisting that costs would only be reduced and coverage extended by removing the profit motive from health care provision.[167] The CNHI wanted universality and compulsion.[168] It preferred funding to come from deductions from payroll taxes and for the program to be administered by a "quasi-public corporation."[169] This exacerbated the second tension: Carter's goal of balancing the budget.[170] Eizenstat informed the CNHI that he detected among the public "the feeling that people were resentful about the Social Security tax increases and that even introducing the subject of more taxes for health care would create a political problem."[171] In contrast, labor believed that this was an excuse used by fiscal conservatives to stall social legislation altogether.[172]

At a typically heated meeting between the administration and the CNHI in late 1977, the UAW's representative became convinced that Carter's staff was opposed to NHI. He reported that while Califano and Mondale, who had become the administration's link with the CNHI, were enthusiastically for its passage, Carter's economic team was pessimistic and, in the case of Charles Schultze, opposed in principle.[173] He ominously stated that further delay would embarrass Senator Kennedy, warning that the battle over health care could precipitate a primary contest.[174] It was certainly true that his work with the CNHI had allowed Kennedy to develop intimate political relationships with liberal groups.[175] The issue of health care provided Kennedy with a distinctive platform, media attention, and a network of single-issue activists whose expertise he could tap.[176]

Ultimately, the CNHI conceded to the administration's demand that private firms be involved, believing that unless a settlement was reached, momentum would subside and the "issue of national health insurance will be shelved for yet another decade."[177] But it could not accept the program Carter put to it in July 1978. Angry at its phased and timid nature, the CNHI lashed out at Carter, dubbing his cost-containment program "a façade, not a solution."[178] But what really killed the plan was Kennedy's eleventh-hour denouncement at the end of tortuous negotiations. The senator was regarded by congressional liberals as their leader on the health care issue. Any plan that Ted did not support was instantly verboten.[179] The administration believed Kennedy was driven by personal ambition, while Kennedy believed that Carter was not committed to traditional liberal policy making.[180] He was also angry at the lack of consultation the White House had offered him.[181] In this manner, the NHI controversy typified relations between Kennedy and the White House.[182]

The cause of NHI legislation formed the moral and thematic core of Kennedy's nomination campaign. His battle for its passage had helped him establish links with a diverse coalition of liberal groups, and it explained his frustrations with Carter as president.[183] It demonstrated that Kennedy's candidacy was not merely a personal one, but one that exploited activist anger toward Carter. It also utilized the coalitions that emerged to protest the president's policies and benefited from an ongoing process of reconciliation between liberal groups. Finally, NHI tapped into the language and spirit of universalism, deepening its support within the party and reaching out to Middle America. In this regard, the Kennedy moment that was yet to come was the culmination of an era of liberal philosophical evolution, internal party reform, and growing activist militancy.

But more importantly, it was also the product of one man's personal political journey. From the early 1960s to the late 1970s, Edward Kennedy evolved from an awkward extra in his family's drama to the lead player. During that time he moved dramatically leftward, although his association with his brothers and their peculiar variety of tough liberalism ensured his continued popularity with working-class and Middle America. For Edward Kennedy, philosophical and personal development were synchronized. He was not simply popular because of his name, and he was not simply fighting for the presidency as a matter of family honor. Rather, he was the leader of the American liberal movement, in all its strengths and weaknesses. It drove and defined him just as much as he drove and defined it. Edward Kennedy was motivated not by personal ambition but by an almost burdensome sense of public duty. Crucially, when he finally came to challenge Carter for the presidency, this meant that the degree of arrogance and self-belief that was necessary to win was absent.

But before he could declare, Kennedy needed a platform, a base, and an organization. Typically, he did not create these things himself. Rather, they were forged in the catastrophic politics of the Carter presidency.

A ten-year-old Jimmy Carter, pictured here barefoot with fishing pole like a latter-day Tom Sawyer, grew up in a rural South that was modest, religious, and conservative.

Edward Kennedy was the son of a wealthy East Coast power broker. His was the "first family" of American liberalism, here gathered at Hyannis Port in 1948 (the men, left to right, are Jack, Joe, Ted, and Bobby). Courtesy of the John F. Kennedy Library.

Kennedy's first political role was as a cheerleader for his brothers. Here, in 1962, he introduces President John F. Kennedy to a Boston Democratic fund-raiser shortly before inheriting his brother's Massachusetts Senate seat. Courtesy of John F. Kennedy Library.

After serving as governor of Georgia, Carter ran a moderate campaign for the Democratic presidential nomination that played on his humble Southern roots. His brother, Billy (left, in the Redneck Power T-shirt), provided some authentic "good ol' boy" charm. © Owen Franken/CORBIS.

After election, Carter tried to maintain his modest, common-man image as president—staying in voters' homes, ending the playing of "Hail to the Chief," and even carrying his own bags onto *Marine One*. Courtesy of Jimmy Carter Library.

Behind the smiles, Kennedy and Carter were natural rivals. While Kennedy was regarded as the tragic heir to his brothers' liberal vision, Carter saw him as a vain, spoiled playboy. Courtesy of Jimmy Carter Library.

After announcing budget cuts to slash inflation and new military outlays to contain the Soviets, Carter faced a rebellion by liberals at the 1978 Democratic midterm convention. Vice President Walter Mondale (left) listens to a speech that was greeted tepidly by a hostile crowd. Courtesy of Jimmy Carter Library.

Shortly before he declared his candidacy, Ted Kennedy met Carter once more at the dedication ceremony of the John F. Kennedy Library in October 1979. The body language of the candidates and their wives, Joan (on Kennedy's left) and Rosalynn (on Carter's left), was noted by the press. Courtesy of John F. Kennedy Library.

Hit by both crises overseas and the press reinvestigation of Chappaquiddick, the Kennedy campaign disappointed voters. In Iowa, the visibly bored candidate judged pig-breeding contests in subzero temperatures. He lost the state 2 to 1, and his presidential run was suddenly all over. © Bettmann/CORBIS.

As the economy worsened and Kennedy's campaign radicalized, he began forging a remarkable new coalition. Even though victory was nearly impossible, he was mobbed in depressed areas like Jersey City, New Jersey. © Bettmann/CORBIS.

Kennedy's campaign reached out to groups typically excluded from the political process. In a gay bar in San Francisco, he pledged his commitment to "compassion for all" and a federal fight against discrimination on the grounds of sexual preference. © Bettmann/CORBIS.

By the time he arrived at the Democratic convention in August, Kennedy was pronounced electorally defeated but morally victorious. Even the timid Joan was overcome by the passion of the crowds and roared her approval. © Bettmann/CORBIS.

3

Judgment at Memphis, 1978

In October 1978 Jimmy Carter moved fiscal policy into a new era.[1] Up to that date, all postwar American administrations had fought unemployment with increased spending. However, a crisis in the international money market in August moved inflation up a notch, and the administration feared another inflationary cycle was due. Therefore, on 24 October Jimmy Carter addressed the nation and committed himself to achieving a balanced budget through cuts that would affect every department, regardless of social priority.[2] That same month, the president was informed by the chiefs of staff that the nation's nuclear arsenal was in need of updating. Since the end of the Vietnam war, the defense department had undergone an endless round of cuts that had left it underequipped. Military advisers urged Carter to invest in the mobile MX missile and the neutron bomb. Both devices were controversial. The MX's mobility was ripe for parody because it was effectively wheeled around the country on the bed of a truck.[3] The neutron bomb was dubbed "the capitalist bomb" because its high-yield plutonium killed large numbers of troops and civilians but left infrastructure and private property intact. Regardless of their tactical necessity, these weapon systems were costly. Acquiring them at the same time as slashing the domestic budget looked callous.[4]

Jimmy Carter was in part responding to popular pressure for some kind of reform of America's fiscal position. In June 1978, Californians voted 65 percent to 35 percent in favor of a ballot initiative called Proposition 13. The initiative placed a cap on property taxes across the state, reducing them by an average of 57 percent. Property holders were angry that as inflation increased the value of their homes throughout the 1970s, they ended up paying out ever-increasing sums in taxes for owning capital that they were probably never going to realize. The proposition was opposed by a coalition of civil rights groups and public service unions who argued, with some truth, that a dramatic reduction in state income would affect schools and welfare recipients. But its passage struck a chord with a Middle America trapped in the viselike squeeze of an inflationary cycle.[5]

Nevertheless, liberals like Edward Kennedy had little sympathy with the president's program. They believed that the full machinery of the state should be used to tackle inflation through controls and equitable tax reform, not cutbacks. They argued that the president had the political muscle necessary to do it. The Democratic Party controlled Congress by a generous margin, and Carter had been elected on a staunchly liberal platform with widespread appeal. Liberal activists felt personally responsible for his election, which was narrow and relied on the commitment of unionists, ethnic minorities, feminists, and white-collar activists. The problems of inflation and unemployment, they believed, made their case for structural reform of the economy even stronger. Now was not the time for fiscal restraint, but rather boldness and activism. The full energies of the federal government should be put behind economic and social reform. Proposition 13 was a challenge, but not a defeat for American liberalism.[6]

Yet their new president had dared to govern in a moderate, almost conservative manner. He cut budgets rather than enlarging them, and he shied away from culturally controversial causes rather than embracing them. Liberals acknowledged that the public was more concerned with reducing inflation than tackling unemployment and that the conservative drift of Congress reflected that mood.[7] However, they believed that Carter should have used the moral authority of the presidency to steer the country in a dynamically liberal direction, that the people were looking for leadership and were receptive to new ideas. Some Democrats even began to note that Republican Gerald Ford, who was forced to negotiate with an aggressively liberal Congress, had been more generous toward their campaigns and ideas than Democratic Jimmy Carter. Ford had lobbied for the Equal Rights Amendment (ERA) and had proposed to Congress a health insurance package that—ironically, given how readily representatives rejected it—was the closest America would come for thirty years toward enacting universal provision of health care.[8]

But how to proceed? The American party system offers little role in policy making to grassroots activists. There is ordinarily only one convention every four years, and only through the painstaking process of finding a liberal candidate, writing him a platform, and forcing it through the convention could he be made to deliver a more liberal outcome. This was a daunting task in and of itself, but it was made all the more complex by the incumbency. Liberals did not yet have the stomach to challenge a sitting president for his own party's nomination. Nor did they have an alternative candidate. George McGovern indicated that he was available, but he was, to put it bluntly, spoiled goods. In the minds of most, he was tarred with the catastrophic defeat of 1972.[9] Moreover, the history of rebellion against party officials within the Democratic Party was an inglorious one. The debates of the 1960s had torn the party apart because there was no accord between activists groups. Nobody wanted a repeat of 1968.

But the political context of the 1970s was more conducive to "orderly" protest and revolt than the 1960s were. Indeed, it was arguably uniquely conducive. The liberals were now more united than they ever had been, or possibly ever would be. What is more, they had a mechanism by which to discipline their president that would only ever be used effectively once in the history of America politics: the midterm convention.[10]

The midterm convention was mandated by McGovern's activists at the Democratic nominating convention of 1972. It was intended to work as a policy review conference, a chance to discuss the party's direction, and, if it should fall in the middle of a Democratic administration, to judge whether or not the president was sticking to the brief given to him by the people who had nominated him. In 1974 the first midterm convention passed without incident. There was no administration to scrutinize, the party was united behind its opposition to Gerald Ford, and liberals were too chastened by McGovern's defeat to create a fuss. Instead, much of the media focused on the warm reception given to George Wallace and his marginally successful attempts to make his party endorse tax relief and expanded police powers.[11] The 1974 midterm convention was an exemplar of how desperate Democrats were to win, how rejuvenated and vindicated they felt by Watergate, and how far they were prepared to temper their differences to project a winning image to the American voter.

By 1978, however, the situation was very different. There were several factors that made an explosive convention more likely. The increasing likelihood of a Kennedy candidacy was one, providing a focal point for opposition and an eloquent spokesman for discontent.[12] Delegates were genuinely angry with the president, and there is plenty of evidence to suggest that many ran for election, took precious time off work, and paid outrageous hotel and travel costs purely so that they could tell Carter what troubled them face-to-face. But Kennedy's ambition and the delegates' dismay would have been nothing without a quiet revolution that had taken place within political activism in just two years.

Innovation within activism in the 1970s is typically associated with the conservative New Right movement. These were organizational (small pressure groups coalesced and pooled resources to support broad, right-wing campaigns) and technical (direct mail canvassing).[13] But they were not limited to conservatives, and liberals borrowed their tactics and stratagems. Perhaps the two most significant campaigns to do so were the Progressive Alliance and the Democratic Agenda. Both provided models of how a relatively small group of ideologues could capture a party and steer it into an entirely new direction. Both provided the grassroots structure and personnel that would later form the core of the Kennedy campaign. Therefore, the attempt by liberals in 1978 to chasten Carter became the blueprint for Ted's candidacy, confirming that he ran as part of a wider movement that was perhaps beyond his control.

The Progressive Alliance

The Progressive Alliance was started by Douglas Fraser, president of the UAW.[14] Born in Glasgow, Scotland, in 1916, Fraser followed his father, who had emigrated to Detroit, Michigan, in 1923. After starting work in an auto factory, Fraser rose quickly through the ranks to eventually replace Leonard Woodcock as head of the UAW. Although Woodcock was certainly a liberal, Fraser was more of a doctrinaire democratic socialist favoring a corporatist-style state with labor and management sharing joint responsibility for the companies in which they worked. Fraser was a leading player in the negotiations over the bailout of the Chrysler Corporation in 1979–1980, securing as part of the deal a bigger role for unions in the governance of the company. As a result he was appointed to the board of Chrysler from 1980 to 1984, a hitherto unique example of corporatism in the United States.[15] Fraser was a firm supporter of Kennedy on a political and personal level. He liked the senator's convivial yet tough-minded style—his ability to mix compassion with a blue-collar sensibility that was rooted in patriotism and the politics of the union hall.

Douglas Fraser was dispirited by the turn of politics in the late 1970s. Growing conservatism in the Congress and White House alarmed him, as did the sense of senseless drift to the right in the wider liberal movement. As a union organizer, Fraser was used to hardball politics. His socialism was born out of struggle: he would relentlessly push for reform because aggression was all that management understood. Militancy was inbred in Fraser: shorter hours, longer holidays, better pay, and increased health benefits had not been won for his workers by compromise and equivocation. It was in this spirit that he decided to organize a Progressive Alliance that would offer radical policy alternatives to high interest rates, spending cuts, and antilabor legislation. Importantly, these alternatives would be backed up by enough political muscle to ensure that Democratic officeholders would have to take notice of them. The solidarity of the workplace would be extended to the polling booth.[16]

Fraser was fascinated by the dizzying and terrifying success of the New Right. New Right gurus pioneered mass mail order schemes that were coordinated with the very latest in computer technology. They sold and exchanged mailing lists with other right-wing organizations to create a bank of grassroots activists and a powerful coalition among pro-life, antigay, pro–prayer in schools, and antitax campaigners. The $10 contributions of thousands of otherwise inactive voters had helped to fund the dazzlingly successful campaigns of maverick conservatives, while liberals still relied on money from big labor and public policy organizations like the National Organization for Women (NOW).[17] Acknowledging the need to match Republican expenditure in state elections, Fraser intended the Progressive Alliance to concentrate its efforts in those areas. Rather than spending their money on atomized issues and candidates, liberal pressure groups that operated "on budgets ranging from $100,000 to $1.4 million a year" would be invited to contribute toward a central fund that was reserved for genuine liberals and wholly liberal causes. The Progressive Alliance would thus offer "powerful and effective advocates before city councils, county commissions, and state legislatures." So too did Fraser attempt to borrow the New Right's technical innovations. He planned to "develop in association with progressive entrepreneurs a computer mailing and fundraising capability similar to that developed . . . for the right wing." It would provide funding for firms that communicated liberal messages in a "cost-effective manner" such as "direct mail."[18]

The Progressive Alliance even tried to appropriate some of the New Right's issue agenda, initiating "activities and programs around . . . the 'state and local tax revolt.'" It developed "positive concrete programs of tax reform and tax relief" and provided "a new piece of congressional legislation aimed at Federal stimulation, encouragement and financial aid to state and local tax reform." This was not an isolated phenomenon, and many liberal-left groups would discuss tax reform in the late 1970s, usually in the context of reducing military expenditure or closing loopholes for business and the wealthy. Nevertheless, it is important to note that the liberal response to tax cuts and referenda was not entirely defensive: they did provide constructive alternatives too. Moreover, the Progressive Alliance avoided association with big government and stressed "more decentralization, less coordination" in federal affairs.[19] In so doing, it perhaps sought to remind commentators that the radicalism of the 1960s was in part a reaction *against* big, authoritarian government and that the New Right had in effect stolen some of the New Politics' clothes.[20]

What Fraser also wanted to offer liberals was a politically neutral space outside of the Democratic Party in which to convene, organize, and plot. His twin objectives were greater unity and cultural counter-revolution—that is, to give impetus and dollars to the fight against the New Right. The Progressive Alliance continued the trend among activist groups of seeking to make mainstream political parties "responsible and accountable" by controlling their manifestos and threatening to withdraw support if they did not honor them once in power. "Party platforms must become contracts made with the American people," argued Douglas Fraser.[21] This was the only method by which the party system might be rehabilitated, reducing the role of private campaign financing, personalities, and the media and restoring the philosophical imperative.[22]

Fraser decided to "use the UAW as a catalyst to organize other unions of like persuasion to join with us" in forming a new liberal coalition of activists in June 1977. Parts of this coalition had been at war with one another for ten years, including the AFL-CIO, NOW, the Committee for a Sane Nuclear Policy (SANE), and the anti-bureaucratic watchdog Common Cause.[23] Why did New Deal and New Politics groups agree to put aside their differences? Ostensibly they were interested in very different, often contradictory issue agendas. If Fraser had attempted to create such a coalition in 1970 or even 1976, it likely would have been impossible. The AFL-CIO, for instance, had disagreed sharply with the UAW over Vietnam. While the UAW had happily campaigned for McGovern, the AFL-CIO had not, and its president, George Meany, had even hinted that he had voted for Richard Nixon in 1972. Meany's virulent anticommunism put him out of step with the New Politics.[24] He was also relatively disparaging of the feminist movement. In the early 1970s he had opposed the ERA and the use of affirmative action, both in federal employment and in efforts to better integrate the Democratic Party. But for all their old disagreements, one thing united the AFL-CIO, NOW, and the UAW: Jimmy Carter.

In 1976 the unions were broadly optimistic about the Carter/Mondale ticket and regarded themselves as indispensable to its victory.[25] In return for their hard campaigning and generous donations, they expected tax, welfare, and labor law reform.[26] The narrow defeat of legislation related to common situs picketing (which would have made it easier to organize on construction sites) in 1977 quickly disillusioned them.[27] Although significant elements of the administration had opposed the legislation outright, Carter could not be directly blamed for its failure.[28] However, the president had not personally canvassed representatives for it either.[29] Carter was disinclined to work for liberal causes that he judged could be easily defeated.[30] After the failure of common situs picketing, labor became more skeptical of the president's loyalty and highly critical of his economic policy.[31] Combined with a tepid increase in the minimum wage, George Meany regarded Carter's legislative record on labor issues as a "bitter disappointment to anyone who looked to this administration for economic justice for the poor."[32]

Labor urged instead a relaxation of fiscal policy, protection, and government assistance to the manufacturing industry.[33] These views were not shaped by philosophical whim, but by an instinct for self-preservation. The UAW, for instance, was keenly aware that recession in the auto industry was precipitating a sharp decline in its membership.[34] Moreover, hamstrung by the restraints it perceived inflation had placed on it, the administration did not grant labor structural influence in government or the economy in the manner to which it was accustomed.[35] Combined with growing issue militancy at a local level, this mood precipitated a dramatic cooling of relations between unions and the administration. At a press conference in August 1978, Meany gave an ominously evasive answer to a question regarding his support for President Carter. Asked if "the course he is taking right now will lead him to an AFL-CIO endorsement for re-election," Meany replied, "I don't know. I don't even know if he's going to be running. . . . We would have to look over the candidates."[36]

Many feminist organizations felt the same. At first Carter was regarded favorably by the women's movement because he committed himself to reproductive rights and passage of the ERA.[37] Rosalynn Carter was heavily involved in campaigning for the latter, and White

House staff and the first family all thought they had done their best to support the amendment.[38] But the administration did not take long to disappoint its erstwhile supporters. Feminists were angered during the 1976 campaign at the Democratic National Committee's (DNC's) decision, supported by Carter, not to insist on 50 percent female representation at the convention in New York.[39] They were also disappointed with the number of women within the new administration.[40] The few who were appointed often faced marginalization. Midge Costanza, a presidential assistant, resigned in 1978 after a "series of humiliations engineered by Carter's Georgia advisers." Her staff was cut, her office was moved to the White House basement, and, in a personally insulting incident, Costanza was allegedly withdrawn at the last minute from a TV show appearance for fears about her radical views.[41] After leaving the administration, Costanza felt free to comment negatively on Carter's support for feminist causes. She told participants of a lesbian, gay, bisexual, and transgender (LGBT) campaign dinner that "she knew Carter was a 'Born again' Christian. . . . 'But I always wondered why he would want to come back as himself'"[42]

A still more damaging sacking took place in January 1979, when Carter fired liberal feminist Bella Abzug as chair of the influential National Advisory Committee of Women.[43] Abzug took the first meeting of the committee as an opportunity to assail the administration's anti-inflationary program and the president sacked her soon after.[44] The incident demonstrated the importance to the women's movement of economics, and half the committee resigned in protest.[45] Feminists sensed that Abzug's firing "was really an excuse to create some distance [from the women's movement] for the re-election campaign."[46] The "Friday Night" massacre represented the maturation of the women's movement. Feminists discovered that mainstream politicians would welcome it when it limited itself to discussion of individual rights, "but it was another matter when feminists moved from equal opportunity to women's deprivations that were deeply embedded in the current distribution of natural resources."[47]

The National Organization for Women also became convinced that Carter was not committed to the state-by-state campaign to ratify the ERA.[48] The ERA had passed through Congress but required ratification by three-quarters of the state legislatures. This number was almost achieved, but well-financed campaigns in a handful of Western and Southern states stopped the requisite number from being met. The White House thought that it had done all that was possible to help ratification.[49] In contrast, the first couple argued that the militant and unaccommodating behavior of the "radical and threatening" feminist movement alienated moderate public support.[50] But NOW did not believe the administration shared its sense of passion and urgency. To quote one activist, "We didn't feel that we got a lot of help. In Indiana the White House said they helped us, but we didn't feel it. . . . We only got through by one vote." When Congress came to pass an extension of the deadline for states' ratification, again, NOW sensed Carter did not offer his full support.[51] This anger was intensified by the administration's budgets, which many feminists believed amounted to a declaration of economic war on their programs and the vulnerable women that benefited from them.[52]

It was common anger that brought the AFL-CIO and NOW together into the fold of the Progressive Alliance. Their collective legislative defeats made them realize just how much they needed each other.[53] Despite his earlier opposition, Meany described ratification of the ERA in 1979 as "a major issue for the labor movement" and expressed the "strong unequivocal commitment of the AFL-CIO to the ERA."[54] One of the first tasks of his successor in 1980, Lane Kirkland, was to establish a committee to investigate "how, whether and in what way could the contribution and role of women and minorities be better reflected in the highest level of the trade union movement."[55] That year, the UAW committed itself to strengthening "the ability to organize women workers and to work with women's groups supporting the organization of women workers."[56] Douglas Fraser developed a close political relationship with NOW, even cochairing its 1979 conference.[57] The more socially conservative unions were beginning to mellow too. The deeply anticommunist American of Federation of Teachers' 1979 convention was attacked by its rival union, the National Education Association (NEA), for rejecting affirmative action and "being in league with the military/industrial complex." Yet the NEA could not ignore that the convention endorsed the ERA, opposed Carter's budget cuts, supported détente, and advocated ending discrimination that was based on sexual preference.[58]

Thus, the Progressive Alliance benefited from a new, convivial atmosphere within internal liberal politics. There were limits. Even Douglas Fraser conceded that the Progressive Alliance would have to avoid direct involvement in electoral politics. If it did not, it would "intensify existing and latent antagonisms among its constituent organizations and seriously weaken its capacity to influence the climate of opinion."[59] But the organization still enjoyed considerable success in bringing together liberal groups ordinarily divided against each other.

Present at its first meeting were representatives from the Americans for Democratic Action (ADA), the Committee for National Health Insurance, the NAACP, the United Farm Workers, the Democratic Agenda, NOW, SANE, Common Cause, the AFL-CIO, the Steel Workers, the Communication Workers, the American Federation of State, County and Municipal Employees (AFSCME), and the UAW.[60] Labor dominated the Progressive Alliance, and its chair was the president of the Machinists.[61] Its agenda was broad; for instance, in June 1979, it lobbied for passage of SALT II, renewable energy, and educational rights for Native Americans.[62] In many regards, its first few months were creditable. It lobbied successfully for liberal appointments to the House Budget Committee and held extensive hearings throughout the country that appeared to generate some activist excitement.[63] It employed two permanent members of staff and received contributions amounting to $132,121.[64]

Although it would enjoy a brief renaissance of influence during the 1980 Democratic Convention platform fight, the Progressive Alliance ultimately faded away.[65] The reasons were threefold. First, it failed to build a positive agenda and quickly became a protest movement that voiced complaints about the administration. The speakers at a February 1979 public meeting in Washington, D.C., though representative of an impressive array of interest groups, merely attacked Carter while avoiding making policy commitments themselves. The president of AFSCME's speech even conceded that public opinion appeared to be against them, pointing out that "78 percent of all Americans said in a poll that they wanted a balanced budget" and that "40 percent of California's public employees voted for the controversial tax cutting referendum, Proposition 13."[66] Second, some differences of interest were irreconcilable. The representative of the dovish New Democratic Coalition urged the Progressive Alliance to support across-the-board defense cuts.[67] But even the UAW, which had opposed Vietnam, protested similar cuts proposed by Carter as a result of their impact on the auto industry.[68] Some groups complained that the primacy of economic and labor issues left them excluded. Tom Hayden's Campaign for Economic Democracy (CED), although an active member of the Progressive Alliance, criticized it for being too focused on preserving blue-collar jobs and ignoring the issues of energy and military expenditure.[69]

The final reason for its decline was that it was eclipsed by the Kennedy candidacy. The Progressive Alliance admitted that "inherent in all of this is the necessity of considering the building of a left challenge

(Edward Moore Kennedy) within the Democratic Party so that Carter cannot play general-election, right wing politics for decades to come. . . . We cannot rely upon rhetoric and threats, we have to organize and show people power." Only the primaries would give the Progressive Alliance the opportunity to flex its muscles, and in this light, it is easy to see how such organizations became quickly absorbed into the Kennedy campaign in late 1979.[70] However, in the beginning of that year, it had to maintain its political integrity by evading clear association with Kennedy, walking "a fine line between creating a political base which could be used to challenge Carter in 1980 while avoiding being part of any overt 'dump Carter' movement."[71] This limited its political options further still.[72] Therefore, the Progressive Alliance was stillborn, eventually both overshadowed by and subsumed within the Kennedy candidacy.

The Democratic Agenda

Far more successful than the Progressive Alliance was the Democratic Agenda, which grew out of an organization called the Democratic Socialist Organizing Committee (DSOC). It was effectively DSOC's voice within the Democratic Party.[73] The Democratic Agenda's story once again illustrates the attempt by activists to "exert discipline" over elected officials and to "require accountability from them." But it also shows the Democratic Party's willingness to flirt with social democracy in the 1970s in its search for new ideas.[74] The Democratic Agenda tried to place European-style social democracy in an American Democratic tradition while encouraging liberals to reject fiscal conservatism.[75] It came up with a winning slogan that appropriated Democratic symbolism to promote socialistic policies: "If we do not go beyond FDR, then the reactionaries will drag us back to Herbert Hoover."[76] To achieve this it would attempt to rebuild coalition politics and offer a vehicle for liberal groups that felt marginalized by the Carter administration.[77]

DSOC was led by the academic Michael Harrington. An estranged Catholic, remarkable polemicist, and fiercely passionate defender of the poor, Harrington had become famous by the publishing of his book *The Other America*, a study of rural and urban poverty in the United States of the 1960s that sparked an outcry and provided a rationale for Johnson's Great Society. Harrington believed strongly that socialists should work within the Democratic Party, and as such, the goal of DSOC was to "influence the Democratic Party in a socialist manner, to adapt its policies, and to make them work better in our interests."[78] The group acted as a caucus, attending Democratic Party meetings and filing delegates. It also sought to act as "a bridge between progressive labor and the Democratic Party." Its major bases of influence were California and New York, the Machinists and the UAW.[79]

In the fall of 1975, Harrington decided to move away from independent lobbying and toward infiltrating the Democratic Party.[80] Aiming to challenge "a growing sense that problems like poverty were becoming intractable," he believed that DSOC needed "an ideological fight back program" and that it could gain influence among liberals at the same time by using the 1976 Democratic Party platform as a vehicle for its philosophical offensive. To this effect, DSOC lobbied for adoption of three policies: the passage of Humphrey-Hawkins, tax reform, and "greater democratic control of investment decisions," which amounted to increased regulation of the free market.[81] Demonstrating its sensitivity to the political climate, DSOC stressed that all three were anti-inflationary, and its tax reform package was designed to capitalize on the tax revolt. For instance, the Massachusetts DSOC branch sympathized with a tax-cutting referendum called Proposition 2.5 as a rebellion against "unfair property taxes." Rather than reversing the measure, it suggested "local aid formula reform to reflect the unequal impact of Prop 2.5 on communities," measures such as "a revision of current sales tax exemptions to generate more revenue," and "a tax on computer software and services."[82] Both the Democratic Agenda's and the Progressive Alliance's involvement in tax reform demonstrated that liberals were conscious of its salience as an issue, and rather than avoiding it, they attempted to appropriate it.[83] In spring 1979, a group called Tax Justice was founded. Its organizers argued that "the need for progressive tax reform is all the more urgent since conservative organizations have taken the initiative in the debate on tax reform to the detriment of consumers, workers, and taxpayers." It was designed to write alternative proposals for tax reform and to create "as broad based a coalition of labor, citizen, and local tax reform groups as possible." Coordinated by the AFL-CIO, its membership included the NAACP, ADA, Urban League, UAW, NOW, and AFSCME.[84]

For socialists, each of their major pledges amounted to a "transitional demand" and was part of a wider "very clear and very conscious" strategy of avoiding overt association with economic socialism to appeal to mainstream liberals.[85] In order to create a momentum behind these proposals and construct an alliance to lobby for them, DSOC coordinated a preconvention conference entitled Democracy '76. It

was at this conference that the Big Three auto unions that would provide funding and personnel for the Democratic Agenda first worked
together: the UAW, AFSCME, and the Machinists.[86] In 1977 the
presidency of the Machinists fell to William Winpisinger, a socialist
who lobbied the AFL-CIO to campaign "for broad social goals, like
national health insurance, rather than concentrate on parochial measures like the common situs picketing bill."[87] Both Douglas Fraser and
AFSCME president Jerry Wurf were vocal socialists too. Although
they were members as private citizens, Winpisinger, Fraser, and Wurf
could not affiliate their unions directly to DSOC. Thus Democracy
'76 became a method of unofficially integrating labor machinery into
organized left-wing activism, an opportunity "for education and ideological formation for [their] cadre."[88] It also tapped into growing militancy within unions.[89]

Democracy '76's ambition was the construction of a liberal Democratic Convention platform and the establishment of a lobby that
would work to ensure that the Carter/Mondale ticket fulfilled it. In
the long run, this small band of New York socialists proved "somewhat
naïve, but effective nonetheless, in pushing forward the idea that [the
platform] should have merit, it should have weight and that the presidential campaign should campaign on ideas that have meaning."[90] Over
1,000 delegates attended Democracy '76, and it achieved its objectives
of gaining national attention and creating an embryonic activist coalition. The convention readily endorsed DSOC's three-point program
and its promotion at the 1976 Democratic convention platform hearings by high-profile liberals. The socialists discovered, to their surprise, that their new professionalism worked. Simply by donning a tie
and jacket and presenting their ideas in a rational, calm manner, they
were able to greatly influence the platform committees. Radicalism
had come of age. The committees were now staffed by equally smart
and suit-wearing members of the once hard left who were happy to
rubber-stamp socialist proposals and dress them up as liberal. Thus,
DSOC noted with deserved pride that the 1976 Democratic Party
platform included almost all of the ideas and language that they had
submitted.

The Democratic Agenda emerged from Democracy '76 as a formal
organization dedicated to holding "the Democratic Party accountable"
to the promises it made in 1976.[91] "When the new administration failed
to live up to its promises," wrote Harrington, "Democratic Agenda
provided a meeting place and a strategy for action." Its coalition represented "the disenchanted who had done the most to elect the Carter/

Mondale ticket: trade unionists, minority leaders, community action groups, feminists, senior citizens, and perhaps for the first time, environmentalists and religious activists."[92] This coalition charged the Carter/Mondale ticket with ignoring its promises and felt a general sense of "dismay." Despite having "a huge Democratic majority," the neoliberals in Congress and the conservatives in the White House frustrated everything DSOC had striven to achieve.[93] To head its fight back, the Democratic Agenda employed a full-time director and three part-time organizers out of its office in Washington. It balanced a $61,500 budget, mostly sustained by annual donations of $10,000 each from the UAW, Machinists, and AFSCME.[94] It ran conferences every year in Washington, organized on a "state by state basis," with the primary ambition of "getting people excited about taking part at the Memphis convention." The effort in individual states meant that the Democratic Agenda was able to generate a degree of representation at the midterm convention that far outweighed its actual numerical strength.[95] In the afternoon session of the January 1978 conference, the delegates marched to the offices of the DNC to protest the administration's policies.[96]

The Democratic Agenda managed to include figures that would not have felt comfortable with DSOC, such as Amalgamated Clothing and Textile Workers Union (ACTWU) president Murray Finley, a passionate anticommunist but a cofounder of the Democratic Agenda.[97] In a private letter to Fraser, an activist reported of the 1979 Democratic Agenda conference that "more than 80 unions, industrial councils, and building trades councils were represented. The excitement generated by their contact with students, environmentalists, retirees, and others was electric."[98] They discussed issues as diverse as "the tenant's movement," "organizing working women," and "union busting and beyond."[99]

Throughout 1977–1978 the Democratic Agenda focused its attention on support for Humphrey-Hawkins.[100] This campaign promised to both strengthen its coalitional process, "reuniting the shattered left," and increase its animosity toward the administration. The Democratic Agenda charged Carter with "purposefully ducking full employment." It established links with the offices of both Humphrey and Hawkins, and Hawkins addressed one of its trade union conferences on full employment in New York. Several prominent members of the Congressional Black Caucus were also members of the Democratic Agenda.[101] Support for Humphrey-Hawkins allowed the Agenda to tap in to mainstream liberal traditions and associate its own brand of socialism with the New Deal era. It became an "indicator of success on any other front. . . . It was the prerequisite for getting advances in health care legislation and environmental legislation" because full employment, and the reduction in inflation that the Agenda calculated it would bring, would create an economic atmosphere more conducive to social spending.[102]

Throughout the late 1970s the Democratic Agenda generated a great deal of news coverage. The media was surprised to find that in an era of apparent electoral conservatism, elements of mainstream liberalism were prepared to flirt with socialism. *Business Week* warned its largely corporate readership that "socialism is no longer a dirty word to labor." It noted with anxiety that all seventeen building unions, traditionally "considered the most conservative element of organized labor," had placed a $700 ad in DSOC's newsletter. "The ad 'proudly salutes' DSOC . . . for its firm and militant support of the American labor movement." *Business Week* blamed anger at the Democratic Congress for the failure to pass common situs picketing legislation and DSOC's strategy of developing apparently innocuous alliances such as the Democratic Agenda for the leftward swing. The magazine ominously stated that DSOC enjoyed a weight of influence within the Democratic Party comparable to that of the Moral Majority within the Republican Party, even though it could muster but a fraction of its numerical support.[103] In short, a calm, businesslike movement that enjoyed nothing more than a four-figure membership came close to achieving what the mass antiwar and New Left movements of the 1960s had only dreamed of.

But after 1978 the Democratic Agenda declined in influence under pressures markedly similar to those faced by the Progressive Alliance. Kennedy's candidacy inevitably diverted attention and resources from the organization and exacerbated internal tensions.[104] Michael Harrington was personally supportive of Kennedy, privately describing the senator as "the odds-on-best man," a view generally held within DSOC.[105] However, some constituent groups within the Agenda (such as Hayden's CED) remained neutral, while others (such as Finley's ACTWU) campaigned for the president.[106] Ultimately the Agenda chose to stay out of the contest, with DSOC voting to endorse Kennedy and run members as delegates to the convention.[107] Once again, with the return of high politics, activist organizations became quickly subsumed within personality-driven campaigns. "In the context of a

direct Kennedy-Carter struggle . . . it was difficult," conceded one activist, "for Democratic Agenda to be as prominent in 1980 Democratic
politics as it was in 1978."[108]

In addition, an acrimonious internal split tore DSOC apart over
primary tactics.[109] Before Kennedy had declared his candidacy, and
buoyed by their recent publicity, some members urged Harrington
to enter the primaries as a protest candidate.[110] The movement had
reached a crossroads, with many activists firm in their belief that the
economic crisis augured well for a socialist ticket. Many more were
determined to avoid splitting the Agenda project and planned instead
to build on their new network.[111] Although the debate was resolved
by Harrington's endorsement of Kennedy, it ruptured DSOC, and
it never regained its momentum or the impressive degree of unity it
had built among the left.[112] Some socialists gravitated toward the Citizen's Party, with Barry Commoner as its presidential candidate and
LaDonna Harris (wife of Fred Harris) as its vice presidential nominee. Its platform was socialist enough, with some farsighted environmentalism thrown in, but it polled poorly in November 1980.[113]
Nonetheless, the primaries helped DSOC to integrate further into
the Democratic Party by fielding candidates for state delegations and
committees under the Kennedy banner.[114] Carter's administration had
created a context within which socialists could expand their membership and influence for the first time in forty years.[115] DSOC, which
reached a membership of 3,000 in 1979, had succeeded in "making life
at least slightly miserable for Jimmy Carter."[116]

The Meeting at Memphis

Both the Progressive Alliance and the Democratic Agenda directed
their efforts and attention to the only forthcoming event that held
out the tantalizing prospect of confronting, embarrassing, and thus
influencing the president: the midterm convention. At Memphis,
the Progressive Alliance initially intended to demand "the President
and Democratic members of Congress keep party platform commitments . . . and the setting up of a task force for party reform to create
a 'stronger, more accountable, more ideological' party."[117] But as it fell
apart and began to drift listlessly without results, it threw its people
and money behind the Democratic Agenda instead.[118]

The midterm convention was the high-water mark of the Democratic Agenda's influence in Democratic politics, and it proudly laid

claim to be the sole "effective opposition presented to the president's budget-cutting programs inside the Democratic Party."[119] It was "the only national effort to put issues discussion on the floor."[120] Harrington rationalized that if the left did not organize, the public would conclude that "the upsurge and tumult in the Democratic Party, which began with the civil rights movement, is over. Former civil rights and anti-war activists have settled down to the 'pragmatic' politics of the late 1970s and are accommodating themselves to the post–Proposition 13 conservatism." But were the convention to descend into well-planned chaos, "people will see a live and lively Party discussing and debating the future of our country. . . . The conclusion will again be obvious: there is a broad and massive constituency which wants and will fight for social progress and economic justice, and that constituency is a force to reckon with in the politics of the 1980s."[121] The midterm convention was therefore crucial for both ensuring the survival of 1960s activism within the Democratic Party and setting an agenda for the 1980s.

But as always, there was another, more covert goal, too. Harrington and Fraser hoped that vibrant opposition to Carter at the midterm convention would encourage Kennedy to run. In many regards, it was an effort to force his rather unwilling hand. They both reasoned that if the senator were to see that activists were angry enough with the president to embarrass him in front of television cameras (thus risking their own jobs and influence), he might conclude that a nomination effort would be considerably easier than he presupposed. There were then two audiences for the Democratic Agenda's efforts: the American people and Edward Kennedy.[122]

Throughout 1978, the Democratic Agenda ran workshops and conferences across the country designed to enthuse sympathizers to run as delegates to the convention.[123] It wanted to encourage the party to be "militant, tough. . . . We want the Democrats in the White House and Congress to shape up. The party asks for and gets support from the constituencies we represent. . . . We want a real discussion at next year's mini-convention."[124] The Agenda benefited from low interest in the meeting, allowing it to "steal a march on the administration" by fielding delegates in uncontested seats. The Agenda believed that gaining delegate strength could allow it to demonstrate its influence, but also hoped that it might force the administration to seek a compromise on isolated points of policy.[125] Depending on the influence of the Big Three unions, some states sent elected delegations that were almost entirely Agenda supporting.[126] The Michigan delegation, where the state party was orchestrated by the UAW and a self-declared socialist had run a respectable second in the 1978 gubernatorial Democratic primary, was dominated by the Agenda.[127] Agenda delegates were also selected from traditionally conservative states, such as Alabama.[128] The Agenda claimed to control 40 percent of the men and women at Memphis.[129]

Against this backdrop, the administration approached the midterm convention with understandable dread and foreboding. Carter loathed the very idea of having to go before his party to explain his policies. Not only did he feel that their necessity was self-evident, but the whole process positively reeked of the kind of dirty party politics that he so despised. His staff was more sensitive to the importance of putting on a good show. White House communications director Gerald Rafshoon wrote to Carter to warn him that while the president's speech "would cite the progress we are making . . . there are some political realities that should be faced." The administration was, after all, "asking Democrats to support an austere budget and cuts in many popular programs. . . . This is not a message all Democrats want to hear."

Rafshoon advised Carter to tell it anyway. The president faced a catch-22 situation: he could avoid conflict and receive a scolding from the press, or speak bluntly and risk a public rupture with his party.[130] Carter's staff chose a three-pronged strategy. The president's speech was worded to suggest that he shared his party's goals, but he was bound by the limitations of stagflation. What little he had achieved was remarkable.[131] He was trying to "get control of the critical issues of the day," a message that mixed idealism with rationality and accumulated wisdom.[132] Meanwhile, the vice president would balance an essentially cautious speech by providing a more liberal one. He told his audience, "We would rather risk reaction—than abandon the Equal Rights Amendment. We would rather contend with controversy— than turn our back on the Humphrey-Hawkins bill. We would rather take on a charged debate—than sign a wasteful [defense] appropriation. And we would rather suffer defeat—than side-step reform of our labor laws."[133] Mondale and Carter spoke to two different audiences, Carter to the general public and Mondale to the Democratic Party.

Finally, as a forerunner to its strategy in the 1980 primaries, the administration decided to aggressively press the flesh. The White House offered one-on-one meetings with the president himself, at which Carter stressed that "his budget decisions will make some interests unhappy, and . . . that there is no single, easy answer to each of our nation's problems."[134] It was hoped that personal contact with prestigious officials might allay fears and/or impress unity on del-egates.[135] Although the administration was determined to treat the convention as an opportunity rather than an inconvenience, its goals pointed to wider fears that the Democratic Party was abandoning the president.[136] Recognizing that the "upcoming session is obviously go-ing to be very difficult on the budget," Carter was even advised to meet with Speaker Tip O'Neill before the convention. Although O'Neill had accepted in principle "the need to cut the deficit . . . he has not focused on where the cuts will come from." Moreover, "the Democratic leadership, who are much easier targets for constant and intensive lobbying," was threatening to disregard even the Speaker's political authority to protest cuts.[137]

The administration's fears were not misplaced. The 1978 and 1980 conventions represented the high tide of an attempt by activists to exert control over party platform and to punish any Democratic ad-ministration that ignored its recommendations.[138] It reflected an ongo-ing generational "tension between party leaders, whose first loyalty is to the White House, and party reformers and liberals, most of whom were drawn in to politics by the Presidential candidacies of Eugene J. McCarthy and Robert F. Kennedy."[139] It displayed publicly the con-stantly evolving nature of Democratic Party institutional reform that had not ceased with 1972 and continued afresh in many state-level or-ganizations. For instance, in California, the Democrats did not intro-duce caucuses for the selection of delegates to the state convention until 1978, a move designed by reformers to effect a "further reduction in the influence of incumbent officials and nominees."[140]

At the 1978 midterm convention, the DNC attempted to craft del-egate selection and voting rules to avoid such a shift in constitutional power.[141] As *Time* explained, DNC chair John White and administra-tion/party liaison Tim Kraft "tried to turn the miniconvention into an exercise in intraparty public relations, a sort of half-time pep rally. . . . White rigged the rules in an attempt to minimize debates on resolutions critical of Carter. But on the eve of the convention he made concessions to liberal groups, led by lame duck Minnesota Con-gressman Don Fraser and UAW President Douglas Fraser, to allow several dissident resolutions to get a full airing on Sunday." Liberals won this concession by threatening to stage a walkout during Carter's speech "and flock instead to Senator Kennedy's session on national health insurance."[142] Don Fraser headed the "Democratic Conference" group, which lobbied specifically for constitutional reform of party conventions.[143] It was founded in 1975 just before the Democratic primaries to "narrow the field and avoid a self-defeating split of liberal strength."[144]

Initially, liberal activists' major goals regarding rules were to maximize debating time, give priority to resolutions generated by petitions, and decrease the required votes necessary for an automatic roll call from 25 percent to 10 percent of elected delegates.[145] Petitions to the DNC to this effect were ignored, and the administration successfully limited voting on resolutions to the last day of the convention—a Sunday, when many activists would be returning home.[146] Although it did agree to increase overall discussion time, many party liberals felt cheated.[147] The liberal activists now threw their weight behind those few controversial motions that White had permitted them to debate.[148] Nevertheless, their efforts were constrained by the DNC's decision that any resolution could only be passed by a majority of all delegates, rather than a majority of those present at the debate.[149] The administration flooded the convention with floor whips,[150] who kept in constant touch with state delegations to avoid embarrassing resolutions.[151]

The press predicted that the convention would prove a disappointment. The DNC had successfully massaged the rules to ensure that attendance at debates would be minimized and "most of the 20-odd resolutions expected to be considered are bland or supportive of Carter policies." A number of high-profile liberals declined to attend the convention altogether, including Gary Hart, Jerry Brown, Frank Church, George McGovern, and Daniel Patrick Moynihan.[152] The strength of the administration's position was demonstrated on the first day when White obtained an overwhelming standing vote to defeat a rules challenge.[153] Again, all of these tactics would return in the 1980 primaries: the rewriting of party rules and the use of personal diplomacy and outright intimidation. Although it proved effective, it arguably dented the president's dignity and made him appear panicked.

The convention consisted of a day of speeches, a day of workshops, and a day of debate.[154] The delegates included all Democratic officeholders and one man and one woman from each congressional district.[155] There were twenty-four workshops, the most heavily attended of which was on inflation.[156] Their subject matter spanned "defense policy and arms control," "energy," "welfare reform," and "the Democratic Party and the independent voter."[157] Panelists, who included White House officials, members of Congress, labor, and other liberal activists, provided a statement of their views and took questions from delegates.[158] The floor then elected members of the platform advisory committee, which would submit a nonbinding report on the discussion to the DNC. These members were ostensibly elected by delegates according to their ability to reflect the opinions expressed in the workshop.[159] These workshops attempted to represent as broad a range of views as possible. Thus, the foreign relations workshop included Henry Jackson, neoliberal representative Pat Schroeder, Kennedy partisan Senator John Culver, and the undersecretary of Defense.[160]

The Carter family moved between workshops, which allowed an unprecedented degree of contact between a sitting president and angry party activists. The contact was not always friendly. Although some activists were thrilled at the chance to meet the president, those that the Democratic Agenda had brought along were made of more militant stuff. These people were a mixture of social workers, single-issue campaigners, and union members. They were not cheerleaders for the administration but rather guardians of ideological purity. When the Agenda's people met the president, they were tough and uncompromising, even disrespectful. The *L.A. Times* reported that in one confrontation between an unemployed delegate and Carter, the president "listened patiently at first. But . . . accustomed to aides who understand his passion against wasting time, began shifting restlessly in his chair as [the] convention delegate demanded in some detail to know the answers to [difficult] questions."[161]

The resolutions presented to White from Democratic state parties were often contrary; they were colored by parochialism and provide fascinating insight into the priorities of ordinary activists.[162] Virginia Democrats demanded funding for a "100-mile transit system" and "a national health insurance program . . . supplemented by general tax revenues." But they additionally wanted "a coordinated program of federal and state legislation to ease the tax burden on Americans."[163] In contrast, the Democratic Agenda focused on securing consideration of a handful of ideologically consistent motions that largely dealt with economic policy. Throughout 1978 it had "worked with Democratic Party activists to develop a series of resolutions, almost all of them based on the 1976 Democratic Party platform and asserting either implicitly or explicitly the proposition that party platforms must be taken seriously."[164] In this regard, the Democratic Agenda's resolutions were an exercise in accountability and activist power. Each resolution began with the phrase "The Democratic Party reaffirms the following statements . . . in the 1976 Democratic Party Platform." They reminded Carter of his commitment to health insurance, Humphrey-Hawkins, and regulation of oil and gas.[165] They also pointed to the central point of activist concern regarding Carter's economic policies. "The problems which confronted this nation in 1976," they suggested, "have not yet been solved, yet it appears that the FY '80 budget will cut many social programs below 'current services' levels, while allowing the military budget to grow."[166] The Democratic Agenda easily gained the 25 percent of signatures required for consideration, which meant that on the last day of the conference, they were discussed as alternative wordings to the resolutions submitted by the administration—a key victory.[167]

Despite his apparent political strength, when Carter arrived in Memphis on Friday, 8 December 1978, the convention's atmosphere was tense.[168] Douglas Fraser had stated on Tuesday, 5 December, that he intended to "support efforts . . . in Memphis to go on record against those apparent budget intentions in the Carter administration" and warned that he had the support of "10 other major unions."[169] He kicked off the convention with a rally against budget cuts, at which one Michigan congressman warned Carter that "we elected him and we can de-elect him."[170] There were blue-and-white Kennedy signs in the air, one year before he was even to declare.[171]

More troubling was that black officials indicated that they too were inclined to break rank with Carter. One hundred black delegates voted to demand a face-to-face meeting with the president to discuss the budget. Representative John Conyers predicted that cuts would "flatly result in [Carter's] defeat in 1980."[172] President of the NAACP Vernon Jordan had led a coalition of urban black leaders to the Oval Office the previous week to signal disapproval with cuts in aid to cities.[173] They had been joined by Detroit mayor Coleman Young, an important black Carter ally, who openly urged the convention to vote against the administration's urban spending plans.[174] A postconvention administration report noted that there had been "intense pressure on black delegates" to support the Democratic Agenda. It also reported that those delegates committed to supporting the administration did so despite "guaranteed grief about it back home."[175]

Carter's opening speech was received politely but without enthusiasm, and the first day of the convention passed without significant incident. He had, as was often the president's stratagem, deflated tensions through reason and banality. "We face tough times ahead," he told them. "We have to cut the budget or else inflation will destroy everything we've ever accomplished." But the activists had heard this message many times before and were unmoved. There was a palpable sense that they were there to see someone else instead.[176]

The next day Edward Kennedy spoke at the workshop on health

care. He was joined by Douglas Fraser, Stuart Eizenstat, and Joe Califano. The workshop was chaired by Carter partisan Bill Clinton in
his first national role after his election as the youngest governor of
Arkansas in history.[177] The workshop began as quietly and on message
as expected. Eizenstat and Califano outlined the hospital cost-containment bill as the first, albeit cautious, step toward health insurance, and
the audience clapped politely in all the right places. But then Kennedy stood up. It is important to note that what he did next was not
a declaration of candidacy at all. It was rather a genuine statement of
philosophical belief, a desperate plea for hope and ambition. Perhaps
the power of his speech came truly from the fact that it was not about
him or his candidacy, but instead about what he believed in.

Kennedy rigorously defended his national health insurance (NHI)
proposal. The audience expected that. But then, his voice getting
louder, Ted launched a startling attack on Carter's cuts in federal
spending.[178] "We cannot accept a policy that cuts spending to the bone
in areas like jobs and health," he growled, "but allows billions of dollars in wasteful spending for tax subsidies to continue and adds even
greater fat and waste through inflationary spending for defense." The
delegates jumped to their feet and applauded wildly.[179] "The party that
tore itself apart over Vietnam in the 1960s," continued Ted, "cannot
afford to tear itself apart today over budget cuts in basic social programs."[180] To be sure, high inflation had dramatically altered the tenor
of political debate. "We know that some things in America today are
wrong," he conceded. "It is wrong that prices are rising as rapidly as
they are." But he could not allow inflation to deflect the Democratic
Party from its historic commitment to the poor. "It is also wrong," he
reminded the delegates and the absent president, "that millions of our
fellow citizens are out of work. It is wrong that cities are struggling
against decay. It is wrong that women and minorities are denied their
equal rights. It is wrong that millions who are sick cannot afford the
care they need."

Senator Kennedy invoked the memories of Roosevelt and his
brother, Jack—presidents, he said, that had demonstrated that a
bold and activist federal government could generate both "economic
growth and price stability." Such a government could do anything if
it put its mind to it. The Democrats were not the "party of Coolidge
or Hoover," but rather a movement that "stood for action, hope, and
progress." The audience hollered and cheered, and the administration officials melted quietly into their seats. His face red and his voice

hoarse, Kennedy concluded, "Sometimes a party must sail against the wind. We cannot afford to drift or lie at anchor. We cannot heed the call of those who say it is time to furl the sail."[181]

The speech electrified the hall. Delegates cried out his name and stamped their feet in joy. Eizenstat visibly seethed, and Califano, who had enjoyed every moment of it, smiled enigmatically. When he heard the news, a resigned Carter presumed that the race for the nomination had finally begun. A fledgling "draft Kennedy" movement took it the same way too.[182] "You couldn't help but look at the '78 convention," recalled Kennedy's pollster Peter Hart, "and realize that the Democrats were in trouble . . . and certainly Kennedy and the liberals were beginning to open up a front on Carter."[183]

There was no doubt in the Democratic Agenda's collective mind that "the idea of a Kennedy candidacy came out of that speech and came out of that convention."[184] The race was on. Said one witness, "The heart, the soul, the pride, and the passion of the party is in its sponsorship of programs. And that is a tradition that Kennedy—and only Kennedy—now invokes."[185] However, it was not an isolated example of dissent. In a panel on cities, U.N. ambassador Andrew Young attacked budget cuts; in the panel on employment, the administration was charged with failing to support Humphrey-Hawkins; and in the panel on foreign relations, Culver asserted that defense spending was "the most inflationary dollar you can spend." However, many of these attacks lacked force because of the administration's successful lobbying. In contrast, Kennedy's speech dominated the news. It was replayed and analyzed again and again by a media that had finally found a story out of Memphis.[186]

The resolutions debate the next day proved equally embarrassing for Carter. Although the administration won every motion, it did so narrowly, and at the cost of exposing the extent of internal disquiet. The floor debate on full employment provided a neat example. The UAW and Democratic Agenda wanted the party to adopt language that would commit the administration to achieving an ambitiously low level of unemployment of 3 percent. On the evening before the debate, Douglas Fraser and his staff met privately with Eizenstat to negotiate compromise language. The administration, which had decided to alter its definition of an acceptable rate of unemployment, hoped to split the UAW off from the Democratic Agenda. This would embarrass militant supporters of Humphrey-Hawkins and also defuse a "draft Kennedy" movement. It was trying to avoid "a headline in the *New York Times* that read that rank and file Democrats had rejected the

President" in favor of the now-godlike senator. But the meeting went badly; neither side was prepared to give ground to the other. Fraser was defending people's jobs and pay. Eizenstat was advocating economic reason in order to stem the tide of inflation. Voices were raised and political threats were made. Infuriated with Carter's intransigence, Fraser suddenly stormed out of the meeting and left his staff to speak for him. The meeting quickly reached an impasse, with both sides recognizing that any settlement that involved conceding ground would be regarded as a political victory. The meeting was symptomatic of the conflict between the administration and its erstwhile liberal constituency.

The next day there was an ugly floor fight. Both the Democratic Agenda and the administration operated a whip; the administration's effort was orchestrated by a young lawyer and governor's wife, Hillary Rodham. The UAW hoped to avoid a vote altogether because it had no desire to embarrass Carter and thus weaken its influence within the administration. However, Don Fraser of the Democratic Conference put forward a motion for a roll call vote. The chair misread the motion to refer to *Douglas* Fraser and announced erroneously that the UAW had requested the vote rather than the mayor of Minneapolis. Fraser was infuriated by the mistake, which put him in an invidious position. He was forced to choose between a loss of face among unionists and antagonizing the administration. His staff argued that after Kennedy's speech, Carter was now a lame duck and Fraser could take a risk. Therefore, reluctantly, Douglas Fraser acknowledged the motion as being by his hand and whipped for its passage. The final vote was close enough for the Democratic Agenda and the UAW to claim a victory, despite actually losing.[187] The precarious campaign by the UAW had successfully shown "the broader anger of Democrats" toward the administration. "It turned into a moment when our side took on Carter and was perceived to have won, even though we lost numerically. . . . It laid the seeds for ultimately turning our back on Carter and backing Teddy Kennedy."[188]

1979

Delegates, journalists, and the president left behind them a divided and battered party at Memphis. They returned home to rising inflation and unemployment, and the president signaled publicly for the first time that he was probably going to allow the country to slip into recession in 1979–1980 rather than bail it out with tax breaks and spending programs. The events of the midterm convention were discussed at the presidential Cabinet on 11 December 1978. John White gave a positive report, indicating that "the Conference had adjourned with a basically united Democratic Party." Mondale interjected to signal his disagreement.[189] He "observed that some delegates to the Conference had unwarranted doubts about the administration and its policies, and that we must work closely with those delegates and the people they represent to resolve their doubts." Revealingly, when Carter spoke next, he alluded immediately to the workshop on NHI. He defended his own proposals and stated that "his commitment to a national health plan is undiminished." Califano closed the discussion by arguing that "the national health issue was part of the larger debate within the Party and across the country over budget and fiscal priorities." He ominously warned that "the debate would intensify in the months ahead." Without naming Kennedy, the Cabinet had acknowledged the true political significance of the midterm convention.[190]

Some commentators judged that Memphis had been a partial success for Carter. He had won, albeit narrowly, every resolution vote on the floor.[191] But the victory was pyrrhic. The Democratic Agenda had embarrassed the president and forced a public debate on the future of administration policy. The backroom negotiations gave activists a new sense of power and importance. Even gay rights activists successfully exploited the administration's weakness. Although they failed to get a resolution on sexual discrimination past the DNC, the LGBT lobby managed to get 406 delegates' signatures toward debating a motion and began to prepare themselves for a floor fight. Eizenstat and White moved quickly to quash the revolt by promising reconsideration of the issue at the 1980 convention. This represented a significant step forward.[192]

The midterm convention marked the emergence of a new liberal alliance. Its most powerful member was labor, and this would stay the case well into the 1980s.[193] "The unions have been Democratic stalwarts since the New Deal," began one typical postconvention analysis, "and until this year, they tended to oppose the militant minorities in the party. In Memphis, however, the dissidents were lead by Douglas Fraser of the UAW. The attitude to George Meany, head of the AFL-CIO, on economic issues is 'right on.'" The potential for labor to undermine the anti-inflation program with wage increases was significant. "Unless the President can make some changes soon, his effort to hold the line on inflation could quickly transform his relations with labor into a state of costly and unnecessary and perhaps self-defeating war."[194] This was an accurate interpretation of the growing militancy within labor. In October 1978 an internal UAW memo suggested that administration inaction was forcing unions to "use our economic power to win political concessions."[195] The wider implication of Memphis was that liberals intended "not to defeat or embarrass the President, but to send him the message that their support cannot be taken for granted." Their "improvised coalition" had successfully sparked debate and garnered national attention.[196] It had also given courage to the senator from Massachusetts to finally take a stand.

Things only got worse for the administration after Memphis. Carter's first attempts at frugality were either weak-willed or misdirected, and the annual rate of inflation reached 11.3 percent in 1979, bumped up by OPEC's decision to raise the price of oil.[197] Carter responded with yet more restraint. In the first half of his administration, the chair of the Federal Reserve, William Miller, had overseen a relatively expansionist monetary policy encouraged by low interest rates. In 1979, Carter appointed Paul Volcker (a liberal Keynesian turned monetarist) as the new head of the Federal Reserve. It was widely expected that Volcker would use the traditional method of curtailing inflation: manipulating interest rates. But Volcker decided that a kill-or-cure solution to inflation was necessary, and as Carter slashed the federal budget, Volcker raised interest rates and reduced the money in circulation by controlling bank reserves.[198] The White House opposed the move, fearing that the inevitable recession would land in an election year. But Carter was forced to acquiesce, and as interest rates soared to 15 percent, he announced new controls on consumer credit. Between them, the president and the banker manufactured a recession for 1980.[199]

As unemployment, inflation, and interest rates mounted up, Carter stumbled from crisis to crisis, his sense of leadership and direction totally lost. Then in July 1979 he appeared for a brief moment to have recaptured the nation's affections and his own sense of purpose. This singular incident of political genius arose from the energy crisis. As OPEC raised prices, supply dwindled, and gas stations were forced to close down. On 24 June 1979, a Sunday when many Americans would have ordinarily taken a leisurely drive, 70 percent of gas stations were closed. Congress held hearings to determine what the causes of rising prices were. Conservatives argued that the problem was regulation and the relatively high cost of extraction: domestic suppliers had to be encouraged to produce more by slashing business taxes and deregulation.

Liberals argued the opposite: corporations were simply exploiting the crisis to make bigger profits. Only more regulation and controls on prices would bring them down. Typically, Carter equivocated and told the public that tough choices were necessary—choices that he refused to elaborate on. He preferred the strategy of conservation and self-discipline, which naturally meant allowing prices to continue to rise. It was a remarkably insensitive position to take.[200]

The next week, OPEC raised prices further still. Carter dashed home from a summit in Tokyo and requested TV time to make a statement on the crisis. Then he changed his mind. Instead, he retreated to Camp David and held a domestic summit. He summoned business and union leaders, community representatives, priests, and even those ordinary members of the public in whose houses he had stayed.[201] The nation was fascinated. There was something Moses-like about Carter's journey up the mountain in search of answers. When he returned back down, he gave an impressive television address that thrilled them further still. In a self-effacing and bold expression of political paralysis, he told viewers that America was undergoing a "crisis of confidence." Its problems were not just economic, but spiritual too. Ever since Watergate and Vietnam, Americans had lost confidence in their nation's ability to get things done. Paralysis and doubt had replaced energy and vision. The speech was perhaps the definitive moment of Carter's career. It offered no easy answers, posed many questions, and was delivered in a quiet, pastoral manner. The president was remarkably candid about the criticism he had received, but this honesty seemed to recapture what had first made Americans fall in love with him: his truthfulness and simplicity. In his conclusions, Carter asked for his people's prayers and that they might dedicate themselves to a "rebirth of the American spirit" of selflessness and discipline.[202]

The speech was initially popular.[203] However, within a week, Carter undermined his own momentum. He requested the resignation of his entire Cabinet. He reappointed the majority, but the action gave the impression of a lack of leadership, and the initial bump in his poll ratings quickly turned into a dramatic nosedive.[204] The legislation he put to Congress on energy was complex and ultimately toothless. This moment of near-triumph turned public relations disaster neatly encapsulated everything wrong about Jimmy Carter's presidency. The problem was not just his inept handling of the political side of his administration. It lay also in the policy proposals themselves. A call to self-sacrifice was admirable and briefly inspiring, but most Americans actually thought that their problems lay in ineffectual government and corporate greed, not in the realm of the spirit.[205]

Walter Mondale did not like the "crisis of confidence" speech and advised Carter not to give it. Its themes of paralysis and the complexity of modern living contradicted the spirit of American liberalism.[206] Edward Kennedy agreed. He dubbed it the "malaise speech," a phrase that Reagan borrowed in the general election of 1980.[207] Many friends and staffers have stated that it was the "crisis of confidence" speech that confirmed Ted's intention to run. It presented a model of the presidency that he found self-lacerating, defeatist, and cowardly. Government should not back down in the face of impersonal forces but should confront and overcome them. Kennedy thought that Jimmy Carter had metaphorically emasculated the presidency. This was an insult to the office as well as to the memory of Jack and Bobby, who had argued that the American people could, in the words of John Wayne often quoted by Ronald Reagan, "lick any problem if they put their mind to it." After Memphis, Kennedy had the issue on which to run (NHI) and the beginnings of a grassroots structure. After the "crisis of confidence" speech, he finally found the anger he needed to force him to take a stand.[208]

4

The Kennedy Moment

By autumn 1979 it was common knowledge that Edward Kennedy was running for the presidential nomination. The Democratic Party prepared itself for civil war. Carter set up field operations in Iowa and the South, poured federal money into the hands of local government officials, and began contacting old friends to call in favors. Kennedy went on a whirlwind tour of the United States. Because he hadn't yet declared, the tour was technically pointless, but the enthusiastic audiences who met him knew exactly what he was doing.[1] The Progressive Alliance and Democratic Agenda amalgamated and reformed as a "draft Kennedy" movement.[2] They created a coalition titled the National Call for Kennedy, its goal being to demonstrate that "there is a large number of concerned citizens who are willing to come forward with their financial support to build a huge groundswell of citizens urging Senator Kennedy to run."[3] The National Call was angry with "a government that is hopelessly paralyzed. . . . Things are getting worse, not better." Senator Kennedy offered movement and action. "He believes," it insisted, "that the rich can take care of themselves. Government is for the ordinary citizen. He has fought—really fought—for a long time on a lot of fronts—for tax reform, campaign finance reform, national health insurance, handgun control, crime laws, the Equal Rights Amendment, arms control, break-up of the big oil companies, clean water, clear air, anti-trust actions against corporate mergers."[4]

In addition to the National Call, a series of wholly autonomous statewide "draft Kennedy" committees were formed by local Democrats.[5] These established links with, and often were staffed by, unions. For instance, the Missourians for Kennedy organization was founded by a St. Louis lawyer and funded and staffed by the state UAW.[6] Of course, not every Kennedy operation was homespun and spontaneous. Some of the Senate staff worked behind the scenes making contacts, developing local organizations, and cultivating friends. For legal and political reasons, it remained unofficial, and none of its operatives participated in the primaries. Although it had been functioning since late 1978, its furtiveness reflected the fact that Kennedy remained uncertain about entering the race and was reluctant to commit himself.[7]

The decision to run for president was not an easy one. On the one hand, Kennedy was riding high in the polls while Jimmy Carter was sinking to new lows. Friends, family, peers, and even sworn enemies told the senator that the nomination was his if he wanted it. All he had to do was declare. But on the other hand, Carter was a sitting president. As such, he had access to money, power, and influence that even a Kennedy could not rival. Moreover, Kennedy had a lot to lose if he lost. Were he a stalking horse, a liberal Don Quixote like George McGovern, then just running and winning a handful of primaries would be glorious enough. But as a Kennedy, Ted had to win, and win big. He would be running in the shadow of his brothers' reputation as political titans. He would have to not just lead the field, but dominate it. Edward Kennedy would have to psychologically commit himself not only to winning a landslide, but winning it easily. And he wasn't even sure that he really wanted to be president.[8]

The decision to run for president was probably harder for Kennedy than it was for any other candidate that year. Chappaquiddick hung over his candidacy like a black cloud permanently threatening to burst. July 1979 was the tenth anniversary of the accident, and the media was suddenly full of investigations and reinterpretations that dredged the scandal up at precisely the moment when it was least helpful.[9] Kennedy apparently hoped that the public cared less about the incident than the press did, that they were more concerned about inflation, unemployment, and dumping a deeply unpopular president than they were about the finer details of the candidate's private life.[10] Perhaps easy reelections in his liberal home state of Massachusetts had shielded him against the wider wrath of public disapproval, or perhaps his commitment to the issues blinded him to the personal dimension of any presidential candidacy. Either way, Kennedy approached Chappaquiddick with an objectivity and distance that implied he wasn't even really there that night, let alone driving the car. Even if Kennedy did not think that Chappaquiddick would matter, his friends warned him that the public would not be that forgiving. After all, the senator was running against a president who had an image of propriety that a clergyman might envy.[11]

And then there was the lingering threat of assassination. Edward

Kennedy had survived two brothers who had both died by assassins' bullets, one while on the campaign trail. There was a risk that if he ran for the presidency, Kennedy might attract the attentions of yet another maniac.[12] So real was that risk that Carter extended the offer of Secret Service protection to the senator a month before he actually declared, on the grounds that the publicity his noncandidacy was getting made him a potential target. Ordinarily candidates do not receive Secret Service protection until they are eligible for federal financial aid.[13] Ted's mother privately told him that she feared for his life and asked him not to run.[14]

Therefore, it took enormous personal courage for Kennedy even to consider declaring. Yet fate demanded it. Carter's disastrous handling of the presidency had descended into farce. His fiscal policies pushed the country further and further toward recession; his energy policy vacillated between taxing gas and oil producers' profits (which curtailed new investment) and allowing prices to rise. His every misstep seemed calculated to make Kennedy declare, as if he were daring the senator to take a stand and to see if he could do any better.

In October Carter and Kennedy met in an iconic public appearance that crystallized all their differences and signaled to the world that the race was on. The occasion was the dedication ceremony of the John F. Kennedy Library in Boston. Both men were scheduled to speak. For Kennedy, it was a family affair, both personal and political. It reminded him of past glories and the role the Kennedys had gladly played in shaping their country's history. For Carter, the meeting was almost a nuisance. It was another reminder of the good old days of Camelot and of the charisma, wealth, and public support that he had always envied and rarely enjoyed. In fact, his preparation for the speech conveyed perfectly the hardened, bitter, confrontational attitude that he felt toward the senator ever since Memphis. Jimmy Carter believed that Edward Kennedy was not a humble public servant but instead an ambitious patriarch willing to use money and naked appeals to the worst excesses of the 1960s to steal the White House away from its rightful occupant. Driven by greed rather than idealism, Kennedy had rejected reasonable negotiations over national health insurance to catalyze a public confrontation that would give him an excuse to run.[15]

Carter decided to fight fire with fire. He had beaten a wide field of liberal Democrats in 1976 to take his party's nomination and threatened that if Edward Kennedy ran, he would gladly beat him too. He had then defeated a well-liked president in the general election. After four years of intense struggle, he was unwilling to surrender his prize. When asked privately what would happen if Kennedy entered the 1980 Democratic primaries, Carter replied, "I'll whip his ass."[16] The intemperate language shocked the president's evangelical supporters. It was the first of many occasions in which Carter would be accused of being mean throughout the campaign. In fact, it was simply a public display of a deep, private bitterness toward an infuriatingly presumptuous heir.

Carter could have played ball that day at the John F. Kennedy Library. He could have just thanked Ted for the invitation, praised his predecessor, applauded the assembled liberals' speeches, and then returned home. Instead, his speechwriters urged him to outshine the senator with a combative oration that lay out a clear message of limits. This was precisely what he did. Carter delivered an excellent speech that effectively threw down the gauntlet to Ted.[17] He pointed out that "the world of 1980 is as different as the world of 1960 was from that of 1940. The carved desk in the Oval Office which I use is the same as when John F. Kennedy sat behind it, but the problems that land on the desk are quite different. . . . We have a keener appreciation of the limits now—the limits on government, the limits on the use of military power abroad." The implications were obvious. Yes, the Kennedy family had done much in the 1960s, but the world had moved on. Ted was out of touch.

If Carter's words defined his presidential style, Kennedy's defined his candidacy. At the podium, he invoked the memory of his brothers, telling his audience that it was Jack that had first taught him to "sail against the wind," to take risks and stand up for his principles. He talked of a commitment to helping the poor and the disadvantaged and finished with words that would become a leitmotif in his campaign: "the spark still glows. The journey never ends. The dream shall never die." He was, in effect, telling the audience that his coming candidacy would be the completion of Jack's and Bobby's. If the message was not obvious enough, his nephew, Joe, delivered a much angrier speech that asked tough questions of the administration. He demanded to know who in modern politics was prepared to defend Americans against "vested interests" such as oil companies and big business.[18] All of these speeches set the stage for a battle that would decide in which direction the Democratic Party should sail: to the left or to the right. Ominously, the press broadly thought that Carter had won. This was not because he was better or that they necessarily agreed with him. It was simply that they expected far less of him than what he actually delivered. By not being excessively rude, fluffing his lines, or falling off the platform, Carter impressed the press corps. In contrast, they expected Kennedy to say exactly what he did say and thus were indifferent toward it. This subtle shift in the dynamics of the race suggested that it was going to be far tougher going than the Kennedy family expected.[19]

The Brilliant Noncandidacy

Carter and his staff have always asserted that Edward Kennedy only considered running for the presidency because he was ahead in the polls.[20] That would hardly have been an unorthodox reason to run for office. Even so, Carter's assertion that Kennedy's actions were governed "simply and only [by] whether or not he thought he could win" contains within it an admission of serious weakness on the part of the president. A Kennedy candidacy appeared viable in 1979—more than that: if the elections had been held in October 1979, Edward Kennedy would have won both the Democratic primaries and the presidency by a landslide.[21]

First, President Carter was vulnerable. In July 1979 the president's public approval rating slumped to an historic low of 25 percent.[22] Some 36 percent of registered Democrats and 41 percent of self-described independent voters stated they would not consider voting for him in 1980.[23] The economy had entered recession and Carter's response to it was widely regarded as weak and indecisive.[24] Sixty-four percent of Americans subscribed to the view that "although well intentioned, at times you begin to wonder if he has the basic competence to do the job."[25] In June 1979, the *New York Times* reported that Carter had an approval rating among Americans of 30 percent and a disapproval rating of 53 percent. His performance in economic and energy policy received a 70 percent disapproval rating. Significantly, 42 percent listed the economy as the most important problem facing the country. Only 19 percent favored his renomination.[26]

An eve-of-campaign poll demonstrated disapproval of his performance in all fields: 53 percent disliked his handling of foreign policy and 65.8 percent his handling of economic policy. A majority of 51.4 percent stated that they desired qualities of leadership most in their presidents and that they thought Carter had demonstrated little of it.[27] Jimmy Carter's decline in the polls corresponded with a decrease in numbers of citizens describing themselves as Democratic, from 51 percent in 1976 to 38 percent in 1979. Importantly, the biggest decreases in party identification took place within the Democratic base, rather than among moderates or conservatives.[28] The number of those describing themselves as liberal identifying with the party fell by 33 percent. The fall was 20 percent among African Americans, 18 percent among union members, and 13 percent among Catholics.[29] These groups were simultaneously greatly attracted to the notion of a Kennedy candidacy, and he enjoyed highly favorable ratings of 81 percent among blacks, 70 percent among Hispanics, 53 percent among Catholics, and 52 percent among union members.[30]

In contrast to Carter's unpopularity, both registered Democrats and the general public greeted a Kennedy candidacy with clear enthusiasm.[31] As a result, many officeholders regarded him as the strongest candidate for 1980.[32] By June 1979, registered Democrats preferred Kennedy by 54 percent to 21 percent and considered his judgment better by 55 percent to 40 percent.[33] In July 1979, the *New York Times* reported that Kennedy's lead over Carter had climbed (61 percent to 33 percent) and that he was preferred as a candidate even in the South (48 percent to 44 percent).[34] The wider public favored Kennedy as an alternative nominee too.[35] In a sample poll from September 1979, 68 percent of all voters thought he should enter the race, and 63 percent thought he could "save the Democrats from almost certain defeat under Carter." Some 56 percent believed that Carter would not win renomination.[36] Americans consistently told pollsters that they thought Kennedy had the characteristics of leadership a president needed.[37] An eve-of-campaign poll by Gallup found that the general public preferred Kennedy to Carter by 53.1 percent to 27.8 percent.[38]

Given his many personal weaknesses, it would be tempting to conclude that Carter was more hated than Kennedy was loved. But this was not so. Kennedy was not only preferred to Carter, he was consistently voted the best presidential candidate in 1979.[39] According to *Public Opinion* magazine, he held a lead over Reagan of 64 percent to 34 percent, and lobbyists were reporting that he "frightens many Republicans . . . because no Republican is close to him in national polls."[40] Reagan's pollster, Richard Wirthlin, detected that Kennedy's support stretched across a spectrum of ideology, holding comfortable pluralities among voters who described themselves as liberal, moderate, and even somewhat conservative. Interestingly, he was narrowly preferred as a candidate by those who told Wirthlin they were somewhat for Reagan, suggesting that he held appeal even for the conservative voter. Kennedy led Reagan in the governor's own polls by 55.1 percent to 40.1 percent.[41] An eve-of-campaign poll by Gallup put the lead at 63.6 percent to 36 percent.[42] Even one of Kennedy's academic critics acknowledged that these figures pointed to a "'landslide' in public sentiment" for Kennedy.[43]

Kennedy's pollster, Peter Hart, confirmed Wirthlin's findings that the public thought his candidate was more likely to square the circle of providing free health care and reducing inflation than his rivals were. Interviewees believed that Kennedy would be better at cutting inflation than Carter, while simultaneously acknowledging that he was more likely to raise government spending. They did rate him poorly on controlling federal outlays, but this was dwarfed by the only other concern about his candidacy: that he might be assassinated.[44] Pollsters regularly found, somewhat paradoxically, that a relatively conservative public, concerned most about inflation, supported a man whom it regarded as moderately to very liberal. For instance, a Yankelovich poll found that Kennedy was preferred as a candidate to Carter among Democrats by 58.6 percent to 25.3 percent and among all voters to Reagan by 54 percent to 34.5 percent. He was also rated by 64 percent of all voters, the highest figure among all candidates, as an "acceptable" president elect. Yet a clear majority identified Kennedy as a liberal. Coincidentally, 41.6 percent described themselves as conservative.[45] This broad support for Kennedy undermines the popular view of the late 1970s as an era of right-wing drift. That he led Jimmy Carter, Ronald Reagan, and Gerald Ford suggests that the country was still receptive to liberal ideas, even if put forward by a man whose private life had undergone considerable and unfavorable scrutiny.

It should be noted briefly that Kennedy was not the only Democrat to challenge Carter for the nomination. Neoliberal governor Jerry Brown declared his candidacy in 1978, building on his success in the 1976 primaries and his landslide reelection as governor.[46] Brown's strategy rested on the assumption that Kennedy was likely to dominate the primaries, to the degree that he publicly urged the senator to declare and thus trigger a contest.[47] He intended to offer himself as a moderate alternative to Kennedy after Carter had been decisively beaten in the first round.[48] Brown ran on a platform of fiscal conservatism and environmentalism—classic neoliberal positions.[49] Having weathered the Proposition 13 referendum, Brown became a supporter of a constitutional convention to mandate a balanced budget.[50] However, the Brown candidacy suffered as a result of the shifting dynamics of the primary season. When Kennedy's fortunes declined, Brown's campaign lost momentum and purpose. The Brown candidacy was not a popular one.[51] His message of fiscal frugality alienated liberals and labor while his conversion to tax capping suggested to the wider public that he was either indecisive or unprincipled.[52] Brown conceded defeat early on in the primaries and rarely took more than 10 percent of the vote.[53] After his withdrawal, most of his former supporters (including peace activist Tom Hayden and his wife, Jane Fonda) happily switched to Kennedy in an effort to forestall Carter's renomination.[54] The ease with which they did so showed how hostility toward the president united a broken liberal coalition.

Kennedy's People

The work of the Progressive Alliance and the Democratic agenda demonstrated that quarrelsome liberals had begun to find greater cohesion toward the end of the 1970s, first by developing policies designed to alleviate unemployment and then by opposing Jimmy Carter. But what really united American liberals (and even some conservatives) was the tantalizing prospect of a Kennedy candidacy. Undoubtedly this was linked to the senator's unique personality and the glamour of his name. But it was also an expression of the healing potential of universalist ideas.

Edward Kennedy's politics had a cross-generational appeal. For instance, Kennedy sympathized with many of the demands of the social movements of the 1960s, including second-wave feminism. He regarded the Equal Rights Amendment (ERA) as the first step toward female liberation.[55] He believed, as did the National Organization for Women (NOW) and the feminist movement, that women were entitled to a "fair share of the economy" even if they were unproductive. Overcoming structural and de jure discrimination would require government intervention and a president prepared to tell federal agencies and private employers how many women to employ and how much to pay them. Therefore, he endorsed an equal pay act, support for widows and single parents, and gendered employment quotas.[56] On most cultural matters, Ted was fashionably hip.

But Kennedy also appealed to the New Deal vanguard of the Democratic Party through association with economic liberalism and structural reform of the economy.[57] Ted rejected "little government as an ideological end in itself." Rather, he preferred to ask "what government must do—and . . . can do well."[58] Later, toward the end of his 1980 campaign, Kennedy endorsed not only increased government spending, the use of taxation to control inflation, and regulation of oil and gas, but also wage/price controls.[59] The administration even accused him of promoting nationalization and socialism. The senator supported the Wisconsin state government's plans to extend public ownership of its railroads in an effort to keep them open and had lobbied for it in the Senate.[60] For the administration, this was evidence of the senator's opposition to the free enterprise system and "another indication of the differences that separate his philosophy and that of the President."[61]

Kennedy's ability to appeal across the liberal spectrum was demonstrated by those who either publicly or intellectually wanted him to run. This encompassed liberals of the New Deal tradition, such as Henry Jackson, Robert C. Byrd, Representative Chris Dodd of Connecticut, Michigan party chair Morley Winograd, and Representative Paul Simon, who marshaled his Illinois campaign.[62] But he also attracted New Politics activists such as George McGovern, Fred Harris, Mo Udall, Birch Bayh, and the controversial mayor of Cleveland, Dennis Kucinich.[63] McGovern stated, "I thought he had tremendous qualities of leadership . . . and he had a commitment to deliver on the kind of policies that we had always fought for."[64] In contrast, "the perspectives, the policies and the priorities of the administration [were] unclear or mistaken from the beginning."[65]

Often support came from liberals who felt marginalized or failed by the Carter administration.[66] The Congressional Black Caucus, representing a constituency thought to be loyal to Carter, endorsed Kennedy because of its perceived betrayal by the administration on the issues of employment and health care.[67] Both Mayor Bill Green of Philadelphia and Andrew Stein of the Manhattan Borough Council backed Kennedy because they believed he would provide aid to now cash-starved urban centers.[68] Stein represented a large group of previous Carter supporters who had defected to Kennedy. He wrote to the president in August 1979 to ask him "for the good of the country [to] announce that you will not seek a second term." Carter's fiscal policies had created an environment within which "the middle class suffers daily under this weight [of inflation], the elderly, the unemployed, and the under-employed suffer more." He believed that in contrast, the "country can unite" behind Kennedy's "leadership." Former mayor of Pittsburgh Pete Flaherty, one of the architects of Carter's victory in the 1976 Pennsylvania primary, came out for Kennedy too.[69] Thomas Salmon, an ex-governor who described himself as "one of Carter's most avid supporters in Vermont," believed that Carter deserved "a D minus in attempting to cope with America's most acute domestic crisis . . . the economy."[70] When the administration tallied its final committed support at the close of the primaries, it would only be able to claim public endorsements from eleven senators and ninety-eight congressmen. Of the senators, only one was from the Northeast, and the rest were from the Deep South and Hawaii. Among the congressmen, only thirteen were from the North. The rest were all Midwestern, and the vast majority from the Deep South.[71]

Much of Kennedy's strength was perceived to be among Northeastern liberals, such as Shirley Chisholm, Walter E. Fauntory, and Louis Stokes, all of them respected voices within the African American community.[72] Nevertheless, in 1979 Kennedy did show signs of attracting the support of some officeholders outside his home region. In September a representative from Hawaii wrote to Carter to register his surprise at the sheer number of representatives who had joined an ad hoc "Kennedy for President" group within his state. They were people who he thought "would never openly endorse a candidate," let alone a challenger. [73] In early November, Kennedy received support from the governor of Colorado, a large number of Floridian senate representatives, Memphis mayor Richard Fulton, and even some Georgians, including the highly respected African American state representative Julian Bond.[74] Southern politicians were wary of Carter's electoral weakness in their own region. A Claiborne Darden poll in July 1979 showed that Kennedy was a preferred candidate to Carter in ten Southern states by a margin of 51 percent to 40 percent.[75]

Thus Kennedy's support was not confined to a particular ideological or regional milieu. One commentator concluded, "Draft Kennedy organizers are, for the most part, pragmatic Democrats with strong local political Democratic bases." In fact the key ones—Florida Democratic National Committee member and 1976 Carter leader Sergio Bendixen, former Iowa executive finance director and 1978 gubernatorial campaign manager Rick Nolan, New York attorney general Bob Abrams, and Cleveland Democratic chairman Tim Hagan—were closer to the Democratic Party establishments in their states than those who backed either Robert or Jack Kennedy. "Most of these organizers did not create the anti-Carter, pro-Kennedy sentiment in their constituencies: they reflect it."[76] Indeed, often it was grassroots pressure that caused officials to endorse Kennedy. While the mayor of Waukegan, Illinois, was "100 percent" behind the president's renomination, he was unable to run as a Carter delegate because of the strength of feeling of Democrats in his city.[77] Connecticut congressman Bob Giaimo told

the administration that despite his sympathy with its economic policies, the fear of ostracism from his own activists meant that he could
not support the president.[78]

Moreover, Kennedy proved intellectually attractive to some perceived to be on the right of the Democratic Party in 1979, including many neoconservatives and neoliberals. Senator Daniel Patrick
Moynihan was a key example of support among the former. A Catholic of Irish descent, Moynihan was John F. Kennedy's assistant secretary for labor.[79] He worked on the Great Society's War on Poverty,
producing a number of controversial reports that argued that welfare
programs bred dependency and encouraged father absenteeism.[80] He
was also critical of the doves within the Democratic Party, and in the
late 1960s he openly attacked the emerging New Left and New Politics
movements.[81] He accepted a position within the Nixon administration
as an urban adviser.[82] Moynihan's backing for the McGovern/Shriver
1972 ticket was cool enough for him to be charged by its supporters with
favoring Nixon's reelection and with membership of a conspiracy to re-
tard social reform.[83] This impression was reinforced when a memo by
Moynihan was leaked to the press suggesting that "the time may have
come when the issue of race could benefit from a period of benign
neglect."[84] Thus, Moynihan was a national figure of hate for the New
Politics, who regarded him in plain terms as a racist. Having served
as an aggressive ambassador to the U.N., he also developed a reputation for being staunchly anticommunist and pro-Israel. Moynihan was
even relatively pro-life, opposing abortion on demand.[85]

Throughout 1979, Daniel Patrick Moynihan let it be known that he
was attracted to the idea of a Kennedy nomination.[86] He was motivated
by a growing unease with Carter's policies. Fellow members of the liberal, anticommunist Campaign for a Democratic Majority were angry
at the president's foreign policy, labeling SALT II "appeasement," and
were frustrated by Carter's decision in early 1979 to delay production
of the neutron bomb.[87] But as a representative from the economically
declining New York, Moynihan's tentative support was in large part a
communication of local anger at Carter's fiscalism.[88] In May 1979, the
New York state party issued a statement questioning Carter's urban
policy.[89] In turn, Moynihan believed that under Carter's stewardship
inflation had reduced the effectiveness of urban aid and the fiscal year
1981 budget threatened further cuts in money to his state.[90] Moynihan,
critical of the balanced budget movement, attacked Carter's attempt
to do the same at the expense of employment and housing programs.[91]
In a controversial article in January 1980, he went so far as to claim

that President Ford had been more generous to New York than the incumbent Democrat.[92] He warned in March 1980 that the president's budget was "unacceptable" and that as "New York's Presidential primary election is on March 25 . . . this is our week to be courted."[93]

In contrast, Moynihan was far closer to Kennedy in philosophical sensibility, sympathizing with his economic liberalism.[94] He also responded favorably to those parts of Kennedy's record that appeared more conservative. In particular, Moynihan was impressed with his position on deregulation, wiretapping, and mandatory sentencing.[95] As a result, Moynihan edged toward endorsing Kennedy.[96] In August 1979, he even offered himself as a favorite-son candidate if Kennedy did not enter the race with a view to pushing the senator to run.[97] He had been privately investigating his own presidential campaign in protest at Carter's policies for over a year.[98] The White House regarded this as a serious threat and began briefing the media against the New York senator.[99]

Moynihan ultimately refrained from endorsing either candidate. This was probably because when Kennedy started losing in early 1980, he hoped that he might be considered an alternative candidate should Carter stumble too. He also wanted to be considered as a potential running mate by either candidate and thus could not afford to totally alienate one or the other.[100] But he publicly explained away his neutral stance as an objection to Kennedy's dovishness.[101] He described himself as "shaken" by Kennedy's stance on competition with the Soviet Union.[102] If this was true, then Moynihan was unusual among the neoconservative Campaign for a Democratic Majority's membership, which largely remained loyal to Kennedy, was unabashedly liberal in its economics, and blamed the president's weak foreign policy for the crises of 1979–1980. Jeane Kirkpatrick, writing in the CDM's newsletter, reassured her readers that the senator's apparent dovishness, though disturbing, was just "electoral posturing" and could be safely overlooked. Kirkpatrick later served as Ronald Reagan's ambassador to the U.N.[103] Anticommunist maverick Henry Jackson would prove to be one of Kennedy's most enthusiastic supporters, endorsing him as early as July 1979.[104] Urging support for Kennedy at a Democratic fund-raiser, he warned that his party faced defeat in 1980 because, under Carter, it had become "resigned to the economics of Herbert Hoover."[105] For Jackson, "Kennedy was the last hope his wing of the party had."[106]

A number of neoliberals would also privately express early support for Kennedy. Gary Hart believed that Kennedy could "bridge the generations" of Democrats. In contrast, he had been highly critical of

Carter since clashing with him in 1977 over appropriations for water projects.[107] Hitherto, Hart had defined himself as a fiscal conservative, which was what gave him his competitive edge in Colorado politics. He favored a balanced budget, cuts in federal spending, and selective tax cuts. Until the late 1970s his voting record was regarded as poor by the AFL-CIO, and he received few campaign contributions from labor. But toward the end of the decade, things began to change. Regardless of philosophical tradition, most Democratic officeholders were critical of Carter's conservative fiscalism when it threatened their constituents' interests.[108] Thus, he dubbed Carter's fiscal year 1981 budget "Hoover economics" and conceded, despite his sympathy for such a proposition, that a balanced budget was undesirable and unattainable that year.[109] He urged the president not to run for reelection in 1980, and like Moynihan, he became a touted favorite-son candidate at the nominating convention.[110] Hart was not alone among Colorado statesmen: neoliberal governor Richard Lamm welcomed a Kennedy candidacy too and later became an organizer of the state's uncommitted delegates.[111] Ex-senator Floyd Haskell claimed that his defeat in 1978 had been due to Carter's unpopularity and stumped for the Massachusetts senator.[112] Disillusioned with Carter, Gary Hart was attracted to a Kennedy candidacy in its own right. In 1978 he was "pretty much in awe" of Kennedy, both out of admiration for the senator's abilities and because he had served as a volunteer for his brother Robert in 1968. The only reason why he did not publicly endorse Edward Kennedy was that "being an incumbent fighting for re-election, you couldn't expect anyone in my situation to get involved in that." This was typical of the dilemma faced by many officeholders who ultimately preferred to avoid conflict with an incumbent president in a difficult election year.[113] Finally, among neoliberals, Kennedy also received the endorsements of Massachusetts officeholders Mike Dukakis and Paul Tsongas.[114]

Support for Kennedy was also driven by his apparent electoral strength and thus by realpolitik.[115] House Speaker Tip O'Neill believed that many representatives simply feared that a renominated Carter would lose them their seats.[116] The *New York Times* reported that "dozens of congressional Democrats . . . are moving toward concerted action to urge Mr. Carter to step aside in 1980." They worried that "so many Democratic voters would stay at home that the party's House candidates would suffer as Republicans did after Watergate." Besides, most of them "took it for granted that Mr. Kennedy would be the nominee, thinking it was virtually all over."[117] The *Washington Post* concluded that Kennedy's economic arguments were a cover story: he was being urged to run simply to protect Senate seats.[118] Professor Arnold Saltzman counseled the president, "Many [representatives] are concerned about their own ability to survive in an election year that could be an 'election of rejection.'"[119] In contrast, the *New York Times* reported that "the widely held view among non-ideological Democratic office holders is that Kennedy is a far stronger candidate for November."[120] Mo Udall expressly endorsed Kennedy on the grounds of his ability to motivate the Democratic base.[121] Even Minnesota state attorney general Warren Spannaus, cochair of Minnesotans for Carter/Mondale, suggested that it "might perhaps be best" if his candidate withdrew for Kennedy.[122] Governor Lamm told the *New York Times* that "Kennedy could get 80 percent of the Democrats in Colorado" and win the general election.[123]

This reflected a body of Colorado Democratic opinion that while Kennedy might motivate urban voters, there would otherwise be a "real, convulsive anti-Carter, anti-Democratic feeling" without him on the ticket.[124] Even some conservative news outlets urged Democrats to "begin thinking the unthinkable, which is dumping Jimmy Carter."[125] A letter distributed to Democrats in Florida from committeemen across the state expressed similar sentiments. While it did touch on Kennedy's "capable, effective, and confident" leadership, the core of its argument focused on a recent opinion poll "taken to determine nation-wide support for Presidential contenders. . . . Our incumbent President lost to all but one of those mentioned Republican hopefuls, while Senator Kennedy easily defeated all of those same Republicans mentioned."[126]

Whether for reasons of political calculation or ideology, Kennedy's appeal reached across philosophical divides within his party. So too did it attract the support of both social protest movements and organized labor. Social protest movements found the primaries a profitable experience. The competition for votes enhanced their influence and Kennedy's campaign furthered the growth of their institutional power. For instance, the gay rights movement had been largely marginalized during the 1972 and 1976 primaries.[127] Although Carter's administration tentatively supported gay rights in principle, it made it clear that the president was "not entirely comfortable with homosexuality" in practice.[128] No gay federal appointments were made, and the administration did little to protest a tide of antigay legislation that swept state governments in the late 1970s.

Despite political marginalization, the gay vote was growing in confidence and significance.[129] Gays had established Democratic clubs, appropriating mainstream liberal ideas and identifying themselves with the civil rights movement to increase their cultural legitimacy.[130] In California, these enjoyed the patronage of senior Democrats like Senator Alan Cranston and Jerry Brown.[131] Congressional Democrats, including Senators Cranston, Tsongas, and Moynihan, had begun to sponsor bills outlawing discrimination.[132] A number of semiprofessional lobbying organizations, such as the National Gay Task Force (NGTF), had built fruitful relationships with groups like NOW and sympathetic Congress members.[133] The coming-out of a growing number of Democratic officeholders helped this process.[134]

Although they were constantly threatened by referenda, a large number of municipal and county authorities had passed antidiscrimination laws in the 1970s.[135] These were in part the product of the growth of gay political coalitions, particularly in Florida and California.[136] In Washington, D.C., gay rights activists had determined the outcome of the 1978 city council elections after a candidate had "declared war on the city's 'fascist faggots.'" Reported the *Washington Post*, "The District's homosexuals have bounded out of the political closet. Through hard work, their ability to raise campaign contributions, assemble platoons of volunteers, and deliver votes, homosexuals have established themselves as a highly sought after political constituency."[137] Gay campaigners believed that local success could be translated into "broker" status in the primaries.[138] A gay Texas group wrote to Carter in 1979 to inform him that "we anticipate at least 600,000 gay/lesbian registered voters in next year's elections. . . . They now constitute a very significant body of voters who increasingly look to the gay/lesbian leadership of our state for political direction."[139]

Kennedy's courtship of the gay vote proved bold and unprecedented, both for the very fact of doing it and for his degree of candor.[140] During the June 1980 California primary, Kennedy targeted the gay vote, assiduously canvassing clubs and bars with his wife and son. The *San Francisco Chronicle* noted the "striking diversity" of the crowd at a fund-raiser in a Castro bar and Kennedy's ability to unite radically different traditions of Democrats. It was composed not just of gays, but labor officials too, like "David Powell, 23, a house painter and painter's union trustee from Stockton."[141] Kennedy's declaration that he was "opposed to discrimination based on sexual preference" and his pledge to issue an antidiscrimination order if elected forced Carter to compete with him for gay votes.[142] Carter announced his support for a bill to lift restrictions on gay immigration to the United States and canvassed the NGTF, pledging, among other things, to "permit the receipt of non-pornographic gay literature in federal correctional institutions."[143] The NGTF endorsed Kennedy. The 1980 convention, attended by many gay Kennedy delegates, became the first to include the phrase "sexual orientation" in the categories listed in the charter's nondiscrimination language, and there was a pronounced liberalization of Kennedy's Massachusetts organization.[144] Most importantly, Kennedy set a precedent. In 1984, presidential hopefuls Walter Mondale, Gary Hart, and Jesse Jackson deluged Californians with pro-gay policies and literature. One activist noted of the nominees, "Eight years ago there was nobody. Four years ago, there was only Kennedy. Now it's all three."[145]

The campaign similarly strengthened the hand of feminists. Preeminent feminist lobby the National Organization for Women initially decided that it could not campaign exclusively for Kennedy, despite his close relationship with the movement, because it would break its rules on partisanship and alienate Republican members.[146] Yet its board unanimously favored the senator. Therefore, NOW chose to allow local chapters to campaign for whomever they wished, after providing a public analysis of the candidates' issue positions that made Kennedy appear more closely aligned to its philosophy.[147] It also issued a statement attacking Carter and refusing to campaign for him in the fall election.[148] However, Kennedy supporters subsequently forced the board to "recommend" to chapters that they endorse the senator.[149] Although NOW took this difficult balancing act upon itself in part out of ideological motivation, it also took the risk of alienating the administration because its board believed Kennedy was almost guaranteed victory.[150] "We must support not only a candidate who is good on the issues," argued NOW, "but a candidate who has the best chance to win and carry other progressive candidates with him." The future of the ERA depended on returning liberals to the Senate.[151] "Senator Kennedy is leading all other candidates, Democratic and Republican, in the presidential candidate polls in all regions of the country."[152] Indeed, NOW's executive believed that because he was so popular across the country and thus did not rely on motivating Southern voters for his electoral majority, Kennedy "could afford to take more risks" on feminist issues.[153]

The feminist organizations that pushed for Kennedy to run wanted to promote liberal policy on broader issues than just women's rights and to revolutionize gender relations within the Democratic Party.[154] One activist summarized, "It wasn't at all before the 1980 campaign that women . . . began to think of ourselves as a real political force."[155]

In Massachusetts, a NOW local established a Women's Advisory Committee (WAC) to organize the state for Kennedy. It aimed to be a "multiracial committee of 70 of the most powerful women in the state," wrote to every citizen, and organized speaker programs.[156] But the WAC did not exist purely to campaign for its candidate. It set up events "designed to attract the 43 percent of American women that work," in order that women might "do what men have always done— participate in these kinds of informal events that establish contacts."[157] It acted as a watchdog for sexism, publicly chastising the campaign if it did not promote women.[158] The WAC became a model for Democratic women's organizations throughout New England.[159] This was a campaign around a cause rather than a candidate, openly manipulating the competition for votes in order to induce change in the party.[160] It lobbied successfully for the Massachusetts delegate slate to be 50 percent female and for the policy to become a plank at the convention.[161]

Similar political dynamics were present within unions, which took much greater risks when choosing whom to endorse. Ostensibly labor was overwhelmingly favorable to a senator who regarded "Union Halls" as his "second home," from which could be forged a "common effort to create a better country."[162] But in the scramble for union votes, the issue of class gained new significance. Edward Kennedy boasted philosophical compatibility. He thought that unions should support him because of his record and that of his brothers: he had taken a stand for them and should therefore expect their gratitude. In contrast, Carter found it absurd that a multimillionaire who had only once worked outside of politics should claim to be the true friend of the workingman. This insulted the president's sense of proud modesty. Carter stressed that Kennedy "has never had to work for a living, so he really does not have any understanding of the problems" faced by real people. As a farmer and small-business man, the president was in a much better position to fight for the common man.[163]

Despite this tentative attempt to exploit class envy, labor still preferred the senator in 1979. Indeed, many labor leaders thought that their hands were forced by their membership's fervor.[164] Unions that had called early for Carter in the summer reported a "tide rising under them" of protest.[165] From Iowa, one Carter staffer complained, "Fears that we will fight inflation with unemployment dominate the discussions. Very few understand the President's record. . . . At this time, Kennedy has a distinct edge in the labor community."[166] The secretary of labor warned the president that "we should have no illusions. Our labor effort is an uphill fight."[167]

Labor would prove to be the backbone of organized campaigning for both candidates, and in most states, it comprised a substantial portion of registered Democrats.[168] They provided free staff and organization. For instance, Kennedy's campaign in Iowa was directed and staffed almost entirely by the Machinists.[169] Such activity was not just a Northern phenomenon, and unions organized Carter's campaigns in Alabama, Oklahoma, and Oregon.[170] Labor's support demonstrated a candidate's appeal to the average Democratic voter and their ability to reach out to a key constituency of blue-collar ethnic white voters.[171] Union endorsements were used to bid for the title of most friendly to the workingman's interests and of the "only candidate to have kept his word and kept his faith with our traditions."[172] Kennedy's endorsements lauded his record, and Carter's trumpeted his support for incremental improvements in the standard of living.[173] Carter let it be known that he would adopt more labor-friendly policies if reelected.[174] He even tried to convince labor leaders that Kennedy was opposed to free collective bargaining, by citing his support of an anticrime bill that permitted the FBI to wiretap labor leaders.[175]

The labor machine, like the party's, would often prove unable to guarantee that an endorsement would reap votes.[176] Carter's support was characterized by his own Iowa staff to be soft, unenthusiastic, and largely patriotic, while Kennedy's was intense.[177] There are more examples of members publicly breaking rank with Carter-endorsing union leaders than vice versa. The Grainmiller's union in Iowa voted to support Kennedy, in opposition to nationally held policy.[178] So too did textile workers in Maine and New Hampshire.[179] President of the Communication Workers of America Glenn Watts endorsed Carter in mid-1979. However, he quickly received "a lesson in the limitations of leaders when he invited President Carter at the union's convention. The applause was standard for Carter's remarks. The ovations came later when Senator Edward Kennedy spoke." Soon after, the Communications union opened its office in New York to a pro-Kennedy group.[180] Moreover the voting patterns of ordinary members appeared to be reflective of national rather than sectional trends. In Iowa, Carter enjoyed the support of the National Education Association, and some UAW locals rebelled and canvassed for him.[181] But in the June California primary, he lost, despite the figure of the combined memberships of unions committed to supporting him being significantly larger than Kennedy's.[182]

The AFL-CIO responded with enthusiasm to Kennedy's economics, noting that his policies were "designed to 'one-up' Carter among

the various disgruntled Democratic Party constituency groups." However, it was displeased with his attempts to woo "McGovernites" and
"feminists." Therefore, it felt "closer to Kennedy on the economic
issues and closer to Carter on the environmental and foreign policy
issues."[183] Many of the wounds inflicted during the battle between the
New Deal and the New Politics had yet to heal. The AFL-CIO, under
its new president, Lane Kirkland, decided to remain neutral in 1979.[184]
"Kirkland preferred Kennedy's unambiguous liberalism to Carter's
indecisiveness and economic centrism," but he was unprepared to
undo a recently signed accord between the federal government and
labor that seemed to offer a new era of cooperation with government
over prices and incomes.[185] The AFL-CIO sent clear guidelines to its
state bodies indicating that they should endorse nobody officially and
unofficially only as private individuals.[186] Despite this, labor's lobbying
power depended on a strong Kennedy candidacy. It found that "when
Kennedy appeared to a viable candidate, Carter began wooing labor
assiduously." However, when the senator performed badly in early
1980, Kirkland publicly complained that Carter stopped returning his
calls.[187]

The Kennedy labor constituency was a broad one that included
many unions that had previously been hostile to one another. Both
the UAW and the Machinists provided moral and practical support: in
Iowa, they handed over their political staffs to Kennedy and canvassed
the entire state.[188] So too did the United Farm Workers, which became
Kennedy's de facto organization in the Southwest.[189] The executive
of the "conservative" American Federation of Teachers (AFT) voted
unanimously to endorse the senator.[190] This experience was atypical,
and many executives divided over the issue. All the black members
of the UAW's executive committee, for instance, voted to support
Carter.[191] The average Kennedy union was nonskilled or semiskilled
and old, had strong central organization, and had a tradition of political campaigning. Carter's labor secretary bemoaned that the Kennedy
unions were "better organized and better experienced politically."[192]
The senator's endorsements came from the auto workers, machinists, rubber workers, textile workers, painters, and woodworkers. The
core of his endorsements from smaller unions came from manual labor
unions, such as warehousemen and bricklayers.[193] In many cases, he
picked up support from groups with parochial grievances with the administration. The United Rubber Workers endorsed Kennedy largely
because Carter's wage guidelines disrupted contract negotiations in
the rubber industry. The International Association of Fire Fighters

favored Kennedy because Carter broke a promise to cut the workweek of firefighters.[194] In contrast, Carter attracted largely white-collar unions, such as teachers.[195] Among blue-collar groups, his endorsers were usually craftsmen and skilled manual laborers, such as carpenters, engineers, and telecommunications workers. The rank and file of the ordinarily conservative Teamsters, although officially neutral, overwhelmingly favored Kennedy.[196]

Kennedy unions tended to regard mainstream liberal causes, such as women's rights and health care, as important to them as labor rights, indicating that the coalition building around universalist policies that had begun in the 1970s influenced their actions. On the day the AFT executive committee voted to endorse Kennedy, it also voted to lobby Congress for more aggressive open housing legislation, equalized pay for male and female teachers, and protection of the U.S. car trade.[197] UAW supporters in Michigan explained that they supported Kennedy "because he has favored labor law revisions, an increased minimum wage, ratification of the Equal Rights Amendment."[198] The bricklayers' union mentioned his fight for "healthcare, education, and housing."[199] These organizations often used the Kennedy candidacy to lobby the wider Democratic Party for liberal policy commitments. The bricklayers were intimately involved in Kennedy's platform fights at the 1980 Democratic Convention. They argued for an increase in government regulation of the economy, enforcement of Humphrey-Hawkins, and price controls.[200] Many of Kennedy's unions campaigned for policy positions ordinarily associated with the New Politics and the McGovern campaign of 1972. Again, this indicated the long-term impact of coalition building within the left. In March 1980 the International Woodworkers of America sent a series of resolutions to the president. These covered several areas of special interest to its members, such as a proposed restriction on logging exports and mill closures. But they also demanded a halt to the building of nuclear power stations and for the "Canadian and American governments to break all relations with Chile" in protest at its long-running civil rights abuses.[201] These resolutions were not merely a parroting of Kennedy's platform but the expression of deeply held liberal sentiment within his labor support.

Kennedy on the Eve of the Primaries

Kennedy was a formidable candidate in the autumn of 1979. Hugely popular among all demographic groups (including self-described conservatives), he appeared to have the potential to bind the Democratic coalition back together. Within the draft movement could be found hawks, doves, feminists, gays, unionists, environmentalists, rabbis, civil rights activists, neoliberals, and even a few Carter partisans from the Deep South. And yet at the very moment of his ascendancy, Kennedy misstepped.

On 4 November 1979, CBS broadcast an interview with Kennedy by Roger Mudd that was all but a declaration of candidacy. In theory, it was a chance to shine and to project an image of confidence that would reinforce the senator's impressive poll numbers. In practice, it illustrated the media's determination to engender controversy and Kennedy's naiveté.[202] Mudd was a friend of the Kennedy family, and the senator consented to the interview specifically because he believed the veteran reporter would defer to him. Thus, little effort was made to decide what questions would or could be asked in advance.[203] But times had changed. Sitting down with a very unpresidential-looking Kennedy (who wore an unflattering polo shirt and seemed throughout the interview to have just woken up), Mudd immediately tore into the senator. He revisited the Chappaquiddick incident and asked insulting questions about Kennedy's marriage. "The relationship" remarked Mudd, "only seems to occur on select public occasions." Halfway through the interview, he showed a video of Mudd visiting the crash site and listed the ways in which Kennedy's account of the accident did not hold up to scrutiny. The whole documentary seemed framed to prove Mudd's personal objectivity and avoid accusations of hagiography. Kennedy was filmed walking alone through the Senate, aloof and even a little lost. There was a close-up of his shaking hand as he asked a question in committee like a nervous schoolboy. The Mudd interview was the first-ever stage-by-stage public debunking of the Kennedy myth. It presented Ted as the lesser brother propelled into the limelight by luck.

Kennedy's performance did not help. Friends say that he expected it to be edited or else that the less favorable sections wouldn't be broadcast.[204] But on camera, Mudd described him as "stubborn, elliptical, and [giving] the impression that he really doesn't want America to know him." He stuttered his way through answers, simply staring helplessly at the interviewer when he didn't know what to say. Most embarrassingly, when Kennedy was directly asked why he was running for president, he could not answer. After the interviewer gave him some extra time to think about it, Kennedy garbled his way through a poorly thought-out statement that contained more criticism of Jimmy Carter than it did good reasons to vote for him.[205]

The impact of the Mudd interview was felt most among the pundits, who took it as evidence that Kennedy would not perform as well as a candidate had been expected to.[206] It is true that he was anxious about the candidacy and still wracked with uncertainty about it. But there was a more complex reason for his awkwardness too. Kennedy believed he was going to win the primaries and so had begun his general election campaign already. In an effort to appeal to moderates and independents, he was avoiding specifics and stressing vague themes like leadership, optimism, and ambition. This was not what Democratic voters watching at home expected to hear. Fortunately, few of them were watching anyway; the interview clashed with the network premiere of *Jaws*. But they were also distracted by some disturbing news that had just come out of the Middle East. On 4 November, staff at the American embassy in Tehran were taken hostage by radical Iranian students. In many regards, the crisis reprieved Kennedy and took attention away from his blundering first steps. Yet events had already started to conspire against him. A bad campaign and a series of foreign policy crises prevented what seemed to many to be the almost inevitable nomination (and even election) of Edward Kennedy. They turned what might have been a glorious revolution into a swan song for liberalism.

5

Iran, Afghanistan, and Defeat in Iowa

When Kennedy officially declared his candidacy at Faneuil Hall on 7 November 1979, he was the strongest candidate for the presidency that year. His support ranged across the Democratic Party and its various constituencies. Importantly, this enthusiasm was driven not only by antipathy to Carter and attraction to Kennedy, but also by the belief that Kennedy was likely to win the Democratic nomination and would be the strongest candidate against Ronald Reagan. Those who had tried to draft him throughout 1979 did so because of his myth, his quantifiable successes, his philosophy, and his perceived ability to get things done. They hoped that he would hold the line against the Republican Party, perhaps even turn the clock back to the heady days of the early 1960s. Kennedy's early supporters thought that his nomination would wipe clean the memory of Jimmy Carter's lackluster and largely conservative four years in power. Buoyed by the polls and visible public anger at the status quo, they looked forward to eight years of uncompromising liberalism in the White House.[1]

Kennedy chose to declare at Faneuil Hall because it evoked images of the American Revolution and distinguished him from his brothers, both of whom had declared in Washington. The hall was packed with cheering supporters, many of them wearing union buttons, and all genuine in their enthusiasm and love for the senator. When he entered, they jumped to their feet, crying "Ke-nne-dy! Ke-nne-dy!", waving "We Want Ted!" signs, and punching the air with their fists. A visibly nervous Kennedy climbed the stage and took the microphone. However, rather than launching into a passionate tirade against Carter, he first waited until the TV cameras were in position, loudly cleared his throat, and began a soft, well-considered speech about the challenges facing America. The senator had been advised to appear presidential and to cool down his oratory to better suit the small screen. All of this was technically good advice, but the disappointment felt in the hall was immediate.[2] The atmosphere chilled. The shouting ceased and the applause became respectful but rare.

The speech set the tone for the first part of his campaign. It emphasized leadership over specific liberal policy, telling the audience that "the energies of our people must be marshaled toward a larger purpose—and that can only be done from the White House." Ted voiced the economic concerns that Americans faced in the 1970s ("wages are rising only half as fast as prices") but avoided proposing solutions. Kennedy reached out to the various groups he calculated added up to a majority in the coming primary. He made reference to the New Deal, promised to guarantee "that opportunity is neither diminished, nor denied for any Americans because they are women, or because they are black, or because they were born to the Spanish tongue," and hinted at a more robust and "coherent" foreign policy. The principle of national health insurance was invoked to appeal to all the Democratic constituency groups while also promising to reduce "spiraling costs" and therefore inflation. These points were well received and emphasized that Kennedy was the only man truly capable of bringing his party back together again.[3]

Yet the speech as a whole was a disappointment. A Carter mole in attendance contacted a member of the administration to give his reaction. "The speech was not that good," he said, "and . . . the UAW people were disappointed." The mole threw a party for his county delegates to the Boston launch and took a straw poll of their responses. Fourteen supported Carter, nineteen Kennedy, and forty-seven were undecided. The negative reaction of this partisan audience demonstrated the damage Kennedy's poor performance would do throughout the campaign.[4]

Very soon, events conspired against Kennedy's remarkable coalition. After his declaration in November, Ted's poll rating dipped slightly as he moved from being a popular insurgent to a presidential candidate.[5] Nevertheless, he continued to hold a commanding lead, and there was no evidence to suggest that voters, faced with the idea that Kennedy might actually win, were beginning to abandon him.[6] All eyes turned to the first-in-the-nation caucus in Iowa. A win in the Hawkeye State, which had not only gone for Jimmy Carter in 1976 but had arguably made his nomination possible, was the perfect opportunity to establish front-runner status. Iowa certainly looked like Kennedy's for the taking. In mid-1979 he led the president among local Democrats and independents by 56 percent to 30 percent, and in

October the campaign received a significant boost when former Iowa senator Dick Clark quit his job as the administration's coordinator for refugee affairs to work full-time for Kennedy.[7] Yet for all his early strength and the extraordinary potential of his coalition, the race in Iowa proved considerably closer than anyone expected.

The Kennedy Strategy

There were really two Kennedy campaigns. The first ran from his declaration in November to the Iowa election in January, and it belied his image as a populist liberal and undermined his electoral coalition.[8] It was an instructive lesson in how to lose friends and disinterest people. The first campaign was staffed by three different generations of activists with different responsibilities and relationships to Kennedy.[9] The result was often structural paralysis and personal conflict.[10] Peter Hart, who was hired to do its polls, regarded it as "a mess. . . . You had so many different factions working, all in their heart, in [the campaign's] best interests, but against each other." The oldest generation were the staff associated with the family and the John Kennedy administration, such as Phil Bakes (the deputy campaign manager), Ted Sorenson, and Steven Smith. The middle generation were the senatorial staff, who enjoyed the greatest personal access to Kennedy. The youngest were the "presidential staff," a combination of younger politicos such as Bob Shrum, Carl Wagner, Paul Kirk, Gary Orren, and Paul Tulley. Much of the latter group had cut their teeth working for Robert Kennedy and George McGovern. "Unlike most Presidential campaigns, where there's a central core and everybody works for that central core, this had three or four different satellite groups . . . all which led to a lot of disorganization and was far from a Kennedyesque model of organization that we'd all heard about and knew about."[11] The "presidential staff," which dictated campaign themes and strategy, was additionally divided internally.[12] Some (Shrum in particular) argued for a traditional liberal campaign, while others (Hart, Orren) pushed for a non-issues-based emphasis on leadership.[13] The latter view, driven by the assumption that the primaries were a guaranteed victory and thus Kennedy should prepare himself for the November fight by appearing presidential, won out.[14] It was not unorthodox: Ronald Reagan, equally confident of the Republican nomination, was also pursuing an image as a moderate.[15]

As they prepared for the Iowa caucus, Hart and Orren argued that

Kennedy should present himself as the "candidate of order and control, Carter [as] the candidate of disorder and lack of control." Kennedy should stress that he was "effective" and that Carter was "the risky candidate." They argued that Kennedy should restrain his public performance, engage mainly in "soft-side events . . . birthdays, anniversaries, St. Valentine's Day," and encourage "identification with movie stars and athletes." Hart specified that the celebrities should have "an All-American quality" and that Kennedy should be seen more with actor Gregory Peck.[16] Orren instructed his candidate "to advance the dialogue . . . in terms of general themes" rather than specific policies.[17] Hart cautioned him to "not cast issues in terms of liberal vs. conservative or new direction vs. same direction dichotomies, but rather speak of the need to provide order, stability. . . . The Kennedy message will be different from what it has been in the past, or at least different from what the press believes it has been in the past."[18] And so Kennedy promised a new era of activist leadership, if not necessarily activist government.[19] As president, he would create an atmosphere in which things might get done, not a specific legislative agenda. He did not identify the means by which all this would happen, but spoke in generalities.[20] He castigated Carter for being a passive president. He drew on the Roosevelt and Kennedy governments in his symbolism, not because they were liberal but because they were vigorous: "This is the same nation that pulled itself out of the Great Depression," he reminded audiences, "that, but a decade ago, put the footprints of America in the valleys of the moon."[21] Kennedy's campaign up to the Iowa caucus was a debate about the style of government, not method.

Thinking beyond Iowa and keen to reach out to fall voters, Kennedy even adapted his tone to appear more conservative.[22] The tactic, again, was Hart's and Orren's, who urged him to embrace conservative platforms such as deregulation and even supply-side economics.[23] His announcement speech restated Kennedy's commitment to contain communism.[24] The administration quickly released a long list of votes Kennedy had put in the Senate to limit or decrease defense spending.[25] *Business Week* noted after an interview in October 1979 that his economics were nearly indistinguishable from Carter's. On defense, he too favored "3 percent more spending in real terms." On inflation, he too supported "voluntary rather than mandatory wage-price rules . . . no attack on high interest rates." He too wanted to cut the federal share of GNP "to 18.3 percent by fiscal 1983" and supported the Federal Reserve's policies on credit control.[26] Kennedy pursued a more fiscally disciplined image, welcoming "a clean break with the New Deal and even the 1960s ... There is now a growing consensus, which I share, that government intervention into the economy should only come as a last resort."[27] Overall, Kennedy avoided committing himself to a specific economic package, preferring instead to attack Carter's record.[28] One activist warned him, "You really need some specifics to back up the theme."[29] Indeed, the administration was able to argue that "Kennedy has no real alternatives to the president's programs in the areas of energy and the economy."[30]

The candidate himself was clearly uncomfortable with the strategy, which resulted in a lackluster campaign style.[31] Even his staff conceded that "the Senator's own performance has been somewhat of a disappointment."[32] Again, the decision to restrain his public appearances was an orthodox and logical one. Kennedy's oratory was naturally variable, and when unscripted, he was often ineloquent.[33] The dramatic stump style he was comfortable with did not translate well to television.[34] But he now appeared "battened down and unnatural ... his hands tied behind him." When he launched his campaign in the union halls of Iowa, he was met with frosty disappointment. Although he was generally greeted with violent enthusiasm, he quickly cooled audiences down by speaking in a bizarre quiet, staccato manner that gave the impression that he was mildly stoned. Booing was not uncommon.[35] According to *Newsweek*, "he sometimes sounds like Dwight D. Eisenhower delivering a Franklin D. Roosevelt speech, dropping malaprops like 'fam farmilies' or 'Roll up your sleeves and your mothers and fathers.'"[36]

In January 1980, 59 percent of Americans polled by Louis Harris described Kennedy as a disappointing campaigner.[37] This in part explained his poor performance in his interview with Roger Mudd, but his new style confused many liberal supporters and weakened Kennedy's appeal to the party's base.[38] One Iowa supporter wrote of his disillusion after a Kennedy campaign appearance. "He sounded like a Senator playing it safe, neither hawk nor dove ... it was HARD to be for him."[39] Letters of complaint from Kennedy's activists flooded the campaign, most of whom "missed the old fire and zeal."[40] One reminisced that "when he came out here in '78 ... it was like a shot of adrenaline in the heart. You had to be for him ... now it's all gone."[41] All of this was compounded by poor marketing and scheduling. The senator would speak to half-empty school halls covered in expensive campaign literature and pale blue balloons. He did silly things like judge pig-breeding contests, and many of those who gathered around him were there to see a celebrity rather than a politician. The money began to dry up. Indeed, Kennedy never spent as much money in any other state as he did in Iowa, and it was all horribly wasted.[42] The Kennedy family itself seemed to be on autopilot. Rose Kennedy was featured in an ad in her tennis clothes, as if she didn't have the time or will to dress properly for the audience at home.[43] When once asked what she thought about the funneling of private family dollars into the campaign, she replied, "It's our money and we'll do what we want with it." The politics of class had resurfaced, and the economic populist was beginning to look like an out-of-touch snob. A Carter staffer jokingly referred to Edward Kennedy as "that fat rich kid," and he quickly gained the nickname FRK among the press corps. FRK was of course RFK turned inside out: a cruel, mocking reminder that Ted's campaign was but a pale shadow of Bobby's.[44]

Carter Fights Back

Meanwhile, the Carter administration was almost delighted that campaigning had finally begun. The spell of tension, suspicion, and paranoia was broken.[45] Now the White House could take on the Kennedy family and make a case for its own policies in the process. Perversely, Jimmy Carter was spoiling for a fight. Although Kennedy's declaration subverted his authority, he wanted the chance to face him publicly. He wanted to expose him as a paper tiger, an ambitious playboy with money and opportunity, but very little in the way of philosophical principle.[46] White House chief of staff Hamilton Jordan had written in January 1979 that Carter might secure victory if he could successfully "minimize differences" in policy between himself and Kennedy. Jordan calculated that the source of Kennedy's appeal to registered Democrats was his perceived platform rather than his personality. Carter agreed enthusiastically with this assessment. The White House's strategy then was to exploit Kennedy's determination to appear presidential, to use it as evidence that he was motivated not by ideology or even patriotism, but rather by greed.[47]

Jordan's prescient memo also advised Carter to use the political and financial largesse of the presidency to secure his renomination.[48] Jordan had noticed that Gerald Ford had refused to use federal money to assist his renomination campaign in 1976, which had proved to be a terrible mistake. Instead, his staff privately urged Carter to do the opposite.[49] The first group of elected representatives to endorse Carter was that which most benefited from federal largesse: state governors.[50] Carter offered generous financial support and political endorsements to those who supported him. He withheld both from those who did not.[51] When Carter met with governor elect John Y. Brown of Kentucky in November 1979 for a routine discussion, he was advised to state that "you believe your administration can work well with his, and hope that will be the case in the coming months and years. You hope that he will work . . . to get our organization structured in Kentucky." Additionally, Carter was told to "ask him how you can help him with his priorities," offering funds and access to Cabinet staff. Brown had flirted with endorsing Kennedy, but he had been disappointed by his performance at a fund-raiser. The purpose of the meeting was effectively to bribe the governor to support the president, and it worked.[52]

The administration used its political and financial authority to influence the outcome of a straw poll in Florida that was held a few days before Kennedy's declaration. The White House threw its efforts behind the merger of Pan American and National Airways. The merger was vital to revenues for Florida, as it would increase cheap transport, and the mayor of Miami lobbied vociferously for it. In May 1979 he wrote to Jordan pleading for the administration's support, on this, "a matter of extreme importance to us in South Florida."[53] The merger was approved, and the mayor endorsed Carter. Later the mayor wrote to Jordan to thank him for a grant of $5 million and to assure him of his support for Carter. A state senator insisted the two were not connected, "in spite of the fact that some newspaper comment ascribed all kinds of motives to the President."[54] Such grants were numerous.[55] Days before the Florida poll, public officials distributed copies of memos to potential Carter supporters that read, "On behalf of President Carter I am pleased to inform you of a grant offer of $1.1 million for rehabilitation." Dade County mayor Stephen Clarke joked to reporters, "We ought to do this more often."[56] Little Havana received $2 million and Gerald Lewis, Florida's controller, complained, "Carter is attempting to buy the election."[57] It worked: Carter pulled off a narrow win. This story was not unique. During the Mach Illinois primary, Jane Byrne, mayor of Chicago, supported that accusation by telling reporters that "[Carter is] on the phone making promises saying he's got 55,000 jobs to hand out . . . going round to committee men saying, 'What does your son want?'"[58] Iowans were given $100 million to improve their railroads.[59] In the Virgin Islands, $55 million "in various special funds or grants" were donated by the federal government, Kennedy's supporters claimed in order to bolster Carter's chances of winning the primary.[60]

The president was also able to offer political endorsements. A

Carter point man in California wrote to the president to advise him to endorse Mayor Dianne Feinstein's candidacy in San Francisco in return for her support. Feinstein was a moderate in a city dominated by New Politics radicals. She was a "close political ally," but one in a tough election that would be grateful for assistance. The letter stressed that Feinstein attracted "liberal supporters" that "we will need the help of . . . in the June primary."[61] In California, the deputy White House press secretary was forced to deny leaks to the *L.A. Times* that suggested the administration would purge Kennedy supporters.[62] To be sure, Kennedy reportedly also threatened activists in Massachusetts with isolation and demotion if they canvassed for the president.[63]

Similarly, although much of labor was enthusiastic about Kennedy's candidacy, some calculated that a Democratic administration under attack from a popular liberal was too good an opportunity to miss. It was likely to be more prepared than unusual to dole out gifts and concessions. Many within the labor movement recognized their newfound power and used it.[64] Lobbying ranged from the petty and personal to the significant and legislative. The president of a UAW local wrote to the president to tell him, "I respect and admire you and believe in your policies. . . . I have approximately 10,000 votes pledged to your support." He went on to request "a personal or special invitation to the convention. Any consideration on this matter would be greatly appreciated."[65] The Glassworkers' Union offered a more substantial trade. It asked that its industry be given "five years of protection . . . in order that they might, if at all possible, adjust to the competition from abroad." At the end of the letter, the correspondent reported, "During a recent visit to Corning, New York where we have more than 4,000 members . . . President Carter's son Chip, who was campaigning for his dad at the plant gate, was made aware of our concern." The letter concluded by stating, "Workers and employers in this industry will be greatly appreciative of [the president's] considerations." His request was granted.[66]

Naturally, Carter did not simply buy his renomination. He ran an effective campaign that played strongly to his personable character and qualities of integrity and humility. As president, he stayed in direct contact with activists and sometimes stayed in their homes. He was a remarkably effective one-on-one campaigner.[67] He also largely maintained the support of born-again Christian and Southern Democrats, who found Kennedy's personal life distasteful.[68] The Carter family, charismatic yet humble, often carried out campaigning on the president's behalf.[69] During the campaign, he made thousands of personal telephone calls to local activists, asking for their support.[70] For the Iowa caucus, his staff compiled an extraordinary index of thousands of cards that identified potential supporters, their phone numbers, a brief summary of their background, and what to say to impress them.[71] For example, former Iowa state legislator Gene Glenn was listed as a "strong Carter/Mondale supporter" from having met the president in 1976. However, his file indicated that he "needs some encouragement to do more for us." Contact was vital because he "carries a certain amount of influence among Wapello County Democrats." The call was made, and at the bottom of the card, Carter wrote, "Supporting us strongly next Monday."[72] Carter even called Democrats that were sick or had ailing members of the family to offer his personal prayers.[73] The irony was not lost on the media that in the same week that Carter had publicly declared that he was too busy to debate Kennedy, "he somehow found time to speak by phone with fifteen people in the little farming community of Anita, Iowa."[74]

The purpose of a clear majority of the calls was to reassure supporters that Carter was not a conservative.[75] However, there were many pockets of moderate to conservative officials who readily endorsed the president. In August 1979, Carter met with members of the United Democrats of Congress, who responded favorably to his overtures. In so doing, Carter exploited historical conflicts. The UDC "was organized in 1972 during George McGovern's candidacy for the presidency, when it was felt that an 'anchor' was needed to stem the party's shift to the left. . . . This group has a higher support record rather than any other." The group's chair was Congressman Gunn McKay of Utah, "a strong and dependable Carter Democrat."[76] The Democratic National Committee (DNC) and the wider party apparatus, which offered him contacts and access to registration networks, also proved helpful.[77]

Finally, Carter cleverly manipulated popular memories of Chappaquiddick.[78] The campaign ran a series of ads that pictured the president with his family and declared, "Husband. Father. President. He's done these three jobs with distinction." Carter was implying that Kennedy had not.[79] His grassroots activists were less subtle.[80] The leader of Jimmy's "peanut brigade" of Georgian activists told reporters that Kennedy "leads a cheater's life—cheats on his wife, cheats in college."[81] A coalition of New Right groups formed the Kennedy Truth Squad with the aim of raising awareness of Kennedy's voting record and private life.[82] After Ted lost Iowa, it quickly regrouped itself into a Carter Truth Squad and leveled several unsavory and absurd accusations at the president.[83] The administration and its allies proved remarkably successful at reminding the public of Kennedy's flaws, keeping him on the defensive and preventing more serious and salient discussion of the issues.[84]

Iran and Afghanistan

However, Carter's presidency was rescued not by his canniness or Kennedy's mistakes, but rather by history. In early 1979 the repressive regime of the shah of Persia, under pressure from a coalition of democrats, communists, and religious fanatics, finally collapsed. Central Asia and the Middle East were quietly changing in a way that neither the first nor the second world could comprehend. As the Soviet Union began to direct aid and advice to prop up a communist regime in Afghanistan, so America attempted to bolster a deeply unpopular pro-Western government in Iran. In both cases, East and West saw the internal revolutions and brewing civil wars in the anachronistic terms of capitalism versus communism. One reason why Carter, who otherwise despised authoritarian regimes of any hue, assisted the shah for so long was that he believed that what was taking place in Iran was not a popular uprising but a Soviet power grab.[85] He was terribly wrong, and neither the Soviets nor the Americans understood the remarkable revival of religious fundamentalism taking place in the slums and fields of Central Asia. Americans living in Iran did. The American ambassador believed America should negotiate with the recently returned religious scholar Ayatollah Khomeini, whom he rightly identified as being at the center of the insurrection. When Carter overruled private talks, the ambassador held them anyway. He predicted that U.S. support for the shah was turning it into a locus for anti-Western sentiment.[86] On 14 February 1979, Iranians marched on the U.S. embassy and detained the ambassador. Khomeini intervened and they let him go. That same day the U.S. ambassador in Afghanistan was seized and murdered.[87] Some within the administration, including the president, began to voice concerns that Americans in the Tehran embassy were perhaps exposed to the risk of kidnap.[88] Despite these tensions, Carter decided to grant the shah a visa to visit America for medical treatment in October. A few weeks later, on 4 November 1979, radical Iranian students took American hostages at the U.S. embassy in Tehran.[89] Then, on Christmas Day 1979, the Soviets invaded Afghanistan to prop up their own government against religious extremists.[90] The clash of civilizations had begun, and just as it redefined the presidency of George Bush Jr. in 2001, so it briefly resuscitated Carter's.

These crises, although arguably prompted in part by the administration's haphazard foreign policy, altered the tenor of the primaries and created a short-term patriotic boost in Carter's opinion poll ratings.[91] Their events shifted the public's attention from economic to diplomatic problems.[92] Coverage of the hostage crisis kept a sudden 1.3 percent leap in the consumer price index off the front pages.[93] Carter responded with reassuring restraint and authority to the Iranian debacle and with tub-thumping patriotism to the Afghanistan invasion. For Iran he froze the regime's overseas assets and began a series of painstaking negotiations that would last for over a year. For the Soviet Union he announced an embargo on grain exports and withdrawal from the 1980 Moscow Olympics. He also asked all Americans to register for the draft. His new Carter Doctrine, unveiled in the 1980 State of the Union address, defined the Persian Gulf as an area of American strategic interest and committed U.S. military power to its defense. It appeared to justify the militaristic policies of 1978–1979 that had so angered grassroots liberals, including the 6 percent increase in defense expenditures, investment in the mobile MX missile, and production of the devastatingly powerful neutron bomb.[94] The Carter Doctrine, rather than Ronald Reagan's policy of confrontation, marked the beginning of the second cold war.[95]

It was also one of the few moments of genuine popular support that Carter ever enjoyed. Kennedy campaign organizer Barney Frank complained to journalists that "Afghanistan hurts Kennedy . . . because it diverts people's attention from the price of oil and the unemployment rate."[96] It also gave Carter the excuse to rule out any kind of public debate so long as the crises continued: ordinary politics were effectively put on hold. Kennedy, like many liberals and peace activists, was dismayed by the wholesale rejection of ten years of détente and disarmament. He pointed out, as did Republican presidential hopefuls in the GOP primaries, that Carter's vacillation and weakness had prompted the crises. America did not need more missiles but rather better leadership. However, his plea for restraint only angered patriotic voters.[97] Ironically, Kennedy's polls found that 72 percent of the public thought Carter's previous diplomatic policies were to blame for the crises. Indeed, many Americans shared Kennedy's analysis of Carter's overseas failures but regarded it as unpatriotic to publicly voice such an opinion. In Peter Hart's polls, a plurality (49 percent) strongly opposed the granting of asylum to the shah, while 75 percent believed the granting of asylum was either wholly or partially responsible for the seizing of hostages. Despite this, 54 percent thought that Kennedy had hurt America by protesting the shah's grant of asylum.[98] As the crisis dragged on, Carter's approval ratings fell, and by April 1980, 60 percent disapproved of the administration's foreign policy.[99] This suggests that Kennedy's early campaign was ineffective in part because the issues on which he had been polling well in 1979 were suddenly off the agenda. Attacks on the president's leadership qualities became poor taste.

The administration noted with some pleasure that "the enunciation of the so-called Carter Doctrine together with announced plans to increase defense spending have added a large measure of breadth to our potential support." Iowa suddenly looked winnable.[100] This is not to say that Carter took pleasure from the crises. Far from it. They consumed his time and dominated his thoughts. His dedication to the release of the hostages in Tehran was admirable, and the tortuous process of negotiations tested his many remarkable gifts as a leader and diplomat. However, there can be no doubt, first, that the crises benefited the administration and, second, that Carter knew it.[101]

Public approval for increased defense spending jumped from 27 to 46 percent in one month, and voter admiration of Carter and his policies skyrocketed.[102] At the beginning of November the *New York Times* reported that only 32 percent thought Carter was performing his job well and 55 percent not. Among all social groups at least a plurality disapproved of his performance. The figures were worst among traditional Democratic groups in the East and among the college educated. But by the end of the month his approval rating had leapt to 51 percent, and a plurality among all groups (bar Republicans) supported him.[103] The Roper Center found that by the end of November 1979, 80.4 percent of interviewees were confident of Carter's ability to handle a crisis, and for the first time in over a year, a majority thought he was performing his job well. He had also become the second most admired man in America, just after Edward Kennedy. This was despite the fact that 55.9 percent predicted that the economy would be worse off in 1980, and majorities of 82 percent and 74.4 percent felt sure that prices and unemployment would rise.[104] Similarly, Gallup found that one week after the taking of the hostages, Kennedy still led Carter by 49.5 percent to 38.6 percent. Only 37.8 percent approved of Carter's handling of his job.[105] But by the end of the month, 51.5 percent approved of Carter's job performance, and he was quickly closing the gap with Kennedy.[106] By early December, 75.5 percent approved of

Carter's handling of Iran, and for the first time in its polls, Carter led Kennedy among all voters as a preferred Democratic nominee.

Afghanistan added an extra fillip to Carter's support. It turned a slim majority of sympathy into a landslide. In the new year, Gallup found that after the invasion and imposition of a grain embargo on the USSR, 73.9 percent of interviewees regarded Carter as capable of responding effectively to a crisis, 61.2 percent were happy with his foreign policy, and 56.2 percent thought that Carter's job performance was good. His lead over Kennedy had increased greatly, and pollsters now put him ahead in Iowa.[107] Similarly, Yankelovich found in January that a majority (64.8 percent) mentioned either Afghanistan or Iran as the most important issue facing the country. Some 38.2 percent said that their opinion of Carter had improved recently, and of that figure, 70.7 percent said this was because of his handling of Afghanistan and 40.1 percent because of the hostage crisis. Carter now led Kennedy, according to Yankelovich, by 66.3 percent to 24.2 percent.[108] Interestingly, an increase in Carter's support did not always correspond with a decrease in Kennedy's. Gallup found that in a hypothetical race in December 1979, Kennedy still led Reagan by 50.5 percent to 39.2 percent.[109] In the new year, that lead actually increased to 58 percent to 41.7 percent.[110] Thus, Gallup's interviewees were showing support for the president rather than obliquely rejecting Kennedy.

Meanwhile, Iran threatened to open up wounds within the Democratic Party that the withdrawal from Vietnam had supposedly healed. Many New Dealers welcomed the president's toughness, and most New Politics people regarded it as irresponsible. For instance, feminist organizations rejected the president's posturing militarism out of hand.[111] In contrast, many blue-collar unions embraced it enthusiastically. The Sheet Metal Workers passed a resolution "supporting [the president's] position in the boycott of the forthcoming Olympic Games." The resolution was sent to the White House; at the bottom was scrawled, "Good show in Iowa!" in reference to the president's new popularity there.[112] The support was still qualified by bad memories. One Sheet Metal Workers local passed a resolution that stated, "Even though many of us have not been very enthusiastic about the past performance of our President, [we] think he is doing a good job in a very difficult situation with Iran."[113] Nevertheless, many more responded enthusiastically to Carter's retaliation to the Soviets, and the president probably forestalled a likely endorsement of either Ronald Reagan or Edward Kennedy by the quixotic Teamsters leadership.[114] Union members often used their industrial muscle to display their support for the administration. In New York, hotel and restaurant workers refused to sell food and beverages that originated in the USSR or Iran. The president of their association wired Carter to explain that this was "to not only help implement your policy of sanctions, but to raise awareness of our fellow Americans to the crisis confronting us." The secretary of labor was instructed to call the association to offer its thanks, but to advise it to return to work as normal.[115] Every labor endorsement that Carter received in 1980 made reference to his "ability to lead America in the search for peace."[116]

Party officials too felt drawn to Carter's candidacy in the wake of the foreign crises.[117] "In December 1979," Jordan informed Carter, the mayor of Comanche, Iowa, had "publicly endorsed Kennedy, but has now reverted to being uncommitted. He is impressed with your foreign policy."[118] Representative Tom Harkin of Iowa bemoaned that although he had to support President Carter out of loyalty, he was "philosophically at one with Kennedy."[119] Patriotic fervor was not limited to Iowa. In a regular letter to Carter, a Maine state senator told the president, "Sentiment was very strong for you and your Soviet position in Afghanistan and the Olympics." As a result, he predicted that Carter could count on the state's support.[120] Congressman Howard of New Jersey informed the *New York Times* that he could no longer campaign for Kennedy because he had to show support for the president in a time of crisis.[121] As with labor, the overwhelming majority of Democratic endorsements for Carter in 1980 made reference to his tough stance against the Soviet Union.[122]

The manner in which Iran and Afghanistan diverted momentum, men, and money from Kennedy to Carter was best illustrated by the wholly venal defection of the United Mine Workers of America (UMWA). The UMWA was tipped to endorse Kennedy.[123] Its reasons were both personal and political. When addressing its annual conference, Kennedy expressed "a special bond with the men and women of this union," primarily because it was among them that his brother Jack had begun "another primary campaign 20 years ago."[124] John Kennedy had secured his 1960 nomination only after winning a key primary in West Virginia, a stronghold of the UMWA. Thereafter, the union and its membership had become enthusiastic members of the Kennedy coalition.

But the UMWA was also thought to be hostile to Carter because of a protracted strike it had led in 1977–1978 over pay and fringe benefits.[125] The administration opposed the industrial action, arguing that it weakened the economy and was inflationary.[126] Its relationship with the UMWA leadership was a complex one. Miners' president Arnold Miller had been elected in 1972 as an anticorruption candidate in a conservative union that shied from wider engagement in liberal politics.[127] Although a weak president, his widely welcomed "liberalizing" of his union, which included establishing a political action committee, corresponded with one of the few areas of growth for union membership in the 1970s. The UMWA raised its cadre by 40 percent in that period.[128] However, inflation increased this new membership's desire for increased pay and benefits, and Miller won reelection in 1977 by agreeing to allow locals to strike without the national's consent.[129] The Carter administration predicted, correctly, that this would spark wildcat strikes.[130]

The administration saw the 1977–1978 strike as politically motivated: Miller was encouraging industrial action because he had lost control of his grassroots organization and could only retain leadership by submitting to its militancy.[131] The administration prevaricated with mediation and public appeals, but eventually Carter threatened to invoke the Taft-Hartley Act, and the UMWA backed down.[132] The AFL-CIO was uncomfortable with the use of Taft-Hartley, regarding the denial of food stamps to striking workers as particularly cruel.[133] It organized a massive campaign to encourage unions to send food and money to UMWA members.[134] The strike was far from an isolated incident. For instance, in 1978 the Brotherhood of Railway and Airline Clerks began a long rail action that threatened to cause significant long-term economic damage.[135] Again, the union's president, Fred Kroll, was facing reelection and was keen to court militant grassroots activists.[136] Similarly, the ironworkers engaged in a record sixteen-week strike in 1977.[137] Thus, the UMWA typified the growth of militancy in an inflationary era that made accommodation with the administration particularly difficult.[138]

But the Iranian crisis and sudden restriction in oil supply made the administration more sympathetic toward the coal industry. This led to an accord between union and president.[139] UMWA leader Sam Church wrote to Carter, "The recent events in Iran once again point out the folly of continued dependence upon foreign energy supplies. . . . Increased utilization of coal [is imperative]."[140] The president agreed and put forward a bill that offered $10 billion to phase out gas and oil utilities, replacing them with coal ones and creating some 9,000 new jobs.[141] Throughout 1979–1980 the union continued to lobby the government, with some success.[142] In return, the UMWA endorsed Carter in Iowa, praising his "coal conversion program" while conceding that

"President Carter and the UMWA have not always seen eye to eye on certain issues." It blamed its defection from Kennedy on the senator's professed environmentalism.[143] The decision was unpopular with UMWA members, many of whom defied Church to campaign for Kennedy in West Virginia.[144] Although it was an uneasy alliance, through a combination of the power of the incumbency and foreign events, Carter had secured the support of a union with 300,000 members. Church recorded radio ads for the president, telling listeners, "His energy program means millions of tons of increased coal production." However, even in these ads, he admitted, "We have not always agreed with President Carter."[145]

Defeat

For all his problems, Kennedy trudged gamely through the sleet and snow of Iowa over Christmas and New Year's. But despite the enthusiasm of his activists and the truckloads of students that poured into the state, Iran and Afghanistan took their toll on his bewildered campaign. Kennedy argued that Carter's weak foreign policy had caused the disasters and attacked the grain embargo on the grounds that it would hurt Iowa farmers. But farmers were actually delighted to play a part in standing up to the USSR, and the state was pleased by the president's newfound resolve. On 21 January 1980 Edward Kennedy went down to a humiliating 2–1 defeat in the Iowa caucus. The message was made all the louder by the historic turnout: in 1976 just 38,000 Democrats voted in the caucuses, but in 1980 the figure was 100,000. Remarkably, the victor had never even set foot in the state. Carter had refused even to debate Kennedy and sat the campaign out in the White House, overseeing the hostage negotiations with the Iranians.

Although Kennedy was always courageous during his campaigning, it was obvious to the press corps that he was in pain. Defeat was difficult to take, particularly because it was the first time that a member of the family had been beaten in the popular vote since 1968. Some counseled a face-saving withdrawal. The long-term impact on the campaign cannot be overstated: before Iowa, Kennedy had raised an impressive $4.6 million. On the morning of 22 January, he had just $200,000 left. Ted's sister, Eunice, tried to comfort him as results came in. "You still have me," she said. "I'd rather have Iowa," he replied.[146]

Iowa gave Carter considerable short-term momentum. In previous years this might have proven short-lived and insignificant. Primary seasons in the past had been overlong and full of highs and lows for various candidates. In 1972, George McGovern did not actually win the first three major primaries he entered. He came seventh in Florida with just 6.2 percent. But this did not matter because the length of the contest gave him plenty of opportunity to perform better in later primaries in liberal states in the North and West. His victory in Wisconsin created a bubble of momentum that saw him through the middle of the season. Likewise, after he had won a handful of victories in states like Massachusetts, he lost Ohio and Pennsylvania to Hubert Humphrey, and the contest once again seemed open.[147]

The dynamics of 1980 were completely different. Since 1976, the Carter-controlled DNC had reformed the nomination procedures to ensure greater front-loading of primaries. This pushed many of the big Southern contests to the beginning of the campaign season. Thus, votes in Alabama, Georgia, and Florida were bunched together and taken before Illinois, New York, or Pennsylvania. The primary season was still long (the first round was in January and the last round was in June), but the early Southern contests were predicted to give a greater impression of early support for the president. In contrast, the last round featured a flurry of big industrial states like New Jersey, Ohio, and California. The DNC's hope was that the incumbent would score well enough in the early rounds in the South to build up an apparently insurmountable delegate lead. No challenger would probably have the money or the guts to suffer these defeats with good grace and wait until the later contests for a comeback.[148] The DNC also attempted to increase the number of delegates selected by state party bosses, although this received a great deal of nonpartisan protest from activists and was largely unsuccessful.[149]

The front-loading of primaries was an inspired idea that achieved its purpose. Carter built up an impressive lead in the early rounds that stacked the delegate count in his favor. Although Kennedy won several impressive victories later in the contest and dominated the last few rounds, he was never able to overcome the president's psychological lead. It could be argued that the primaries were over long before Carter officially won them, that the front-loading and the president's early victories made Kennedy's own breakthroughs nothing more than a liberal chimera. But it is wrong to place too strong an emphasis on the machinery of the contest when trying to understand Carter's eventual victory. The logic of front-loading only worked if the incumbent had momentum. He needed to win Iowa (and to win big) in order to dominate the primaries in the next few months. It was Iran and Afghanistan that won Carter Iowa, and it was Iran and Afghanistan that gave him the momentum he needed to scoop the primaries that followed. If Kennedy had won Iowa—that is to say, if the crises had never happened or if he had run a better, more overtly liberal, campaign—then front-loading might have made the contest tighter but certainly not unwinnable.[150]

Above all else, the crises overseas determined the outcome of the early primaries, while front-loading gave these primaries a mathematical significance that they had never before enjoyed. The importance of Afghanistan and Iran was illustrated not only by Carter's 59 percent to 31 percent win in Iowa, but also by what happened next. From January to late March the president continued to enjoy a high rating in the polls that won him primary after primary. Edward Kennedy began to turn the tide by developing a new strategy and a whole new campaign that would eventually bear fruit as a populist, popular protest against the country's poor economic situation. For all the despair of Iowa, the defeat at least forced him to reengage with the party's base and return to his core principles. But the public was not yet ready for this message. It was only when the crises overseas became a cause not for commending Carter's leadership but rather for condemning it that the public turned its attention to other matters. In 1980, the country entered a full-blown recession, and it was against this backdrop that Kennedy's new coalition was formed.

6

"We Gotta Fight Back!"

The Carter Spring and the Kennedy Summer

On 28 January 1980, a few days after the Iowa defeat, a humbled Kennedy gave a speech at Georgetown University in Washington, D.C., that stunned the press corps and radically redefined his candidacy. Kennedy criticized not only Carter's economic strategy, but his foreign policy too. Hitherto, an unspoken consensus had dictated that it would be unpatriotic to publicly question the president's handling of the Iranian and Afghani crises. Kennedy brushed this consensus aside, contemptuously dismissing the view that politicians should "stand silent in the ranks even if we have a different view of the national interest." He argued ominously, and with evident frustration, that "the silence that has descended across foreign policy has also stifled the debate on other essential issues." In short, deference to national interest had mutated into deference toward Jimmy Carter and prevented a proper debate about the effectiveness of his administration and the efficacy of its policies.

Kennedy broke with mainstream public opinion to argue that American support for the bloodthirsty regime of the shah of Persia had triggered the Iranian revolution. The U.S. government had nobody to blame for the wave of fundamentalism sweeping the Middle East but itself. He even opined that the USSR's invasion of Afghanistan did not represent any real threat to American strategic interests. Most Americans, after all, did not even know where Afghanistan was. Communist aggression, and the massive stockpile of nuclear weapons behind it, necessitated a measured rather than militaristic response. "Let us not," pleaded the senator, "foreclose every opening to the Soviet Union." But the big applause lines of Kennedy's speech were reserved for the economy. Having lifted the veil of deference that had shrouded the campaign thus far, Kennedy promised to use his pitch to fight the "oil companies and the other elements of the military-industrial complex." He would adopt emergency powers to put controls on wages and prices, implement a six-month freeze on inflation, force through equality legislation for women and gays, bail out collapsing farms, and institute a public health care system.[1] Kennedy said he wanted to use his presidency to realize the liberal "dream of social progress."[2]

Jimmy Carter hated the Georgetown speech and dismissed it privately as a wail of desperation. "The speech will win back the liberal activists but hurt him in the general election," said one White House insider. Campaign director Robert Strauss commented, "I'm rather speechless about the speech. It didn't excite me, and I suspect the American public feels the same way."[3] Nevertheless, everyone recognized its significance. The Kennedy campaign was changing direction. Just two months earlier the senator had been the front-runner for the Democratic nomination. Ted thought that his main opponent was Ronald Reagan rather than Jimmy Carter and so had adopted a moderate, centrist tone in an effort to appeal to independents and Republicans. Now that he had to fight to win over rank-and-file Democrats, the contest changed shape. Those within his campaign who had argued for a liberal, principle-driven crusade were vindicated by the failure of the moderate strategy. They were back in control and quickly set about redefining Kennedy's candidacy. The senator, they argued, was still running for the presidency—but now he was battling for the soul of the Democratic Party too. From now on, Kennedy would run as a Kennedy, speaking unscripted and from the heart. Rather than the contest being about the choice between two different men, it became a choice between two different visions of America.[4]

To be sure, the Georgetown speech did not change Kennedy's fortunes overnight—far from it; for the next couple of months, he suffered defeat after defeat. But the speech's significance lay in the psychological boost it gave to the campaign. It redefined Kennedy as a candidate, liberating him from the constraints of presidential behavior and freeing him up to say exactly what he truly thought. The public was not yet ready for this message, but the message was certainly a massive improvement on the one that had bored Iowans. Kennedy's campaign performance dramatically changed. Gone was the nervous, heavily scripted, pitifully banal Edward Kennedy. In his place was a raucous, charismatic fighter, bellowing at packed speaker meetings and forever pounding available surfaces with his fist.[5] The press noticed the improvement, and it marked the thawing of relations with a media that had hitherto done little but comment on Chappaquiddick.[6] "What a pleasure it is to see," wrote conservative William Safire, "a favorite get knocked on his ear. What an even greater pleasure it is to see the chastened man shake his head clear, get up off the floor and—by dint of the emotional and intellectual effort of a powerful speech—give his political campaign life and give his political life meaning."[7]

Georgetown gave Kennedy a hidden momentum that was disguised by the defeats that followed in February and March. Activists were coming back to the campaign. Georgetown gave them a reason to endorse Kennedy that went beyond political calculation: they now had a crusade.[8] New York's most senior rabbi was so delighted with it that he mailed a copy to most of the city's Jewish population, highlighting those passages that showed the candidate was finally starting to say something about the unemployment that dogged the city.[9] Since Iowa, the cash-strapped campaign had begun to lay off large numbers of its paid staff.[10] After January, Georgetown became its rallying cry and featured heavily in publicity material.[11] As a result, donors slowly trickled back, and the campaign was able to focus small amounts of cash on states that it thought it might perform well in, like Illinois and New York.[12] The speech even helped heal some of the rifts within the campaign staff too, providing a mantra on which to focus and thus overcome its structural dysfunction.

Where Kennedy had previously tried to appear presidential, he now presented himself as a populist fighting for ignored Americans. The imagery of control versus disorder remained; Kennedy still regarded himself as the more competent of the two candidates. One particularly effective ad that was relayed in English and Spanish showed Carter playing baseball and missing a pitch, with a comical slide whistle effect dubbed over it.[13] But the senator was campaigning now "not for a candidate, but for a cause." Kennedy told audiences that while they were "out of political fashion this year," he was happy to be their champion, to "stand against the temporary tides of reaction—against a politics and a Presidency that may see injustice, but then quietly looks away." An appeal to and for the underdog was politically convenient. It suggested that while a Kennedy success was possible, a defeat was martyrdom against insurmountable political odds.[14]

Perhaps the best ad of the campaign season was a classic piece of class warfare starring popular TV actor Carroll O'Connor. O'Connor played Archie Bunker in the hit U.S. sitcom *All in the Family*. Bunker was a blue-collar icon, a rough, rude, racially prejudiced patriarch struggling to come to terms with the cultural changes of the 1970s. He railed against the hippie his daughter was dating, against the African American family who moved in next door, and most of all against the liberals in government who raised his taxes and spent the money on blacks and bums. A good example of Archie Bunker philosophy came from a 1977 episode during which he gave his opinions on the energy crisis to his long-suffering wife, Edith. "Ah, let me tell ya, I am so sick of Washington and all its works," he sighed, "all them politicians down there and all them congressmen. And the congressmen! Boy! I bet you won't find any of them congressmen turning down their electric blankets tonight. 'Cause if they did their secretaries would get up and go home."

But in 1980, Archie Bunker became a liberal. In Kennedy's ad, Archie Bunker/Carroll O'Connor spoke directly to the camera and warned viewers in his thick Queens accent, "Carter is the most Republican president since Herbert Hoover." He solemnly predicted that "Jimmy's depression is going to be worse than Hoover's." The spot's tagline was "Kennedy for president. We gotta fight back!"[15] An equally culturally powerful ad featured Will Geer, the actor who played Grandpa Walton in the Depression-era soap *The Waltons*, sitting in a rocking chair and talking about Franklin Roosevelt. At the end, the ad shouted, "Take a stand. Vote Kennedy!"[16] Both these ads signaled Kennedy's newfound determination to win back to the Democratic Party the conservative working-class voters who had begun to abandon it.

The Carter Spring

The momentum that Carter enjoyed after his victory in Iowa overshadowed the improvements in Kennedy's campaign. There was a glimmer of hope on 11 February in Maine, when the senator reduced the president's lead in the first open primary to just 4 percent. The press noticed that students protesting the registration for the draft had flooded the state.[17] However, later that month Kennedy was defeated in New Hampshire by a 47.1 percent to 37.3 percent margin and in early March in Vermont by a decisive 69.1 percent to 25.5 percent.[18] In New Hampshire, a Kennedy state coordinator told reporters, "It was the flag. People kept saying that in a time of crisis, they had to support the president." The only people who went for Kennedy in New Hampshire were voters under the age of thirty. The campaign had briefly reopened an old generational divide between those who thought that confrontation with the USSR was America's painful duty and those who feared they might actually have to spill their blood fulfilling it.[19]

Kennedy's only primary success in February and March was a solid victory in his own state of 65.1 percent to 28.7 percent.[20] Early precinct caucuses also favored Carter, with the president winning Delaware, Oklahoma, Hawaii, and Washington State in voting on 13 March 1980. That day Kennedy won a surprise 2–1 victory in Alaska, assisted, in a pattern that would become typical of a number of smaller states, by a large turnout of minority voters. In this case, Eskimos provided the margin of victory.[21] Yet Alaska and Massachusetts were not states that traditionally determined the outcome of presidential primaries. Kennedy went on to a disappointing 23 percent to 61 percent loss in the Florida primary on 11 March, and continuing support for Carter's foreign policies and front-loading helped the incumbent establish an impressive early lead of 351 to 179 delegates.[22] Although small donations to the Kennedy candidacy increased after the January lull, the senator's campaign was still desperately underfinanced.[23] In March it cut its budgets so drastically that the director of finance, who had put $4,000 of his own savings toward the primaries, had to resign. He had not received a paycheck since the Iowa defeat.[24] Throughout the rest of the primaries, Carter consistently outspent his rival.[25]

Buoyed by improving crowds and a growing sense of purpose, Kennedy dismissed contests like Iowa and Florida as atypical and ultimately unimportant. One was a caucus and the other a Southern state neighboring the president's own.[26] Instead, Ted pinned his hopes on a victory in Illinois on 18 March. Illinois, an industrial Northern state gripped by recession, seemed perfectly suited to the senator's new, angry message.[27] What is more, Kennedy had received the endorsement of Chicago city mayor Jane Byrne.[28] Byrne's support was indicative of Kennedy's earlier strength: she believed Carter would be an electoral "disaster" in the general election while Kennedy could bring out traditional Democratic voters.[29] However, the story of Illinois was symptomatic of the decline of the Democratic machine.[30] Byrne's surprise election to the mayoralty had elevated a controversial figure that exposed the fault lines of Illinois liberalism.[31] She courted the gay community, moved the mayor's residence to a poor black neighborhood, and attempted to wrest state politics from the domination of former mayor Richard Daley's Cook County machine.[32] She was a combative iconoclast given to holding impromptu press conferences in which she angrily denounced her opponents, both real and imaginary. In gaining Byrne's endorsement, Kennedy lost the sympathy of the wider Illinois Democratic Party.[33] Byrne's political opponents supported the president, such as County Assessor Thomas Hynes, who controlled local party fund-raising, or former lieutenant governor Neil Hartigan,

whose wife was running against a Byrne legislative aide for a committee post.[34] They did so purely to defy the mayor's early endorsement.
One committee member told a journalist, "People who never accepted
Jane's victory are now taking sides in the presidential fight."[35] The
greatest embarrassment for Kennedy came on the St. Patrick's Day
march when, walking alongside the mayor, he was repeatedly booed.
One drunken onlooker followed him down the parade route shouting, "Where's Mary Jo?" This was home turf for the liberal stalwart,
and its rejection hurt. Later, a car backfired somewhere on the parade route, and Kennedy visibly flinched. The twin specters of Chappaquiddick and the deaths of his brothers haunted him even in a city
where he ought to have felt most at home.[36]

Kennedy's hopes for a comeback in Illinois were cruelly dashed. His
family had spent one hundred days in the state in total, most of which
saw Kennedy battling a crippling bout of flu.[37] Nevertheless, he was
defeated by a stunning margin of 65 percent to 35 percent. The cost
to the people who had backed the senator was enormous. In down-
state Morgan County, Democratic Party chairman Leonard Kramp
was stripped of his control over hiring local census takers by regional
census director Manker Harris. With it went the power to give jobs
to friends and relatives. "You're a nonperson," explained Harris to
Kramp. "You decided to back the wrong man for President. You understand politics, and this is politics." His career was finished.[38]

This was the pinnacle of Carter's new popularity, and the greatest
depth to which Kennedy's struggling campaign would sink. The state
was predicted in 1979 to go easily for Kennedy.[39] The result neatly
encapsulated how drastically the political wind could change its direction in a mere matter of months. Kennedy was damaged slightly by his
positions on busing and abortion.[40] The endorsement of Mayor Jane
Byrne undermined party establishment support for the senator but
ultimately had little effect on the final result.[41] Kennedy performed
best in Cook County, where Byrne was most unpopular.[42] The senator was, however, hurt by media attention on Chappaquiddick.[43] By
the time of the primary, 36 percent of all American voters said they
were less likely to vote for Kennedy because of the accident.[44] With
Carter's leadership rating inflated by Iran and Afghanistan, the issue
of character had become more important during the campaign, and
Kennedy lost voters who rated honesty most highly as a qualification
for the presidency by a margin of 4 to 1.[45] Carter won Illinois on issues
of trustworthiness (by 60 percent to 30 percent) and leadership (by 58
percent to 40 percent) in response to foreign crises.

More importantly, 50 percent approved of Carter's handling of foreign policy, and he received the votes of 77 percent naming foreign crises as the issue most affecting their choice. A majority did consider economic problems preeminent, and Carter did badly among those who disapproved of his policies in that field. However, Illinois voters actually interpreted the economy as being significantly healthier than New Hampshire voters had the previous month. Crucially, only 35 percent thought that their financial situation worsened during 1979. Forty percent thought that Carter was handling the economy well.[46] This was despite respondents supporting Kennedy's liberal measures to fight inflation and unemployment.[47] By large majorities, they supported wage/price controls and opposed the building of more nuclear plants, but citizens holding those positions still voted for Carter. By a plurality, it was believed that the administration was not helping minorities enough. Voters often adjusted their judgment of the economy according to their perception of the president's current diplomatic performance.[48]

Finally, in Illinois, Kennedy was somewhat hurt by crossover voting among Democrats for a maverick liberal running in the Republican primaries named John B. Anderson. With Kennedy's campaign in apparent decline, liberals switched affiliations, causing the scale of Carter's victory to be exaggerated.[49] Carter's campaign was now better organized and considerably richer. The president spent $1 million on personal advertising to Kennedy's $200,000.[50] He offered up to $59 million in urban aid to Chicago.[51]

To Illinois, Carter had run a near-perfect campaign that had benefited enormously from historical accident. In 1979 the Democratic nomination belonged to Edward Kennedy. He had pulled together the various liberal factions of the 1970s and appealed even beyond his party to a nation desperate for leadership in difficult times. Hamilton Jordan had described his boss's chances of winning the nomination as "a long shot."[52] But then came Iran and Afghanistan, and the president had an opportunity to impress his people with his resolve and resilience. For three months, they repaid his defiance of the Soviet Union and the Iranian fanatics with one solid election victory after another. Illinois seemed to confer the nomination upon him.

But as the returns flooded in, Kennedy's prospects were not as dim as they at first appeared. The senator had won the votes of liberals, those paid by the hour, and the very poorest. Ominously, he won 65 percent of that 35 percent who had told pollsters their economic situation had worsened, pointing to the foundation of a new Kennedy constituency that would grow throughout the primaries. Although the Georgetown speech had not yet enjoyed the impact that his staff hoped, Kennedy at least had found an electoral foothold that had eluded him before. Had he continued to campaign simply as a pragmatic, careful states-man, Kennedy would probably have continued to be beaten well into June. But his bitter, pointed rhetoric had begun to identify a new co-alition of dissent.

The Kennedy Comeback

After Illinois, the next big state to vote was New York. If the presi-dent could win there, then he could secure the nomination and force Kennedy out of the race. A private poll conducted for Carter confi-dently predicted that a landslide in New York was likely, by 58.5 per-cent to 19.8 percent. Even in the urban centers and among Catholic voters Carter was heavily favored, with Kennedy enjoying the major-ity support of no demographic group at all.[53] A pro-Carter commen-tator reported that "the suspicion in some quarters is that Kennedy will surrender unless New York voters astonish everyone by rejecting the President."[54] Recognizing that this was the last stand, both candi-dates threw everything they had at the primary. Kennedy stumped the state strongly, appearing at union halls, street corners, synagogues, and packed auditoriums. So poor was the campaign now that it was reduced to handing out photostatted, often inaccurate leaflets.[55] The Carter family toured the state too, and the president announced a new injection of federal aid, which was trumpeted by his key supporters, Lieutenant Governor Mario Cuomo and New York City mayor Ed Koch.[56] There was a small wobble in support for the president after an incident at the U.N. cast doubt on the administration's support for Israel. Yet again demonstrating the disintegrating structure of com-mand within the White House, a U.S. representative at the U.N. had either deliberately or accidentally misinterpreted his instructions and voted to condemn Israeli seizures of Palestinian land. New York City's large Jewish population was incensed, but pundits still predicted a 2–1 victory for the president.[57]

The opposite happened. On 25 March, Kennedy upset all the odds and took 58.9 percent to Carter's 41.1 percent. On the same day, he won a much narrower but no less gratifying victory in Connecticut by 46.9 percent to 41.5 percent. When the results came in, the Kennedy camp was ecstatic. Finally, they had won a victory and proved their point. The president was unpopular, the senator was electable, and the country was not slipping to the right (at least it wasn't in New York).[58] The joy was not misplaced, and the reasons for both victories were the same: the growing fear of recession and a new willingness to consider Kennedy's solutions. Both joblessness and inflation had inched up since January, and there was talk of yet another increase in interest rates. The results, coming just one week after Illinois, demonstrated a tectonic shift in priorities among voters.[59] This time, the economy was the most important issue, and only 35 percent supported Carter's foreign policy.[60] Many commentators claimed the victory was a response to the mishandling of the U.N. vote on Israeli settlements.[61] But this alone did not count for the scale of the defeat. Certainly only 13 percent of Jewish respondents considered Carter to be an ally of Israel, and they trusted and voted for Kennedy in larger numbers than gentiles. But Jewish voters emphatically listed inflation (by 42 percent) as a more important issue than support for Israel (28 percent). Of the entire electorate, only 10 percent said Israel was a deciding factor for candidate preference.[62]

New York was the first primary when respondents voted with their pocketbooks. ABC News reported that 70.6 percent voted for candidates on the basis of their platforms rather than their characters, a reading starkly different from Illinois. Fifty-eight percent of voters thought that tackling inflation was the most important issue, and 70.3 percent thought that the candidate they had chosen was best suited to tackle it. Only 14.7 percent mentioned the hostage crisis as a decisive influence on voting.[63] Sixty-four percent of those interviewed by the *New York Times* who favored wage controls, 63 percent who supported domestic spending increases, and 67 percent of those who wanted national health insurance voted for the senator.[64] Throughout the primaries, Kennedy's vote increased the greater his voters regarded their financial situation to have worsened.

But this was not merely a rejection of Carter. Kennedy led Carter by 39 percent to 26 percent in leadership capability and by 49 percent to 46 percent in trust.[65] Arguably New York proved that early support for Carter was a hiatus for Kennedy caused by crises abroad.[66] Kennedy's main support came from those traditional Democratic groups that polls indicated he initially led among in 1979. The size of his victory was dependent on support from Jews, liberals, working-class whites, and blacks. He carried New York State by dominating the returns in the city. He won twenty-eight of the thirty-nine congressional districts, including all of the city's sixteen full districts and two partial districts. He won all five boroughs by margins of up to 2 to 1 and all but ten of the city's assembly districts. In the Bronx, he won by 65,114 to 33,504.[67] Rightfully, the Kennedy campaign was jubilant. The senator had let rip in the Big Apple as had never been done before, barnstorming the state with a rough and rowdy message of economic democracy. When the results poured in, the sense of surprised joy was so infectious that even, for perhaps the first time, Joan Kennedy caught the election fever. Usually shy of media attention, she took the microphone at the victory rally and sang "I Love New York." Ted and the audience looked on, bemused but charmed.[68] At the White House, the news was received in stony, shocked silence. Defeat had not been predicted, and everyone knew that it meant the race would go on for a few primaries more at least.[69]

It was Kennedy's first win, and it was both big and trendsetting. New York not only rescued the campaign, but it also demonstrated that a return to basic liberal principles was a sound strategy. New York had been hit hard by the 1970s and by Jimmy Carter's spending cuts. The city had gone into debt and faced bankruptcy in 1975. The Ford White House was forced to offer it a federal loan that amounted to a bailout, but even this was not enough. As Carter tightened his budgets and inflation reduced the value of government grants, states like New York began to lose more in taxes than they gave to the federal government and than they received back in aid.[70] New York was a sick city, its urban centers blackened with pollution and depopulated, leaving only crime, drug addiction, and joblessness behind. Around it grew vast new stretches of suburbia, the so-called white flight of Middle America from its industrial origins. The city (largely black, Hispanic, and poor) and suburbia (almost entirely white and moderately, but precariously, affluent) were divided against each other. But for all of their mutual suspicion and vastly different cultural prejudices and expectations, their anger was toward the same thing: economic and social decline.[71] While conservatives like George Wallace had made appeals to the rage of the suburbs and radicals like George McGovern had tried to soothe and direct the trauma of the ghettos, Kennedy did something no one else had done in the 1970s. He spoke for them both.

The Kennedy Coalition Revived

Often Kennedy polled well among Wallace Democrats. In many regards, the Kennedy and Wallace constituencies were very different.

For instance, Wallace's spectacular victory in the 1972 Democratic Michigan primary was due largely to defecting Republican voters. In contrast, Kennedy's strength in the 1980 Michigan caucuses was reliant on union support and heavy voting in Detroit and Flint.[72] Wallace's vote was almost solely white, Protestant, and male.[73] In the 1972 Massachusetts primary, he performed best in South Boston, the racially conservative district that Kennedy lost in 1980, and his narrow defeat in Indiana was due to solid black support for his opponents.[74] Perhaps unsurprisingly, Wallace endorsed Carter in 1980, although his Alabama state party chair was a Kennedy supporter.[75] Nevertheless, in the Maryland primaries, Kennedy and Wallace both polled well in industrialized areas and among people who worked with their hands. They shared many of the unionized voters in Districts 7 and 8, concentrated in the Baltimore suburbs.[76] Wallacites were the quintessential Archie Bunker voters, and they often went for Kennedy too.

Similarly, both George McGovern and Edward Kennedy enjoyed the consistent support of "students, suburbanites, and intellectuals," and there are points of comparison between the campaigns.[77] Kennedy often relied strongly on student activism, motivated by the issues of the draft and nuclear power.[78] He performed well in most of the districts that had gone for McGovern in 1972: both easily swept New Jersey.[79] But McGovern's culturally hip campaign appealed best to suburban white middle-class voters. In the 1972 California primary, he polled poorly among blacks and blue-collar union members, groups that went heavily for Kennedy in 1980.[80] In the 1972 New York primary, McGovern did better among rural voters than Ted did in 1980.[81] Moreover, Kennedy attracted far more labor and Democratic office-holder support than McGovern, appealing to both the party machine and antiestablishment activists. Kennedy's coalition, then, was unique. His majorities were typically built on uniting divergent voting blocs; he drew to the polls large numbers of liberals, minority voters, and blue-collar conservatives, all angry with the status quo. In this manner, Kennedy both revived and expanded the Democratic coalition, expressing, among contrasting groups, common anger at a decline in the standard of living. Unsurprisingly, he performed best in industrialized areas hit by recession, even though this citizenry often comprised a traditionally conservative demographic.[82]

Some commentators suggested that Edward Kennedy re-created the mythical "Kennedy coalition" of "blacks and liberals and blue-collar conservatives, all united at their anger at the way things were," typically associated with his brother Robert. It is often argued that

Robert Kennedy's macho liberalism managed to create a bridge between idealistic campus liberals, frustrated working-class whites, and poorer, marginalized groups like Hispanics. This was key to his victories in the 1968 Democratic primaries. In fact, Bobby was not as successful at constructing this coalition as his myth implies. Historian Brian Dooley has convincingly demonstrated that Robert Kennedy's performance among white voters was poor and that he won by energizing minorities alone. Dooley points out that his key victory in the Indiana primary was largely the result of a huge turnout among African Americans, and he demonstrated little appeal to down-at-the-heels whites. If Edward Kennedy did assemble the Kennedy coalition, then he was the first Kennedy to do so.[83]

And it was here in New York that Ted first did it. Carter held those congressional districts that he had won in the primaries of 1976, the agricultural and conservative areas upstate. Kennedy took those areas that had gone to Carter's opponents that year: Henry Jackson and Mo Udall. Jackson and Udall spoke for very different elements of the Democratic coalition and represented the extremes of experience within their party.[84] Udall's were the youngest and the most likely to self-define as liberal; they enjoyed the highest instance of college education and were the wealthiest. Jackson's were the eldest, poorest, and least educated. Both groups of supporters were the most heavily unionized and thus represented the most activist branches of the party. They were located almost exclusively in the urban and suburban districts within New York State.

Jackson ran well in ethnic white districts; 54 percent of his support was unionized, and 51 percent worked in manufacturing. He comfortably carried the Archie Bunker districts in Queens, securing every delegate. Four years later Kennedy would win some of his largest votes in that same neighborhood, notably carrying 27,716 votes to Carter's 11,853 in Queens's eighth congressional district. But Kennedy also took the twentieth congressional district in the Bronx, where Udall had won all the delegates in 1976, by 30,066 votes to 14,523 votes.[85] In short, Kennedy had done something that had long been the dream of New York Democratic politicians. His vote encompassed Catholic and Jewish, rich and poor, middle- and working-class, liberal and conservative, young and old neighborhoods.[86]

New York did not start an immediate turnaround in Kennedy's fortunes; popular momentum took longer to build than the landslide suggested it might. Although the media was thrilled to suddenly have a much closer contest on its hands, the senator still had a long way to go to catch up with the president. Carter recouped with a victory in Wisconsin on 1 April, prompting many to suggest that the revolt was fading. In fact, the Iranian crisis had once again staved off defeat. Having received news from Iran that a contact had been made with radical student leaders, the administration spun a minor step forward as a major breakthrough. On the morning of the primary, a breathless president held an impromptu press conference at which he implied that the hostages were close to release. Approval of Carter's foreign policy among Democratic voters shot to 48 percent (during Kennedy's New York win, it was only 35 percent), and once again, it outpolled the economy as the most important issue. He carried the primary comfortably, some 36 percent of voters deciding whom to vote for on the day.[87] This was despite the fact that 59 percent opposed Carter's decision to allow gasoline prices to rise (as did Kennedy), 51 percent opposed the building of nuclear power plants to replace oil demand (as did Kennedy), and 51 percent thought that inflation was out of control enough to demand the imposing of wage or price controls (as did Kennedy).[88] The views of voters on what should be done about the economy showed that it was Wisconsin, not New York, that was the blip.

On 12 April, Hispanic Kennedyites caused a surprise upset when they helped him to win the Arizona primary. Local farm organizer and iconic hero of the American left, Cesar Chavez, was an old friend. He had campaigned with Robert in 1968 after the senator joined him in a fast in protest at the treatment of migrant workers. Ted had kept in touch with Chavez's United Farm Workers of America (UFW), supporting their campaigns in Congress and regularly joining their picket lines. The UFW was also part of the Progressive Alliance/Democratic Agenda machine. So popular were the Kennedys that it was not unusual in Hispanic homes to find a photograph of Robert hanging next to a painting of Jesus Christ.[89] Honoring a political debt, Chavez threw the manpower of the UFW behind the senator. Chavez calculated that the state could be tipped if Kennedy were to "win in predominately Mexican-American areas by a 3 to 1 margin" and if the UFW kept its presence quiet "so as not to arouse opposing forces until it is too late." As well as winning one for his old friend, Chavez wanted to "demonstrate that the United Farm Workers is a power to be reckoned with" and that Carter could only ignore Hispanic politics at his peril.[90] He succeeded, handing Kennedy a 55 percent to 45 percent victory, which the administration was shocked by and blamed entirely on dissident union organization.[91] The president had been endorsed by the state governor and had outspent Kennedy enormously, even sending

Rosalynn to campaign personally for Jimmy.[92] But Kennedy brought out Hispanic voters in record numbers, winning the heavily Chicano tenth district with a 4–1 margin and the eleventh by 12–1.[93]

After the sideshows of Wisconsin and Arizona had produced contradictory results, all eyes turned to the Pennsylvania primary scheduled to take place on 22 April. Kennedy stepped up his rhetoric, and despite being hugely outspent, he threw himself into a make-or-break test of support in another ailing industrial state. With only two days of preparation, aides organized a rally in Pittsburgh attended by 10,000 people—a far larger crowd than what had greeted the Steelers after they won that year's Super Bowl. Kennedy drew his loudest reaction when he called on Carter to leave the Rose Garden and campaign actively, bawling, "You've got to come out and face the American people sometime!"

On voting day, his voice breaking with strain and his face windswept and white with exhaustion, Kennedy took to the streets of Philadelphia. A midday rally, timed to catch office workers pouring into the streets for lunch, drew a crowd over 2,000 strong that cheered and roared its way down Main Street. There, Ted, in a scene reminiscent of Bobby's 1968 campaign, was torn and grabbed at by fevered admirers as he shouted hoarsely into a microphone. "I say it's time to say," he said in a speech that would be eagerly replayed in Republican ads in the fall, "noooo more high interest rates, noooo more high inflation, noooo more hostages, and noooo more Jimmy Carter!" Angered by joblessness and soaring prices, Philadelphia bellowed its approval. The media noted that Kennedy was "more effective on the stump than in any previous state."[94] His raw emotion paid off. In all the primaries that he won after New York, Kennedy secured a clear majority of those who made their minds up in the last week before voting, thus demonstrating the impact of recent events, the recession, and Kennedy's revived campaign.[95]

Kennedy narrowly won Pennsylvania by 45.7 percent to 45.4 percent.[96] *Time* magazine nicely communicated the despair of the White House. "On primary night," it reported, "the first problem was how to tell the President that he had been . . . defeated. Said an aide: 'Thank God we had him prepared, or it would have been very unpleasant breaking the news.'" The president was still apparently very upset. "Said Jody Powell, with what sounded like a hint of understatement: 'He is a graceful loser, but he is not a good loser. He was not at all happy.'"[97]

Carter's anger in part reflected the fact that ordinary working-class voters—those who had voted patriotically for him in Iowa and

Illinois—were now abandoning their president. Once again, Kennedy's appeal was not limited to liberals (of whatever hue) and ethnic minorities. He also attracted the support of a surprising number of self-proclaimed conservative voters, the blue-collar ethnics that had started to tell pollsters they were thinking of voting for Reagan in the general election. Pennsylvanians leaving the voting booths told pollsters that inflation was the biggest influence on how they voted. Kennedy led Carter 2–1 among Democrats most concerned about the economy. A plurality of voters thought that their financial situation had declined, and 58 percent of this vote went to Kennedy. Interestingly, 54 percent stated that they did not think that the federal budget needed to be balanced.[98] Although Carter beat him 3–1 on issues of character and trust, Kennedy thrashed the president by 6–1 on issues of leadership.[99] As in New York, Kennedy's vote was an urban and suburban one, easily carrying Philadelphia (where he lost only one district), its suburbs, and the cities of Scranton and Wilkes-Barre. He performed badly in the rural areas and ran narrowly behind Carter in some mining towns. Interestingly, the voting intentions of union members were dictated by locality: rural labor went for Carter and urban labor for Kennedy.[100] Some commentators blamed Kennedy's views on gun control and abortion for these results.[101]

An ABC News–Harris exit poll explained that Kennedy had won big majorities in 1980 among blacks and self-described liberals, pulling even with Carter among moderates and losing among conservatives.[102] However, a CBS/*Times* poll disagreed. Its findings demonstrated that Kennedy had in fact secured majorities among self-described liberals and conservatives, while Carter had led strongly among moderates.[103] Looking at an electoral map of Pennsylvania, the CBS/*Times* poll proved the more accurate. Kennedy swept the angry cities and suburbs, taking the votes of both the left and right and leaving the president as the figurehead of a rapidly disintegrating center. A comparison with how candidates in other elections have performed is most illuminating. As in New York, Kennedy combined the votes of those who had supported Jackson and Udall in 1976.[104] He easily took Udall's liberal suburb of Montgomery and the unionized blue-collar areas of Philadelphia that had gone for Jackson and cast a smaller share of votes for Wallace.[105] The senator also combined the votes of Clinton and Obama supporters in 2008. Excepting the rural west (which went heavily for Clinton), Kennedy took the Clinton districts of Montgomery, Schuylkill, Lackawanna, Carbon, and Luzerne and the Obama districts of Chester, Delaware, and Philadelphia.[106]

April belonged to Kennedy. Louis Harris published a poll that insisted it was "a mistake to say the Democratic race is over. . . . Kennedy is now, albeit belatedly, putting together the traditional, gut vote in the Democratic Party. Carter's coalition consists of small-town conservatives and Protestants. Furthermore, Carter is now falling and Kennedy is on the rise for the first time since he declared."[107] This was probably an overstatement, given that Carter still enjoyed a healthy lead after the landslide in Illinois and there were still more votes to come from Southern states. Indeed, the American media often has a habit of sustaining interest in campaigns some time after their victory has probably become a statistical unlikelihood. In 2008, Hillary Rodham Clinton continued to campaign beyond the point when it was likely that Barack Obama had enough delegates to clinch the nomination. Not until the last round did the media proclaim the race was over, for fear of depriving the public of a good story. But this should not detract from the fact that Clinton did indeed pull off several last-minute impressive victories in 2008, any more than it should detract from similar wins by Edward Kennedy in 1980. Even though Carter had established a probably insurmountable lead, more people than ever before volunteered for, supported, and voted for the senator's campaign. The existence of this new momentum, foolhardy or not, was undeniable. On 27 April Kennedy won the Michigan primary in an effort largely managed by the UAW and the Democratic Agenda.[108] Meanwhile, some earlier results were overturned in delegate-selecting caucuses, suggesting that local activists were reviewing the latest results and starting to change their minds.[109]

Victories in big industrial states in the East began to give Kennedy the momentum needed to win more conservative Western ones too.[110] At the beginning of May, Carter was predicted to win a 2–1 victory at the Colorado nominating convention.[111] But after Kennedy stumped the state, support began to move in his direction.[112] The *Colorado States-man* found that although 94 percent of Democratic county chairs believed Carter was guaranteed renomination, "rival Edward Kennedy's support among them is as high as it's ever been. Thirty percent of the chairmen prefer Kennedy for president, compared to 47 percent who favor Carter." Moreover, Kennedy narrowly won a surprise victory in the precinct caucuses on 5 May, taking 842 delegates to Carter's 816. Kennedy won eight house districts, Carter only two. Kennedy's strength was located in Denver and its suburbs, like the chic university town of Boulder. But he also swept Denver's poorest white-dominated rural county, Los Alamos.[113] Only after intensive lobbying at the state convention itself could Carter secure a precarious overall victory of 805 to 799 votes, giving him fourteen national convention delegates to Kennedy's twelve. This skillful piece of last-minute jockeying could not disguise the fact that it was the senator who had won the popular vote.[114]

Carter took several big, easy primary victories throughout the rest of May in mostly Southern states like Tennessee, Arkansas, Maryland, Kentucky, and North Carolina. Kennedy only pulled off a single, small triumph in Washington, D.C. (which he won 62 percent to 37 percent). But Carter's winning streak looked like a poor consolation prize after losing the psychologically significant state of Pennsylvania. Besides, Kennedy was spending all his time and money on the last round of primaries on 3 June. And this round belonged to Kennedy. Winning the popular vote by 2.6 to 2.4 million, the angry senator from Massachusetts took California, New Jersey, Rhode Island, South Dakota, and New Mexico, giving him a final tally of 1,239 delegates to Carter's 1,964.[115] With some justification, he pointed out that "we have carried the states that are the heartland of the Democratic Party . . . the states that a Democratic nominee must carry to prevail in November."[116] Importantly, he had won a number of conservative Western states too.

Kennedy dominated the last round by attracting a coalition of liberals and conservatives. But he also did it by motivating large numbers of ethnic minorities to come to the polls. His surprise victory in New Mexico was secured by combining the votes of urban and suburban voters with the mobilization of Hispanics. This support represented a rebellion against the organized Democratic Hispanic machine. Although polls showed that Kennedy led Carter 2–1 among their community, the Hispanic American Democrats convention in December 1979 endorsed Carter in a floor vote by 40 percent to 24 percent, an example of the discrepancy between ethnic leadership and ethnic voters. Eduardo Pena, the previous convention president, tried successfully to use the threat of a Kennedy landslide to win concessions from the administration.[117] The president heeded his warning and appointed the first-ever Hispanic ambassador to Mexico.[118] But symbols were not enough to scoop the support of a community hard hit by unemployment.

The writing was already on the wall for the administration. In the 3 May Texas primary, the White House's attempts to woo the Spanish vote were similarly successful at the level of the party machine, but a failure at the ballot box. Carter ran a liberal campaign, claiming that he had fought hard to create jobs for Hispanics.[119] The strategy worked at a community-leader level, and on occasion Hispanic community leaders proved to be Carter's most ardent supporters. Like blacks, they depended on financial and political support from the incumbent and were unwilling to sacrifice a growing influence within the administration.[120] In Illinois the prominent Hispanic community leader Joseph N. Gomez fought off threats of political death and a lucrative job offer from city hall to continue his support of Carter. He organized the ten Hispanic delegates that went for the president and raised $23,000 in December 1979.[121] Nationally, the official Hispanic Democratic group Mexican American Democrats (MAD), which donated $750,000 to his renomination effort, supported Carter. However, in early primaries, Hispanic voters spontaneously came out for Kennedy in numbers that troubled the administration. In Texas, MAD dominated the Hispanic leadership, as did the Carter-friendly teaching union, the National Education Association. Nevertheless, while in the 3 May primary Kennedy was beaten soundly (55.9 percent to 22.8 percent), he won a landslide victory among Chicanos (68 percent to 27 percent). They amounted to 58.5 percent of his support, and where they turned out in the biggest numbers, Kennedy performed best.[122]

In the 3 June New Mexico primary, where conservative Democrat George C. Wallace had run second in 1972, Kennedy again "beat the party machine and surprised a lot of people."[123] Carter enjoyed the support of the governor, the mayor of Albuquerque, and the state party chair. But following on from its triumph in Arizona, the UFW brought out enough voters to secure Kennedy a 46.3 percent to 41.8 percent victory.[124] He ran strongest in Hispanic counties, taking 3,067 votes to Carter's 1,410 in Taos and 4,324 to 1,089 in Rio Arliba.[125]

But the New Mexico primary also showed the attraction to Kennedy of another minority just finding its feet in primary politics. Native Americans are often a conservative voting bloc and sometimes went for George Wallace in primaries and Republican candidates in general elections.[126] But in New Mexico in 1980, Kennedy carried the Native American district handsomely, by 3,119 votes to Carter's 1,828.[127] On the same day, they also provided the margin of victory in South Dakota, where Kennedy's shoestring campaign cost just $5,000.[128] Although Kennedy polled well in unionized urban areas such as Minnehaha, he won his biggest margins of victory in counties dominated by Native Americans.[129] For instance, he took the Shannon reservation by 356 to 84 votes.[130] With a statewide majority of just 1,497 votes, Native American support effectively clinched the primary for Kennedy.[131] It was a repeat of the senator's earlier victory in Alaska, which was thanks to a coalition of environmentalists and Eskimo voters formed to protest budget cuts in wilderness preservation programs.[132]

On 3 June, African Americans voted strongly for Kennedy too. This had not always been so. The president enjoyed a well-documented rapport with black voters, particularly conservative and religious Southerners.[133] In the primaries, blacks began as a solid bloc of support for the administration but closed the season overwhelmingly favorable toward the senator, regardless of region or ideology. Thus, in the 11 March Alabama primary, they voted 67 percent to 29 percent for the president, and in Illinois 57 percent to 39 percent. Like unionists and Democratic officeholders, black leaders were beholden to the administration, aware of its ability to break "their programs, their communities, and their careers." In March this picture began to change, and in Pennsylvania, 59 percent of blacks voted for Kennedy.[134] By the time of the May primaries (in which Kennedy barely competed), the senator's vote was reliant on black urban dwellers.[135] The administration noted with some anxiety the growing sophistication of the African American vote, which was increasingly influenced by pocketbook issues.[136] Like Hispanics, blacks largely ignored the advice of community leaders. In Philadelphia, Carter enjoyed the "unanimous endorsement of all black ward leaders" and the city's religious community. But blacks went overwhelmingly for Kennedy.[137]

Jewish voters never vacillated, and they came through for Kennedy in the last round too. In the early Florida primary, Kennedy led Carter only among students, self-described liberals, and Jews.[138] Jewish votes would also prove vital in the November election, with 11 percent of them defecting from the Democratic ticket.[139] Jews voted disproportionately to the rest of the nation for John B. Anderson's independent candidacy, by 17 percent (contrasted with 8 percent among whites), and Anderson's total deprived Carter of many electoral votes in the Northeast.[140] Thus, Kennedy's candidacy had energized and exploited constituencies that could provide the margin of victory in key states.

Naturally, ethnic minorities are not enough to win an election, and the scale of Kennedy's victory on 3 June was dependent on once again drawing together an alliance of conservatives and liberals. In the last round of voting, Carter was forced to "split the moderate vote." In contrast, "Kennedy managed to put together a coalition of disaffected working-class conservatives and middle-class, white-collar liberals." Much of Kennedy's vote on 3 June planned to switch to another candidate in the fall. "Roughly half of the pro-Kennedy liberals, especially those with a college education, were ready to go for Mr.

Anderson." More surprisingly, more than "40 percent of the pro-Kennedy conservatives were ready to go for Reagan."[141] Overall, 34 percent of Kennedy's supporters intended to vote for Anderson in November, and 22 percent planned to vote for Reagan.[142] Kennedy's New Jersey victory of 56.2 percent to 37.8 percent was achieved by winning a majority of 3–2 among voters who thought that their economic situation had declined, regardless of their political philosophy.[143] He ran very strongly among those who prioritized the reduction of unemployment and more modestly ahead of those who prioritized inflation. He combined conservative and liberal voters.[144] Kennedy swept every single congressional district, despite being heavily outspent, again performing best among urban dwellers.[145] He did so despite the Democratic governor's early endorsement of Carter. Indeed, in a reversal of the outcome of the Illinois primary, some members of county Democratic organizations indicated that they voted for Kennedy as much out of spite for the governor as discontent with the president.[146]

California repeated the experience of Pennsylvania and New York. To be sure, Kennedy targeted the votes of minorities, particularly Latinos. "Speaking beneath a 'Viva Kennedy' banner in the familiar UFW colors of red and black, the Massachusetts Democrat pledged that the political goals Hispanics have sought for years—often promised and infrequently delivered—would finally be fulfilled under a Kennedy administration."[147] Despite its association with MAD, the administration had ceased courting the Hispanic leadership after his victories in the early primaries. Polls indicated that it was likely to win in California, and so a last-minute push on behalf of the president seemed unnecessary.[148] Therefore, Hispanic groups began coalescing around the senator instead, giving him their much-needed money, activist labor, and voters.[149]

Beyond Hispanics, Kennedy broadened his appeal considerably.[150] His campaign was aimed at the Democratic base, accusing the administration of "failing the historical and traditional commitments to the Democratic Party."[151] In the last week of the campaign, Kennedy spoke in gay clubs, an Irish cultural center, a black church, the Lockheed plant at Burbank, and an overflow rally in downtown San Jose.[152] His ability to strike the same degree of fervor among crowds that, according to the national media, were otherwise at loggerheads over cultural values was remarkable. But then California Democrats told pollsters that their greatest concern was the economy, not sex, drugs, or race. They rated the candidates' positions on the issues and their leadership and experience skills as the most important factors in

influencing their vote.[153] Kennedy swept Los Angeles and the industrialized north of the state, as well as black, unionized, and Hispanic
voters.[154] Moreover, of his total, 40 percent indicated that they would
refuse to vote for Carter in November. Of that number, 45 percent
said they would defect to Anderson and 37 percent to Reagan. Thus,
roughly 218,000 California Kennedy supporters also favored Ronald
Reagan.[155] While in this state Kennedy did not win a majority of the
conservative vote, he nevertheless attracted a remarkable proportion
of it.[156] Moreover, on the day of the California primary, as voters gave
Kennedy a clear plurality, they also voted by 61 percent to 32 percent
to reject by referendum a proposal to slash the income tax in half.[157]
Pundits concluded that Californian politics had suddenly taken a surprise turn to the left.[158]

The Lingering Appeal of Liberal Economics

It is tempting to suggest that all of these victories were won in spite
of, rather than because of, Kennedy's liberalism. Voters, it could be
argued, were angry with Carter and prepared to vote for the senator
precisely because they knew he could not win. Kennedy was then a
glorified protest vote. Such a proposition is unfair and inaccurate. The
people who voted for the senator shared his liberal views on economics. For instance, Kennedy's campaign did not focus solely on alleviat-
ing unemployment; it also proposed a comprehensive system of controls to be placed on wages and prices in order to curtail inflation. Such
a policy was gaining support among both business and labor, both of
whom predicted their return, given the spiraling rate of inflation.[159]
"Some think this will happen not long after Senator Edward M. Kennedy, the first candidate to advocate controls, is no longer regarded as
a threat by President Carter," reported one journalist. "The President
presumably would then feel free to adopt his rival's position without
seeming to yield to him."[160]

Putting federal controls on wages and prices might appear contrary to traditional American attitudes toward state intervention, but
it was a tremendously popular idea. In February 1980 the *New York
Times* declared that "the people want economic controls," a recent poll
showing that 65 percent thought that they were desirable.[161] By June
1980 the figure had climbed to 71 percent.[162] Remarkably, a February
Gallup poll found that of voters who described themselves as most
conservative, about half said they would be more likely to vote for a

candidate because he favored controls.[163] Voters leaving the polls in the later primaries consistently told pollsters that they knew Kennedy's economic platform and approved of it. Indeed, the senator's campaign proved effective in promoting his popular policy positions. In New Hampshire at the beginning of the primary season, only 37 percent realized Kennedy supported wage and price controls. By the time of voting, 56 percent did, and 57 percent supported this position.[164] New Hampshire is ordinarily characterized as a fiscally conservative state, and therefore its stance demonstrated that Kennedy's policies had a cross-regional appeal. Massachusetts Democrats who went heavily for Kennedy thought, by 39 percent, that spending on domestic programs should be increased.[165] But New Hampshire and Florida Democrats, who voted overwhelmingly for Carter, supported increased social spending by even larger percentages than in Massachusetts: by 46 percent and 49 percent, respectively.[166]

Kennedy often won the support of those who thought that their financial situation had gotten worse and those who favored increased government spending and greater regulation of the economy.[167] In offering radical alternatives to orthodox fiscal policy, Edward Kennedy was not alone. John B. Anderson's candidacy had first gained public attention when he proposed a new gas tax of 50 cents a gallon to reduce consumption. The revenues were to be put into dramatic cuts in Social Security payroll taxes.[168] Governor Reagan's supply-side (literally, encouraging supply by stimulating the profitability of business) economic program called for lowering interest rates, slashing taxes, and increasing defense expenditure. Perhaps surprisingly, in an era characterized by tax revolt, the American public agreed with economic orthodoxy that such a program would fan further inflation and broadly opposed it.[169] At the height of the 1978 tax revolt, one pollster reported that the threat of a GOP landslide had dissipated because "while the public is very angry over property taxes and government waste, it's not turning towards traditional conservatism. People want to spend more, rather than less, on most government services."[170] Louis Harris confirmed this reading, which some more liberal members of the administration used as evidence of the need to increase spending while reducing bureaucracy and waste.[171]

Nevertheless, the L.A. Times pointed out the historical quirk that in Carter, the Democrats had a candidate who favored less spending and a balanced budget, and the Republicans had a candidate who championed largesse. "The President seeking re-election insists on a balanced budget. . . . His challenger calls for a 30 percent slash in tax rates. . . .

This contest sounds like a classic confrontation between a conservative Republican in the White House and his liberal Democratic opponent. In the Alice-in-Wonderland world of modern economics, however, it is Democrat Jimmy Carter who is spooked by red ink."[172] Reagan and Kennedy both favored the economics of jam today and jam tomorrow. As such, they appealed to very similar voters. Thus, 1980 was "a vote of no confidence in an incumbent" and in "policies which called for sacrifice, constraint, and unemployment without ever remotely suggesting why." That many Americans demonstrated enthusiasm for Kennedy's liberal ideas in the primaries but turned to Reagan in November suggests that they only did so because "they had nowhere else to go."[173]

In 1980, Americans were not ideologically liberal or conservative, just desperate for solutions and open to strong appeals from either left or right. This created a paradox. One study declared ironically that "the message Americans are giving on tax and spending is clear: Reduce taxes; maintain 'big government.' . . . It is not an easy one to respond to."[174] Although the message was muddy, it contrasted clearly with Carter's one of limits and of doing little at all. According to Louis Harris, 69 percent of Americans still believed that a president had it within his power to prevent a recession.[175] The American Federation of State, County, and Municipal Employees union used a private poll that found Americans favored wage/price controls, public works jobs, and increased Social Security payments to argue forcefully that "voters are demanding action from the federal government on the economic front."[176]

Nor was the American public as socially illiberal as Reagan's election might appear to suggest. Both Reagan's and Kennedy's pollsters found that U.S. voters by large margins supported the Equal Rights Amendment (ERA) and legalized abortion.[177] Taking the ERA as an example, pollsters throughout the late 1970s detected steady support for the amendment, assisted in large part by its backers' campaign to educate the public.[178] In 1977, 56 percent of the population endorsed the ERA. This figure fell to 55 percent in 1978 and rose back to 56 percent by 1980. In short, the many years of conservative, antifeminist, and Christian fundamentalist attacks on the ERA had barely any impact on public support for it.[179] Sympathy for the ERA was unsurprisingly highest among self-described liberals and Democrats, but it also enjoyed large support among "the young, the poor, the less educated, blacks, and women themselves."[180] It was lowest in the South, but Southerners still supported it, according to Louis Harris, by 49 percent to 44 percent. In the East, 63 percent wanted its passage.[181] Many feminists believed that a facade of public antipathy toward the ERA in key states was in fact sustained by the targeted lobbying of conservative and fundamentalist organizations like the Moral Majority. It was not an accurate picture of how ordinary Americans felt about women's rights.[182]

In 1980, Louis Harris reported that "if the public has turned somewhat conservative on the role of the federal government in the economy, it has not turned conservative on social issues." The ERA was supported by 56 percent of Americans, and 60 percent wanted abortion to remain legal. Additionally, 78 percent favored registration of handguns, and "clear-cut majorities favor[ed] federal affirmative action programs in jobs and higher education for women and minorities."[183] The public often told pollsters that they opposed employment discrimination against gays.[184] These positions were particularly strongly held among the growing suburban, college-educated middle class. This class was a new force that tended "to counterbalance the influence of conservatives by also turning out in larger numbers."[185] Social liberalism cut across religious and ethnic backgrounds, although blacks were typically more tolerant than whites.[186] Abortion was supported by almost all religious groups, including Roman Catholics. Only white evangelicals favored a ban.[187] A Yankelovich poll in 1981 reported that the social conservatism of the New Right was "out of step with public feelings." Some 56 percent wanted to keep abortion legal, 60 percent wanted mandatory handgun registration, 61 percent wanted passage of the ERA, and 70 percent wanted sex education in classrooms.[188] In sum, Kennedy's perceived social liberalism might not have been as much of a handicap as one might presuppose.[189] Indeed, political feminists argued that a strong commitment to social liberalism had the potential to mobilize women and create a powerful new voting bloc that (through numerical superiority) could easily mitigate the support of evangelical Christians for the GOP.[190] In sum, Americans voted for Kennedy in such large numbers because they broadly agreed with his program.

Therefore, Kennedy's success in the later primaries was due to his ability to pull together a coalition of the disaffected and financially vulnerable—which, in the economic climate of the 1970s, constituted a majority of Americans. The senator energized the poor, ideological liberals and ethnic minorities, much as his supporters had predicted he would in 1979. Although there is often a temptation to dismiss such voters as automatically Democratic by dint of education, income, or birth, their role in the general election of 1980 (assessed in the following chapter) proved pivotal. It proved every bit as important for nominees to motivate their natural base as it did to reach out to independents—indeed, while Kennedy won New York, New Jersey, Pennsylvania, and Michigan in the primaries, Carter lost these typically Democratic states in the fall. Kennedy's campaign illustrated that a return to populist, tub-thumping economic themes had the capacity to win back to the Democratic Party voters who otherwise might have stayed at home.

Such a strategy could also appeal to so-called Reagan Democrats. Kennedy tapped into a nascent desire among Americans to see their government do something, *anything* (even something liberal), to lift the country out of recession. It is undeniable that Americans in the 1970s regarded themselves as overtaxed by an unwieldy federal bureaucracy and believed the reduction of inflation should be prioritized over creating employment. Many also thought that they were culturally under assault by feminists, gays, pacifists, black militants, and hippies. But Americans consistently told pollsters that for all their reservations toward 1970s liberalism, they still did expect government to relieve unemployment, provide health insurance, protect jobs, use controls to fight inflation, and safeguard the basic civil rights of all Americans regardless of creed, color, and (even) sexuality.

In this climate of ideological flux, panic, and anger, Americans were prepared to turn to Edward Kennedy as the man who could restore their confidence in their country. This is quite remarkable considering the candidate's image problem. The evidence suggests that the media's intense reinvestigation of the Chappaquiddick accident did have an impact on the way voters regarded Kennedy as a candidate for the presidency.[191] Louis Harris found that Chappaquiddick especially hurt the candidate among his natural constituency of Catholics in the early primaries.[192] The issue narrowed the margin of his victory in Pennsylvania.[193] The further west or south the state, the greater Chappaquiddick's impact was.[194] In Wisconsin, 40 percent stated that his behavior after the accident disqualified him from being president, and 70 percent had little or no faith in his account of events.[195] In Massachusetts, only 18 percent thought that he had lied, and 42 percent that he had told the truth.[196]

And yet millions of Americans voted for Kennedy all the same. This is probably because Chappaquiddick only mattered when voters thought that the homely Carter was an attractive alternative. But when the debate returned to domestic issues, Kennedy won hands down. It is also worth noting that had Kennedy won the primaries (that is, if Iran and Afghanistan had not happened), then it probably would have mattered much less in the fall election against Reagan. The Republican's campaign team decided early on that if Kennedy were nominated, it would not use Chappaquiddick in the general election. To do so would have been seen as in poor taste, callous, and mean. Evidently, Jimmy Carter was not quite so gallant. Reagan was hungry for a straightforward philosophical contest; Carter understood that the only way to win was to minimize differences between Kennedy and himself and exploit Ted's checkered personal history.[197] Iran and Afghanistan created the necessary distraction from domestic problems that made Chappaquiddick into a real issue. When the crises overseas declined in importance, so too did Kennedy's private life.

Had Iran, Afghanistan, and (to a lesser extent) Chappaquiddick not been deciding factors in the early primaries, it is highly likely that the Democratic Party would have nominated Kennedy and that he would have entered the fall election on a popular platform at the head of a reinvigorated Democratic coalition. Of course this argument is purely a "what if?", but it is a very big "what if?" that offers a significant challenge to the way we see postwar American politics.

7

Letting the Dream Die

The Democratic Convention of 1980

On 5 June, Kennedy met with Carter at the White House to discuss the terms of his withdrawal from the race.[1] The meeting was tense, and after a brief exchange of pleasantries, the two quickly settled down to trading accusations. Carter complained that Kennedy had attacked his record unfairly and improved Reagan's prospects in the fall. Arguing that he had won the popular vote, a clear majority of the convention delegates, and, effectively, the presidential nomination, Carter demanded Kennedy's immediate withdrawal and endorsement. Typically, at a decisive moment, Ted was elliptical and fumbling. Carter complained that he mumbled his way through a poor set of excuses as to why he should continue to run. In fact, considering his recent performance, Kennedy was remarkably humble. He indicated that he would concede defeat if the president joined him in a televised debate on policy—a reasonable demand given that the contest had become one of ideas and issues rather than personality.[2]

After six months on the campaign trail, neither man had grown as a politician or evolved significantly as a personality. Jimmy remained stubborn and haughty; Ted was still inarticulate and frustrating. The meeting lasted over an hour and achieved absolutely nothing. Buoyed by his recent success, Kennedy genuinely believed that he could still win.[3] An open convention—that is, a convention wherein delegates were free to vote for whomever they wished—might ignore the overall will of the people and nominate the better-qualified candidate. History was on the senator's side. As recently as 1968, a Democratic presidential candidate was nominated without winning a majority of the elected delegates. Kennedy saw little reason to be contrite.[4]

Desperate to be rid of this meddlesome senator, Carter considered his proposal of a debate very seriously. He raised it at a meeting the next day, telling his closest staff that he was inclined to accept

158

it. Given Kennedy's notorious ineloquence and tendency to shout on television, Carter thought that he could probably win. In the process, he could even get some free airtime. The Cabinet enthusiastically agreed, hoping that this would bring an end to their long nightmare. The only man whom Carter did not consult was Walter Mondale, who was away on a tour. After the Cabinet meeting, the president retired to Camp David and put a call through to Mondale to discuss the format for a potential debate. The vice president was horrified by the idea of an on-air discussion and argued vehemently against it. He pointed out that Carter had won the primaries handily and that such a meeting would unnecessarily elevate Kennedy and degrade the presidency. By defending the dignity of his office, Mondale appealed directly to Carter's pride, and the president immediately telephoned his Cabinet to announce that he had changed his mind. The debate was off.[5]

Logical though Mondale's position was, refusal to debate Kennedy removed his one avenue of dignified retreat and was a gross strategic error. Ted angrily told reporters that he had decided to see the race through to the convention.[6] To keep his dream alive, he opted to follow a two-pronged strategy: agitating for an open convention on the one hand, and fighting for the passage of a liberal party platform on the other. Although the Democratic platform was not technically binding on the nominee, it would help define the general election campaign and validate Kennedy's claim on the soul of his party.[7]

Both propositions would be considered by the Democratic National Committee's (DNC) various convention committees in late June and then voted on by delegates on the convention floor in August. Kennedy recognized that the DNC establishment was unlikely to agree either to an open convention or a nakedly liberal platform, so his only hope was to build up anger toward the administration throughout the summer and convince ordinary delegates to vote his way at the convention.[8] It was a gamble that sustained the contest long after it should have finished. Indeed, it should be stressed that Kennedy almost certainly could not win the nomination with his existing delegate total. Just to open the convention would have required over 350 delegates to switch to him, which was highly unlikely, given that they were committed to the president. Arguably, the media's interest in keeping the race interesting gave the convention and Kennedy's presence there undue attention.[9] Nevertheless, the senator's grim determination opened the way to the last genuinely exciting and unmanaged convention in U.S. political history.

Preparing for a Fight

The DNC convened to consider Kennedy's proposals shortly after his meeting with Carter. The senator's call for an open convention was a direct challenge to Rule F(3)(c) of the standing orders of the DNC, which bound elected delegates to the candidate on whose platform they had been elected.[10] The rule was the product of a commission chaired by Michigan Democratic Party chair Morley Winograd. The commission was created to find ways of avoiding the chaotic delegate fights of 1968 and 1972 while protecting the newfound status of primaries in the selection of the presidential nominee. Its logical conclusion was that primaries should continue to select delegates, but that those delegates should not be allowed to change their stated candidate preference at the nominating convention. A delegate elected on a Carter slate had to vote for Carter in August.[11]

Kennedy began pushing for the repeal of Rule F(3)(c) shortly after winning the New York primary, arguing that Iran and Afghanistan had distorted the outcome of earlier primaries. Now that the issue agenda had returned to economics, Kennedy's later victories were good enough reason to reopen the nomination process and start all over again.[12] Many commentators concurred that whether the results indicated growing support for Kennedy or not, the 3 June round of primaries had equated to a "referendum on Carter."[13] Seeing an open convention movement as a chance to dump the president from the ticket, several high-profile officeholders came out in support of it. These included Patrick Moynihan, Scoop Jackson, Richard Lamm, and Robert Byrd. Conservative Senate leader Robert Byrd had an added incentive to support the movement that he kept to himself: Kennedy had just offered him the number two spot on his presidential ticket.[14]

Support for an open convention began to gather steam, although it probably reflected renewed doubts about Carter's political strength rather than enthusiasm for Kennedy.[15] The left-wing Democratic Conference organization polled House members and claimed that 60 percent favored the rules challenge, counting "15 avowed supporters of President Carter including 4 Carter delegates."[16] House liberals formed the Committee to Continue the Open Convention, with a starting fund of $200,000 and an office in Washington.[17] A *Washington Post* survey found that 41 percent of delegates supported its cause and warned that "mutiny" was once again in the air.[18] This was a classic example of the kind of media hyperbole that hyped up the convention's significance and paved the way for Kennedy's moral coup: the

41 percent that the *Post* counted almost certainly represented the 41 percent of delegates that Kennedy controlled. Arguably the greatest impediment to a rules challenge was antipathy among Carter delegates toward Kennedy.[19] Although they wanted the opportunity to consider an alternative to the incumbent, hostility among the president's delegates toward the senator remained strong. As such, the media and several insiders began touting Secretary of State Edmund Muskie or Vice President Walter Mondale as alternative presidential candidates. Even some of Kennedy's supporters urged him to withdraw in order to make defeat of F(3)(c) more likely and bring a final end to the Carter presidency.[20]

Despite growing public support, the DNC's Rules Committee quickly rejected the idea of an open convention. Carter had stuffed the committee with White House appointees, and his team enjoyed a twenty-five-vote advantage.[21] The ease with which he manipulated the DNC shocked some, but it merely reflected his determination to use the authority of the White House to make the convention work to his advantage. For instance, he cannily appointed House Speaker Tip O'Neill as convention chair, forestalling a likely endorsement for his good friend Edward Kennedy, and tying up one of the best party leaders who might otherwise have negotiated an alternative outcome. Of course, O'Neill was pleased with the appointment because it allowed him to stay above the fray of a divisive battle: his own family was split on whom to vote for.[22] As a presidential appointee, the chair of the DNC, John White, was a Carter partisan. He had criticized the idea of a Kennedy candidacy throughout 1979 and in May 1980 had called for the senator's withdrawal.[23] Carter was thus able to use the DNC to pressure state delegations to vote against a repeal of F(3)(c) on the convention floor itself.[24]

After it had dismissed Kennedy's rules challenge, the DNC turned its attention to the party platform. At a series of public hearings on economic, social, and foreign policy, liberals took the opportunity to berate the administration and demand a return to traditional Democratic priorities.[25] Kennedy's victories in the later primaries were commonly cited as evidence of the unpopularity of Carter's conservatism and of the need to return to base principles.[26] In a typical statement, the president of the American Federation of State, County, and Municipal Employees, a public-sector union, told the platform committee, "In recent months the President and many congressional Democrats have been acting like conservative Republicans on the bread and butter economic issues. We must reverse this slide toward economic conservatism, before it totally alienates key party constituencies."[27] Perversely, many of Carter's most fervent supporters agreed. They had supported the president throughout the contest with their heads, but their hearts had steadily drifted to Kennedy.[28] The pro-Carter National Education Association testified against attempts to balance the budget, endorsing immediate passage of national health insurance and the Equal Rights Amendment (ERA).[29] The Garment Workers' union asked for protection of U.S. industry to help save jobs, wage/price controls to curtail inflation, and a commitment to not enact tax cuts for big business.[30] Senator Abraham Ribicoff, who had a few days before lobbied the rules committee against allowing an open convention, testified in favor of Kennedy's economic ideas and congratulated him on his "imaginative" and "intelligent" proposals.[31]

Again, the DNC's platform committee was stacked in Carter's favor, and he easily defeated the draft proposals that Kennedy put before it.[32] Kennedy accused the Carter staff, unfairly, of playing "hard-ball throughout the Standing Committee Meetings, virtually refusing to give an inch."[33] In fact the administration did offer to negotiate, but with the senator's increased electoral clout, "the atmosphere was not conducive to compromise." The Carter staff modified and proposed large sections of its own draft platform to appeal to liberals, including inserting an admission that the country was in recession. But Kennedy rejected every concession.[34] He believed that the public mood was such that he could get his proposals passed in full at the August convention. Ominously, Carter's own delegates on the DNC committees broke from his whip to vote in favor of pro-abortion and anti–nuclear power language. It was a hint of the trouble to come.[35]

After the platform hearings in June, Carter's position only got worse. Even his own family let him down. Jimmy had always had a certain image problem when it came to controlling the antics of his brother, Billy. Billy was an unrepentant good ol' boy who swore, spat, and drank live on camera, almost on cue. He was once filmed by reporters discreetly relieving himself on an airport runway. In July 1980, Billy was accused of receiving Libyan money in return for softening U.S. policy toward the al-Gaddafi regime. For the first time since the Lance affair, Carter was tainted by association with corruption, and to the general public, his inability to control his own family was a perfect metaphor for his inability to control the economy.[36] In August, Louis Harris reported, "President Carter is showing signs of dropping into third place behind Ronald Reagan and third party candidate Representative John Anderson." In a clear three-way race, Reagan stood to take

53 percent, Carter 26 percent, and Anderson 18 percent. But when asked how they would vote if Anderson had "a real chance of winning," Americans gave Reagan 49 percent, Anderson 25 percent, and Carter just 23 percent.[37] Regardless of the stubbornness of the DNC and Carter's delegates, Democratic voters favored an open convention by 65 percent to 31 percent, and 48 percent preferred that the party select a candidate other than the incumbent president.[38] Carter resolved "Billygate" deftly with an eleventh-hour television statement just before the convention began. He convincingly pronounced his brother innocent of everything but ineptitude in business and diplomacy. But it cast a shadow over his lackluster convention performance.[39]

Meanwhile, Kennedy had a happy summer. Although his nomination was only a distant possibility, the threat of an open convention strengthened Ted's platform challenges.[40] It also protracted the Democratic nomination battle, forcing Carter to continue throughout June and July to court delegates already theoretically committed to vote for him.[41] He invited over 400 delegates to the White House for a briefing and made personal calls to every one of those apparently already running on his slate. Arguably, what little dignity Carter had preserved by not debating Kennedy on TV was soon lost as he begged his own delegates to vote for him.[42] In contrast, Kennedy went on a tour of the country and was greeted by large, enthusiastic crowds. With the campaign over, Ted was able to relax, and he looked happier and healthier than ever before.[43] When he shared a podium with the president in mid-June to speak in favor of the ERA, the difference between the two was immediately apparent. A haggard president was greeted politely by the mix of union activists and feminists. A tanned, jovial Kennedy was warmly cheered.[44]

The Rumble in the Garden

The 1980 convention at Madison Square Garden, New York, was not a show of unity against a remarkably conservative Republican nominee, but rather a showdown between different philosophies of government. It also highlighted the various regional and class prejudices that the primaries had brought to the fore. When the convention opened on 11 August, Northern industrial Democrats committed to Kennedy sat unhappily alongside Southern middle-class Democrats committed to their president. A rules change mandating that half the delegates be women dramatically increased the representation of feminists, the vast bulk of whom were Kennedyites. The Kennedy campaign arrived bullish and on the attack. While Carter's people wore their candidate's traditional green-and-white colors, Kennedy's activists proudly wore their man's color of blue, and they carried bullhorns that they frequently used to disturb the speeches of their opponents. As tempers flew out of control, fistfights were not uncommon.[45] Arizona representative Mo Udall opened the convention with a typically laid-back speech that helped to break the tensions between delegates. "Let me recommend Dr. Udall's Patented Unity Medicine," he joked. "Take one tablespoon, close your eyes, and repeat 'President Ronald Reagan'!" But even the keynote speaker could not disguise his partisanship. He described Kennedy's campaign as the "most genuine draft movement in history," and the floor roared in agreement.[46]

To defeat Kennedy, Carter put in place an admirable whipping operation. It was staffed by campaign chief Hamilton Jordan and his "gerbils": young volunteers, most of them male and Southern, who used the latest radio technology to manage the floor from trailers parked outside the auditorium. Kennedy's organization was chaotic, relying on individual leaders of single-issue groups to direct the troops under their control. Both sides attempted to bribe support from delegates, and Chicago mayor Jane Byrne and her loyal sewers commissioner toured the Illinois delegation in a mafialike fashion, offering jobs and a pension to anyone who switched sides. The president put his family to work again. One journalist noted, "Even Chip Carter pitched in, returning breathless from the Louisiana delegation at one point to announce that he had won two more delegates. 'I tried it on the merits but it didn't work,' he grinned. 'Finally I just begged 'em. It works so much better.'"[47]

The convention's first piece of business was to consider the F(3)(c) rules challenge. Initially it looked as if momentum might swing Kennedy's way when word swept the media box that the Illinois delegation had changed its mind and was considering supporting an open convention. Mayor Jane Byrne was boasting that she could deliver fifty or sixty votes from the state, which could start a domino effect across the convention. It turned out to be a hyperbolic bluff, and only ten of Carter's delegates switched, reflecting recognition that the administration's support was simply too big to overcome. The rules challenge was easily beaten by a floor vote of 1,936 to 1,390.[48] Ted watched the returns in his convention suite, surrounded by Joan and the rest of the family. Seeing that nine months of grueling struggle had finally come to the end, he flatly announced he would withdraw his candidacy.

Nobody protested. His aide put a call through to the White House and asked to be connected with the president. In a humiliating twist, the politically unaware operator thought Kennedy's aide was a regular member of the public and told him the president was too busy to talk. The aide demanded to speak to her supervisor, who immediately recognized the historical significance of the moment and connected Kennedy with Carter. The senator solemnly announced his withdrawal. In turn, the president asked the senator if he would join him in a display of unity at the convention podium after his acceptance speech. Kennedy did not answer.[49]

But the campaign was not over, and on the second day, it moved from discussing rules and personalities to debating ideas and first principles. The full Kennedy platform presented to the convention on 12 August was titled "A Rededication to Democratic Principles." The rededication embraced two priorities. The first was a return to activist government, conceding that while "we have learned what government cannot do," the Democratic Party must evaluate "what government can do."[50] Government could, it determined, "reindustrialize America," "rebuild our cities, reform our tax and welfare systems, and guarantee decent medical care for every American." The rededication's second priority was to reject the administration's fiscal policy. "We must not," it stated, "rely on policies of unequal sacrifice that make America divided against itself. . . . We must not fight inflation by depriving millions of their jobs." Finally, the rededication expected obedience to the platform by elected representatives, accountability, and discipline. It mandated the creation of a Special Commission on Platform Accountability, implying the potential withdrawal of Democratic Party endorsement from those who did not implement it.[51] This subtle attempt to exert discipline was designed to ensure that even if Carter were the nominee in fact, Kennedy would be the victor in principle.[52]

The administration- and DNC-approved platform proposals were deliberately vague, promising to fight inflation "in ways not designed or intended to increase unemployment," to continue an unspecified number of antirecessionary programs, and to pursue a deregulated, free-trade economic policy. In contrast, the Kennedy platform would "take all actions necessary" to immediately create full employment and pledged to take "no fiscal action, no monetary action, no budgetary action" that would increase unemployment. The centerpiece of the rededication was a "12 billion dollar anti-recession jobs program," a "1 billion dollar railroad renewal program," and the construction of

"200,000 new units" of housing. While Kennedy conceded the necessity of deregulation and tax breaks for business, he trumpeted a "freeze and then controls on prices, wages, interest rates, profits, dividends, and rents."[53] In addition, his other planks supported passage of the ERA, abortion on demand, a moratorium on nuclear power, national health insurance, and an end to draft registration.[54]

Kennedy's platform was by far the more popular of the two. Democratic voters strongly agreed with it. Louis Harris found that the jobs package was supported by 68 percent of Democrats, 62 percent favored passage of national health insurance, and 59 percent were opposed to balancing the budget "if it means cutting out funds for those who are poor or on welfare."[55] Among all likely voters, the jobs package was supported by 52 percent to 42 percent, giving priority to jobs over inflation by 55 percent to 34 percent and implementing mandatory wage/price controls by 55 percent to 35 percent.[56] The recession had worsened and the prospect of joblessness had forced Americans to reconsider their economic priorities. By July 1980, Louis Harris reported that "people's worries about the rising cost of living have become considerably less intense." In contrast, "a record 88 percent" worried that their jobs might be at risk.[57]

Elated to have won the nomination and keen to give Kennedy whatever was required to secure his support in the fall, Carter made perhaps his biggest mistake yet. Thinking that his advantage in delegate numbers would allow him to easily win the platform votes anyway, the president agreed to allow the debate over the economic part of Kennedy's platform to take place during prime-time television. The Kennedy campaign was allotted an hour in which the senator was scheduled to speak for thirty minutes commending his proposals. In hindsight, this reasonable attempt to appease Kennedy and bring the debate to a swift end looks foolish. It gave a prime-time platform to the senator from which he could restate the rationale for his candidacy, despite having actually lost. It handed him a moral victory.[58]

On the night of 12 August 1980, Kennedy gave what was widely regarded as the best speech of his career.[59] It was written mostly by Bob Shrum and contained a compendium of slogans from the campaign. Several journalists, in fact, complained that they had heard it all before.[60] But the convention had not, and it was spellbound. Conceding defeat, Kennedy told the delegates, "I have come here tonight not to argue as a candidate but to affirm a cause. I am asking you to renew the commitment of the Democratic Party to economic justice." He castigated Reaganite economics, but he argued that "the blue-collar workers Ronald Reagan is courting will not desert the Democratic Party in 1980 if we respond again . . . to their needs at a difficult time."[61] He reminded his audience, "We are the Party of the New Freedom, the New Deal, and the New Frontier. We have always been the party of hope. . . . To all those who are idle in the cities and industries of America let us provide new hope for the dignity of useful work. Democrats have always believed that a basic civil right of all Americans is their right to earn their own way." He finished with a phrase that he had used throughout his campaign and that had come to define it: "For all those whose cares have been our concern, the work goes on, the cause endures, the hope still lives, and the dream shall never die."[62]

The speech was received rapturously, and although O'Neill banged his gavel repeatedly to bring the auditorium to order, he could not. A genuinely spontaneous demonstration broke out that lasted for half an hour. Delegates chanted, "We want Ted! We want Ted!" and the band struck up "Happy Days Are Here Again" over and over to try to drown them out. There was a brief fight on the floor when one of Kennedy's New York delegates grabbed for the state's standard and tried to parade it down the aisle. Incredibly, the Carter people fought back, and Queens borough president Donald Manes refused to let go. Someone punched Manes in the stomach, and he disappeared beneath the delegates' feet. The standard was liberated and carried away into the cheering throng.[63] In the Carter headquarters, a stunned Robert Strauss, watching the demonstration on the TV monitors, shook his head, repeating to himself, "Good speech . . . good speech." In the Kennedy headquarters, the staff asked themselves why he had never performed so well on the campaign trail and wondered aloud what might have been if he had. When the riot had finally subsided, the votes were held, and every single Kennedy platform proposal was passed.[64]

Hamilton Jordan believed that the speech played to a convention dominated not by "the many faces of American life . . . but instead the many faces and representatives of special interest groups."[65] Delegates were voting, in effect, for a handout to themselves. Yet Kennedy's speech received a 64 percent to 19 percent favorability rating among all American voters and 73 percent to 12 percent among Democrats. Some 57 percent of independent voters thought it was an excellent speech, and so too did a narrow plurality of registered Republicans.[66] Although many historians have argued that the Kennedy candidacy saddled the Democratic Party with an unattractive platform, public approval of the jobs program suggests otherwise. Moreover, adopting a liberal platform was crucial to convincing various constituency groups to campaign for Carter in 1980. Commitment to the ERA and reproductive rights persuaded the National Organization for Women to reverse its refusal to campaign for Carter and effectively endorse the Democratic ticket.[67] Similarly, the platform encouraged Douglas Fraser and the UAW to support the president too.[68] Fraser admitted that he could not "paint Carter as a great, charismatic progressive—that says in effect, either he has changed, we have changed or we were wrong." Instead, he planned to explain to union members that the platform demonstrated that "we own this party. . . . Carter is our instrument; he accepts our victory and will carry out our program with competency."[69] It is possible that, had Kennedy's platform not been passed, many liberals would have remained neutral in the general election.[70]

The convention represented a philosophical victory for Kennedy and a joyless one for Carter. Eventually Carter was nominated 2,129 votes to 1,150. Even though Kennedy had withdrawn, many of his supporters insisted on voting for him. On 14 August, the president gave his own speech, a carefully crafted bore that offered excuses for the past and more sacrifice for the future. He restated his themes of limits, telling delegates that in four years, "I've learned that only the most complex and difficult task comes before me in the Oval Office. No easy answers are found there, because no easy questions come there." Carter was received with tepid approval and was even booed when he defended registration for the draft. He seemed distant, occasionally checking his watch as if exhausted by his own performance. At one point he paid tribute to "Hubert Horatio Hornblower," instead of Hubert Horatio Humphrey, and some delegates could be heard laughing. In a final indignity, the bright blue balloons suspended above the hall by a net failed to fall when cued to do so at the end of the speech. "His hour of triumph," wrote one witness, "was shadowed by a rush of nostalgia for his defeated rival . . . and by the plain unenthusiasm of his party for him or his prospects."[71]

At the close of the convention, the Carter family and various notables shuffled onto the podium to receive the crowd's applause. When Kennedy had conceded, the president had asked him directly to join him on the podium. Ted did not leave his hotel suite until Carter's speech had finished so as not to distract the media, but he then got stuck in traffic and so arrived late. He glumly moved around the podium waving at friends in the hall and shook Carter's hand in a polite but not effusive manner. It was hoped that he would seize Carter's arm and hold it aloft in the traditional victor's style, and several times the president hovered near him and looked hungrily at his hands. The joint salute never came. The gesture would have been inappropriate, but its absence was interpreted by the media as a final, perhaps mean-spirited, snub. After taking some cheers, Kennedy slipped out of the auditorium and into the warm summer's night. He had lost the nomination but won the convention.[72]

The 1980 Democratic convention was the most democratic convention in history, with the largest proportion ever of delegates being directly elected.[73] It was the last time when the DNC's proposed platform was influenced and rewritten by the floor. All of this was a high-water mark for party reformers. In 1981 the DNC revised convention rules to introduce new superdelegate primaries that would weaken the chances of outsiders taking the nomination. Comprising popularly elected and appointed party officials, the superdelegates were designed to bolster the influence of the Democratic establishment on the outcome of the primaries. Weighing up experience and popularity, it was hoped that they would make sure that only the most electable candidates could be chosen. In 1984 they stepped in to help nominate Walter Mondale over antiestablishment candidate Gary Hart at the convention in San Francisco. Likewise, in 2008 they were pivotal to deciding whether Clinton or Obama received the nomination after running so close to each other in the primaries. Although Obama did not have a majority of the elected delegates, his lead among the super-delegates allowed him to carry the convention.[74] These changes were the direct result of the Kennedy primary challenge.

8

Giving It to the Gipper

The Elections of 1980

In the aftermath of the convention, a thick mist of photo-op love descended over the Democratic Party. Wounds were quickly tended and healed, friendships repaired, slights forgotten, and unity forged. In October, Carter signed into law a reorganization of the mental health acts that pumped new money into the system. Kennedy joined him, along with Rosalynn and Joan. The stage-managed event showed the two shaking hands and praising each other lavishly for their devotion to social progress.[1] Behind the scenes, negotiations ended in Carter reluctantly agreeing to help Kennedy cover some of his debts and pledge not to hurt his supporters. In return, Kennedy offered to film ads for the president praising his leadership and experience.[2] The senator then toured the nation endorsing his new best friend with a degree of passion that bordered on the convincing. Sometimes his presence reminded voters of the opportunity that they had lost by not voting for him. Speaking in Texas, he was greeted by an overflow crowd of 2,000 Mexican Americans waving "We Want Ted!" placards. The warm welcome was taken by the press as an indirect snub of the president.[3]

Kennedy's enthusiasm reflected the fact that the dynamics of the election changed dramatically after the convention. He had certain venial concerns to consider first, such as paying off his debts and letting the party know that he was loyal and partisan enough to deserve its support in 1984. But more importantly, the enemy was now not Carter, but rather Ronald Reagan. An antitax, anticommunist social conservative, Reagan's election threatened everything that liberals like Kennedy had worked for since the New Deal. He offended moderates like Carter with his threat of conflict with the Soviet Union and disregard for good fiscal management. Recognizing the need to reunite the Democratic Party and to energize its base in a totemic fight against a philosophical conservative, the administration lurched to the left. Carter reached out to Kennedy and his voters. Amazingly, he almost succeeded.[4]

Although the outcome of presidential elections is often predetermined by long-term trends and fixed political contexts, they can turn on accidents, mistakes, and events—particularly if they are close. The 1980 campaign has a reputation for being a realigning election: a landslide judgment on the postwar U.S. political settlement in which millions of Americans rejected liberalism in favor of ideological conservatism. Looking backward, from the perspective of Reagan's ten-point margin of victory and the Republican sweep of the Senate, it is tempting to assume that Carter's defeat was inevitable. In fact, the 1980 general election was remarkably close. *Time* magazine reported just two days before voting that "Jimmy Carter and Ronald Reagan remain just where they were at the beginning of their long campaign—locked in a virtual tie among registered voters." At the start of October, they were fixed, according to *Time*'s Yankelovich poll, in a 39 percent to 39 percent dead heat. On 3 November, Carter actually led Reagan by a statistically insignificant margin of 42 percent to 41 percent.

The reason was simple: Americans were unsatisfied with the choice. "Forty-three percent of Reagan's voters," reported *Time*, "indicate they are more interested in voting against Carter than for Reagan. The President does not fare much better. Thirty-seven percent of Carter's supporters say they are really just anti-Reagan." Americans were concerned about the direction of the country and believed Carter was doing a poor job of leading it. However, they also suspected that Reagan lacked the national experience necessary to be an effective president and were broadly unhappy with his ideological conservatism. In this regard, the 1980 election provided a fitting conclusion to the 1970s. It told not a single story of conservative triumph and liberal collapse, but rather a collection of smaller, more complex narratives that suggested that the nation was fundamentally uncertain about which direction to take. The 1970s concluded with the election of one of the most philosophically conservative leaders in U.S. history. But there were other stories to tell too, most notably the narrow race throughout October, John B. Anderson's popular, liberal independent candidacy, and the enormous energy, enthusiasm, and money that grassroots activists put into defending the Senate seats of John Culver, George McGovern, Frank Church, and Birch Bayh. Although the 1980 general election ended in victory for the GOP, its actual meaning was far from clear. The spirit of Kennedy's insurgency remained, and liberalism did not die with it.[5]

The Republican Nomination

For all its acrimony, the 1980 Democratic Convention, with its consistent themes of anti-Reaganism and commitment to economic liberalism, provided Carter with a desperately needed bounce of support.[6] Afterward, Carter began campaigning like a Democrat again, pressing home his endorsement of jobs programs, arms control, and a sizable increase in the minimum wage. The crowds became bigger, doubtless a reflection of nonpartisan curiosity at meeting the president in part, but they were becoming more fervent too.[7] Almost overnight, Carter reduced Reagan's lead from twenty points to just six. Louis Harris determined that the cause was "party-based rather than personal." House Democrats turned a close 45 percent to 44 percent edge over Republicans into a substantial 51 percent to 41 percent lead, while Jimmy Carter's personal rating remained low. Some 32 percent said they could not vote for the president, 29 percent could not vote for Reagan, and 24 percent could not vote for independent John B. Anderson. Harris concluded that "the gains made by Carter can be traced directly to a firming up of the ranks of the Democratic Party, mainly because of the platform that the party adopted at its convention and the strong and basic appeal of Senator Edward M. Kennedy."[8] The general election of 1980 was, until the last week, remarkably close. Most surveys gave Reagan a narrow lead.[9] Patrick Caddell found the public tied between the two candidates.[10] Yankelovich too put the race at a dead heat, with Reagan beating Carter by just 38.3 percent to 38.1 percent and with 13.2 percent undecided.[11] Gallup even gave Carter a healthy lead over Reagan of 41.5 percent to 35.3 percent with 6.6 percent undecided.[12] Not one published survey detected the Reagan landslide, and the Carter campaign began to believe victory was possible.[13]

The cause of Carter's revival was partly Kennedy's reconciliation, but it was also the Democratic Party's exploitation of what was arguably the greatest weakness of the Republican campaign: its nominee. Reagan's conservatism was not as popular with the electorate as many commentators assume, and he was hurt by an image of shooting from the hip, fueled by extemporaneous remarks about defense, environmental, and racial issues.[14] In lighter moments, he suggested that nuclear disarmament was "none of our [that is America's] business" and that the greatest polluter on earth was not man, but trees.[15] His policy positions were at odds with those of the public, who broadly did not favor confrontation with the USSR, across-the-board tax cuts, or his variety of social conservatism. The administration in fact welcomed the Reagan candidacy because they believed he would be the easiest candidate to beat.[16] Carter wisely made Reagan's perceived weaknesses the center of his campaign, although this increased charges of "meanness."[17] Liberal commentators Richard Scammon and Ben Wattenberg concluded that Carter's "main hope is to just hammer away at [Reagan] . . . just as organized labor did against Wallace in 1968."[18]

Many liberal leaders felt emboldened to press the Carter administration for concessions on policy by Reagan's nomination. As the president of the National Organization for Women (NOW) recalled, "We thought we could take risks, push Carter more . . . you've got Reagan as the nominee and none of us thought we'd get a second rate actor in the White House."[19] Douglas Fraser was hopeful that Reagan would secure the nomination because he would be "easier to beat . . . just goes to show you've got to be careful what you wish for."[20] The same polls that showed Kennedy leading Carter throughout October and November 1979 also showed Carter decisively beating Reagan. For instance, a mid-October Gallup poll, which found Kennedy beating Carter 53 percent to 32 percent, gave Carter a lead over Reagan of 54 percent to 45.9 percent. Kennedy also beat Reagan 63.6 percent to 36 percent, and the surveyed voters preferred former president Gerald Ford as the Republican nominee by 51.8 percent to 32.3 percent.[21]

Throughout the primaries, Reagan was haunted by the specter of Ford, who often polled better among independent and moderate voters.[22] In 1979, many journalists and politicians privately concurred that the most probable and strongest candidate in 1980 was Ford.[23] October 1979—ironically, the month that he publicly refused to enter the race—began a trend of the former president leading Reagan in the polls.[24] For the first time, he was preferred over Reagan among Republican voters as a candidate by a narrow 27 percent to 26 percent.[25] It is likely that the media was cheering on a chimera for the sake of making an apparently closed contest more open. Ford had indicated scant interest in running, and Reagan had an impressive field machine in operation and a body of loyal voters in the South and West who could have probably guaranteed him the election. Nevertheless, while Reagan trailed Carter among all voters by 52 percent to 35 percent, Ford led the president by 55 percent to 42 percent.[26] Ford continued to be a preferred nominee by all voters up to the Republican convention, largely because he was perceived to be both "experienced" and a "moderate."[27]

Nor were the 1980 primaries as easy for Reagan as many accounts of his presidency suggest. For much of the time he was stalked by an attractive, preppy ex–CIA director called George Bush. Although unquestionably a conservative, Bush had a certain Episcopalian gentility and a set of moderate views on social and diplomatic issues that appealed to Republicans in the old GOP strongholds of the Northeast.[28] Choosing, like Kennedy, to remain above the fray and to moderate his image in the early primaries, Reagan avoided campaigning in the first-in-the-nation primary in Iowa and handed Bush a surprise early victory. As a result, Bush was catapulted into the limelight and his support among Republicans leapt from 6 to 27 percent, "one of the most precipitate and startling rises in modern political history."[29] By February 1980, Bush was beating Reagan as first choice among Republicans by 32 percent to 29 percent, forcing Reagan to debate him and to step up campaigning.[30]

Much like Ford's noncandidacy in the winter of 1979, Bush's campaign in the spring of 1980 was probably given more credibility by the media than it really deserved. He could not match Reagan's field operation or his near-godlike status among primary voters in the South and West. After a satisfying victory in Pennsylvania, Bush conceded defeat. Registered Republicans were now considerably to the right of the country as a whole and the domination of the delegate count by the South and West ensured Reagan's nomination. Nevertheless, although Reagan saw off all of his potential challengers, their existence implied that even Republicans were cautious toward the Reagan candidacy. Cleavages between North and South, East and West, still existed. Perhaps in recognition of this, Reagan picked Bush to be his vice president even though he had described the Californian's tax plan as "voodoo economics."

In September 1980, Reagan contributed to a narrowing of the polls by "his remarks about the Ku Klux Klan, Taiwan, and evolution."[31] Throughout the year and into the fall, both candidates remained equally unpopular.[32] Gallup noted that "personal enthusiasm for both Carter and Reagan is lower in this Presidential year than it has been for leading candidates in other Presidential election years since 1952."[33] Both were rated poorly by the public for their perceived ability to govern.[34] Louis Harris expressed the dilemma voters faced thus: "By a substantial 56–41 percent, a majority of the voters agrees with the claim that 'there is no way President Carter's record during his first four years in office justifies another four years.' . . . However, by a narrow 49–46 percent, a plurality of the same voters agrees with the claim that 'even though Carter's first-term record has not been good,

Ronald Reagan would be an even greater risk in the White House."[35]
Two popular jokes neatly summed up the sense of apathy that clouded
the 1980 campaign. In the first, someone chases a voter down an alley,
points a gun to his head, and demands an answer: "Carter or Reagan?"
After thinking for a moment, the voter replies, "Shoot." The second
came from Arnold Reisman of Shaker Heights, Ohio. When asked by a
journalist whom he was voting for in November, he replied, "Probably
Carter. At least we all know what he's *not* capable of."[36]

The Anderson Difference

Dissatisfaction with the two major contenders was enough to justify
a third-party run, and Carter found himself forced to compete not
only with Reagan on his right, but John B. Anderson on his left. Much
overlooked by historians, in 1980 John Anderson became the second
most successful independent candidate in postwar U.S. presidential
elections. He provided a model of third-party activism for Ross Perot
and Ralph Nader, tapping into their themes of frustration with the
political status quo, rejection of partisan politics in an age that seemed
to demand something more, and outright eccentricity.

John B. Anderson rounded off a period of "little men" doing great
and unexpected things. Sporting a mop of startlingly white hair and
owlish glasses, Anderson served the rural, heavily Republican six-
teenth district of Illinois from 1961 to 1981 and was elected chair of the
House Republican Conference in 1969. Initially his voting record was
conservative, and Anderson voted against the Civil Rights and Voting
Rights acts and for the Vietnam war. He was a born-again Christian,
although he defied the trends of his party by refusing to discuss his
religious beliefs in public. He regarded them as too solemn to be de-
graded by rhetoric. Throughout the 1970s he became more socially liberal, though he remained fiscally conservative.[37] He publicly lamented
his vote to authorize the Vietnam war and apologized sincerely for
his previous attitudes toward states' rights. In 1978 he faced a tough
primary campaign against a New Right challenger that he almost lost.
This experience left him feeling isolated in his own party and skeptical of its direction.[38] In 1979, no longer guaranteed of renomination
and having decided to step down from office, Anderson entered the
Republican presidential primaries. Favoring equal access to abortion,
gun control, and energy conservation, Anderson won a great deal of

editorial support in late 1979.[39] Like McCarthy, McGovern, and even Carter, Anderson was regarded as an outsider and a "no-hoper" who merely took television time away from bigger, better candidates.

But Anderson well understood the mood of his decade and its desperate search for something different, something untainted by politics as usual. Deciding that defeat was a foregone conclusion, Anderson began to take risks, moving beyond the cautious moderate Republicanism of George Bush and reaching out instead to a nascent radicalism that, in 1979 at least, Kennedy was failing to energize. The turning point was a debate in Iowa shortly before the party's statewide caucus. While the other candidates assailed the president for a grain embargo that was hurting Iowa farmers, Anderson endorsed it and excoriated his opponents for their lack of patriotism. While the other candidates urged Carter to contemplate military intervention in Iran, Anderson supported the commander in chief's efforts and urged calm. Most boldly, he made a passionate case for a reduction in gasoline consumption, facilitated by a 50-cent-per-gallon gas tax, so as to rescue the environment and reduce dependence on foreign oil.[40] As a result, he carved out an image of being "the only Presidential candidate who is authentic—who has not tailored his positions to attract the broadest constituency."[41] Pleasantly surprised viewers were thus introduced to the "Anderson Difference": a perception of honesty and independence built around ambitiously controversial policy positions.[42] With his distinctive shock of white hair and defiantly unfashionable dress sense, Anderson was every inch the angry professor. He did not tell audiences what they wanted to hear. He preferred instead to warn them, in great extemporaneous and breathless speeches, that they were on the brink of destruction. Suspecting that he might have a point, people started to listen.[43]

As predicted, Anderson polled poorly in Iowa, but the debate had made good television and was widely repeated and discussed. Anderson came in a narrow second in the Massachusetts and Vermont Republican primaries, just 1,200 votes behind George Bush in the former and 600 votes behind Ronald Reagan in the latter.[44] His cash-starved and disorganized campaign polled an impressive 36.7 percent to Reagan's 48.4 percent in Illinois the following week.[45] Anderson benefited enormously from Democratic crossover voting, allowing him to sweep Chicago and suburbs like Everton, a college town that he took by a 3–1 margin. Voters rated Anderson highly for his candor and ideas. Anderson enjoyed a slight edge among moderates and led Reagan among liberals by a 4–1 margin. His voters were largely college educated or students, and they favored the Equal Rights Amendment (ERA) by 2 to 1.[46]

Nevertheless, Anderson conceded that the Republican Party was sufficiently conservative to deny him the nomination, and he withdrew from the primaries and declared as an independent. Thereafter, he achieved highs of 25 percent in the polls, which reflected public dissatisfaction with Reagan and Carter as well as fascination with the Anderson Difference.[47] His strategy was to manipulate public perceptions of Carter as incompetent and Reagan as too conservative, offering a "competent, acceptable, middle-of-the-road alternative."[48] He never expected to sweep the whole country; Anderson relied on winning enough electoral votes in the Northeast and West for victory. His battlegrounds were ordinarily Democratic states.[49] As of June 1980, Anderson's support held steady at 23 percent of the popular vote. But when pollsters were asked for whom they would vote if they thought the congressman could win, Anderson's vote leapt to 29 percent, with Reagan at 35 percent, and Carter at 31 percent. In the Northeast, he finished ahead of Carter 36 percent to 31 percent and ahead of Reagan 36 percent to 29 percent.[50]

Anderson's strength reflected public dissatisfaction with the choice of mainstream contenders.[51] A June 1980 poll found that 55 percent of voters registered discontent with Reagan and Carter, and 64 percent welcomed Anderson's entry into the race for the alternative choice that it offered.[52] The *Congressional Quarterly* predicted that "Anderson's campaign has the potential to be the most successful candidacy ever mounted outside the two party system." Carter's staff feared that this broadly liberal defection could deny the president victory.[53] Although ultimately an electoral failure, Anderson's greatest success was perhaps getting his name on the ballot in every state, which set new legal precedents for other third-party campaigns.[54] Close to 1.5 million people signed petitions to get Anderson on the slate in 29 states and in Washington, D.C.[55] In Massachusetts, 39,245 signatures were required and 101,000 were gathered. In California, 101,377 were required and 400,000 were gathered.[56] His was the first-ever third party on the ballot in postwar Michigan.[57] Anderson absorbed what remained of McCarthy's 1976 campaign, and between the two of them, these otherwise forgotten outsiders laid the ground for all third-party efforts in the future.[58]

To reverse Anderson's gains, Carter refused to debate him, forcing Reagan and Anderson to debate alone.[59] When Reagan agreed to do so, the gesture appeared magnanimous, and the exercise proved more beneficial to the Republican than to the independent. Anderson did not fluff his appearance in the two-man presidential debate (the first time a third-party candidate appeared in such a forum in history); he simply failed to give the impression of a winner. Carter's absence highlighted Anderson's dip in the polls, and while he and Reagan lashed out at the president, it reinforced his hopelessness. Meanwhile, the White House painted Anderson, with some accuracy, as a late-comer to social liberalism and an enemy of labor.[60] The campaign was successful, and the unions remained largely hostile to the Anderson Difference. But Anderson's image worked because it was purposefully vague. One reporter noted, "Anderson's appeal thus far appears to be primarily to the young, college-educated liberals disenchanted with President Carter but unable to swallow the conservatism of Reagan." However, "they may be surprised to discover that he is somewhere in the middle of the political spectrum, between Carter and Reagan."[61] Democrats were frustrated that a "moderately conservative Republican" was drawing the votes of "perhaps millions of disgruntled supporters of Senator Edward M. Kennedy."[62]

Anderson's Democratic critics misunderstood the evolving nature of the congressman's campaign, which became decidedly more liberal when he quit the primaries in an effort to woo and keep those Kennedy votes.[63] At face value, the Anderson platform remained "fiscally conservative and socially liberal" while striking a "middle ground between the fiscal pronouncements of the two major party platforms."[64] However, it was a middle ground on which liberals could feel comfortable. Anderson denounced supply-side economics.[65] But he also accused Carter of trying to "fight inflation through unemployment" and lacking a "viable, realistic national healthcare plan." The president had "gutted the Humphrey-Hawkins bill and postponed its deadlines for reducing unemployment."[66] In contrast, Anderson claimed to be a "vigorous and vocal supporter of the Humphrey-Hawkins bill," such statements clearly reaching out to H.R. 50's supporters and economic liberals.[67] To be sure, he opposed bailing out failing manufacturers, but he supported industrial policy in language that consciously echoed the New Deal.[68] Historian Arthur Schlesinger Jr. voted for Anderson specifically because he was "the only one of the three candidates with a Rooseveltian belief in affirmative government. . . . In a time when the country has moved to the right, he has moved to the left—not the very far left, but definitely to the left of Mr. Carter and Mr. Reagan."[69] After he declared as an independent, Anderson's economic platform shifted even further. His argument that "we must not balance the budget on the backs of the poor" was borrowed directly from Kennedy.[70]

Moreover, Anderson's social liberalism defined the candidacy and was stressed over his fiscalism. Anderson was running in defiance of the New Right, speaking out against its "anti-women, anti-family, anti-children beliefs."[71] Believing that women and students were his principal constituency, Anderson focused his campaign on a number of policies designed to appeal to them.[72] He was for the ERA, abortion rights, and conservation of wildlife areas and opposed to nuclear power and the draft.[73] Anderson courted the gay community, explaining, "My commitment to ensure that no American is denied constitutional protections because of sexual or affectional preferences was a logical outgrowth of my strong support for the civil rights and women's rights movements of the 1960s."[74] He was staunchly pro-Israel too, something he emphasized to appeal to the traditionally Democratic voting bloc of American Jews.[75] Anderson chose a New Politics liberal Democrat as his running mate, former Wisconsin governor Patrick Lucey. A tubby, jovial politician, Lucey had campaigned aggressively against Vietnam and, later, for Kennedy, and his appointment was clearly designed to reach out to the senator's supporters and the remnants of the McGovern/McCarthy crusades.[76] Anderson's staff elected a number of Democrats for Anderson committees and tried, in vain, to elicit an endorsement from Douglas Fraser.[77] Finally, Anderson indicated that he would reconsider his candidacy if Kennedy were selected as the Democratic nominee. He was photographed outside the senator's office in Congress after a lengthy, private discussion about the problems facing the country. Here Anderson departed from Eugene McCarthy, Ross Perot, and Ralph Nader. He told reporters that he was a "supporter of the two-party system" and if it offered a true contest of philosophies, he would allow politics to return to normal.[78]

As a result of this strategy, Anderson became an alternative candidate for many liberals unhappy with Carter.[79] He boasted the acclaim of that other invention of the 1970s: the celebrity liberal. Stumping for the Anderson Difference were veterans of McGovern's campaign: Lauren Bacall, Margot Kidder, Julie Christie, Gore Vidal, and Paul Newman.[80] While Nixon had played with fire by courting his own alternative set of celebrity admirers, Carter set a new tone of contempt for actors and actresses that flirted with the real world. "The financial backing for John Anderson's bizarre presidential bid provided by Hollywood's left-liberal set provides a rare insight into the nature of the Anderson candidacy," said Carter's press officer.

"For the Los Angeles film crowd knows as much about life in south Boston or Detroit as John Anderson knows about being President of the United States."[81] It is interesting to note how much celebrity liberalism had changed by 1980. In 1972, actors like Warren Beatty or Shirley MacLaine had a direct influence on McGovern's policies. In 1980, celebrity support was strictly limited to public events and fundraisers. As politics had become more populist and less sophisticated, so celebrity liberals lost some of their once glamorous cachet. Since 1980, celebrity liberalism has become a double-edged sword; it attracts money and attention, but it provokes reverse snobbery and not a little derision.

Several notable Democrats stumped for Anderson, most clearly identified with either the New Politics or New Left, including Floyd Haskell and Cissy Farenthold.[82] Farenthold protested, "I still consider myself a Democrat . . . but a vote for Jimmy Carter is an irresponsible vote."[83] During the primary season, feminist Gloria Steinem divided her time between the Democratic and Republican primaries, fundraising for both Kennedy and Anderson.[84] Privately, many Democratic officeholders, such as George McGovern, welcomed Anderson's presence on the ballot as though he were a proxy Kennedy: a liberal presidential candidate that would draw key Democratic constituencies to the polls.[85] Publicly, Mo Udall suggested that "the Anderson candidacy, while damaging to Carter, actually could assist the rest of the Democratic ticket."[86] A former president of Americans for Democratic Action, which endorsed Anderson, pointed out that "Carter's re-election could not possibly be as important from the standpoint of liberalism as the re-election of McGovern, Nelson, Bayh, Culver, Church, Eagleton, Udall, and all the other fine Democratic leaders being challenged by the right wing. Many in this group know that Anderson is their best bet to get young people and independents to the polls."[87] The New York Liberal Party, Common Cause, and *New Republic* magazine also supported Anderson.[88] The Liberal Party castigated Carter for embracing "laissez-faire economics" and denying liberals "recognition as a positive force in progressive politics."[89] Anderson ran on a joint liberal ticket with Republican Jacob Javits in New York.[90] In Michigan, his campaign was staffed by a significant number of Democratic Agenda activists.[91] Indeed, it is a testament to disaffection with Carter that a self-described fiscal conservative was able to win the enthusiastic support of self-proclaimed "Democrat[s] with socialist leanings."[92] Liberals explained this paradox by defining Anderson's economics as "realist" and stressing its subservience to social liberalism. Thus his campaign was "based upon fiscal conservatism, admirably balanced by a commitment to human rights."[93]

Anderson also curried favor among liberal Republicans.[94] Each member of the Rockefeller family donated the maximum $1,000 to the campaign.[95] Mary Dent Crisp, chair of Anderson's National Unity Campaign, was a former chair of the Republican National Committee (RNC).[96] Her defection reflected anger among many female Republicans over their party's pro-life, anti-ERA platform. "The Republican Party left me," she told voters. "It has been taken over by religious and political zealots."[97] Anita Miller, a Reagan appointee to the California Commission on the Status of Women, told reporters she was "supporting Anderson because she believes Reagan has 'abandoned the women of this country.'"[98] Miller was far from alone, and Anderson's most fervent supporters were to be found in the feminist community, drawn by Anderson's commitment to their policy positions.[99] Ms. Robbin Setzer of North Carolina wrote to Anderson to express familiar sentiments among feminists. "I like what you said about energy, gun control, and national defense, however the biggest reason I'm considering voting for you is your stand on abortion. I AM PRO-CHOICE AND I VOTE."[100] Another Anderson feminist was Catherine East, a cofounder of NOW, member of the Kennedy Commission on the Status of Women and a preeminent activist, described by Betty Friedan as "the midwife to the contemporary women's movement."[101] East was an early supporter of Anderson, changing her party registration to vote for him in the Republican primaries.[102] She composed speeches for Anderson and believed that his candidacy, if not actually successful, would create momentum for passage of the ERA.[103]

As with Kennedy, NOW allowed local organizations to endorse and campaign for Anderson while avoiding stating a national position.[104] Nevertheless, the growing politicization of NOW was evident in its annual convention in October 1980 when a group of Anderson activists attempted to force the board to endorse their candidate.[105] However, the political mood had altered since Kennedy was no longer the likely Democratic nominee.[106] "Fear of Reagan," complained an Anderson activist, "seemed to be the dominating emotion among delegates." The NOW conference withdrew its 1979 resolution not to campaign for Carter's reelection and offered an alternative one attacking Reagan's record.[107] Fear of Reagan was Anderson's undoing, causing many liberals to withdraw support and return, albeit reluctantly, to the Carter/Mondale ticket.[108] The more voters believed he could not win, the smaller his popular vote became.

The 1980 Senate Elections

Meanwhile, as the election entered the fall, several Democratic senators found themselves facing probable and catastrophic defeat. Two
had debilitating primary campaigns that either took them out of the
race early or else made victory nearly impossible in November.[109] The
passing of Alaska's Mike Gravel and Georgia's Herman Talmadge truly
marked the end of an era. New Politics crusader Gravel was predicted
to win the general election but was defeated within the Democratic
primary by a conservative opponent. He was finally expelled not by
his people but by his party, and he took its decision badly. He slipped
into debt and went bankrupt twice before throwing his hat into the
2008 presidential primaries with a typically New Politics ticket of
tax reform and disarmament. His effusive, almost violent rhetorical
style and stringent fiscal conservatism left the Democratic base cold.
He eventually found a more natural home in the Libertarian Party.[110]
Georgia's Herman Talmadge was nearly defeated by his liberal primary
opponent, Zell Miller. Miller appealed to blacks and union members
with a legislative program of health insurance and support for Humphrey-Hawkins. He also charged Talmadge, not unfairly, with racism.
Stung by the attacks, Talmadge fought a poor fall campaign, and for
the first time since Reconstruction, Georgia gained a GOP senator.
Later Miller became a moderately liberal governor before becoming a
very conservative senator. He endorsed President Bush in 2004.[111]

The Senate Democrats faced a rejuvenated New Right movement
and an enriched RNC that intended to spend $1,924,000 on defeating
ten high-profile senators alone.[112] Their closest attention was focused
on the defeat of six liberals: Gary Hart, Alan Cranston, Frank Church,
George McGovern, John Culver, and Birch Bayh.[113] They all responded differently to this challenge. Bayh, Hart, Cranston, Church,
and McGovern moderated their images to adjust to the more conservative climate.[114] Hart stressed his fiscal conservatism and support for
a balanced budget. Church manipulated a diplomatic crisis that arose
from the discovery of Soviet advisers in Cuba to appear more macho,
and McGovern challenged the very definition of the word *liberal*.[115] In
his election material, McGovern was invariably portrayed carrying a
gun and extolling the virtues of a balanced budget.[116]

But one man bucked the trend and tried, like Kennedy and Anderson, to tap into a resurgence of liberal activism and political defiance.
John C. Culver was a handsome, one-term senator from Iowa elected
in the landslide of 1974. Angered by Carter's slide into conservatism,

Culver decided to turn the election into a referendum on liberalism and its political heritage. It became an exercise in grassroots campaigning and motivating the Democratic base.[117] This last-ditch strategy proved surprisingly effective, turning on voters, audiences, and the otherwise demoralized senator. A casually dressed and angry Culver told his growing audiences, "These days if you have a little compassion in your heart . . . you're a jerk. And if you're mean and hard hearted— why you're one smart s.o.b."[118] Rather than shy away from big government, Culver defended it. "The principal danger," he argued, "is not government taking over our lives, but powerful and privileged special interests taking over our lives and our political system. . . . I do not believe we are ready to surrender the power to govern our lives."[119] Like Kennedy, Culver tried to tap into and redirect the anger of the late 1970s, deflecting criticism of big government into criticism of big business and little politicians. Like Kennedy and Anderson, the excitement—and money—that Culver generated testified to liberalism's residual strength.

McGovern's campaign was more typical. By 1980 McGovern's South Dakota state party was in poor shape. It began the campaign $50,000 in debt, was forced to fund-raise and organize through lists left over from the 1972 presidential campaign, and was described as being "on the verge of shambles."[120] McGovern repeatedly faced the charge of providing poor constituency services and rarely being in the state.[121] A high-profile trip to Europe in 1979 led to accusations of absenteeism.[122] McGovern's Republican rival, Jim Abdnor, was an anti-Washington conservative who boasted that he rarely left South Dakota.[123] Cheerfully ignorant of a number of national issues, Abdnor was, however, committed to unrestricted gun ownership, loggers' rights, and across-the-board tax cuts.

Moreover, the key issue in the election was abortion, which Abdnor avowedly opposed.[124] The issue even divided the state Democratic Party, which refused to accept a pro-choice plank in its platform.[125] A pro-life Democrat provided McGovern with his first-ever primary challenge, hoping to raise awareness of the veteran senator's voting record on abortion. He was easily defeated, but he won some counties in rural western South Dakota. McGovern complained that the issue was being used "to defeat humane Senators because of their progressive domestic and policy views," and he spoke with some accuracy.[126] He was singled out by two out-of-state organizations: the National Conservative Political Action Committee (NCPAC) and the Life Amendment Political Action Committee (LAPAC).[127] The NCPAC constructed a "Target '80" plan to defeat incumbent liberals, which included "the use of sophisticated polling services, massive mailing to registered voters in these states, as well as an entirely independent radio and television and newspaper advertising program." It hoped that the defeat of McGovern would "put all the other liberals on notice."[128] Its strategy was to send mailings to voters illustrating McGovern's voting record and to start early enough to create the political atmosphere within which a Republican might feel emboldened to challenge the senator.[129] Had it not done so, it is doubtful that a popular local Republican would have risked campaigning against the unbeaten McGovern at all; certainly the convivial Abdnor often praised the senator and appeared reluctant to run against him.[130] LAPAC was motivated purely by the abortion issue and was the face of NCPAC in South Dakota; NCPAC recognized that abortion was the issue for which the senator had the most embarrassing record.[131] It spent $200,000 in both 1979 and 1980 informing Dakotans how McGovern had voted on right-to-life cases.[132]

Although McGovern complained about outside money, the 1980 campaign also witnessed the largest effort to date of special-interest funding by liberal groups. McGovern received his greatest financial and personnel contributions from NOW and the National Abortion Rights Action League (NARAL). NARAL regarded the election as a test of its strength: defeat could mean reversal of everything it had gained in the 1970s.[133] "If any or all of these incumbents lose," it warned, "we will have a Congress ever more cowed into submission by anti-choice groups than the one with which we now wrestle."[134] In an echo of Target '80, NARAL formed "Impact '80," which raised $327,000 for McGovern alone.[135] According to an impressed Gloria Steinem, the "LAPAC issue" had generated $250,000 in support money.

Some of the old magic was returning too, and the New Politics began to reconfigure and reorganize in South Dakota. Robert Redford and Shirley MacLaine stumped for their old friend, and folksingers Peter, Paul, and Mary performed an emotional reunion concert in support. The decade had been tough on them too; they had split acrimoniously and pursued unsuccessful solo careers. But there was no evidence of that when they gladly came together to sing "Blowing in the Wind" and a host of other anthems from a happier, more ambitious age.[136] In the true spirit of '72, there was even a brief scare that the campaign was being monitored by the CIA. McGovern staff reported that every day at lunchtime, a dark man in a black suit and shades would sit on a bench in the small park opposite the campaign headquarters in Sioux

City and stare menacingly at passing activists. Eventually one of the secretaries plucked up the courage to confront him. As soon as she demanded to know who he was, he jumped up from his seat and ran into the trees. The secretary told her story to the police, and they wearily explained that the park was a well-known cruising area for gay men. The "secret agent" was probably looking to pick someone up during his lunch hour. The campaign staff laughed at their own naiveté, but it is interesting to note that the world had moved on dramatically in just eight years—too fast even for McGovernites to keep up.[137]

Finally, the New Right challenge in states like South Dakota sped the reconciliation of New Deal and New Politics groups. At a national level, the DNC shared its electoral and polling information with NOW. In return, NOW provided activists and money in the general election. In South Dakota, Henry Jackson barnstormed the state in support of his onetime opponent, George McGovern. Even an idol of the antiwar movement was preferred by some neoconservatives to the untested, bellicose, and fiscally conservative Ronald Reagan.[138]

The Landslide

Yet McGovern recognized that he shared the ticket with an unpopular president and that, as such, any landslide for Reagan was likely to sweep him away too. Into the very last week of campaigning, that landslide was still not identifiable. As a result of indecision, a large proportion of voters decided how to vote at the last minute.[139] For this reason, the presidential debate assumed a significant degree of importance. In negotiations over format, Carter pushed for a series of debates that would allow him to show Reagan up as weak on detail. However, Reagan whittled him down to one meeting in the last week of the campaign. At the debate, the president performed poorly, appearing to suggest in one of his answers that he sought advice on national defense issues from his twelve-year-old daughter, Amy. His performance typified his campaign. It was defensive and mean-spirited, and it was aimed squarely at a set of special-interest groups; his answers were divided neatly up into policy positions designed to appeal to minorities, women, and labor. In contrast, Reagan was relaxed, jovial, and reassuringly on message. In his closing statement, he asked the audience, "Are you better off than you were four years ago?"—and thus defined the election squarely as a referendum on his opponent. It is interesting to note that radio listeners gave the debate to Carter and TV viewers to Reagan. This was precisely what happened in 1960, when Jack Kennedy's cool, tanned performance defeated Richard Nixon's quarrelsome, shifty one.[140]

The election eve was the anniversary of the seizure of the hostages at the American embassy in Tehran, and the networks ignored images of the president submerged in enthusiastic crowds of voters terrified by the thought of a Reagan victory to instead review the crisis day by humiliating day.[141] Patrick Caddell found that this, combined with the failure of a last-minute attempt to release the hostages in Iran, swung the election for the challenger.[142] The chair of the Carter/Mondale reelection campaign, Robert Strauss, similarly concluded that the outcome was decided by "the events." Historian Leo P. Ribuffo, concurring, wrote, "In short, Jimmy Carter occupied the White House at a time when the consumer price index rose by 14 percent annually, inflation tipped the economy into recession, and American diplomats were taken captive in Tehran."[143] In a sense, the party had come full circle from 1968. Humiliated by a prolonged foreign crisis, its administration was defeated in spite of the residual popularity of its welfare programs.

On 4 November 1980, Reagan beat Carter by a landslide margin of 50.7 percent to 41 percent. Jimmy Carter accepted defeat early in the evening, before polling had finished on the West Coast. It was a matter of pride: he didn't want commentators to say that he had held out conceding until the last minute. However, it probably discouraged Democrats from voting out West and may well have lost Frank Church his Senate seat. Even in defeat, Carter's prideful personality angered his own party. Carter conceded onstage to the tune of "Happy Days Are Here Again," ordinarily associated with the joys of the New Deal era. "I promised you four years ago that I would never lie to you," he said, "so I can't stand here tonight and say that it doesn't hurt."[144]

The result produced a lopsided victory in electoral votes of 489 to 49. It saw a swing of ordinarily Democratic groups, many of which Kennedy had appealed to in the primaries, toward the Republican ticket. The Republicans also gained control of the Senate for the first time since 1952, and the swing of twelve seats was the largest since 1958.[145] McGovern went down to a 58.2 percent to 39.4 percent loss. Statewide polling in the last few weeks of the campaign put the candidates neck and neck.[146] The *Daily Republic* even gave McGovern a lead, but reported that 15 percent of voters were undecided.[147] The size of the percentage of voters who decided how to vote in the last few days gives weight to McGovern's argument that he was hurt by the

Reagan coattail.[148] McGovern had regained some ground by challeng-
ing Abdnor to a debate; the Republican had refused and thus appeared
cow-ardly.[149] In a campaign fueled by good memories, McGovern
cheerfully pointed out that "only two men have ever refused to debate George McGovern: Richard Nixon and Jim Abdnor." McGovern
also made an issue of out-of-state funding for Abdnor, who was forced
to publicly denounce NCPAC.[150] "What Senator George McGovern
did to turn the campaign around," surmised one editor, "may have
significance beyond South Dakota." Approaching November, the tide
began to turn against the New Right as state Republican organizations started to ask them politely to be quiet and leave moderate voters
alone.[151] However, the focus of the campaign on abortion in a state
that, according to McGovern's own polls, was overwhelmingly pro-
life doomed his reelection.[152]

Reagan's victory did not represent a conservative realignment.
Carter's inability to energize his liberal constituency was as important
to understanding the final result as the defection of "Reagan Democrats." Larger percentages of registered Democrats and independents
self-defining as liberal switched to the Republicans than conservatives
did, and minority voters proved as important in the general election as
they did in the primaries.[153] The administration had taken the results
in the Western primaries as evidence that it could not rely on Hispanic votes, and it was right.[154] There was a swing of 16 percent among
Hispanic voters from Carter to Reagan in November—the largest
swing among any individual ethnic group, including whites.[155] In addition, Carter's vote dropped among Jewish citizens by 11 percent and
in households with union activists by 8 percent. Overall, 11 percent of
registered Democrats abandoned the president.[156] More importantly,
there was a clear correlation between the "Kennedy Democrats" and
the blue-collar voters who would leave their party in 1980 to become
"Reagan Democrats."[157] In August 1980 the *New York Times* reported
that "only 23 percent of Mr. Kennedy's Democratic followers say they
plan to vote for Mr. Carter." Despite Kennedy's eventual endorsement
of Carter, 27 percent of his primary supporters switched to Reagan
in November, most of them blue-collar men.[158] Many of the Reagan
Democrats were Kennedy Democrats too. The 1980 election was determined by the public's anger toward Carter.[159] Postelection analysis
seemed to suggest that "a large share of the 43.2 million Americans
who voted for Ronald Reagan appear to have been motivated more by
dissatisfaction with President Carter than by any serious ideological
commitment to the Republican's views."[160]

This was further demonstrated by Anderson's vote, which had been rapidly declining in the last months of the campaign but rallied in the final week. He took 6.6 percent, and he won large enough percentages in Maine, Vermont, New York, Massachusetts, Connecticut, Michigan, Wisconsin, and Delaware to deny Carter 105 electoral votes.[161] Anderson's vote represented the defection of liberals and traditional Democratic constituencies. He received the support of 6 percent of registered Democrats, 11 percent of liberals, 7 percent of Catholics, 14 percent of Jews, 11 percent of college graduates, 11 percent of students, and 9 percent of Easterners.[162] Although this liberal slide did not deny Carter the election, it did exaggerate Reagan's victory. If one presumes that Anderson's voters would have preferred the moderate Carter to the conservative Reagan, then had Anderson not been in the race, the president might have been defeated by the relatively small margin of 50.7 percent to 47.6 percent. Carter would have amassed 154 electoral votes, dominating the Northeast, and political scientists would have probably interpreted the election quite differently.

Ultimately, Anderson's campaign ended a failure, reduced to single figures and denied even equal billing in a debate with the president. Nevertheless, an overall defeat did not mean that the Anderson Difference had not enjoyed its moments of triumph. It had demonstrated the damaging impact of liberal defection on Carter's reelection and residual enthusiasm for liberalism among a significant number of Americans. Propounding a message of dynamic, albeit limited, liberalism in a straightforward, dramatic, and convincing manner, Anderson gave hope to a generation of young activists who otherwise felt denied a candidate in 1980. On election night, Anderson's supporters cheered as it became evident that he had cost the president several states. Anderson told them that the vote was "a decision deferred."[163] It showed how weak Reagan was perceived to be that Anderson could have confidently predicted another run in 1984. But the decision proved final. By 1984 the country was experiencing a relative boom, and its people had learned to love their new president. Anderson endorsed the Democratic nominee and declined to enter the race, and by 2000, he was a member of the Green Party. The Anderson phenomenon marked the end of an era, not the beginning of a new one.[164]

If Carter was defeated because he failed to mobilize his base, this had a ripple effect on the states. McGovern's defeat was a personal one in a traditionally conservative state that wanted to protest both his record and that of the administration. It was highly unusual for its scale. Culver was beaten 53.5 percent to 45.5 percent, Bayh 53.8 percent to

46.2 percent, and Church just 49.7 percent to 48.8 percent.[165] Each faced apparently insurmountable odds, in Culver's case a predicted 2–1 defeat. Had this been a true ideological landslide, one would have expected these margins to have been bigger. Moreover, each ran better than Jimmy Carter did.[166] Notably, Cranston's impressive 56.5 percent to 37.1 percent victory in California was against Paul Gann, popular coauthor of the income-tax-cutting Propositions 13 and 9.[167] Once again, American voters demonstrated their antipathy toward conservative fiscalism.

Wider conclusions about the political state of the nation should not be drawn from the Senate results. Most contemporary commentators predicted that the Democrats would lose five or six seats.[168] Of all the Senate Democrats defeated in 1980, only one came from the ordinarily Democratic Northeast (John Durkin, New Hampshire) and one from the typically Democratic Midwest (Gaylord Nelson, Wisconsin). Four were from the South, three the West, and two the Republican Midwest.[169] They were running in the middle of a recession, sharing the ballot with a deeply unpopular president. The four defeated liberals shared several factors in common. First, they all represented seats in rural, traditionally non-Democratic areas. Second, partly as a result of geography, the defeated liberals were all encumbered by state parties that were either indebted or low in activism. Third, all four were accused of providing poor constituency services.[170] Cranston and Hart, who were predicted to lose but did not, developed strong state parties and campaigned in their states every week.[171] Fourth, they were all targeted by New Right organizations that masked partisanship behind single-issue campaigns.[172] The New Right set the political agenda for each state, turning the election into a referendum on the incumbent's position on one contentious issue. Thus, McGovern was targeted by the pro-life lobby, Church by anti–Panama Canal treaty campaigners, and both Culver and Bayh by a mixture of anti-SALT, pro-life, and anti-ERA groups.[173] The proliferation of these organizations demonstrated the growing power within parts of the United States of the religious right and social conservatives.[174] Democrats faced opposition from the Committee to Defeat Union Bosses, Stop the Baby Killers, and Restore School Prayer.[175]

As even McGovern discovered, to his frustration, Dakotans continued to hold some liberal views. His pollsters told him, "They tend to think that the government can do something about energy and inflation, while at the same time feeling that such action is highly unlikely." Although majorities opposed wage/price controls and favored a balanced budget, clear majorities also supported national health insurance, gas rationing, and SALT and opposed nuclear power. The poll's conclusions echoed those of the Culver campaign: that the Democratic base needed to be energized. To win, McGovern had to "reinforce his bases of support to offset weaknesses elsewhere. . . . Strengthen ties of important segments of the traditional Democratic constituency," while reaching out to "those aged 18–25 and women."[176]

In 1980, then, there was no realignment, and there had been no realignment because the American people were not in fact conservative in the truest sense of that word. It was only much later in the 1980s, when Reagan had won a landslide reelection victory, that historians began to reassess what 1980 had really meant. At the time, pollsters and politicians concluded that something far simpler, much less significant, had taken place. Fingerhut-Granados, who polled for Carter in the general election, stated that polling data "strongly suggest that reports of the demise of the Democratic majority, and the demise of the fundamentally populist perceptions undergirding that majority, are not merely premature. They are dead wrong." Rather, the "Republican margin in the 1980 presidential election came overwhelmingly from millions of defecting Democratic voters rejecting economic conditions under Jimmy Carter."[177] Louis Harris agreed that the election had been a referendum on Carter. He emphasized the continuing importance of motivating the liberal base, pointing out that "for all of the disenchantment with the Carter record, the nation still is Democratic by a 42–31 percent margin."[178] Reagan's success lay in motivating a sizable conservative base to attend the polls. "Ronald Reagan won his stunning victory last week not because the country as a whole went conservative, but because the conservatives—particularly the white moral majority—gave him such massive support."[179] In a thoughtful postelection analysis, Peter Hart remarked that 1980 "was not a strictly ideological win for the conservatives. The United States is basically a centrist country, and Americans vote pragmatically rather than ideologically. In 1980, voters perceived that the status quo was not working the way they wanted in economics, defense policy and government efficiency. The electorate decided that it was time to try something different than what the incumbents had to offer." Hart concluded that "the beneficiaries of this negative mood were the challengers—who often turned out to be conservative Republicans" but who just as easily could have been Kennedy or Anderson.[180]

Many Democrats and liberals were convinced that they were most hurt by Carter and identified no rejection of their philosophy within the results. The DNC's own study of the election concluded that Democratic performance was undermined by poor organization, disaffection among Democrats, and Reagan's coattails.[181] Tip O'Neill's staff advised him that "the vote was not a repudiation of the Democratic Party; it was a repudiation of the leadership of Jimmy Carter." They insisted that "there was no massive shift of Democratic voters to Republicans but rather a refusal of Democratic voters to vote. . . . Although the over-all Democratic vote from the various groups supporting us in the past dropped (except among blacks), the drop does not appear to have been all that substantial—except among Jews and Catholics, two groups never happy with a Southern Baptist. . . . Given the economic situation, it is no wonder that our normal blue-collar vote would decrease."[182] The Speaker himself pointed out shortly after the election, "We are still the largest party in America. Our political position in 1980 is significantly better than that of the Republicans in 1976."[183] Noting that the RNC had spent $109 million on the congressional campaign while the Democrats had spent only $16 million, he postulated, "Our opposition is at a cutting edge of a technological revolution taking place in American politics that has given Republican candidates a definite advantage."[184]

Even Carter partisans agreed. Many claimed that Kennedy's campaign had damaged the president enough to cost his reelection, yet that the primaries had been a short-term, almost parochial problem.[185] The traditional Democratic label was still popular. New York's lieutenant governor, Mario Cuomo, argued, "I do not believe our recent election losses should be allowed to panic our party into a desperate search for a new philosophy. Our commitment to ideals and emphases is as valid as ever, although it does require better articulation."[186] John White, while not explicitly blaming the president, believed that 1980 marked a failure to energize the Democratic base. Overall, there had been "no drop-off in the number of Americans who identify themselves as Democrats, and, despite the Reagan victory, the Republicans gained very little in party affiliation."[187] Both concluded that the 1980 result did not require a rethinking of Democratic liberalism. To a certain extent, their analysis would be validated by the 1982 midterm elections when the Democrats recouped twenty-seven House seats and won 54.1 percent of the popular vote.[188]

Conclusion

After his defeat, Carter spent two inglorious months continuing to fight for the release of the American hostages. Perhaps with the goal of humiliating the outgoing president, the Iranian militants waited until the first few moments of the new presidency to release them. The media interpreted the coincidence of their release with Reagan's inauguration as a sign that the Republican was ushering in a new era of hopefulness and confidence.[1] Arguably, he did. "Reaganomics" saw a 25 percent cut in the federal income tax, simplification of the tax code, and moderate deregulation. While domestic spending was essentially frozen, the Defense Department grew exponentially. Reagan, inheriting Carter's second cold war, pursued confrontation with the Soviet Union and tried to contain the spread of socialism in Central America. Reelected by a massive landslide in 1984, Reagan claimed that it was "morning again in America."[2] In fact, the country experienced the harshest recession since the 1930s from 1981 to 1982, undoubtedly worsened by deep cuts in social spending and jobs programs. Although there was massive economic growth with very low inflation from 1983 onward, many parts of the country remained trapped in unemployment and poverty for decades to come.[3] Although his domestic record will always be controversial, there can be no doubt that Reagan offered a tough remedy to the "crisis of confidence" and the malaise-ridden 1970s. He was the anti-Carter: charismatic, imperial, idealistic, simplistic, and nationalistic, as well as able to make common cause with the common man.

Meanwhile, Jimmy Carter enjoyed possibly America's most successful postpresidential period.[4] In 1982 he established the Carter Center in Atlanta, which was designed to promote human rights and alleviate unnecessary suffering in the developing world. It has helped to promote democracy worldwide, negotiating between rival political groups and overseeing elections: it has monitored seventy elections in twenty-eight countries since 1989. The center has also worked on disease control, and one of its biggest accomplishments has been the elimination of more than 99 percent of cases of infection by the debilitating parasite the Guinea worm, from an estimated 3.5 million cases in 1986 to fewer than 10,000 cases in 2007. In 1994 Jimmy Carter was personally involved in the resolution of crises in North Korea and Haiti. In North Korea he negotiated an understanding with dictator Kim Jong-il that saw the Koreans agree to freeze plutonium enrichment in return for assistance with its peaceful energy program and diplomatic recognition. In Haiti, Carter's mission managed to forestall a United States–led invasion of the island in order to restore to power the democratically elected president, Jean-Bertrand Aristide. In 2002, Jimmy was awarded the Nobel Peace Prize.[5]

Arguably, Carter found a degree of authority and international recognition that he had never enjoyed in office.[6] Similarly, Edward Kennedy, after accepting that he would never be president, also discovered a new sense of purpose. During the painful recession of 1981–1982, he considered running for the Democratic nomination once again. He almost certainly would have swept the primaries if he had.[7] However, as Reagan's poll numbers improved, he changed his mind. Ted personally liked the new president too, although he disagreed with almost all of his policies. He admired the way Reagan used the office, restoring to it its sense of dignity and potential. In many regards, Reagan's ability to mix glamour with ordinariness made him a very Kennedyesque president.[8] In addition, Ted's marriage to Joan finally ended; the two divorced amicably in 1982, leaving him without someone to play the role of first lady, and open to fresh rumors of scandal.[9] In a wise move, the senator sat out the 1984 elections. He watched ex–vice president Walter Mondale go down to a massive 2-to-1 defeat.[10]

Thereafter, Kennedy devoted himself to building a remarkable legislative record. His signature was on practically every single bipartisan bill that passed through the Senate in the next twenty years, including overriding Reagan's 1986 veto on economic sanctions against Apartheid South Africa, the 1990 Family and Medical Leave Act, the 1996 Kennedy-Kassenbaum Act that allowed employees to keep their health insurance after leaving a job and prohibited health insurance companies from refusing to renew coverage on the basis of preexisting medical conditions, expansion of the minimum wage, the 2001 No Child Left Behind Act, and the 2003 Medicare prescription drug program.[11] In addition, he kept up the fight for free health care by spearheading President Clinton's failed efforts to introduce a form of national health insurance (NHI) in 1993.[12] By the 1990s, Edward Kennedy had become a symbol of the liberalism of ages past. Although reviled by conservative commentators, he was nevertheless loved and adored by Democratic Party stalwarts. To be sure, Carter achieved the same kind of partisan affection that had once eluded him too. In both cases, the passage of time and collective defeats made bad-weather friends out of old enemies. Their endorsements in post-1980 presidential primaries became a seal of establishment approval. In 2008, Edward Kennedy's surprise decision to endorse Barack Obama over Hillary Rodham Clinton arguably helped swing the primaries in the Illinois senator's favor.[13]

Both men received a rapturous reception at that year's convention. Sadly, Ted had been diagnosed with a brain tumor and would die one year later. In his poignant, moving speech, he used many of the same images and ideas that he had evoked in 1980. At its climax, he said of his brother and the 1960s, "When John Kennedy called of going to the moon, he didn't say it's too far to get there. We shouldn't even try. Our people answered his call and rose to the challenge, and today an American flag still marks the surface of the moon. Yes, we are all Americans. This is what we do. We reach the moon. We scale the heights. I know it. I've seen it. I've lived it. And we can do it again." At the end of his speech, he told a tearful audience, "The work begins anew. The hope rises again. And the dream lives on." The resonance of those words illustrated the continuing power of the Camelot dream and the Kennedy myth, thirty years after many political scientists had pronounced the death of American liberalism. Arguably, Barack Obama was the Jack Kennedy of his generation.[14]

Liberalism Reunited

There are two broad conclusions that can be drawn from the Kennedy and Carter fight of 1980. First, although American liberalism experienced a great deal of trauma at the beginning of the 1970s, by 1980 it was united and undergoing a revival of activism. Several factors facilitated reconciliation within Democratic groups. New Deal liberals accepted the institutional triumph of the New Politics and the wave of new social protest movements, minorities, and white-collar activists that it brought into the Democratic coalition. Indeed, while historians have often written disparagingly of the divisive New Politics revolution of the early 1970s, its triumph eventually led, for better or worse, to a greater degree of congruity among liberals.[15] Social and racial conservatives would never enjoy the leverage within the Democratic Party that they exercised before 1968, and thereafter, albeit haltingly, both labor and the Democrats would commit themselves to gender, racial, and sexual equality. With greater qualification, they also accepted much of the antiwar movement's critique of American foreign policy, especially during the dirty wars in Central America and the later war on terror in the Middle East.

The 1980 primaries also encouraged liberals to unite around a common platform and to try to avoid protracted nomination battles. For example, the death of George Meany and the ascension of Lane Kirkland as president of the AFL-CIO in 1979 marked the beginning of an era of accord between labor and the Democratic Party. Kirkland, a more conciliatory figure than Meany, also had a greater appreciation of the powerful role that equalities issues were coming to play in American politics. In the early 1960s, he had coordinated the federation's campaign against racial discrimination by its own affiliates and lobbied successfully for the inclusion of a fair employment practices provision in the 1964 Civil Rights Act. As president, Kirkland nominated the first woman to the AFL-CIO's executive council and dramatically increased the role of African Americans, Latinos, and Asian Americans in the organization. Thanks to his efforts, the Teamsters, the United Auto Workers, the United Mine Workers, the Brotherhood of Locomotive Engineers, and the International Longshore and Warehouse Union rejoined the federation.[16] Stressing the importance of unity, he pontificated that, regardless of their errors, "All sinners belong in the church." In 1981, Kirkland organized a massive "Solidarity Day" rally in Washington, D.C., to dramatize labor's opposition to the conservative policies of Ronald Reagan. Over 250,000 people marched with him.[17] The experience of 1980 taught Kirkland not to shy away from the primary and presidential election process but instead to involve labor fully, so as to ensure the correct candidate was nominated and elected. Thus, he endorsed Walter Mondale in 1984.[18] The failure to pass key liberal legislation in the late 1970s and the election of Ronald Reagan in 1980 had forced labor and the New Politics activists to realize they needed each other. The triumph of conservatism slowed liberalism's advance, but it did force it to become more cohesive and to bury much of its factionalism.

Greater unity was also helped by a change in issue agenda. The recession of the 1970s, often regarded as confounding liberals, in truth encouraged them to return to basic economic issues around which a more perfect consensus could be formed. Political debate returned to health care, jobs, and Social Security. While inflation divided many Democrats over funding priorities, defending the legacy of the New Deal and Great Society against cuts, proposed first by Jimmy Carter and later Ronald Reagan, reunited many more with their core constituencies. Even neoliberals like Gary Hart, although supportive of the principle of a balanced budget, were forced to emphasize the need to protect essential social programs and support increased funding for job creation. Similarly, feminists and civil rights activists realized that joblessness threatened their legal triumphs and returned to economic themes developed in tandem with New Deal liberals. Universalist policies like NHI that protected minorities and the poor while offering support to the middle class played a key role in binding liberals back together and reaching out to the middle class. Time and again, NHI would form the central plank of the Democratic Party platform, even under the centrist Bill Clinton.

Ironically, liberalism was unified and revitalized by opposition to the policies of a Democratic president. Jimmy Carter did not govern as a liberal. Yet he pledged himself to many policy positions dear to liberal groups when running for the presidency in 1976. This political strategy was a disaster. Frustrated liberals, who thought that Carter owed his narrow election to their campaigning, were surprised and then outraged as their president, despite comfortable control of Congress, apparently reneged on his promises. Carter must take a lion's share of responsibility for the failure to enact key liberal legislative goals. To be sure, any judgment of his personal efforts to pass the Equal Rights Amendment (ERA) or tax or labor law reform is inevitably subjective. It is also true that his room for maneuver was limited by inflation and the antitax mood of the late 1970s. But Carter was not personally committed to the passage of liberal economic legislation, regardless of its inflationary impact. His administration chose to prioritize balancing the budget and increasing defense expenditures over enacting health insurance or achieving full employment. A structuralist critique of the 1970s should not deny or excuse Jimmy Carter's personal responsibility for either his triumphs or failures. His relationship with his liberal constituency was poor, as was amply demonstrated by the Anderson candidacy and the massive defection of liberal voters in November 1980. This was a failure he could have avoided. The lesson that future administrations should take from Carter is that it is important to reach out to the center ground, but failure to communicate a message that seems driven by a coherent ideology can be counterproductive. Alienating one's core constituency can be simply ruinous. This was a lesson that Republican George Bush Sr. learned in 1992 when he faced a grassroots challenge by conservatives irate at his decision to raise taxes. The internecine conflict that this decision sparked tarnished his image and contributed to his defeat in the general election.[19]

Opposition to Carter sped the process of reconciliation among liberals, while the Kennedy candidacy completed it. That Kennedy was able to garner the support of the UAW, the National Organization for Women (NOW), the American of Federation of Teachers, the United Farm Workers, the Congressional Black Caucus, and a variety of neoliberals, New Politics activists, New Dealers, New Leftists, and even neoconservatives, is a testament to his personality. But it also attests to the slow process of reconciliation described here and the anger that Carter generated among Democrats. Opposition to Carter literally radicalized liberals. It intellectually returned them to the critique of capitalism contained within the New Deal. Discussions around the enactment of Humphrey-Hawkins, wage/price controls, and the massive program of public works that Kennedy proposed to stimulate aggregate demand suggest that liberals were convinced they could spend and manage their way out of a recession. The longevity of such ideas and the influence of New Deal economics imply that the prognosis of the death of American social democracy was premature.[20] Rather, the return of economic themes allowed socialist groups like the Democratic Socialist Organizing Committee and the Democratic Agenda to enjoy a remarkable degree of political influence. While the 1970s was an era of renaissance for the right, it was for the left too, and such organizations should not be excluded from its narrative. It corresponded with the birth of a set of new liberal issues that welcomed a fresh generation of activists into the Democratic Party's ranks. These included opposition to the draft and nuclear power and the battle to ratify the ERA. They would stay for many years to come.

Opposition to Carter tapped into and accelerated the progress of the party reform movement. Starting in 1968, liberal activists came to believe that the party had the right to exert discipline over elected officials, holding them accountable to the platform on which they had been elected. Arguably this went beyond even the ambitions of the McGovern-Fraser Commission, stretching its principle of representation into one of accountability. The 1978 and 1980 conventions represented the pinnacle of the reform movement. At Memphis, Democrats were given the opportunity to publicly challenge and even vote against the policies of their own administration. At New York, although its success depended on momentum driven by the Kennedy candidacy, the movement rewrote the party platform and effectively repudiated the policies of the president it subsequently renominated. This was a high-water mark for the party reform movement. In 1981 the Democratic National Committee revised convention rules to emasculate the midterm and introduce superdelegates into the 1984 primaries that would weaken the chances of outsiders taking the nomination.[21]

Parallels can be drawn between the experience of the Democratic Party and that of the Labour Party in Great Britain. In 1974 a Labour government was elected on a relatively radical manifesto that was composed in consultation with the party's left. The manifesto was committed to achieving full employment, increased public spending, and greater state management of the economy, and it was ratified by the party's national conference.[22] However, the 1974–1979 governments of Harold Wilson and James Callaghan reneged on these commitments, largely because they deemed them to be inflationary.[23] In response, a coalition of trade unions and left-wing activists formed organizations such as the Campaign for Labour Party Democracy that sought the exercise of discipline over elected officials, the right of the party to elect parliamentary leadership, and a greater role for activists in writing the manifesto.[24] The CLPD, like the Democratic Agenda, couched its Alternative Economic Strategy in the language of its recent past. While American liberals urged a return to the principles of the New Deal, British socialists spoke of the need to revive "the spirit of 1945," when a markedly more socialist government was elected under the premiership of Clement Attlee.[25] The climax of this movement was the deputy leadership election of 1981, in which centrist Dennis Healey narrowly beat left-wing Tony Benn. The divisions within Labour that the election exposed contributed to its defeat in the 1983 general election.[26] Although there were many differences between the two case studies, they demonstrate that the problems and dilemmas that center-left governments and activists faced in the late 1970s were universal. Economic crisis during a period of government forced social democrats to return to first principles.

Popular Liberalism

The second conclusion that can be drawn about liberalism in 1980 is that it was considerably more electorally viable than both historians and political scientists have hitherto judged. Nineteen eighty saw an election of rejection rather than realignment, and the model of re-alignment so often forced on it does not fit. Certainly a degree of dealignment was apparent in ticket splitting, the Anderson candidacy, and defection to Reagan. But 1980 was a judgment on the record of Jimmy Carter rather than liberalism or its major legislative achieve-ments. This was evident from the electoral success enjoyed by Demo-crats throughout the 1970s (which was not entirely due to Watergate) and the Democratic revival in the congressional elections of 1982. Poll-ing at the close of the decade showed that while Americans thought that they were overtaxed and that they were concerned about the size of government, they continued to support NHI, Social Security, and jobs programs. The population showed more tolerance for the agenda of the New Politics in 1980 than in 1970. Clear majorities favored ac-cess to abortion, passage of the ERA, environmental legislation, and détente.

At the end of the 1970s, many liberals did not think that America had become more conservative. Within the administration, Walter Mon-dale and others sensed that frustration with inflation and the hostage crisis led to a referendum on Carter's leadership, but not a mandate for a conservative revolution in the 1980s.[27] "America was changing," judged Mondale, "and institutions have to change with it. The old New Deal stuff and the Great Society stuff, a lot of it survived because it made sense. Social Security, Medicare, Medicaid, aid to education, all the civil rights stuff. They tried to get rid of all of that, or change it or weaken it. They couldn't do it, because it had a solid national constit-uency."[28] Outside of the administration, George McGovern "certainly did not feel that there had been any movement to the right. . . . Politi-cians certainly acted as though there had been, but I didn't perceive it."[29] He wrote in 1980, "While some pollsters might disagree with me, I still feel that liberalism is a vital and dynamic force in American poli-tics. . . . I still think that a majority of Americans look to their gov-ernment to solve our problems."[30] Douglas Fraser concurred, blaming defeat on Carter's failures and Reagan's personal charm, but not the legislation he had campaigned to pass.[31] Eleanor Smeal and NOW "al-ways knew that the country was with us, that public opinion still is." Indeed, the country had become self-evidently more socially toler-ant by the close of the decade, but Carter's unpopularity and a strong conservative lobby gave an opposite, false impression. Kennedy's few victories testified to liberalism's potential, while in November, "An-derson distorted the scale of Reagan's victory and made it look much bigger than it really was."[32] Activists like consumer advocate Heather

Booth were excited by the increase in social protest organization and coalitions that the 1970s witnessed: "We got thousands of people into the streets to campaign on oil and energy." However, received wisdom about conservative realignment crowded out their message: "You have to understand the growing power of corporate lobbies at that time. . . . It was an opportunity lost."[33]

Gary Hart thought that the country "did go to the right," but that this was made possible by the lack of "an imaginative response" by Democrats. The true story of the 1970s was not conservative growth, but the failure of liberals to project a clear identity.[34] Interestingly, fellow neoliberal and governor of Massachusetts Mike Dukakis suggested that 1980 was not a reversal, but merely a hiccup in the process of liberal reform. Dukakis, although defeated by a conservative rival in 1978, was reelected Massachusetts governor in 1982, "and I went right back to doing what I had done before. Look at what we did [in the 1980s]—health insurance, jobs, education." The tax revolt within his state was "to do with property taxes and nothing else. They were too high. We lowered them and then got back to work."[35] Rather, most liberals believed that Carter's presidency triggered a rejection of the status quo that engulfed the Democrats. Fred Harris argued that "Carter lost because he was not bold enough . . . the public didn't agree with Reagan on a single issue position."[36] Peter Hart, who conducted polling for John Culver and Frank Church, detected "no shift to the right. . . . It was like a leaking bag of water. A leaking bag doesn't drip; it explodes all at once. That's what happened in 1980. The disasters of the previous four years just became enough for voters."[37]

The actions of liberals toward the Carter administration should be contextualized by the body of contemporary opinion that concluded that they argued from a position of electoral strength. Throughout 1979, liberals thought that Edward Kennedy's nomination and election were likely or even inevitable. Throughout 1980, they believed that the public would prefer Carter to Reagan and return a Democratic administration. So convinced was the Democratic Agenda of Kennedy's election that they staged a "Eurosocialism Conference" in December 1980.[38] The purpose of the conference was to "write the policy that would become Kennedy's economic policy in his first term."[39] Participants included Willy Brandt, François Mitterand, and Tony Benn, and they debated an international strategy for social democracy in the 1980s. That Edward Kennedy attended the conference offers a hint of what kind of economic program his administration would have implemented.[40] Liberals made tough demands of the Carter administration not simply because they were willful or impatient, but because they believed they could afford to.

Kennedy Liberalism

The Kennedy candidacy was a barometer of American politics in the late 1970s. It comprised essentially two campaigns, both of which illustrated the residual appeal of liberalism. The pre-Iran campaign of 1979 was framed by the public's overwhelming belief that Kennedy should be both the Democratic nominee and president. He consistently led Carter and his potential Republican opponents by large margins among all voters. The width and depth of support for Kennedy indicate that it was not simply a referendum on Carter. Nor was it entirely personal. Certainly his perceived qualities of leadership were probably related to the public's memory of his brothers. But the public also associated Kennedy with Chappaquiddick. Kennedy was in many regards a highly flawed candidate, and that the public could still support him, despite all his personal problems, indicates that they saw some other quality in his candidacy than just his name. In 1979, Americans were searching for relief from stagnation and the status quo. For that year at least, they put their faith in a man associated with activist government and the economics of growth. Polls consistently showed that the public knew Kennedy's policy positions and approved of them, and when they did vote for him in 1980, they voted for him on that basis.

The second Kennedy campaign was a return to basic liberal principles after Iran and Afghanistan changed the character of the nomination battle. The foreign crises gave Carter a brief spurt of popularity that, combined with canny manipulation of the incumbency, allowed him to defeat Kennedy in the early primaries. Kennedy responded by dropping his campaign's emphasis on personality (a key strategic error) and instead running a campaign of economic protest. His primary victories were built on a coalition of voters unique in postwar Democratic primaries. It included liberals of New Deal and New Politics traditions, ethnic minorities, and blue-collar conservatives. Although this coalition is most often associated with Robert Kennedy, it was Edward Kennedy who actually assembled it. Ted's ability to appeal to these groups on a platform of increased government spending and wage/price controls suggests that Americans were prepared to consider a liberal alternative to Carter. The massive popular support that his individual policy positions garnered proves that at the end of the

1970s, Americans still looked to government for solutions to their problems.

The Anderson candidacy and the massive defection of Democratic constituency groups to both the independent and Republican candidates demonstrated that maintaining the support of liberal voters and ethnic minorities was as important to the outcome of the 1980 election as reaching out to conservatives. Kennedy showed an ability to energize and win over precisely those groups that left Carter for Reagan and Anderson. This book does not ask historians to believe that Kennedy could, or should, have won, but rather to finally acknowledge that he had a chance. That Reagan benefited from the backlash against Carter rather than having to fight Edward Kennedy was arguably the product of tactical error and historical accident. The rejection of Carter in 1980 was caused not by a conservative revolution but by a set of far more complicated factors that could just as easily have put a liberal in the White House.

In many regards, the Kennedy and Reagan candidacies were very similar.[41] They both campaigned against the elected establishment. They both challenged Carter's economic record. They both believed that consumption and growth could heal the economy. They both believed that government could be an instrument of economic recovery, be it through increased spending or tax cuts. They both identified themselves with the apogee of activist government, Franklin Roosevelt, tapping into popular memories of the 1930s. They were both highly rated for their qualities of leadership, which placed them in stark contrast with Carter's perceived lack of will. They both appealed to those who thought that their financial situation was worsening, including many blue-collar workers. In the boldness of their platforms and their defiance of contemporary economic orthodoxy, they were unanimous in asking Americans to "sail against the wind." In voting for both, many Americans sought a government that would actively relieve their suffering rather than passively manage decline. This characterized the 1980 voter more accurately than simply nativist conservatism.

The (very) qualified success of the Kennedy campaign means that historians must be careful not to put the late 1970s into a conceptual straitjacket. It was a period of frustration with government and rejection of a political establishment that liberals had come to dominate. It is undeniable that the 1980 election severely wounded the Democratic Party and that it failed to command a majority of the popular presidential vote until 2008. However, liberals should not be excluded from the decade's narrative, nor should they be blamed exclusively for their party's problems. Equally, the American public cannot be neatly defined as undergoing a conservative realignment. Failures of leadership, historical accident, and the impact on the public imagination of Carter's apparently hamstrung presidency should be weighed in the balance.

The lessons that modern liberal activists can take from 1980 are both encouraging and cautionary. On the one hand, coalition building has a great deal to offer activists. Within the Democratic Party, it gave social protest movements entrance into the mainstream, a voice in policy making, and a mandate to pressure the Carter administration to uphold its manifesto commitments. The positive contribution that single-issue activists and labor made in 1976 gave them the moral right to effectively author the Democratic platform in 1980.

On the other hand, liberal coalition partners quickly discovered that the support of the administration for their agenda depended on its popularity with the wider electorate. Jimmy Carter was not prepared to take risks for causes that he judged to be lacking in political capital. Democratic administrations are always hamstrung by the party's fear of appearing extremist or too radical. As feminists learned in the late 1970s when they attempted to shift dialogue on women's rights onto the underlying economic causes of discrimination and inequality, liberal ideas will only be tolerated insofar as they contribute to reelection and remain relatively uncontroversial. Carter's firing of Bella Abzug as the chair of the National Advisory Committee of Women was a turning point for many feminists and illustrated the problem of dealing with administrations that are happy to accept support from any quarter but inclined to be selective about what parts of their agenda they actually push. Sadly, Carter's U-turn on health care and fiscal policy demonstrates that before liberals form a coalition with Democratic nominees, they should be sure of their sincerity. For this reason alone, they might do well to coalesce early in the primary season around an electable liberal with a dependable record rather than simply regrouping around the eventual nominee and hoping that a hearty welcome for campaign contributions will translate into action when elected.

For Democratic presidential nominees, the most important lessons to be taken from the 1970s relate to how to run for office, and what to do when they get there. For presidential hopefuls, the message of Kennedy's campaign is to develop specific themes early on in the primary season and stick to them. Kennedy performed poorly when he vacillated and tried to distance himself from his old ideas and friends. This was not suitable in an election that hinged on giving specific answers to particular problems. The American public in the late 1970s was looking for an alternative to Carter's politics of pain. So desperate was the economic situation that they would happily have elected either a radical conservative or a radical liberal. What they wanted most from government was leadership and activism. But esoteric though these themes might appear, they were tied to a complex politics of symbolism that expressed concrete ideas and policies through image making. Hence, Ronald Reagan's image as a cheerful California cowboy was not simply theater; it was a way of communicating policy points. The cowboy was a symbol of rugged individualism, self-sufficiency, and even antistatism. Similarly, Edward Kennedy's image as a Kennedy was more than a dim reminder of happier times but, when unbundled, a hymn to activism, civil rights, and social reform. When both Kennedy and Reagan fled their images and their old causes at the start of the primary season, their popularity fell. When both returned to those themes later in the campaign, their popularity rose. Politicians who are defined by radicalism lose much when they attempt to disavow it. They abandon the very characteristics of integrity and dynamism that made them so appealing to a troubled electorate in the first place.

When running for office, Democratic nominees would do well to emphasize economics and exploit the potential of universalism. Although Americans were considerably less socially conservative in the late 1970s than historians have claimed, unquestionably, cultural issues remain inherently divisive, and any campaign that emphasizes them is likely to polarize the electorate. It creates wedges within traditionally Democratic voting groups, particularly blue-collar and working-class white ethnics. George McGovern's 1972 loss was exacerbated by the issues of "amnesty, acid, and abortion," Geraldine Ferraro and John Kerry both received opprobrium for being pro-choice Catholics, and Mike Dukakis was excoriated in 1988 for his opposition to the death penalty and use of prison furloughs as governor. In contrast, liberal economic ideas and social programs were consistently popular throughout the late 1970s. Although tax revolts did take place, these did not equate to a wholesale rejection of government intervention into the economy or federal spending on welfare, education, and health. A universalist approach to economics removes the element of special-interest politics from liberal spending proposals. The 1980 Democratic primaries suggest that a candidacy built around populist economics that offers tangible benefits to Middle America has the potential to generate a coalition of need that crosses racial, class, and cultural boundaries. This is what Kennedy achieved, and rebuilding that coalition should be the ambition of every liberal contender.

When in office, Democratic administrations should also try to maintain good relations with their core liberal constituencies. This does not simply mean distributing political favors or listening politely to their advice before ignoring it. Carter was not openly dismissive of the coalition that elected him. Indeed, despite his claim to being a centrist above special-interest politics, he went out of his way to court individual organizations and voting blocs. Lines of communication were always kept open, and he arguably began the now-established practice of dividing up government departments and jobs according to ethnicity or special interest, as illustrated by his creation of an Office of Hispanic Affairs. But cooperation does not equate to partnership. Carter made a list of promises that he not only could not keep but did not intend to keep. Grassroots activists of any hue do not judge an administration by its words but by its actions. Carter's failure to deliver on NHI or proper full employment legislation alienated liberal officeholders, activists, and core voters. It is vitally important to note that Carter's biggest decreases in popularity in the late 1970s were among traditionally Democratic voters, not conservatives or moderates. The advice of his pollsters to reach out to the center ground and even try to gain political capital out of distancing himself from liberals proved foolish. Carter's presidency illustrates well the importance of motivating a party's core constituency and delivering what has been promised to them.

The final message from 1980 is simply that the American public cannot be typified or stereotyped. Humans do not fit neatly into sociological straightjackets. Despite the reputation of the late 1970s for being a period of conservative ascendance, many Americans seriously considered voting for Edward Kennedy. Large numbers of self-defined conservatives actually did so. Despite the popular nostalgia associated with his presidency, the American public was initially ambivalent toward Ronald Reagan. The campaigns of 1980 were decided by random historical factors, the skillful manipulation of events, terrible mistakes, poorly chosen words, and unforeseeable consequences. A voting public that showered love, hate, and disinterest on both liberal and conservative candidates defied clear definition, and their overarching philosophy should probably not be second-guessed by historians, political scientists, or public policy makers.

Perhaps the paradox of 1980 was best summarized during the New York Democratic primary by a Queens resident and Kennedy supporter who was asked how he would vote in November. "I'm a liberal," the man stated. "Carter's a disaster. I think what the country really needs is a father figure, so I'm voting for Ronald Reagan."[42]

Notes

Introduction

1. For representative work on the political and cultural state of liberalism in the 1970s, see Peter N. Carroll, *It Seemed Like Nothing Happened: American in the 1970s* (Piscataway, N.J.: Rutgers University Press, 1990), 348; William C. Berman, *America's Right Turn: From Nixon to Bush* (Baltimore, Md.: Johns Hopkins University Press, 1994), 58–59; Bruce J. Schulman, *The Seventies: The Great Shift in American Culture, Society and Politics* (Cambridge, Mass.: Da Capo Press, 2002), 121–143; Edward D. Berkowitz, *Something Happened: A Political and Cultural Overview of the Seventies* (New York: Columbia University Press, 2006), 227; David Frum, *How We Got Here: The Decade That Brought You Modern Life—For Better or Worse* (New York: Basic Books, 2000), 12; Michael Barone, *Our Country: The Shaping of America from Roosevelt to Reagan* (London: Collier Macmillan), 572.

2. "Remarks of Senator Edward Kennedy: Workshop on Healthcare, Democratic National Committee Mid-Term Convention, Memphis," 9 December 1978, Papers of Adam Clymer, 1958–1999, John F. Kennedy Library, Boston, Mass., Box 9.

3. "Lackluster Convention Lights Up," *Washington Post*, 10 December 1978, A1.

4. "Carter Is Sworn in as President: Asks Fresh Faith in Old Dream," *Washington Post*, 21 January 1977, A01.

5. For a specific analysis of the emergent radicalism of the New Politics, see Gareth Davies, *From Opportunity to Entitlement: The Transformation and Decline of Great Society Liberalism* (Lawrence: University Press of Kansas, 1996), 219–243; Dominic Sandbrook, *Eugene McCarthy: The Rise and Fall of Postwar Liberalism* (New York: Alfred A. Knopf, 2004), 219–221; John A. Farrell, *Tip O'Neill and the Democratic Century* (Boston: Little, Brown, 2001), 525; and Maurice Isserman and Michael Kazin, *America Divided: The Civil War of the 1960s* (New York: Oxford University Press, 2003), 221–240. A more balanced view of the New Politics can be found in LeRoy Ashby, *Fighting the Odds: The Life of Senator Frank Church* (Pullman: Washington State University Press, 1994), 347.

6. For the impact of the New Deal/New Politics divide on the Democratic Party's electoral performance and its political significance, see Arthur H. Miller, Warren E. Miller, Alden S. Raine, and Thad A. Brown, "A Majority Party in

Disarray: Policy Polarization in the 1972 Election," *American Political Science Review* 70 (1976): 753–758; Steven M. Gillon, *Politics and Vision: The ADA and American Liberalism, 1945–85* (Oxford: Oxford University Press, 1987), 231; William G. Mayer, *Divided Democrats: Ideological Unity, Party Reform and Presidential Election* (Boulder, Colo.: Westview, 1996), 45; Ronald Radosh, *Divided They Fell: The Demise of the Democratic Party, 1964–1996* (New York: Free Press, 1998), 178.

7. Introduction to Steve Fraser and Gary Gerstle, eds., *The Rise and Fall of the New Deal Order, 1930–1980* (Princeton, N.J.: Princeton University Press, 1989); James L. Sundquist, *Dynamics of the Party System: Alignment and Realignment of Political Parties in the United States* (Washington, D.C.: Brookings, 1983), 437; Everett Carll Ladd Jr., "The Brittle Mandate: Electoral Dealignment and the 1980 Presidential Election," *Political Science Quarterly* 96 (1981): 1–25; Stanley B. Greenberg, *Middle Class Dreams: The Politics and Power of the New American Majority* (New York: Random House, 1997), 141.

8. Norman Podhoretz, "The New American Majority," in *Party Coalitions in the 1980s*, ed. Seymour Martin Lipset (New Brunswick, N.J.: Transaction Books, 1981); William Schneider, "Democrats and Republicans, Liberals and Conservatives," in Lipset, *Party Coalitions*, 229; John Kenneth White, *New Politics of Old Values* (Lebanon, N.H.: University Press of New England, 1988), 54.

9. W. Carl Biven, *Jimmy Carter's Economy: Policy in an Age of Limits* (Chapel Hill: University of North Carolina Press, 2002), 85.

10. Kenneth S. Baer, *Reinventing Democrats: The Politics of Liberalism from Regan to Clinton* (Lawrence: University Press of Kansas), 2; "How the Seventies Changed America," *American Heritage Magazine*, July/August 1991, 39; Stanley B. Greenberg and Theda Skocpol, eds., *The Real Majority: Toward a Popular Progressive Politics* (New Haven: Yale University Press, 1998), 13.

11. "What Is a Conservative?," *New York Times*, 31 August 1980, SM3.

12. Introduction to David Brian Robertson, *Loss of Confidence: Politics and Policy in the 1970s* (University Park: Pennsylvania State University Press, 1998). This structuralist interpretation is supported by administration memoirs: Jimmy Carter, *Keeping Faith: Memoirs of a President* (New York: Bantam, 1983), 99; Hamilton Jordan, *Crisis: The Last Year of the Carter Presidency* (New York: Putnam Adult, 1982), 363–365. The dissenting voice is Joseph A. Califano, who felt Carter was simply naïve and dismissive of long-term liberal legislative goals: Joseph A. Califano, *Governing America* (New York: Simon and Schuster, 1981), 14–15. This was also the view of the administration at the time: Memo, Al MacDonald to President Jimmy Carter, 19 December 1979, Office of the Staff Secretary, Handwriting Files, Jimmy Carter Library.

13. Kenneth E. Morris, *Jimmy Carter, American Moralist* (Athens: University of Georgia Press, 1996), 17–19; "Carter was a moral trustee that would ignore the special interests including the Northern liberals and the labor unions": interview with Walter Mondale, 7 June 2007.

14. Charles O. Jones, *The Trusteeship Presidency: Jimmy Carter and the United States Congress* (Baton Rouge: Louisiana State University Press, 1988), 216.

15. This is the view of most of Kennedy's biographers. These include Joe

McGinniss, *The Last Brother* (New York: Simon and Schuster, 1994), 614; Thomas Maier, *The Kennedys: America's Emerald Kings* (New York: Basic Books, 2003), 545–548; Thomas R. Burner and David West, *The Torch Is Passed: The Kennedy Brothers and American Liberalism* (New York: Atheneum, 1984), 244–245.

16. Sundquist, *Dynamics of the Party System*, 436.

17. For analyses of the campaign that place it in the context of the decline of liberalism, see Peter G. Bourne, *Jimmy Carter: A Comprehensive Biography from Plains to Post-Presidency* (New York: Scribner, 1997), 450; Burton I. Kaufman, *The Presidency of James Earl Carter Jr.* (Lawrence: University Press of Kansas, 1993), 172; Larry M. Bartels, *Presidential Primaries and the Dynamics of Public Choice* (Princeton, N.J.: Princeton University Press, 1988), 219–236; Seymour Martin Lipset, "Party Coalitions and the 1980 Election," in Lipset, *Party Coalitions in the 1980s*. The only account of the campaign favorable to Kennedy is Adam Clymer, *Edward M. Kennedy: A Biography* (New York: William Morrow, 1999), 276–320.

18. Marcia Chellis, *The Joan Story: One Woman's Victory over Infidelity, Politics and Privilege* (New York: Simon and Schuster, 1995).

19. John W. Sloan, *The Reagan Effect: Economics and Presidential Leadership* (Lawrence: University Press of Kansas, 1999), 45.

20. Farrell, *Tip O'Neill*, 539.

21. Lipset, "Party Coalitions and the 1980 Election."

22. "A Candidate in Search of a Myth," *Progressive* 44, no. 19 (1980): 32–37.

23. Elizabeth Drew, *Portrait of an Election: The 1980 Presidential Campaign* (New York: Routledge and Kegan Paul, 1981), 162.

24. Lester David and Irene David, *Bobby Kennedy: The Making of a Folk Hero* (London: Sidgwick and Jackson, 1986), 300–316.

25. Brain Dooley, *Robert Kennedy: The Final Years* (Keele: Ryburn, 1995), 122–127.

26. Mayer, *Divided Democrats*, 45.

27. Marie Cieri and Claire Peeps, eds., *Activists Speak Out: Reflections on the Pursuit of Change in America* (Basingstoke: Palgrave, 2000), 8.

28. William Julius Wilson, *The Truly Disadvantaged: The Inner City, the Underclass and Public Policy* (Chicago: University of Chicago Press, 1988), 120. For the definitive discussion about universalist policy, see Theda Skocpol, *Social Policy in the United States: Future Possibilities in Historical Perspective* (Princeton, N.J.: University of Princeton Press, 1995). For its influence on the Democratic Party, see Jonathan Bell, *The Liberal State on Trial: The Cold War and American Politics in the Truman Years* (New York: Columbia University Press, 2004), 273–274; Timothy Nels Thurber, *The Politics of Equality: Hubert H. Humphrey and the African American Freedom Struggle* (New York: Columbia University Press, 1999), 233.

Chapter 1: Jimmy Carter Goes to Washington

1. Perhaps Jimmy Carter's philosophy was best expressed through his appreciation for the theologian Reinhold Niebuhr, who stressed the responsibilities of

Christians to establish temporal justice while casting doubt on their capacity ultimately to do so given the conditions imposed on them by the Fall. "The sad duty of politics," wrote Niebuhr as quoted by Carter in his first memoir, "is to establish justice in a sinful world." Jimmy Carter, *Why Not the Best?* (New York: Bantam Books, 1976), 9.

2. "Carter Is Sworn in as President: Asks Fresh Faith in Old Dream," *Washington Post*, 21 January 1977, A01.

3. Kenneth E. Morris, *Jimmy Carter, American Moralist* (Athens: University of Georgia Press, 1996), 21–52.

4. Carter, *Why Not the Best?*, 24.

5. Erwin C. Hargrove and James Sterling Young, *Jimmy Carter as President: Leadership and the Politics of Public Good* (Baton Rouge: Louisiana State University Press, 1988), 2–3.

6. Carter spoke out against the use of busing to desegregate schools, visited a private whites-only school, and said that as governor, he would invite George C. Wallace to visit the state. Burton I. Kaufman, *The Presidency of James Earl Carter Jr.* (Lawrence: University Press of Kansas, 1993), 9.

7. Ibid., 19–20.

8. Betty Glad, *Jimmy Carter: In Search of the Great White House* (New York: Norton, 1980), 204.

9. Nixon promoted McGovern's link with the New Left to dislodge New Deal liberals and labor from his candidacy: Letter, Nixon to John Mitchell, 6 June 1972, H. R. Haldeman Notes of White House Meetings, 1969–1973, Roosevelt Study Center, Middelburg, Holland, File 18.0071; Robert Mason, *Richard Nixon and the Quest for a New Majority* (Chapel Hill: University of North Carolina Press, 2004), 162–164.

10. "Labor's Al Barkan," *New Republic*, 24 March 1973, 13–15. In contrast, Meany enjoyed relatively good relations with Richard Nixon considering he was a Republican president. Meany praised Nixon's foreign policy: Letter, Nixon to Meany, 23 December 1971, Haldeman Papers, File 88.0071; and the AFL-CIO endorsed his position on Vietnam: Memo, Haldeman to Nixon, 14 May 1970, Haldeman Papers, File 9.0003; Nixon was encouraged to pursue good relations as a means of expanding his electoral base into labor: Letter, Leo Marks to Nixon, 15 March 1973, Haldeman Papers, File 72.0057.

11. "Humphrey Resolved to Fight to Finish Despite Risks of Widening Party Rifts," *New York Times*, 7 July 1973, 10.

12. Bruce Miroff, *The Liberals' Moment: The McGovern Insurgency and the Identity Crisis of the Democratic Party* (Lawrence: University Press of Kansas, 2007), 250–253.

13. "The Fear of McGovern," *Washington Post*, 23 May 1972, B7.

14. "Reforms Within Democratic Party," *New York Times*, 7 March 1972, 38.

15. Letter, Karen DeCrow to NOW Politics Taskforce, 5 December 1972, Papers of the National Organization of Women, 1958–2002, Schlesinger Library, Radcliffe Institute, Harvard University, Boston, Mass., Box 48.

16. Thomas H. Hammon, "Another Look at the Rules in the 1972 Democratic Presidential Primaries," *Western Political Quarterly* 33 (1980): 50–72.

17. Byron E. Shafer, *Quiet Revolution: The Struggle for the Democratic Party and the Shaping of Post-Reform Politics* (New York: Russell Sage, 1983), 529–539.

18. Kandy Stroud, *How Jimmy Won: The Victory Campaign from Plains to the White House* (New York: William Morrow, 1977), 185–185.

19. Garland A. Haas, *Jimmy Carter and the Politics of Frustration* (Jefferson, N.C.: McFarland, 1992), 51–59.

20. Hargrove and Young, *Carter as President*, 15.

21. Morris, *Jimmy Carter, American Moralist*, 197; Glad, *Jimmy Carter*, 446–447.

22. Hargrove and Young, *Carter as President*, 1–13; Glad, *Jimmy Carter*, 487–507.

23. Interview with private source, 29 August 2006.

24. Jules Witcover, *Marathon: The Pursuit of the Presidency, 1972–1976* (New York: Viking Press, 1977), 113–127.

25. Charles O. Jones, *The Trusteeship Presidency: Jimmy Carter and the United States Congress* (Baton Rouge: Louisiana State University Press, 1988), 21–28.

26. "New Class: Tapped in to Post Watergate Anxiety About Government," *Washington Post*, 5 September 1976, 12; "The Clean Feeling of Achievement," *New Republic*, 14 March 1970, 9–11.

27. Introduction to Bob Woodward, *Shadow: Five Presidents and the Legacy of Watergate* (New York: Simon and Schuster, 2001).

28. Mark J. Rozell, *The Press and the Carter Presidency* (Boulder, Colo.: Westview, 1989), 235.

29. Herbert D. Rosenbaum and Alexej Ugrinsky, eds., *The Presidency and Domestic Policies of Jimmy Carter* (London: Greenwood Press, 1994), 126.

30. "Carter's Secret," *New York Magazine*, 22 March 1976, 25.

31. "Political Patter," *New Republic*, 7 February 1976, 2.

32. Peter N. Carroll, *It Seemed Like Nothing Happened: America in the 1970s* (Piscataway, N.J.: Rutgers University Press, 1990), 207–208.

33. Ronald Radosh, *Divided They Fell: The Demise of the Democratic Party, 1964–1996* (New York: Free Press, 1998), 112; for general literature on the antiwar movement, see Tom Wells, *The War Within: America's Battle over Vietnam* (Berkeley: University of California Press, 1994), 13–37; Melvin Small, *Antiwarriors: The Vietnam War and the Battle for America's Hearts and Minds* (New York: SR Press, 2002), 55–74.

34. Kevin M. Kruse, *White Flight: Atlanta and the Making of Modern Conservatism* (Princeton, N.J.: Princeton University Press, 2005), 234–258.

35. "'Welfare Queen' Becomes Issue in Reagan Campaign," *New York Times*, 15 February 1976, 51; Susan Douglas, *The Mommy Myth: The Idealization of Motherhood and How It Has Undermined All Women* (New York: Free Press, 2004), 193; Dan T. Carter, *From George Wallace to Newt Gingrich: Race and the Conservative Counter-Revolution 1963–1994* (Baton Rouge: Louisiana State University Press, 1996), 1–23.

36. Bruce J. Schulman, *The Seventies: The Great Shift in American Culture, Society and Politics* (Cambridge, Mass.: Da Capo Press, 2002), 1–20.

37. Richard Scammon and Ben Wattenberg, *The Real Majority* (New York: Coward-McCann, 1970), 35–45.

38. "NOW Origins: A Chronology of NOW, 1966–87," Papers of the National Organization of Women, 1958–2002, Schlesinger Library, Radcliffe Institute, Harvard University, Boston, Mass., Box 1.

39. Estelle B. Freedman, *No Turning Back: The History of Feminism and the Future of Women* (New York: Ballantine Books, 2002), 89–93.

40. Lisa McGirr, *Suburban Warriors: The Origins of the American New Right* (Princeton, N.J.: Princeton University Press, 2002), 217–261.

41. Donald T. Critchlow, "Mobilizing Women: The 'Social Issues,'" in *The Reagan Presidency: Pragmatic Conservatism and Its Legacies*, ed. W. Elliot Brownlee and Hugh Davis Graham (Lawrence: University Press of Kansas, 2003).

42. Donald T. Critchlow, *Phyllis Schlafly and Grassroots Conservatism: A Woman's Crusade* (Princeton, N.J.: Princeton University Press, 2005), 1–11; UPI report by Sarah Fritz, 21 November 1977, in Files of the Office of the First Lady, Jimmy Carter Library, Box 52.

43. Schulman, *Seventies*, 170.

44. For an excellent summary, see Allen Matusow, *Nixon's Economy Booms, Busts, Dollars and Votes* (Lawrence: University Press of Kansas, 1998); for liberal perspectives, see Press Release: "The Humphrey-Hawkins Bill: Lame Duck or Historic First?," undated, Hawkins Papers, Box 82; Letter, Keyserling to Hawkins, 24 May 1975, Hawkins Papers, Box 35; Letter, Hazel Henderson to Jerry Jasinowski, 14 September 1976, Hawkins Papers, Box 35; Letter, Keyserling to Jeff Goolsby, 15 November 1974, Meany Papers, Box 16.

45. "The Whirlwind Confronts the Skeptics," *Time*, 21 January 1974, 22.

46. Iwan Morgan, *Deficit Government: Taxing and Spending in Modern America* (Chicago: Ivan R. Dee, 1995), 116–117.

47. Alonzo Hamby, *Beyond the New Deal: Harry S. Truman and American Liberalism* (New York: Columbia University Press, 1973), 297–303; Form letter, Hawkins and Reuss to House Sponsors, 9 January 1975, Hawkins Papers, Box 82.

48. Edward D. Berkowitz, *Something Happened: A Political and Cultural Overview of the Seventies* (New York: Columbia University Press, 2006), 166.

49. "Economic Policy," *Congressional Almanac*, 1975, 91.

50. Michael Barone, *Our Country: The Shaping of America from Roosevelt to Reagan* (London: Collier Macmillan, 1990), 572; "Mutiny in California," *New Republic*, 3 June 1978, 5; "Massachusetts," *New Republic*, 4 November 1978, 20; Interview with Mike Dukakis, 14 September 2006.

51. Gary M. Fink and Hugh David Graham, *The Carter Presidency: Policy Choices in the Post–New Deal Era* (Chapel Hill: University of North Carolina Press, 2001), 95–117.

52. Schulman, *Seventies*, 121–122.

53. John Robert Greene, *The Presidency of Gerald R. Ford* (Lawrence: University Press of Kansas, 1995), 19–36.

54. Gerald R. Ford, *A Time to Heal: The Autobiography of Gerald R. Ford* (New York: Harper and Row, 1979), 351–353.

55. John Robert Greene, "A Nice Person Who Worked at the Job: The Dilemma of the Ford Image," in *Gerald R. Ford and the Politics of Post-Watergate America*, ed. Bernard J. Firestone and Alexej Ugrinsky (Westport, Conn.: Greenwood Press, 1993).

56. Craig Shirley, *Reagan's Revolution: The Untold Story of the Campaign That Started It All* (Washington, D.C.: Intercollegiate Studies Institute, 2008), 92.

57. "The Shooting: A Victory Celebration That Ended with Shouts, Screams and Curses," *New York Times*, 6 June 1968, 21.

58. Frank Kusch, *Battleground Chicago: The Police and the 1968 Democratic Convention* (Westport, Conn.: Praeger, 2004), 31–42; "Police Battle Demonstrators in the Streets: Hundreds Injured," *New York Times*, 29 August 1968, 1.

59. Mark J. Rozell and William D. Pederson, eds., *FDR and the Modern Presidency: Leadership and Legacy* (Westport, Conn.: Praeger, 1997), 6.

60. William E. Leuchtenberg, *The FDR Years: On Roosevelt and His Legacy* (New York: Columbia University Press, 1995), 283–305.

61. Ronald Edsforth, *The New Deal: America's Response to the Great Depression* (Oxford: Blackwell, 2000), 255; John M. Allswang, *The New Deal and American Politics: A Study in Political Change* (New York: Wiley, 1978), 113–132.

62. Samuel Lubell, "The Roosevelt Coalition," in *New Deal: Analysis and Interpretation*, ed. Alonzo Hamby (New York: Longman, 1981), 143–164; Stephen Lubell, *The Future of American Politics* (New York: Harper and Row, 1965), 44.

63. Jonathan Bell, *The Liberal State on Trial: The Cold War and American Politics in the Truman Years* (New York: Columbia University Press, 2004), 18; Carl Solberg, *Hubert Humphrey: A Biography* (New York: Norton, 1994), 457.

64. William E. Leuchtenburg, *In the Shadow of FDR: From Harry Truman to Ronald Reagan* (Ithaca, N.Y.: Cornell University Press, 1993), 121–160; Donald F. Kettl, "The Economic Education of Lyndon Johnson: Guns, Butter, and Taxes," in *The Johnson Years*, Volume 2, ed. Robert A. Divine (Austin: University of Texas Press, 1988).

65. "Again, Signs in the Air That the Democrats Plan Bloc Party," *New York Times*, 7 March 1976, E15; Robert Gordon Kaufman, *Henry M. Jackson: A Life in Politics* (Seattle: University of Washington Press, 2000), 323–340.

66. Haas, *Politics of Frustration*, 16–17.

67. For work on New Politics, see Byron E. Shafer, *Partisan Approaches to American Politics* (London: Chatham House, 1998), 102; David Gopian, Derek J. Hackett, Daniel Parelman, and Leo Perotta, "Coalitions in the Eighties: A Reassessment of Ladd's Old Class/New Class Explanation of Intra-Party Conflict," *Western Political Quarterly* 40 (1986): 247–264; Everett Carll Ladd Jr., *Where Have All the Voters Gone?* (New York: Norton, 1978), 37; Everett Carll Ladd Jr. and Charles D. Hadley, *Transformations of the American Party System: Political Coalitions from the New Deal to the 1970s* (New York: Norton, 1975), 182–191.

68. Theodore White, *The Making of the President, 1972* (New York: Scribner, 1985), 96–97; Patrick Cox, *Ralph W. Yarborough, the People's Senator* (Austin:

University of Texas Press, 2001), 255–262; "The Party's Over," *Atlantic Magazine*, March 1972, 33–39; Interview with Don Lippincott, 16 September 2006.

69. "Power Struggle," *New Republic*, 16 December 1972; "McGovern: Why His Team Keeps Winning," *Life*, 2 June 1972, 38–46.

70. Letter, McGovern to ADA membership, 28 April 1972, Moynihan Papers, Box 382; This included attacking defense appropriations: Memo, William E. Timmons to Nixon, 1 August 1972, Annotated Nixon Papers, File 235.

71. Howard E. Covington, *Terry Sanford: Politics, Progress, and Outrageous Ambitions* (Durham, N.C.: Duke University Press, 1999), 246–257.

72. Robert Sam Anson, *George McGovern: A Biography* (New York: Holt, Rinehart and Winston, 1972), 275.

73. "What to Do About the Economy," *New Republic*, 7–14 August 1971, 16–18.

74. "The Democratic Party," *New Republic*, 24 November 1973, 16–19.

75. Norval D. Glenn, "Class and Party Support in 1972," *Public Opinion Quarterly* 39 (1975): 1–20; "Nader on Antitrust," *New Republic*, 26 June 1971, 11–12; Ralph Nader and Mark J. Green, introduction to *Corporate Power in America* (Harmondsworth, U.K.: Penguin, 1977).

76. "Strip Mine Bill Veto Is Upheld by House on a 3 Vote Margin," *New York Times*, 11 June 1975, 89.

77. Norman Mailer, *Miami and the Siege of Chicago: An Informal History of the American Political Conventions of 1968* (London: Weidenfeld and Nicolson, 1969), 83.

78. "Harris Bows Out," *Time*, 22 November 1971, 22.

79. Interview with Fred Harris, 8 August 2006.

80. "Harris Regards Key Issue as Need to Fight Privilege," *New York Times*, 26 December 1975, 1.

81. "George Wallace Again?," *New York Times*, 6 July 1975, 131.

82. Jody Carlson, *George C. Wallace and the Politics of Powerlessness: The Wallace Campaigns for the Presidency, 1964–76* (New Bunswick, N.J.: Transaction Books, 1981), 157–172.

83. Much of labor in fact held back from supporting Jackson in the hope that Senator Hubert Humphrey might enter the race. This was another good example of the debilitating division within the party's ranks. Kaufman, *Henry M. Jackson*, 332.

84. Witcover, *Marathon*, 206–235.

85. Marlene M. Pomper, ed., *The Election of 1976: Reports and Interpretations* (D. McKay, 1977), 10–18.

86. Haas, *Politics of Frustration*, 26–32.

87. "Wallace Defeat," *New York Times*, 25 March 1976, 34.

88. "The Well Planned Enigma of Jimmy Carter," *New York Times*, 6 June 1976, 195; Jones, *Trusteeship Presidency*, 25–35.

89. "Working in the System," *New Republic*, 3–10 July 1976, 13.

90. John A. Farrell, *Tip O'Neill and the Democratic Century* (Boston: Little, Brown, 2001), 442.

91. Paul E. Tsongas, *Journey of Purpose: Reflections on the Presidency, Multi-

culturalism, and Third Parties (New Haven, Conn.: Yale University Press, 1995), 16.

92. Letter, O'Neill to Olin E. Teague, 26 November 1974, Leadership Files, O'Neill Papers, Box 1; Letter, Lonnie McCain to William Welch, 2 December 1974, Hart Papers, Box 53. For comprehensive studies on this phenomenon and its effect on legislation and the whipping system, see essays in Joel Silbey, ed., *The Modern American Congress 8, 1963–1989* (New York: Carlson, 1991); Iwan Morgan, *Beyond the Liberal Consensus: A Political History of the United States Since 1965* (London: Hurst, 1994), 134.

93. "Brown: Test by Rorschach," *Time*, 31 May 1976, 8.

94. "Brown: How the Guru Governs," *Time*, 26 April 1976, 19.

95. "Brown's 16-Month Record Shows Perplexing Array of Ambition and Accomplishment," *New York Times*, 7 June 1976 22.

96. "Proteus Californias," *New Republic*, 28 January 1978, 19.

97. "Brown Ahead of 3 in Gallup Poll," *New York Times*, 3 April 1976, 12.

98. "Brown Cites Differences with Carter in Quest for Oregon Write-in Victory," *New York Times*, 23 May 1976, 32.

99. "Stop Carter Bloc Keeping Up Fight against the Odds; but Loose Alliance Shows Signs of Weakness and Lacks Key Support," *New York Times*, 30 May 1976, 1.

100. Haas, *Politics of Frustration*, 35–44.

101. Interview with Stuart Eizenstat, 21 September 2006; Carter later expressed the view that it was this period of negotiation that weakened both his presidential candidacy and his administration, tying him to promises he could not fulfill. Interview with Jimmy Carter, 29 November 1982, Miller Center, University of Virginia, Jimmy Carter Presidential Oral History Project, 43.

102. Interview with Don Stillman, 25 September 2006.

103. "Carter Faces the 'Fuzziness' Issue," *Time*, 31 May 1976, 10.

104. "Carter and Co. Meet New York," *Time*, 21 July 1976, 14–21.

105. Dennis G. Sullivan, "Party Unity: Appearance and Reality," *Political Science Quarterly* 92 (1977): 635–646.

106. "Detractors and Supporters Agree His Positions Are Genuine; Mondale: A Liberal Who Sometimes Gives Up," *New York Times*, 18 July 1976, 113; "Give a Little, Take a Little," *Wall Street Journal*, 25 June 1976, 32.

107. "AFL-CIO Pledges Support to Carter," *New York Times*, 20 July 1976, 1.

108. "Election Shows Labor's Return to Democrats," *L.A. Times*, 4 November 1976, B3.

109. Kaufman, *Presidency of James Earl Carter Jr.*, 16–18.

110. "Legionnaires Boo Carter on Pardon on Draft Defiers," *New York Times*, 25 August 1976, 1.

111. "Carter's Comments on Sex Cause Concern," *New York Times*, 23 September 1976, 36.

112. "Ethnics Score Ford on Europe View," *New York Times*, 8 October 1976, 1.

113. Privately circulated copy of Memo, Caddell to Carter, 10 December 1976, Papers of President Douglas Fraser, UAW Collection, Walter P. Reuther Library, Wayne State University, Detroit, Mich., Box 49.

114. Jones, *Trusteeship Presidency*, 6–9.

115. Jonah Raskin, *For the Hell of It: The Life and Times of Abbie Hoffman* (Berkeley: University of California Press, 1996), 226; DNC daily political report no. 100, Papers of Sarah Weddington, Jimmy Carter Library, Box 39.

116. Leaflet, "The Fight for the Equal Rights Amendment," undated, Box 89.

117. Press Release, "AFL-CIO," 23 October 1973, NOW Papers, Box 47; Letter, Heide to Meany, 22 October 1973, Box 192.

118. "Fact Sheet: Coalition of Labor Union Women," undated, Box 89.

119. "Labor Is Key to ERA's Big Victory Bid," *Sunday News*, 2 October 1977, Box 139.

120. Resolution (adopted unanimously) at NOW conference, Virginia, 12 August 1979, Box 194; many labor activists thought that "the forces behind the ERA defeats—big business and its government— . . . disguise the fact that the ERA issue is a class issue": "The Fight for the Equal Rights Amendment," article, undated, in Box 89.

121. "List of Organizations Running ERA Fight," undated, Box 177.

122. Letter, Lizzie M. Corbin and Barbara G. Lomax to NOW Executive, 18 November 1977, Box 177; Article in *Richmond Times Dispatch*, 6 January 1978, in Box 177.

123. Article in *Washington Post*, 31 October 1977, in Box 177.

124. David Garrow, *Privacy and Sexuality: The Right to Privacy in Roe vs. Wade* (New York: Macmillan, 1994), 473–599.

125. Shifting attitudes toward individual issues are detectable throughout the decade: "Tolerance on Sex Is Found Growing," *New York Times*, 12 August 1973, 21; "Gallup Study Finds Greater Tolerance of Mixed Marriage," *New York Times*, 19 November 1979, 57; "Homosexuals Are Moving Toward Open Way of Life as Tolerance Rises Among the General Population," *New York Times*, 17 July 1977, 34; "Catholics in Survey Back Some Abortion," *New York Times*, 11 November 1979, 43.

126. This is demonstrated by a comparison of two polls from 1972 and 1976. In 1972, 58 percent of respondents listed either "social issues" or "Vietnam" as the most pressing problem facing America. Just 24 percent listed inflation or joblessness. In 1976, 58 percent of respondents listed either inflation or joblessness as their most pressing concern, and just 12 percent listed a social or diplomatic issue. Gallup Poll, 13–15 October 1972, Roper Center and CBS/*New York Times* Poll, 4–8 November 1976, Roper Center.

127. "What the Voters Want," *New Republic*, 23 October 1976, 16.

128. Joel Paddock, "Beyond the New Deal: Ideological Differences Between Eleven State Democratic Parties, 1956–1980," *Western Political Quarterly* 43 (1990): 181–190.

129. "Employment Planning Bills May Be '76 Issues," *Congressional Quarterly*, 6 December 1975, 2628; Letter, Hawkins to Prof. R. A. Nixon, 8 May 1973, Hawkins Papers, Box 84.

130. Letter, Humphrey to Sar A. Levitan, 20 July 1977, Case Files, Humphrey Papers, Box 2; Press Release, "Humphrey on Welfare," 1972, Humphrey Papers, Box 150.K.9.3(B); Timothy Nels Thurber, *The Politics of Equality: Hubert H.*

Humphrey and the African American Freedom Struggle (New York: Columbia University Press, 1999), 247.

131. "Jobs for all is a majority issue; it directly affects the lives and working conditions of over 80 million employed adults, not merely the un- or nonemployed minority." "Full Employment as a Policy Issue," undated, Hawkins Papers, Box 82; Hawkins explained, "Racializing an issue defeats my purpose—which is to get people on my side. Blacks might profit from it, but it affects all people in the country. A job is a right in this country and we are trying to see that everyone who is willing and able can work." "The Other, Unknown Half of Humphrey-Hawkins," *Washington Post*, 1 February 1978, 16.

132. William Julius Wilson, *The Truly Disadvantaged: The Inner City, the Underclass and Public Policy* (Chicago: University of Chicago Press, 1988), 120.

133. "Conservatives who are opposed to large governmental programs of social provision understand well that Social Security is hard to cut back as long as it has middle-class support. . . . Americans will accept taxes that they perceive as contributions toward public programs in which there is a direct stake for themselves." Theda Skocpol, *Social Policy in the United States: Future Possibilities in Historical Perspective* (Princeton, N.J.: Princeton University Press, 1995), 7, 270. For comprehensive essays on this debate, see Margaret Weir, Ann Shola Orloff, and Theda Skocpol, eds., *The Politics of Social Policy in the United States* (Princeton, N.J.: Princeton University Press, 1988).

134. Press Release, "Reordering Economic Priorities," undated, Hart Papers, Box 54. Hart supported a "Full Employment Economic Policy" because he wanted "to replace the demeaning system of handouts with the dignity of self-sufficiency." Press Release, "An Agenda for Colorado," undated, Hart Papers, Box 54. Note that in the 1990s, some Democrats would return to the concept of government-supported employment as an alternative to employment: Mickey Kaus, *The End of Equality* (New York: HarperCollins, 1992), 136–148.

135. "Democratic Consensus," *New York Times*, 13 June 1976, 29; "1976 Democratic Party Platform," undated, Records of the Office of Congressional Liaison, Jimmy Carter Library, Box 8; note the nominee's "passionate" support for H.R.50 throughout the election: Carter told reporters, "I'd put my emphasis on employment and take my chances on inflation." "Carter's Economics," *New York Times*, 14 July 1976, 65; "No economic theory received more of a steady sounding from candidate Carter than the need for full employment": Article in the *St. Louis Post Dispatch*, 17 September 1977, in Hawkins Papers, Box 84.

136. "Many Votes Split; G.O.P. Loses Senate Seats in 6 States and Picks Up 4 Others: Democrats Retain Control of Both Senate and House," *New York Times*, 8 November 1972, 1.

137. Importantly, these elections all but wiped out Republican gains from 1966 to 1972, weakening the unofficial "conservative caucus" in the House: Christopher J. Bailey, *The Republican Party in the U.S. Senate* (Manchester: Manchester University Press, 1988), 54.

138. "'76 House Vote Portends Problems for the GOP," *Congressional Quarterly*, 31 March 1979, 571.

139. Jack M. Mcleod, Jane D. Brown, and Lee B. Becker, "Watergate and the 1974 Congressional Elections," *Public Opinion Quarterly* 41 (1977): 181–195.

140. "A New Candidate Wins with an Old Coalition," *Congressional Quarterly Almanac*, 1976, 820–821; "Moynihan and Carter Breathe New Life into an Old Coalition," Empire State Report, December 1976, in Moynihan Papers, Box 429.

141. Arthur H. Miller, "Partisanship Re-instated? A Comparison of the 1972 and 1976 U.S. Presidential Elections," *British Journal of Political Science* 8 (1978): 129–152; "Election Shows Labor's Return to Democrats," *L.A. Times*, 4 November 1976, B3.

142. Alfred E. Eckes Jr. and Eugene H. Rosenboom, *A History of Presidential Elections, from George Washington to Jimmy Carter* (New York: Macmillan, 1979), 336.

143. "Democrats Add One More Governorship," *Congressional Quarterly Almanac*, 1976, 834–835.

144. "Democrats vs. Mr. Carter," *New York Times*, 1 September 1976, 4.

145. "Patrick Moynihan, Liberal," *New Republic*, October 30 1976, 6–7; Memo, untitled (postelection analysis), November 1976, Moynihan Papers, Box 490.

146. Memo, "Votes Cast on November 2, 1976," undated, Moynihan Papers, Box 490.

147. This was the publicly stated view of Moynihan: "The Liberal's Dilemma," *New Republic*, 22 January 1977, 57.

148. Memo, John E. Barriere to Spenser S. Smith, undated, Leadership Files, O'Neill Papers, Box 1; this interpretation was supported by other pollsters too: CBS/*New York Times* Poll, 4–8 November 1976, Roper Center; "Candidates Far Apart on Jobs and Inflation," *Congressional Quarterly*, 18 September 1976, 2221.

149. Unquestionably, the absence from the race of both Hubert Humphrey and Kennedy skewered the returns and took away any heavyweight challenge that Carter might have faced. "Humphrey and Kennedy?," *New York Times*, 1 June 1976, 35.

Chapter 2: The Man from Massachusetts

1. Adam Clymer, *Edward M. Kennedy: A Biography* (New York: William Morrow, 1999), 21.

2. Thomas R. Burner and David West, *The Torch Is Passed: The Kennedy Brothers and American Liberalism* (New York: Atheneum, 1984), 247.

3. Garry Wills, *The Kennedys: A Shattered Illusion* (London: Orbis Books, 1980), 290.

4. Collier and Horowitz argue that much of Edward Kennedy's behavior can be explained through the paradoxical mix of power and irresponsibility that was the result of his status as the youngest brother. Thus, by turning down the nomination in 1968, he was "asserting his right to be the youngest, beyond obligation and responsibility." Peter Collier and David Horowitz, *The Kennedys* (Ontario: Summit Books, 1984), 365.

5. "Teddy Kennedy Has No Regrets," *New York Magazine*, 14 August 1980, 26.

6. Burton Hersch, *The Shadow President: Ted Kennedy in Opposition* (New York: Steerforth Press, 1997), 100.

7. Rose Fitzgerald Kennedy, *Times to Remember* (New York: Doubleday, 1974), 156.

8. Clymer, *Edward Kennedy*, 21–24.

9. Arthur Schlesinger, *Robert Kennedy and His Times* (Boston: Houghton Mifflin Harcourt, 2002), 371.

10. "Edward Kennedy Tours in Vietnam," *New York Times*, 25 October 1965, 7.

11. "Ted Kennedy: The Dogged Achiever," *Time*, 14 April 2006.

12. Burner and West, *Torch Is Passed*, 224–225.

13. Garry Wills, *The Kennedy Imprisonment: A Meditation on Power* (Boston: Houghton Mifflin, 2002), 9.

14. "Teddy's Ordeal," *Time*, 26 June 1964, 21.

15. Clymer, *Edward Kennedy*, 59–64.

16. Wills, *Kennedy Imprisonment*, 89.

17. Collier and Horowitz, *Kennedys*, 364–365.

18. "Text of Edward Kennedy's Tribute to His Brother in Cathedral," *New York Times*, 9 June 1968, 56.

19. Burton Hersch, *The Education of Edward Kennedy: A Family Biography* (New York: William Morrow, 1972), 283.

20. William Homes Honan, *Ted Kennedy, Profile of a Survivor: Edward M. Kennedy After Bobby, After Chappaquiddick, and After Three Years of Nixon* (New York: Quadrangle Books, 1972), 47.

21. Thomas Maier, *The Kennedys: America's Emerald Kings* (New York: Basic Books, 2003), 512.

22. "Kennedy Is Rated High for '72 Race," *New York Times*, 9 March 1969, 46.

23. "The Non-Candidacy of Edward Moore Kennedy," *Time*, 29 November 1971, 16.

24. "Can Teddy Kennedy Survive His Reputation?," *New York Times*, 24 May 1970, SM13.

25. Leo Damore, *Senatorial Privilege: The Chappaquiddick Cover-up* (Washington, D.C.: Regnery Gateway, 1988), 1–14.

26. "Kennedy's Career Feared Imperiled; Friends Express Concern over Accident's Effects," *New York Times*, 21 July 1969, 19; Mel Ayton, *Questions of Controversy: The Kennedy Brothers* (Sunderland, U.K.: University of Sunderland Press, 2001), 309–333.

27. Wills, *Shattered Illusion*, 53–56.

28. "Can Teddy Kennedy Survive His Reputation?," *New York Times*, 24 May 1970, SM13.

29. "Kennedy Ousted as Whip," *New York Times*, 22 January 1971, 1.

30. Robert Dallek, *An Unfinished Life: John F. Kennedy, 1917–1963* (Boston: Little, Brown, 2003), 295, 786–787.

31. Ayton, *Questions of Controversy*, 289–307.

32. Lester David, *Good Ted, Bad Ted: The Two Faces of Edward Kennedy* (New York: Carol Publishing Group, 1993), 239–240.

33. This overt covering up of the breakdown of their marriage was not isolated; see "Joan Kennedy: Her Search for Herself," *Ladies' Home Journal*, May 1973, in Clymer Papers, Box 24; "The Vulnerable Soul of Joansie," *Time*, 5 November 1979, 19.

34. Susannah Lessard Powell, "Kennedy's Women Problem—Women's Kennedy Problem," originally to appear in print in *New Republic*, but withdrawn and printed in *Washington Monthly*. Undated, in White House Press Office, Jimmy Carter Library, Box 17.

35. Article in the *Boston Globe*, 13 July 1973, in Clymer Papers, Box 24.

36. "The events are a millstone around his neck that just won't go away." Tip O'Neill with William Novak, *Man of the House: The Life and Political Memoirs of Speaker Tip O'Neill* (New York: Random House, 1987), 326. Bumpers didn't think it could work out either: "I just didn't think that with Chappaquiddick especially in the background he could overcome that." Interview with Dale Bumpers, 20 April 1998, Clymer Papers, Box 3.

37. "Themes: Notes on the Campaign," Theodore C. Sorenson (Chaikin), 1928–: Papers, 1934–94, JFK Library.

38. "Kennedy Question Mark," *New York Times*, 22 July 1971, 33; "Teddy: Will He Run or Won't He?," *Newsweek*, 14 November 1971, 37.

39. Interview with Paul Kirk, 6 July 1992, Clymer Papers, Box 4.

40. Kennedy was taking 29 percent in Gallup predictions, a good 8 percent ahead of his nearest competitor, Muskie; "Despite His Lead in Gallup Polls Kennedy Won't Run," *New York Times*, 23 May 1971, 30; "Kennedy Gets Lead on Muskie," *Washington Post*, 26 December 1971, A22; "Draft Kennedy Talk Rises," *Washington Star*, 6 April 1972, A6; "Kennedyites Aid McGovern, but Their Hearts Belong to Kennedy," *Miami Herald*, 13 April 1972, 31A.

41. Article, "Marianne Means," *Washington Post*, 25 April 1972, in Correspondence Files, Humphrey Papers, Box 150.J.13.10(F).

42. "CBS News Special with Roger Mudd," MR2002-11 Q, Kennedy, Edward Moore, 1932–: Audiovisual Archives, JFK Library.

43. "Edward Kennedy: Now the Hope," *Time*, 20 November 1972, 28.

44. "George McGovern Finally Finds a Veep," *Time*, 14 August 1972, 15.

45. Fred Emery, *Watergate: The Corruption and Fall of Richard Nixon* (New York: Touchstone, 1995), 33, 106.

46. "Kennedy Quiet Until the Storm," *Boston Globe*, 12 April 1972, 14.

47. Letter, Haldeman to Nixon, 16 June 1970, Annotated Nixon Papers, File 80; Memo, Bruce Kehrli to Charles Colson, 27 January 1972, Annotated Nixon Papers, File 204; Private Notes at Cabinet Meeting, 30 October 1971, Haldeman Private Notes; "Mitchell Sees Kennedy Plot," *Boston Globe*, 1 May 1972, 12.

48. "Jackson up Front in 1976 Pack," *New York Times*, 8 February 1974, 8.

49. "Kennedy Is Ahead of Ford in Poll Despite Disavowal of Candidacy," *New York Times*, 10 August 1975, 33; "Kennedy Is First in Gallup Survey," *New York Times*, 25 May 1975, 44.

50. "Still Bored with Ford," *New York Times*, 21 August 1975, 802.

51. "Winners and Losers," *Time*, 26 August 1974, 21.

52. "Kennedy's Son Ends Treatment for Cancer," *New York Times*, 7 June 1975, 57.

53. "Kennedy Noncampaign: Some Read a No as Yes," *New York Times*, 18 November 1971, 20; "Kennedy Candidacy Is Denied by O'Neill," *New York Times*, 1 August 1975, 37.

54. "Kennedy and Brown Ahead of Ford in California Poll," *New York Times*, 29 November 1975, 20.

55. "Carter's Plan to Scoop It Up," *Time*, 14 June 1976, 12.

56. Wills, *Shattered Illusion*, 196.

57. "Kennedy, in Minor Role, Still Shining Like a Star," *New York Times*, 15 July 1976, 27; Article in *Boston Globe*, 14 July 1976, in Clymer Papers, Box 24.

58. Collier and Horowitz, *Kennedys*, 576.

59. Burner and West, *Torch Is Passed*, 241–243.

60. Ronald P. Formisano, *Boston Against Busing: Race, Class, and Ethnicity in the 1960s and 1970s* (Chapel Hill: University of North Carolina Press, 1991), 203–221.

61. "Kennedy Jeered on Boston Busing," *New York Times*, 10 September 1974, 1.

62. Interview with Bob Bates, 21 September 1994, Clymer Papers, Box 3.

63. Formisano, *Boston Against Busing*, 236.

64. Maier, *America's Emerald Kings*, 546–548. He was an open advocate of women serving as priests. Interview with Natalie Jacobson, 29 October 1994, Clymer Papers, Box 4.

65. Interview with Paul Tsongas, 12 December 1994, Clymer Papers, Box 5.

66. Interview with Joseph P. Kennedy III, 10 January 1995, Clymer Papers, Box 4.

67. Interview with Bob Bates, 21 September 1994, Clymer Papers, Box 3.

68. Interview with Drummond Ayres, 28 August 1997, Clymer Papers, Box 3.

69. "Kennedy Gives Priority to Antitrust Policy and to the Criminal Code," *New York Times*, 5 January 1979, A24.

70. "Kennedy for Eastland," *Washington Post*, 27 March 1978, 8.

71. Letter, Kennedy to O'Neill, undated, Personal Files, O'Neill Papers, Box 19; Press Release, "The Economy," 7 February 1980, Legislative Files, O'Neill Papers, Box 41.

72. Press Release, "We Must Let Our Airline Service Slip Away," 9 August 1980, McGovern Papers, Box 809; Interview with George McGovern, 27 July 2006. It also led to conflict with some unions: Memo, Gail Harrison to Mondale, 10 August 1979, Bill Smith Files, Mondale Papers, Box 2.

73. O'Neill, *Man of the House*, 88.

74. Interview with Walter Mondale, 7 June 2007.

75. John A. Farrell, *Tip O'Neill and the Democratic Century* (Boston: Little, Brown, 2001), 454–456.

76. Memo, Spencer M. Smith Jr. to John E. Barrier, 16 November 1976, Leadership Files, O'Neill Papers, Box 30; Arthur H. Miller, "Partisanship Re-instated? A Comparison of the 1972 and 1976 U.S. Presidential Elections," *British Journal of Political Science* 8 (1978): 129–152.

77. Jimmy Carter, *Keeping Faith: Memoirs of a President* (New York: Bantam, 1983), 77.

78. Minutes, Leadership Breakfast Meeting, 3 May 1977, Staff Files, O'Neill Papers, Box 9.

79. Letter, Butler Derick to O'Neill, undated, Leadership Files, O'Neill Papers, Box 1.

80. "Crowd Delighted as Carters Shun Limousine and Walk to New Home," *New York Times*, 21 January 1977, 1.

81. "Carter's New TV Ads Stress Complexity of His Job; Grasp of Complex Issues Drama in a Town Meeting," *New York Times*, 7 September 1977, 33.

82. Edward D. Berkowitz, *Something Happened: A Political and Cultural Overview of the Seventies* (New York: Columbia University Press, 2006), 105–107.

83. "To Fashion a Blanket of Pardon," *New York Times*, 10 January 1977, 14.

84. John Dumbrell, *The Carter Presidency: A Re-evaluation* (Manchester: Manchester University Press, 1995), 12–15.

85. "Lancegate," *New York Times*, 11 August 1977, 17.

86. Farrell, *Tip O'Neill*, 448.

87. "Here Comes Mr. Jordan," *Time*, 30 July 1979, 22.

88. Charles O. Jones, *The Trusteeship Presidency: Jimmy Carter and the United States Congress* (Baton Rouge: Louisiana State University Press, 1988), 2–9.

89. Ibid., 21–23.

90. Garland A. Haas, *Jimmy Carter and the Politics of Frustration* (Jefferson, N.C.: McFarland, 1992), 63–67.

91. "Tax Rebate Reversal Criticized by Muskie," *New York Times*, 27 April 1977, 13; Farrell, *Tip O'Neill*, 459.

92. Press Release, 21 February 1977, Hart Papers, Box 183.

93. Press Release, 14 June 1978, Hart Papers, Box 55.

94. "Hart Admits Recession Has Made a Balanced Budget Unlikely," *Greeley Tribune*, 14 May 1980, 5.

95. "Hart Calls Carter's Policies 'Hoover Economics,'" *Greeley Tribune*, 28 April 1980, 5.

96. "$459.2 Billion Budget Approved by Senate," *New York Times*, 10 September 1977, 9.

97. "Cattle, Hog and Pork Bellies Soar to Limits; Soybeans and Grain Also Show Increase," *New York Times*, 23 March 1978, D12.

98. Speech by George Meany on the administration's economic proposals, November 1978, Meany Papers, Box 86.

99. "Carter May Ask Delay in Pay Raise," *New York Times*, 8 December 1978, D1.

100. Haas, *Politics of Frustration*, 93–96.

101. Iwan Morgan, *Deficit Government: Taxing and Spending in Modern America* (Chicago: Ivan R. Dee, 1995), 128.

102. "The Great Energy Mess," *Time*, 2 July 1979, 14–27.

103. Burton I. Kaufman, *The Presidency of James Earl Carter Jr.* (Lawrence: University Press of Kansas, 1993), 116.

104. Haas, *Politics of Frustration*, 65.

105. W. Carl Biven, *Jimmy Carter's Economy: Policy in an Age of Limits* (Chapel Hill: University of North Carolina Press, 2002), 3–4.

106. Adam Clymer, *Drawing the Line at the Big Ditch: The Panama Canal Treaties and the Rise of the Right* (Lawrence: University Press of Kansas, 2008).

107. Carter, *Keeping Faith*, 283–284.

108. Dumbrell, *Carter Presidency*, 12–15; William B. Quandt, *Camp David: Peacemaking and Politics* (Washington, D.C.: Brookings Institution Press, 1986), 237–258.

109. Erwin C. Hargrove and James Sterling Young, *Jimmy Carter as President: Leadership and the Politics of Public Good* (Baton Rouge: Louisiana State University Press, 1988), 128.

110. Charles O. Jones, *The Presidency in a Separated System* (Washington, D.C.: Brookings Institution Press, 2005), 159–160.

111. "Bold Plan by Carter Presses for Upset in the Reagan Power Base," *New York Times*, 22 September 1980, B4; "Carter and Kennedy Ads Go Their Separate Ways," *New York Times*, 19 March 1980, B10.

112. Steven M. Gillon, *The Democrats' Dilemma: Walter F. Mondale and the Liberal Legacy* (New York: Columbia University Press, 1994), 256.

113. "Carter at Midterm: Satisfied So Far but Ready to Admit His Mistakes," *New York Times*, 6 November 1978, 1.

114. Kenneth E. Morris, *Jimmy Carter, American Moralist* (Athens: University of Georgia Press, 1996), 55.

115. Letter, Albert Shaw to Hawkins, 2 April 1979, Hawkins Papers, Box 15.

116. Memo, Eizenstat to Carter, 24 May 1977, DPS, Jimmy Carter Library, Box 22.

117. Interview with Walter Mondale, 7 June 2007.

118. Memo, Lance to Carter, 31 May 1977, DPS, Jimmy Carter Library, Box 22.

119. Memo, Lyle E. Gramley to Schultze, 12 July 1977, DPS, Jimmy Carter Library, Box 22.

120. "Carter Endorses Modified Version of Humphrey-Hawkins Job Bills," *New York Times*, 15 November 1977, 85; "The Humphrey-Hawkins Bill: Lame Duck or Historic First?," undated, Hawkins Papers, Box 82.

121. "Humphrey-Hawkins Debate: House Rejects GOP Move to Set Inflation Target," *Congressional Quarterly*, 11 March 1978, 617; Article in *Washington Post*, 24 November 1977, in Hawkins Papers, Box 82.

122. Article in *Washington Post*, 15 November 1977, in Hawkins Papers, Box 82.

123. Article in *Business Week*, 20 March 1978, in Hawkins Papers, Box 82; "Humphrey-Hawkins Outlook," *Congressional Quarterly*, 9 September 1978, 2422.

124. "Public Law 95-523" (H.R. 50), 27 October 1978, Hawkins Papers, Box 11; Article in *Washington Post*, 13 October 1978, in Hawkins Papers, Box 82.

125. "Humphrey-Hawkins Bill: A Victory of Sorts for Labor," *Congressional Quarterly*, 21 October 1978, 3102.

126. Article in *Washington Post*, 27 September 1978, in Hawkins Papers, Box 82.

127. Article in *Baltimore Sun*, 27 May 1977, in Hawkins Papers, Box 82. He was given an embarrassingly reserved reception at a Congressional Black Caucus fundraiser in September 1977, forcing him to extemporaneously promise immediate

action on H.R. 50: "Congressional Black Caucus Gathers for Session Marking Ten Years of Growth," *New York Times*, 26 September 1977, A12.

128. Memo, Eizenstat and Moore to Carter, 9 August 1978, DPS, Jimmy Carter Library, Box 22.

129. Emphasis added; Memo, Eizenstat, Schultze, Moore, Gerald Rafshoon, Anne Wexler to Carter, undated, DPS, Jimmy Carter Library, Box 22; on administration officials pushing for passage, see "Carter Aides List Bills for Priority in Final Weeks of Congress Session," *New York Times*, 24 July 1978, A7.

130. Letter, Douglas Fraser to Carter, 8 November 1977, Fraser Papers, Box 15; Memo, Peter Gould and Bill Spring to Schultze and Eizenstat, 22 July 1978, DPS, Jimmy Carter Library, Box 22.

131. "The Threat Behind Humphrey-Hawkins," *New York Times*, 13 October 1978, F12.

132. Elizabeth Drew, *Portrait of an Election: The 1980 Presidential Campaign* (New York: Routledge and Kegan Paul, 1981), 248.

133. Interview with Adam Clymer, 19 September 2006.

134. Stephen Skowronek, *The Politics That Presidents Make: Leadership from John Adams to Bill Clinton* (Cambridge, Mass.: Harvard University Press, 1993), 395.

135. Kant Patel and Mark E. Rushefsky, *Politics, Power and Policy Making: The Case of Health Care Reform in the 1990s* (New York: M. E. Sharpe, 1997), 8.

136. Berkowitz, *Something Happened*, 85.

137. Jacob S. Hacker, *The Divided Welfare State: The Battle over Public and Private Social Benefits in the United States* (Cambridge: Cambridge University Press, 2002), 221.

138. Haas, *Politics of Frustration*, 81–82.

139. "Lackluster Convention Lights Up," *Washington Post*, 10 December 1978, A1.

140. "Closing hospitals . . . means that blacks, Puerto Ricans and the poor will be sick more often. . . . Only national health insurance can end this fundamental form of discrimination." "Address to the Association for the Betterment of New York City," 5 March 1980, Clymer Papers, Box 9.

141. "Remarks of Senator Edward M. Kennedy: Montgomery, Alabama," 27 May 1980, Clymer Papers, Box 9.

142. Jill S. Quadagno, *One Nation Uninsured: Why the U.S. Has No National Health Insurance* (New York: Oxford University Press, 2005), 109–138.

143. "Comprehensive National Insurance Act of 1974," 2 April 1974, Social Security Department Papers, UAW Collection, Walter Reuther Library, Wayne State University, Detroit, Mich., Box 105; Interview with Stuart Altman, undated, Clymer Papers, Box 4.

144. Remarks by Leonard Woodcock before Executive Committee, 15 June 1977, Social Security Papers, UAW, Box 110; "Healthy Skepticism," *New Republic*, 29 April 1978, 10.

145. Memo, Mary to McGovern, 27 June 1979, McGovern Papers, Box 981.

146. "Insurance Bills for Health Fade," *New York Times*, 30 April 1973, 13.

147. Letter, Glasser to Woodcock, 3 October 1973, Social Security Papers, UAW, Box 105.

148. Letter, McGovern to Woodcock, 1 November 1975, Social Security Papers, UAW, Box 105.

149. Letter, Fraser to Kennedy, 7 September 1977, Social Security Papers, UAW, Box 105.

150. "Carter Gives Us New Hope for Action," speech by Fraser at conference on health care, 16 June 1977, Social Security Papers, UAW, Box 105.

151. Memo, Fine to CNHI Committee, 14 January 1976, Social Security Papers, UAW, Box 107.

152. Leaflet, "Why Unions Support NHI," by Vicki Kalmar, 13 January 1977, Minutes, Executive Meeting, 22 November 1977, Social Security Papers, UAW, Box 111.

153. Press Release, "Fraser Tells U.S. Senate Hearing of Health Disarray in Michigan," 23 October 1977, Social Security Papers, UAW, Box 111; Letter, Califano to Reginald H. Jones, 22 December 1977, Meany Papers, Box 39.

154. "Carter Backed by Auto Union Chief and Wins Praise of Henry Ford," *New York Times*, 8 May 1976, 10.

155. ". . . Domestically, He Is Going a Little Slower," *New York Times*, 27 February 1977, 135.

156. "Kennedy and Unions Said to Seek Revived Bill on Health Insurance," *New York Times*, 27 March 1978, A1.

157. Memo, Califano to Carter, 3 November 1977, Social Security Papers, UAW, Box 111.

158. Letter, Califano to Meany, 30 January 1978, Social Security Papers, UAW, Box 111.

159. "Carter's Social Security Proposal Raises Funding and Benefit Issues," *New York Times*, 16 May 1977, 60; "Health Insurance Backed at White House Session," *Washington Post*, 7 April 1978, A4; Memo, Glasser to Fraser on meeting with Califano, 3 January 1978, Social Security Papers, UAW, Box 111; Letter, Schlossberg to Butler, 2 December 1977, Social Security Papers, UAW, Box 75; Memo, Bert Seidman to Meany, 5 July 1978, Meany Papers, Box 39.

160. Minutes, CNHI Executive, 25 May 1978, Social Security Papers, UAW, Box 110.

161. "President Carter's National Health Plan Legislation," 12 June 1979, DPS, Jimmy Carter Library, Box 241; *Washington Post*, 30 June 1978; "Comparison of President Carter's National Health Plan and Other National Health Insurance Proposals," undated, Hart Papers, Box 8.

162. Press Release, CNHI, 18 March 1980, Social Security Papers, UAW, Box 111; "Broad National Health-Insurance Plan to Be Proposed Soon, Carter Indicates," *Wall Street Journal*, 27 June 1978; "Senate Panel Approves Hospital Cost Control," *Congressional Quarterly*, 19 May 1979, 988.

163. Speech at Yale by Leonard Woodcock, 3 June 1977, Fraser Papers, Box 73.

164. Press Release, "Fraser Urges Congress to Reject So Called Catastrophic Health Insurance," 29 November 1979, Social Security Papers, UAW, Box 107; Statement of Kennedy before Senate Finance Committee, 21 June 1979, DPS, Jimmy Carter Library, Box 241.

165. Memo, Bert Seidman to Meany, 28 June 1978, Meany Papers, Box 39; "Carter Announces National Health Plan," *Congressional Quarterly*, 16 June 1979, 1108.

166. Statement by Fraser before EEC Committee, 25 May 1978, Social Security Papers, UAW, Box 110; Memo, Bert Seidman to Meany, 5 May 1978, Meany Papers, Box 39.

167. Press Release, 7 August 1978, Social Security Papers, UAW, Box 107.

168. Minutes, CNHI Executive, 26 September 1978, Social Security Papers, UAW, Box 110.

169. Minutes, CNHI Executive, 20 March 1978, Social Security Papers, UAW, Box 110; Letter, Glasser to Beverly Meyers, 30 January 1978, Social Security Papers, UAW, Box 111.

170. "Kennedy Says Budget 'Undermines' U.S. Health Care," *New York Times*, 27 January 1979, 7.

171. Memo, Glasser to Fraser, 3 January 1978, Social Security Papers, UAW, Box 111.

172. Statement by the AFL-CIO Council on Health Legislation, 6 August 1979, Executive Minutes, Meany Library; "Administration's Health Policy in Trouble on Several Fronts," *Washington Post*, 22 June 1978, A2.

173. For Mondale's role, see Letter, Glasser to Fine, 9 December 1977, Social Security Papers, UAW, Box 111; "Advisers Ask Carter to Curb Health Insurance Plan," *New York Times*, 21 June 1978, A1.

174. Notes from meeting with Peter Bourne, 8 November 1977, Social Security Papers, UAW, Box 111.

175. Memo, Glasser to Fine, 20 December 1974, Social Security Papers, UAW, Box 105.

176. "Work Plan," 1978–1979, Social Security Papers, UAW, Box 110.

177. Letter, Fraser to James C. Corman, 15 June 1978, Social Security Papers, UAW, Box 54.

178. Press Release, 12 June 1979, Social Security Papers, UAW, Box 107, 970.

179. "Around the Nation," *New York Times*, 29 June 1978, A18; He reintroduced NHI as the Kennedy-Waxman Plan, essentially identical to his earlier proposals: "Kennedy, Labor Coalition Outline Comprehensive National Health Plan," *Congressional Quarterly*, 19 May 1979.

180. Memo, Bill Smith to Mondale, 15 January 1980, Bill Smith Files, Mondale Papers, Box 4.

181. Minutes, White House Leadership Meeting, 3 April 1979, Staff Files, O'Neill Papers, Box 9.

182. Carter, *Keeping Faith*, 84–87; Memo, Eizenstat to Carter, 6 April 1978, DPS, Jimmy Carter Library, Box 7; Interview with Eizenstat, 19 April 1992, Clymer Papers, Box 5.

183. "Kennedy, in Challenge to Carter, Introduces National Health Plan," *New York Times*, 15 May 1979, A1.

Chapter 3: Judgment at Memphis, 1978

1. Memo, James T. McIntyre and Moore to Carter, undated, *Handwriting Files, Jimmy Carter Library*, Box 111.

2. "Carter Imposes Voluntary Anti-Inflation Plan," *Congressional Quarterly*, 28 October 1978, 3118.

3. "MX: Tick, Tick, Tick," *New York Times*, 21 October 1980, A19.

4. Statement by the AFL-CIO Executive on the federal budget, 19 February 1979, Executive Minutes, George Meany Library, National Labor College, Washington, D.C.

5. Arthur O'Sullivan, Terri A. Sexton, and Steven M. Sheffrin, *Property Taxes and Tax Revolts: The Legacy of Proposition 13* (Cambridge: Cambridge University Press, 1995), 1–14.

6. Memo to participants in 9 February 1978 White House briefing, 9 February 1978, Meany Papers, Box 77; "AFL-CIO Hits Carter's Economic Package," *John Herling Labor Letter*, 15 January 1977; Letter, Leonard Woodcock to International Board Executive membership, 1 February 1978, Fraser Papers, Box 15.

7. Press Release, 20 January 1978, Meany Papers, Box 77; Press conference transcript, 19 February 1979, Meany Papers, Box 100.

8. "What Will They Do for New York?," 27 January 1980, *New York Times Magazine*, in Moynihan Papers, Box 2445.

9. "Keeping His Options Open," *Argus*, 12 August 1979, C1.

10. "Democrats to Meet in Memphis in '78," *New York Times*, 10 December 1977, 13.

11. "Missouri Compromise," *New York Times*, 10 December 1974, 45.

12. "Democrats Girding for Midterm Parley," *New York Times*, 7 December 1979, A20.

13. Andrew H. Busch, *Reagan's Victory: The Presidential Election of 1980 and the Rise of the Right* (Lawrence: University Press of Kansas, 2005), 23.

14. Memo, Steve to Fraser, 4 October 1977, Fraser Papers, Box 68; *L.A. Left* newsletter, September 79, Mandler Papers.

15. "Fraser Board Role Riles Critics, Raises Questions; New Role Staked Out by UAW's Fraser," *New York Times*, 26 November 1979, D1.

16. Interview with Douglas Fraser, 19 February 2007.

17. Nancy E. McGlen, *Women's Rights: The Struggle for Equality in the Nineteenth and Twentieth Centuries* (New York: Praeger, 1983), 309.

18. Memo, Lee Webb to Fraser, 26 December 1978, Fraser Papers, Box 68; Memo, Bill Dodds to Fraser, 4 June 1979, Fraser Papers, Box 68.

19. Memo, Howard Young to Fraser, 13 October 1978, Fraser Papers, Box 68.

20. Memo, Schlossberg to Fraser, 6 February 1979, Fraser Papers, Box 68.

21. Minutes, Progressive Alliance meeting, 28 February 1979, Fraser Papers, Box 68.

22. Memo, Howard Young to Fraser, 11 October 1978, Fraser Papers, Box 68; also see Letter, Fraser to Carter, 19 October 1978, Fraser Papers, Box 68.

23. The NCEC, or National Campaign for an Effective Congress, was a New Politics group established to reverse the growth in executive power. This was, broadly speaking, the goal of John Gardiner's Common Cause too: Memo, Steve to Fraser, 9 June 1977, Fraser Papers, Box 4.

24. Bruce Miroff, *The Liberals' Moment: The McGovern Insurgency and the Identity Crisis of the Democratic Party* (Lawrence: University Press of Kansas, 2007), 239; Letter, Richard Wagner to Meany, 12 August 1972, Meany Papers, Box 32.

25. "The Labor Scene; COPE's Impact on Election Outcome Labor: Effects of COPE's Aid in the Election," *New York Times*, 20 December 1976, 67; "The Annual Sunbath," *New Republic*, 12 March 1977, 12.

26. Letter, Meany to Carter, 9 November 1978, Handwriting Files, Jimmy Carter Library, Box 111.

27. "Council Presses Campaign for Key Legislative Goals," *AFL-CIO News*, 26 February 1977.

28. Memo, Eizenstat and Bill Johnston to Carter, undated, White House Central Files: LA-7, Jimmy Carter Library.

29. "Promises, Promises Well, at Least Some of Carter's," *New York Times*, 19 March 1977, 15.

30. Memo, Moore, Eizenstat to Carter, 25 August 1977, Leadership Files, O'Neill Papers, Box 20.

31. "Labor Turning from Lobbying to New Political Tactics in Growing Struggle for Influence on Legislation," *New York Times*, 23 June 1977, 15; "The George and Jimmy Show," *New Republic*, 21 May 1977, 28.

32. "Defeat of Situs Picketing," *John Herling Labor Letter*, 26 March 1977.

33. Letter, I. W. Abel, President, Industrial Union Department, AFL-CIO, to Carter, 5 March 1977, White House Central File: LA-7, Jimmy Carter Library; Letter, Meany to Carter, 14 February 1977, Meany Papers, Box 77; Telegram, Leonard Roque to Carter, 4 April 1980, Cabinet Secretary, Jimmy Carter Library, Box 3.

34. Letter, John Smith to Marc Stepp, 4 September 1979, Fraser Papers, Box 31; "Runaway Plants," *New Republic*, 26 May 1979.

35. Memo, Butler to Carter, 7 December 1978, Handwriting File, Jimmy Carter Library.

36. Press conference, transcript, 7 August 1978, Meany Papers, Box 100.

37. Letter, Elizabeth Niranga to Carter, 9 September 1976, NOW Papers, Box 207; Midwestern Wayne County chapter of NOW survey of candidates' views, undated, NOW Papers, Box 207.

38. Telegram, Elaine Cartrocelli to Carter, 17 December 1976, NOW Papers, Box 207; Letter, Valerie Adams to Carter, 8 December 1976, NOW Papers, Box 192; Memo, Bill Albers, Barbara Haugen to Weddington, 12 May 1980, Weddington Papers, Box 58.

39. NOW complained, "We are angry at [Carter's] betrayal. He talks about a new morality for the country, but practices the same old false morality of keeping women in a subservient place." Statement by Elaine Latourell, NOW legislative vice president, undated, NOW Papers, Box 54.

40. "Feminists Movement May Nag Carter a Long While," *Washington Star*, 31 January 1977, 11; Letter, Ann Kolken to East, 9 August 1978, East Papers, Box 27.

41. "Midge Costanza: Keeping Her Humor Despite Woes and Canceled Show," *Washington Post*, 26 July 1978, Style, 1; "How Jimmy's Staff Operates," *Time*, 25 April 1977, 21.

42. "Carter Is Butt of Jokes in Midge Costanza Routine," article unsourced, in Papers of Gerald Rafshoon, Jimmy Carter Library, Box 2.

43. "Booting Bella," *New Republic*, 27 January 1979, 9.

44. "Bella Abzug's Ouster and Limits of Dissent; News Analysis," *New York Times*, 16 January 1979, A9.

45. "Women's Committee Still Fights Aftermath of Abzug Dismissal," *Washington Star*, 18 March 1979, A6.

46. Interview with Eleanor Smeal, 25 February 2007.

47. Susan M. Hartman, *From Margin to Mainstream: American Women and Politics Since 1960* (New York: Knopf, 1989), 152.

48. Private notes by Smeal on ERA campaign, 1979, NOW Papers, Box 87.

49. Interview with Walter Mondale, 7 June 2007.

50. Rosalynn Carter, *First Lady from Plains* (Boston: Houghton Mifflin, 1984), 101; Jimmy Carter, *Keeping Faith: Memoirs of a President* (New York: Bantam, 1983), 80.

51. "Rights Amendment Fight Nears Decision in Illinois," *New York Times*, 10 May 1980, 8.

52. Minutes, Study Group on Social Security meeting, March 1979, NOW Papers, Box 96.

53. "Two Skillful Meany Victories in Congress," *New York Times*, 12 October 1977, 76.

54. Statement by Executive on Council of ERA, 22 February 1979, Executive Minutes, Meany Library.

55. Minutes, Executive Committee, 19 November 1979, Executive Minutes, Meany Library.

56. Daily summary, UAW National Convention, 6 June 1980, Fraser Papers, Box 53.

57. Letter, Muriel Fox to Fraser, 29 November 1979, Fraser Papers, Box 53.

58. NEA Report on 1979 Convention, Shanker Papers, Box 10.

59. Memo, Fraser to officers of Progressive Alliance, 3 May 1979, Fraser Papers, Box 68.

60. List of organizations at October 17 planning meeting, undated, Fraser Papers, Box 68.

61. Memo, Winpisinger to nomination committee, undated, Fraser Papers, Box 68.

62. Minutes, Progressive Alliance meeting, 29 June, 1979, Fraser Papers, Box 68.

63. Memo, Mildred Jeffrey to Fraser, 5 January 1979, Fraser Papers, Box 68; Letter, Mary Wessel to Bill Dodds, 25 June 1979, Fraser Papers, Box 68.

64. Budget, 1979–1980, undated, Fraser Papers, Box 68; Budget, 29 June 1979, Fraser Papers, Box 68.

65. Memo, Bill Dodds and Bob Carolla to Fraser and Jerry Wurf, 26 June 1980, Fraser Papers, Box 68.

66. Minutes, Progressive Alliance meeting, 28 February 1979, Fraser Papers, Box 68.

67. Minutes, Progressive Alliance meeting, 1 March 1978, Fraser Papers, Box 68.

68. Letter, Fraser to Carter, 6 February 1978, Fraser Papers, Box 68.

69. Letter, Hayden to Fraser, undated, Fraser Papers, Box 68.

70. "The Progression of Our New Democratic, Progressive Alliance": Memo, Stu Fraser to Fraser, undated, Fraser Papers, Box 68.

71. Memo, Lee Webb to Fraser, 26 December 1978, Fraser Papers, Box 68.

72. Memo, Schlossberg to Fraser, 26 December 1979, Fraser Papers, Box 68.

73. "Return to Good Nature," *New Republic*, 5 March 1977, 12.

74. Interview with Don Stillman, 25 September 2006; "The Passionate Socialist," *New Republic*, 26 March 1977, 17.

75. Interview with Jim Wallace, 27 September 2006.

76. Leaflet, "The Democratic Agenda Convention," undated, Fraser Papers, Box 6.

77. Interview with Ruth Jordan, 26 February 2007.

78. Interview with Jack Clark, 25 September 2006.

79. Interview with Harold Meyerson, 22 September 2006; Transcript of Interview for *Democratic Left*, 20 September 1980, Mandler Papers.

80. Norman Binbaum article, "Building of an Opposition," unsourced, Papers of AFL-CIO President, Lane Kirkland (unprocessed), George Meany Library, National Labor College, Washington, D.C., Box 52.

81. Interview with Jack Clark, 25 September 2006.

82. "Progressive Caucus Amendments at 1981 Massachusetts Democratic Issues Convention," 11 April 1981, Mandler Papers; Yankee Radical Newsletter, May 1981, Mandler Papers; also see the activities of the Massachusetts Tax Reform Association, in Yankee Radical Newsletter, March 1981, Mandler Papers; Minutes, Cambridge, Mass., branch of DSOC meeting, 2 December 1980, Mandler Papers.

83. Letter, Fraser to Carter, 8 November 1977, Fraser Papers, Box 15.

84. Tax Justice report by Vice President Hardy, 8 May 1979, Executive Minutes, Meany Library.

85. Interview with Jack Clark, 25 September 2006.

86. Letter, Harrington to DSOC key contacts, 15 August 1978, Fraser Papers, Box 4; Letter, Harrington to Fraser, undated, Fraser Papers, Box 4.

87. "Wimpy Takes Command," *Time*, 11 July 1977, 51.

88. Interview with Jack Clark, 25 September 2006.

89. In a typical speech in 1978, Winpisinger told the Chicago Chapter of DSOC, "In the tradition of Gene Debs and Norman Thomas, we are going to raise enough hell that sooner or later the American people are going to wake up." Calling for industrial action to protest administration policies, he proclaimed, "I'm fed up with the idea that the trade union movement has to prove its respectability

by accepting and endorsing the ground rules of big business." "Wimpy on the Attack," *John Herling Labor Letter*, 19 May 1980.

90. Interview with Ruth Jordan, 26 February 2007.

91. Interview with Jack Clark, 25 September 2006.

92. Letter, Harrington to Fraser, 20 April 1979, Fraser Papers, Box 53.

93. Interview with Harold Meyerson, 22 September 2006; Leaflet, "Remember November," Fraser Papers, Box 4.

94. Democratic Agenda Budget, undated, Fraser Papers, Box 53; Letter, Harrington to Fraser, 11 January 1979, Fraser Papers, Box 53.

95. Interview with Ruth Jordan, 26 February 2007.

96. Interview with Jack Clark, 25 September 2006.

97. Interview with Harold Meyerson, 22 September 2006.

98. Letter, Jordan to Fraser, 11 December 1979, Fraser Papers, Box 53.

99. List, "Mini Plenaries and Workshops," 5 November 1979, Fraser Papers, Box 1.

100. Letter, Fraser to Harrington, 7 December 1977, Fraser Papers, Box 53.

101. Interview with Jack Clark, 25 September 2006; Letter, Harrington to Fraser, 18 November 1977, Fraser Papers, Box 53.

102. Interview with Harold Meyerson, 22 September 2006. In an article entitled "Full Employment and the Presidential Campaign," Harrington wrote, "It is the single most important reform on the Democratic agenda. Without it all other reforms tend to turn sour, or cannot get off the group. . . . It is probably the only single issue capable of getting the united support of all the members of the coalition and acting as the coalitions' unifier." *Socialist Forum* 1, no. 2, Mandler Papers.

103. "Socialism Is No Longer a Dirty Word for Labor," *Business Week*, 24 September 1979, 130.

104. "Whom Should the Left Support in 1980?," *Yankee Radical*, February 1980, Mandler Papers.

105. Letter, Harrington to Fraser, 16 January 1980, Fraser Papers, Box 53.

106. Letter, Harrington to Fraser, 11 December 1979, Fraser Papers, Box 53.

107. *Democratic Socialist New York Newsletter*, November/December 1980, Mandler Papers; Special newsletter: "DSOC Members Running for Kennedy Delegate Slots," undated, Mandler Papers.

108. 1981 DSOC Convention journal, Maxine Phillips Papers.

109. "DSOC Convention: New Goals Set, Anti-Carter Mood," *Democratic Left* 7, no. 3, Mandler Papers.

110. *DSOC Michigan Newsletter* No. 8, 10 December 1978, UAW Regional 1 Papers, Box 232.

111. "Citizen's Party," *L.A. Left*, August 1979, Mandler Papers.

112. A good indicator of the tempo of debate can be taken from the magazine *Socialist Forum* 1, no. 2, undated, Mandler Papers. One activist argued, "We must cultivate our own leadership"; another noted that the Democratic Agenda is "an unprecedented success," and yet another that "Democratic Agenda deserves a decent burial."

113. "Citizen's Party Born in Unorthodox Way," *New York Times*, 13 April 1980, 15.

114. *Yankee Radical*, April 1980, Mandler Papers; "Socialists Rally for May Elections," *Washington Socialist*, May 1980, Mandler Papers.

115. "DSOC Helps Liz to Victory," *New York Democratic Socialist Newsletter*, October 1980, Mandler Papers.

116. "The Left, Labor and Leadership," *Boston Phoenix*, 6 March 1978, 24.

117. Press Release on meeting to consider formation of "New Alliance," 26 September 1978, Fraser Papers, Box 68.

118. Letter, Fraser to regional UAW directors, 25 October 1979, Papers of the UAW Region 1 Local, Walter Reuther Library, Wayne State University, Detroit, Mich., Box 232.

119. "New Deal Dems Fight Raw Deal Dems," *Democratic Left* 7, no. 1 (January 1979), Mandler Papers; Letter, Harrington to Fraser, 20 April 1979, Fraser Papers, Box 53; "Miniconvention," *New Republic*, 23–30 December 1978, 13.

120. *Democratic Left* 7, no. 10 (December 1978), Mandler Papers.

121. Letter, Harrington to initiators of Democratic Agenda, Marjorie Phyfe and Jack Clark, 24 October 1978, Fraser Papers, Box 53.

122. Letter, Harrington to Fraser, 23 November 1977, Fraser Papers, Box 53.

123. Ibid.

124. Letter, Harrington to Fraser, Fraser Papers, Box 4.

125. Interview with Harold Meyerson, 22 September 2006.

126. Memo, Richard Moe to Rick Hutcheson, undated, Richard Moe Files, Mondale Papers, Box 2.

127. Ferency won 25 percent of the vote to William Fitzgerald's 40 percent— outspent by 5 to 1. He polled best among Jews and blacks: "Democratic Party News," *CAL-LEFT* newsletter, September 1978, Mandler Papers; *DSOC Michigan News*, September/October 1980, Mildred Jeffrey Papers, UAW Collection, Walter Reuther Library, Wayne State University, Detroit, Mich., Papers.

128. Interview with Ruth Jordan, 26 February 2007.

129. Interview with Harold Meyerson, 22 September 2006; Letter, Harrington to the initiators of the Democratic Agenda, 24 October 1978, Fraser Papers, Box 53.

130. Memo, Rafshoon to Carter, 29 November 1978, Office of White House Communications, Jimmy Carter Library, Box 55.

131. Memo, Rafshoon to Carter, 4 December 1978, Staff Secretary, Jimmy Carter Library, Box 111.

132. Draft of conference film, undated, Communications, Jimmy Carter Library, Box 55.

133. Midterm convention speech, 10 December 1978, DPS, Jimmy Carter Library, Box 182.

134. Talking points, undated, Papers of Robert J. Lipshutz, Jimmy Carter Library, Box 13.

135. Memo, Watson and Larry Gilson to Eizenstat, 6 December 1978, DPS, Jimmy Carter Library, Box 182.

136. Interview with Walter Mondale, 7 June 2007.

137. Memo, Moore to Carter, 7 December 1978, Staff Secretary, Jimmy Carter Library, Box 111; "An Unlikely Cult Figure," *New York Times*, 11 February 1978, 18.

138. Letter, Harrington to Fraser, 26 October 1978, Fraser Papers, Box 53.

139. "Activists Upset by Limits on Democratic Conference, May Boycott Carter Speech," *L.A. Times*, 2 December 1978, A27.

140. "Democrats to Test Reforms at Area Caucuses," *L.A. Times*, 3 December 1978, A1.

141. "Now's the Time, Party Is Told, to Aid Carter," *L.A. Times*, 7 December 1978, A2.

142. "For Democrats, a Madhouse in Memphis," *L.A. Times*, 6 December 1978, E7.

143. "Key Democrat to Shun Midterm Parley," *Washington Post*, 4 December 1978, A3; Press Release on convention, 5 October 1977, Fraser Papers, Box 53.

144. Letter, Democratic Conference to delegates, 5 July 1978, Staff Files, O'Neill Papers, Box 3.

145. Letter, Harrington, Phyfe, Clark to "initiators of Democratic Agenda," 24 October 1978, Fraser Papers, Box 53.

146. Letter, Thomas Booth to DNC, undated, Fraser Papers, Box 53.

147. Article in *Commercial Appeal*, 30 November 1978, in Ruth Jordan Papers; Letter, Wisconsin Delegates to DNC, 5 July 1978, Staff Files, O'Neill Papers, Box 3.

148. "Democrats Seeking to Curb Floor Fight," *Washington Post*, 1 December 1978, A17.

149. "Democrats Turn Aside Rules Challenge Backed by Liberal Alliance," *Washington Post*, 30 November 1978, D1.

150. "Carter Ready for Democratic Parley," *L.A. Times*, 8 December 1978, B14.

151. "Carter's Role in Memphis: A Politician as Well as President," *New York Times*, 10 December 1978, 42.

152. "Key Democrat to Shun Midterm Parley," *Washington Post*, 4 December 1978, A3; Memo, Larry to Gary, 8 December 1978, Hart Papers, Box 149; Memo, Abrams to Moynihan, 18 July 1978, Moynihan Papers, Box 2445.

153. "President Links Budget Austerity and Social Goals," *Washington Post*, 9 December 1978, A1.

154. Agenda, Cook Convention Center floor, 8 December 1978, Lipshutz Papers, Jimmy Carter Library, Box 13.

155. "Final Call for the 1978 Nat. Party Conference," 9 June 1978, Mildred Jeffrey Papers, Box 30.

156. List of workshops, 5 December 1978, Papers of the White House Press Office, Jimmy Carter Library, Box 17.

157. List of workshop, undated, White House Press Office, Jimmy Carter Library, Box 17.

158. Instructions for workshop panelists, undated, Lipshutz Papers, Jimmy Carter Library, Box 15.

159. Workshop rules of procedure, draft for Paul Sheehan, undated, White House Press Office, Jimmy Carter Library, Box 17.

160. List of panelists and moderators, undated, White House Press Office, Jimmy Carter Library, Box 17.

161. "Delegates at Conference Lecture Carter and Aides," *L.A. Times*, 10 December 1978, OC1.

162. List of motions, undated, First Lady's Files, Jimmy Carter Library, Box 5; Press Release, Delegate Resolutions: An Analysis, 1 June 1978, Staff Files, O'Neill Papers, Box 3.

163. *The Commercial Appeal*, 28 November 1978, in Mandler Papers.

164. Letter, Harrington to Fraser, 26 October 1978, Fraser Papers, Box 53.

165. "Democratic Agenda Resolutions," undated, Papers of the Special Adviser on Inflation, Jimmy Carter Library, Box 13.

166. Resolution supported by petition, 10 December 1978, First Lady's Files, Jimmy Carter Library, Box 5; for the validity of this statement, see "Key Members Question Need for Higher Defense Spending in Fiscal 1980," *Congressional Quarterly*, 10 February 1979, 239.

167. "Liberals Press Floor Fights Before Democratic Parley," *New York Times*, 8 December 1978, A21.

168. "Miniconvention," *New Republic*, 23–30 December 1978, 13.

169. "Debate over Domestic Budget Cuts Heats as Democratic Parley Nears," *New York Times*, 6 December 1978, A16.

170. *Arkansas Herald*, 10 December 1978, in Clymer Papers, Box 24.

171. Letter, Walter Beach and Valerie Earle to all members, 1 June 1978, Shanker Papers, Box 70.

172. "President Links Budget Austerity and Social Goals," *Washington Post*, 9 December 1978, A1.

173. "Carter's Dual Role in Memphis: A Politician as Well as President," *New York Times*, 10 December 1978, 42.

174. "Carter's Inflation Plans Draw Fire as Democrats Convene at Midterm," *New York Times*, 9 December 1978, 1.

175. Memo, Jane Fenderson to Tim Kraft and Richard Hutchenson, 15 December 1978, First Lady's Files, Jimmy Carter Library, Box 5.

176. "President Links Budget Austerity and Social Goals," *Washington Post*, 9 December 1978, A1.

177. Timetable for final day, undated, Lipshutz Papers, Jimmy Carter Library, Box 15.

178. "Democrats Seeking to Curb Floor Fights," *Washington Post*, 1 December 1978, A17; "Kennedy Assails Carter on Budget at Midterm Meeting of Democrats," *New York Times*, 10 December 1978, 1.

179. "Memphis Blues," *New Republic*, 23–30 December 1978, 2.

180. "Kennedy Warns of a Party Split by Arms Outlays," *Washington Post*, 10 December 1978, A1.

181. "Remarks of Senator Edward Kennedy: Workshop on Healthcare, Demo-

cratic National Committee Mid-Term Convention, Memphis," 9 December 1978, Clymer Papers, Box 9.

182. Interview with Stuart Eizenstat, 21 September 2006; Interview with Harold Meyerson, 22 September 2006; "Memphis Blues," *New Republic*, 23–30 December 1978, 2.

183. Interview with Peter Hart, 25 September 2006.

184. Interview with Harold Meyerson, 22 September 2006.

185. "Kennedy Exposes a Gaping Carter Weakness," *Washington Post*, 13 December 1978, A21.

186. "Kennedy Warns of a Party Split by Arms Outlays," *Washington Post*, 10 December 1978, A11.

187. "The Nation: Carter Fights for Hearts and Minds of Democrats," *New York Times*, 17 December 1978, E4.

188. Interview with Don Stillman, 25 September 2006.

189. Interview with Walter Mondale, 7 June 2007.

190. Minutes of the Cabinet Meeting, 11 December 1978, Jimmy Carter Library, Box 8.

191. "Delegates Back Carter's Budget-Cutting," *L.A. Times*, 11 December 1978, B1.

192. "State's Delegates Take Activist Stance," *L.A. Times*, 11 December 1978, B6.

193. "Labor Dissidents Confront Carter with a 'High Noon' Challenge," *L.A. Times*, 14 December 1978, D11.

194. "Labor Joins the Dissidents," *Washington Post*, 12 December 1978, A1.

195. Memo, Schlossberg to Fraser, 9 October 1978, Fraser Papers, Box 62.

196. "From Memphis: A Liberal Message to Carter," *Washington Post*, 20 December 1978, A1.

197. "Sharp Rise in Supply of Money; $2.7 Billion Jump Expected to Push Rates Up; M-2 Rises $4.7 Billion Fed Funds Rate at 11-3/8," *New York Times*, 14 September 1979, D1.

198. Memo to Carter, 30 March 1979, DPS, Jimmy Carter Library, Box 211; Eizenstat statement before DNC Platform Committee, 12 June 1980, Papers of the Counsel to Butler, Jimmy Carter Library, Box 71.

199. Iwan Morgan, *Deficit Government: Taxing and Spending in Modern America* (Chicago: Ivan R. Dee, 1995), 134.

200. Edward D. Berkowitz, *Something Happened: A Political and Cultural Overview of the Seventies* (New York: Columbia University Press, 2006), 130–131.

201. William B. Quandt, *Camp David: Peacemaking and Politics* (Washington, D.C.: Brookings Institution Press, 1986), 426.

202. Robert Gordon Kaufman, *Henry M. Jackson: A Life in Politics* (Seattle: University of Washington Press, 2000), 392.

203. "Carter's Poll-Taker Seems to Voice 1980s Catchwords: Spiritual Values and Patriotism," *New York Times*, 14 August 1979, A14.

204. "Carter's Ratings Drop to Lowest Yet After Speech and Cabinet Shake Up," Louis Harris Poll, 31 July 1979, NOW Papers, Box 200.

205. "Reshaping of Carter's Presidency," *New York Times*, 22 July 1979, 1.

206. Interview with Walter Mondale, 7 June 2007.

207. Kenneth E. Morris, *Jimmy Carter, American Moralist* (Athens: University of Georgia Press, 1996), 6.

208. Richard E. Burke, William Hoffer, and Marilyn Hoffer, *The Senator: My Ten Years with Ted Kennedy* (New York: St. Martin's Press, 1992), 195; Elizabeth Drew, *Portrait of an Election: The 1980 Presidential Campaign* (New York: Routledge and Kegan Paul, 1981), 78; "Kennedy Presses Leadership Issue in Philadelphia," *New York Times*, 23 October 1979, A16.

Chapter 4: The Kennedy Moment

1. "Home State Labor Backs Kennedy," *New York Times*, 29 September 1979, 1.

2. Interview with Meyerson; Letter, McGovern to Darrel G. Wells, 22 October 1979, McGovern Papers, Box 323.

3. Letter, Victor S. Kamber to Fraser, 18 July 1979, Fraser Papers, Box 68.

4. Letter, Winpisinger to members, undated, Fraser Papers, Box 68; the National Call raised $750,000 in 1979, with an average donation of $19 per respondent: Letter, Winpisinger to National Call supporters, late 1979, McGovern Papers, Box 323.

5. Memo, Monica Borkowski to Mondale, 18 January 1980, Mondale Papers, Box 25.A.0.10(F).

6. Copy of *St. Louis Post Dispatch* article, 12 July 1979, Fraser Papers, Box 68.

7. Interview with private source, 27 September 2006.

8. "Themes: Notes on the Campaign," Theodore C. Sorenson (Chaikin), 1928–: Papers, 1934–1994, JFK Library.

9. "Ted Kennedy: Haunted by Past," *New York Times*, 3 February 1980, SM114.

10. "The Drafting of a President," *New York Times Magazine*, 30 July 1979, 31.

11. John A. Farrell, *Tip O'Neill and the Democratic Century* (Boston: Little, Brown, 2001), 531; Joseph A. Califano, *Governing America* (New York: Simon and Schuster, 1981), 432.

12. "Advice to Kennedy and Other Candidates: Avoid Political Macho," *New York Times*, 14 September 1979, A25.

13. "Out to Stop Kennedy," *Time*, 1 October 1979, 20.

14. Thomas Maier, *The Kennedys: America's Emerald Kings* (New York: Basic Books, 2003), 455.

15. "The President and the Phantom," *Time*, 29 October 1979, 34.

16. "Carter Declares He Can Whip Kennedy in the Test," *New York Times*, 6 October 1979, 27.

17. Indeed, the administration took the event very seriously. If Carter's speech were delivered "thoughtfully and gracefully," then it was predicted that it might outshine Kennedy's and "be remembered" as a definitive statement on the "changes

that have occurred in the nature of our problems and in our political structure." Memo, Cutler to Jordan, 16 October 1979, DPS, Jimmy Carter Library, Box 229.

18. "Carter and Kennedy Share Stage at Library Dedication; Attack on Oil Companies," *New York Times*, 21 October 1979, 1.

19. Peter Collier and David Horowitz, *The Kennedys* (Ontario: Summit Books, 1984), 428–429.

20. Hamilton Jordan, *Crisis: The Last Year of the Carter Presidency* (New York: Putnam Adult, 1982), 20; Jimmy Carter, *Keeping Faith: Memoirs of a President* (New York: Bantam, 1983), 464.

21. Interview with Mark Segal, 27 September 2006.

22. "Gas Shortage Spurs Carter Decline in Poll," *New York Times*, 13 July 1979, A1; In fact, it slipped further to just 22 percent in July 1980: ABC News Harris Poll, 30 July 1980, NOW Papers, Box 200.

23. "ABC/Harris Poll: President Carter's Chances of Re-election in 1980 Seem Dim," 5 July 1979, Clymer Papers, Box 18.

24. ABC News Harris Poll, 9 July 1979, NOW Papers, Box 200; "Confidence in President Carter's Economic Politics Slipping," Louis Harris Poll, 1 March 1980, Mondale Papers, Box 4.

25. "ABC/Harris Poll: Carter Faces Uphill Battle for Democratic Nomination," 6 August 1979, NOW Papers, Box 139; "ABC/Harris Poll: President Carter's Ratings on Personal Characteristics Spell Trouble," 6 July 1980, NOW Papers, Box 139.

26. CBS/*New York Times* Poll, June 1979, Roper Center.

27. CBS/*New York Times* Poll, 29 October–3 November 1979, Roper Center.

28. The process began as early as fall 1977. Private polls for the administration found that the decrease in Carter's approval rating had taken place largely among Catholics, Democrats, liberals, and union members: "An Analysis of Political Attitudes Towards the Carter Presidency," October 1977, Richard Moe Files, Mondale Papers, Box 3.

29. "ABC/Harris Poll: President Carter's Chances of Re-election in 1980 Seem Dim," 5 July 1979, Clymer Papers, Box 18.

30. Reagan Polls by Richard Wirthlin, Clymer Papers, Box 18.

31. Gallup Poll, 17–20 August 1979, Roper Center; "Americans Feel Kennedy Has the Characteristics a President Should Have," Louis Harris Poll, 27 June 1979, Mondale Papers, Box 4.

32. "The Baron Report: Pressure on Kennedy," 8 June 1979, Papers of NOW, Box 139.

33. "Public Opinion," October/November 1979, Clymer Papers, Box 18.

34. "ABC/Harris Poll: President Carter's Chances of Re-election in 1980 Seem Dim," 5 July 1979, Clymer Papers, Box 18.

35. "*New York Times*/CBS Poll: Presidential Politics," 9 June 1979, Moynihan Papers, Box 86.

36. "ABC/Harris Poll: Democratic Party Allegiance Down Sharply Since 1976," 18 June 1979, Papers of NOW, Box 194.

37. "Americans Believe Kennedy Could Be More Depended upon in a Crisis Than Carter," Louis Harris Poll, 10 October 1979, Mondale Papers, Box 4.

38. Gallup Poll, 28 September–1 October 1979, Roper Center.

39. Gallup Poll, 7–10 September 1979, Roper Center; Gallup Poll, 3–6 August 1979, Roper Center.

40. "Kennedy Beats Them Both," *Public Opinion Magazine*, October/November 1979, 23; "Many Republicans Are Fearful of a Kennedy Candidacy," *New York Times*, 24 October 1979, A18.

41. "Reagan for President Poll: Nationwide," April 1979; "Polling Conducted by Peter Hart on Behalf of Senator Kennedy," December 1979, Clymer Papers, Box 18.

42. Gallup Poll, 12–13 October 1979, Roper Center.

43. Everett Carll Ladd Jr., "The Brittle Mandate: Electoral Dealignment and the 1980 Presidential Election," *Political Science Quarterly* 96 (1981): 1–25.

44. "Reagan for President Poll: Nationwide," April 1979; "Polling Conducted by Peter Hart on Behalf of Senator Kennedy," December 1979, Clymer Papers, Box 18.

45. Yake Poll, 21–23 August 1979, Roper Center.

46. "The Carter-Brown Economic Message," *New York Times*, 29 January 1979, A16; Baron Report, 3 March 1978, Staff Files, O'Neill Papers, Box 3.

47. "Brown Says Kennedy Race in '80 Could Help the Democratic Party," *New York Times*, 14 September 1979, B4.

48. "The Brown Strategy," *New York Times*, 3 September 1979, A15.

49. "Boos Turn to Cheers as Gov. Brown Addresses California Democrats," *New York Times*, 21 January 1979, 14.

50. "Brown Confounds Predictions, Weathers the Tax-Revolt Storm," *New York Times*, 16 July 1980, A1.

51. "A Solid No on Brown," *San Francisco Chronicle*, 15 May 1979, 2.

52. "Jerry Brown Seen to Be in Political Trouble with Party and Electorate," Louis Harris Poll, 16 April 1979, Mondale Papers, Box 4.

53. "Gov. Brown, His Dream Ended, Returns to California," *New York Times*, 3 April 1980, 34.

54. "Whatever Happened to Jerry Brown?," *New York Times*, 8 March 1980, SM9.

55. "Kennedy Assails Carter in Appeal to Women Voters," *New York Times*, 5 December 1979, A28.

56. Speech, "Equality and Justice for Women," 16 February 1980, Clymer Papers, Box 9.

57. "Kennedy and the Liberals," *New Republic*, 10 November 1979, 18.

58. Speech, at JFK School of Government, 12 February 1980, Clymer Papers, Box 9.

59. "On the Issues: Edward M. Kennedy; Activist for Underprivileged, a Shift Perceived," *New York Times*, 20 March 1980, B12.

60. Press Release, "Senator Edward M. Kennedy Criticizes the Carter Administration for Abandoning the Milwaukee Railroad Track," 28 February 1980, Clymer Papers, Box 9.

61. Press Release, undated, White House Press Office, Jimmy Carter Library, Box 9.

62. Memo, Borkowski to Mondale, 26 February 1980; Memo, Borkowski to Mondale, 19 March 1980; Memo, Borkowski to Mondale, 24 April 1980; Memo, Borkowski to Mondale, 26 February 1980; Memo, Borkowski to Mondale, 19 March 1980, all in Mondale Papers, Box 25.A.O.10.F.

63. "Dumpster's Convention," *New Republic*, 7–14 July 1979, 12; Memo, Borkowski to Mondale, 11 February 1980, Mondale Papers, Box 25.A.O.10.F.

64. Interview with George McGovern, 27 July 2006.

65. Letter, McGovern to Gula L. Jackson, 26 September 1979, McGovern Papers, Box 323. Privately, McGovern pointed out to Democrats angry with his decision that Carter was a consistent supporter of the Vietnam war and had been a ringleader of the 1972 "Anybody but McGovern" movement: Letter, McGovern to Russell W. Ballard, 25 September 1979, McGovern Papers, Box 323; However, McGovern also charged the administration with failing his constituents directly through its agricultural policies and the 1980 grain embargo: Press Release, "McGovern Faults Administration Farm Program," 22 February 1978, McGovern Papers, Box 505.

66. "Feeling Left Out," *New Republic*, 21 May 1977, 12.

67. "Four Black Caucus Members Ask Support for Kennedy in Primaries," *New York Times*, 7 March 1980, D16.

68. Letter, Andrew Stein to Carter, 3 August 1979, Cabinet Secretary, Jimmy Carter Library, Box 32.

69. Stein's letter preempted the massive support of Jews for Kennedy's campaign by citing the "little sensitivity" that Carter had shown on the issue of Israel. Letter, Andrew Stein to Carter, 3 August 1979, Cabinet Secretary, Jimmy Carter Library, Box 32; "In Which Carterites Stalk A. Pride of Mayors," *New York Times*, 16 March 1980, CN20.

70. Letter, Thomas P. Salmon to Senator Esther Sorrell, 29 October 1979, Cabinet Secretary, Jimmy Carter Library, Box 32; Kennedy enjoyed the support of two ex-governors of Vermont, both of whom had stumped for Carter: Memo, Borkowski to Mondale, 23 February 1980, Legal and Procedural Files, Mondale Papers, Box 219.

71. "Carter/Mondale Endorsements," undated, Records of the White House Office of Administration, Jimmy Carter Library, Box 9.

72. "Four Black Caucus Members Ask Support for Kennedy in Primaries," *New York Times*, 7 March 1980, D16.

73. Letter, Rep. David M. Hagino to Carter, 24 September 1979, Cabinet Secretary, Jimmy Carter Library, Box 32.

74. "Carter and Kennedy Camps Mount Strong, Last-Minute Efforts for Florida Caucuses Today," *New York Times*, 13 October 1979, 6.

75. "Poll Shows Carter Is Trailing in South; Survey Finds Kennedy Is Leading President by 11-Point Margin," *New York Times*, 8 July 1979, 13.

76. Baron Report No. 74, 8 June 1979, NOW Papers, Box 139.

77. Letter, Mayor Bill Morris to Carter, 5 November 1979, Cabinet Secretary, Jimmy Carter Library, Box 32.

78. Letter, Hubert L. Harris to Jordan, 29 October 1979, White House Press Office, Jimmy Carter Library, Box 9. In addition, a leading Maine Democrat wrote to tell Carter that he was "not prepared to say that I would support you" for precisely the same reasons. Letter, James B. Longley to Carter, 10 March 1980, Cabinet Secretary, Jimmy Carter Library, Box 32.

79. "1976 Campaign Biographical Sketch," undated, Moynihan Papers, Box 383.

80. Introduction to Daniel Patrick Moynihan, *Maximum Feasible Misunderstanding: Community Action in the War on Poverty* (New York: Free Press, 1969); Introduction to Daniel Patrick Moynihan, *Politics of a Guaranteed Minimum Income: The Nixon Administration and the Family Assistance Plan* (New York: Random House, 1973).

81. Article in *Washington Post*, 18 June 1976, in Moynihan Papers, Box 383.

82. "Moynihan Raised to Cabinet Rank," *New York Times*, 5 November 1969, 1.

83. "Department of Amplification," *New Yorker*, 1 March 1973; "Moynihan's support of Nixon's re-election is only the political corollary of a concerted intellectual assault on the goal of social and economic equality. . . . Moynihan and co. are able to assert simultaneously that ghetto residents are poor because they are apathetic and disorganized and that our 'fragile' social order is endangered by the strident protests of these same unorganizable slum people." Press Release, "Daniel P. Moynihan and the Assault on Equality," by the New American Movement (Harrington socialists), Moynihan Papers, Box 382.

84. "Text of the Moynihan Memorandum on the Status of Negroes," *New York Times*, 1 March 1970.

85. "Moynihan in Search of His Own Time," *L.A. Times*, 22 April 1976; Letter, Cardinal Cooke to Moynihan, 17 August 1976, Moynihan Papers, Box 383.

86. Interview with Adam Clymer, 19 September 2006.

87. *Face the Nation* transcript, 17 June 1979, Moynihan Papers, Box 50; "Jackson Vows Senate Fight over SALT II," *Washington Post*, 18 June 1979, 13; "Reflections: The SALT Process," *New Yorker*, 26 November 1979, 19; Letter, Moynihan to Ernst Cramer, 11 April 1978, Moynihan Papers, Box 1.

88. Letter, Moynihan to David Broder, 24 March 1979, Moynihan Papers, Box 1.

89. "State Democratic Group Adopts Resolution Criticizing President; Carey Offers a Moderate View," *New York Times*, 9 May 1979, D18.

90. Speech at Sarana Lake, N.Y., 10 April 1980, Moynihan Papers, Box 2445.

91. Letter, John H. Chafee to Northeast coalition members, 23 January 1979, Moynihan Papers, Box 775.

92. "What Will They Do for New York?," 27 January 1980, *New York Times Magazine*, 9.

93. Statement of Moynihan on the Carter proposals to balance the budget, 18 March 1980, Moynihan Papers, Box 775.

94. "Vice President in Syracuse Stumping for Carter Campaign," *Aubern* [*N.Y.*] *Citizen*, 29 January 1980, 1.

95. Memo, Moynihan to Elliot Abrams, 8 February 1979, Moynihan Papers, Box 375.

96. Interview with Moynihan, 26 July 1995, Clymer Papers, Box 4.

97. "Moynihan Opens Way for Favorite-Son Draft," *New York Times*, 2 August 1979, B9.

98. Memo, Michael Novak to Moynihan, 3 August 1978, Moynihan Papers, Box 2834.

99. Moynihan piece by Douglas E. Schoen, Moynihan Papers, Box 263.

100. Memo, Raymond Polin to Kenneth Lipper, 18 November 1979, Moynihan Papers, Box 2834.

101. "Moynihan Rips into Kennedy," *Staten Island Advance*, 11 January 1980, 1.

102. "Moynihan Shaken by Ted's Statements," *Saratogian*, 11 January 1980, 1.

103. *Political Observer*, March 1980, Shanker Papers, Box 70.

104. "Jackson Decries Cabinet Upheaval and Says Kennedy Will Run in '80; 'A Real Political Barometer,'" *New York Times*, 25 July 1979, A15.

105. "Jackson, Attacking Carter, Says Reagan May Win," *New York Times*, 23 May 1980, A14.

106. Burton I. Kaufman, *The Presidency of James Earl Carter Jr.* (Lawrence: University Press of Kansas, 1993), 395.

107. Interview with Gary Hart, 29 August 2006; "Gary Hart's Idea Collection," *New Republic*, 26 March 1984, 12; Press Release, 14 May 1978, Hart Papers, Box 55.

108. Press Release, 21 February 1977, Hart Papers, Box 55.

109. Article in *Greeley Tribune*, 28 April 1980, in Hart Papers, Box 182; Article in *Greeley Tribune*, 31 May 1980, in Hart Papers, Box 182.

110. Unsourced article, undated, in Hart Papers, Box 182; Article in *Rocky Mountain News*, 8 August 1980, in Hart Papers, Box 182.

111. Article in *Rocky Mountain News*, 21 May 1980, in Hart Papers, Box 182.

112. Article in *Colorado Camera*, 8 November 1980, in Hart Papers, Box 182.

113. Interview with Gary Hart, 29 August 2006; Birch Bayh recalled that given his election in 1980, he simply "couldn't afford to get involved with either one." Interview with Senator Birch Bayh, 3 September 1995, Clymer Papers, Box 3 .

114. Interview with Mike Dukakis, 14 September 2006; Interview with Paul Tsongas, 12 December 1994, Clymer Papers, Box 5.

115. ABC News Harris Poll, 7 August 1979, Clymer Papers, Box 15; Interview with John Culver, 17 February 2007.

116. Interview with Tip O'Neill, 23 November 1993, Clymer Papers, Box 4.

117. "Move Grows at Capitol to Urge Carter to Shun Race," *New York Times*, 13 September 1979; Interview with Adam Clymer, 19 September 2006.

118. "Stress on Economy Seen as Cover Story," *Washington Post*, 13 September 1979, 9.

119. Memo, Arnold A. Saltzman to Eizenstat, 7 April 1980, PL-5: Political Affairs Files, Jimmy Carter Library.

120. "If Winning Is Important, Winning First Is More So," *New York Times*, 7 October 1979, E4.

121. "Udall Backs Kennedy; Asserts He Can Unite Party's Constituencies; Stand on Issues Cited," *New York Times*, 9 December 1979, B14.

122. Article, unknown source, undated, in White House Press Office, Jimmy Carter Library, Box 9.

123. "Carter's Woes and New York; Many Democrats Study Alternative to President," *New York Times*, 13 March 1979, B7.

124. *Denver Post*, 7 August 1980; "He Doesn't Plan to Die in the Senate," *Colorado Statesman*, 14 June 1980, 8.

125. *Gainsville Sun*, 17 May 1979, in Cabinet Secretary, Jimmy Carter Library, Box 32.

126. Letter, "Florida for Kennedy Committee" to Floridians, undated, White House Press Office, Jimmy Carter Library, Box 9.

127. In 1972 Shirley Chisholm had received their backing, but McGovern kept quiet about early attempts to garner their support. Norman Mailer, *St. George and the Godfather* (New York: Arbor House, 1972), 52–53; "The Gay Vote," *New Republic*, 12 February 1972, 10.

128. Letter, Robert S. Havely to Joan O'Leary, 4 October 1976, Office of Public Liaison, Jimmy Carter Library, Box 22; News Release, California Gay People for Carter-Mondale, undated, Office of Public Liaison, Jimmy Carter Library, Box 22.

129. David Deitcher, ed., *The Question of Equality: Lesbian and Gay Politics in America Since Stonewall* (New York: Scribner, 1995), 53.

130. Introduction to Stonewall Democratic Club, undated (1979–1980), Bunch Papers, Box 3.

131. It should be stressed that the California gay movement had begun trying to integrate itself into California Democratic politics before 1980. As evidence by the thriving Stonewall Democratic Club, a supporter of the senator: "A Tribute to Morris Knight" with correspondence from Jerry Brown and Alan Cranston, undated, and "Stonewall Democratic Club" brochure, undated, Bunch Papers, Box 62.

132. List of bills before Senate, 7 April 1980, NOW Papers, Box 47; "The Senator Makes a Connection," *Village Voice*, 29 October 1979, 4.

133. Letter, Jean O'Leary to Smeal, 6 April 1978, NOW Papers, Box 47; NOW letter to all state coordinators, 3 November 1975, Papers of Midge Costanza, Jimmy Carter Library, Box 28; "On Capitol Hill, It's Time," *NGTF Newsletter*, bonus issue, undated, Costanza Papers, Jimmy Carter Library, Box 28.

134. Press Release, "Gay Civil Rights and the Democratic Party," undated, NOW Papers, Box 47.

135. "Anita Bryant Is Mad About Gays," *New Republic*, 7 May 1977, 13; Gay rights protections in the United States and Canada, 2 March 1977, Costanza Papers, Jimmy Carter Library, Box 28.

136. "Mayor Shaw Is Adamant—The City's Gays Must Go," *Fort Lauderdale News*, 30 November 1976, 1A; "Commission Hopeful Seeks Endorsement of Gay Community," *Fort Lauderdale News*, 15 January 1977, 2B; "California—A Gay Activist Campaign," *Washington Post*, 8 April 1977, B10; "Gays in the Streets," *New Republic*, 9 June 1979, 9.

137. "District Gays Believed Factor in Council Race," *Washington Post*, 21 April 1979, A6.

138. Letter, Thomas F. Bastow to Robert Strauss, 28 December 1979, Weddington Papers, Jimmy Carter Library, Box 58.

139. Letter, lesbian/gay democrats of Texas to Carter, 13 December 1979, Weddington Papers, Jimmy Carter Library, Box 58.

140. Letter, BJ Willhite to Carter, 11 December 1979, Weddington Papers, Jimmy Carter Library, Box 58.

141. "Kennedy Campaigning Hard," *San Francisco Chronicle*, 1 August 1980, 14.

142. "Primary Season," *San Francisco Chronicle*, 31 May 1980, 2; "Campaign Steps Up," *L.A. Times*, 25 May 1980, 6.

143. Letter, Robert Strauss to Mr. Brydon and Ms. Valenska, 3 March 1980, White House Press Office, Jimmy Carter Library, Box 89.

144. Memo, unknown to Carter, undated, Records of the White House Office of Administration, Jimmy Carter Library, Box 9; Interview with Gwirtzman, 3 April 1993, Clymer Papers, Box 4.

145. "San Francisco Homosexuals Find Democrats Now Listen," *New York Times*, 4 June 1984, B10

146. National Agenda, 25 July 1980, NOW Papers, Box 18.

147. Executive notes, undated, NOW Papers, Box 18; Minutes of Executive Meeting, 9 December 1979, NOW Papers, Box 4.

148. "Board of NOW to Oppose Carter, Charging Lag on Women's Issues; 'Must Be Held Accountable,' NOW Leaders to Oppose Carter, Charging Lag on Their Concerns Meeting Scheduled in January Account Challenged by Author," *New York Times*, 11 December 1979, A1; "Draft Kennedy" notes and discussion among executive board of NOW, undated, NOW Papers, Box 100.

149. Judith Shapiro's notes on meeting, 8 December 1979, NOW Papers, Box 18; Press Release on motion of endorsement, undated, NOW Papers, Box 4.

150. "Statement of the Connecticut Women's Advisory Committee for Kennedy," undated, Papers of Nancy F. Korman (1976–2000), JFK Library, Box 2; Interview with Eleanor Smeal, 25 February 2007.

151. Private notes by unknown, undated, NOW Papers, Box 87.

152. Draft Kennedy statement, undated, NOW Papers, Box 100.

153. Minutes of Executive Committee meeting, undated, NOW Papers, Box 87.

154. Letter, Nancy Korman to Edward M. Kennedy, 9 July 1980, Korman Papers, Box 2; "There was, until late, very late in the '70's . . . an old boy network that ran the Kennedy staff," Interview with Judith Lichtman, 30 March 1995, Clymer Papers, Box 4.

155. Interview with Judith Lichtman, 30 March 1995, Clymer Papers, Box 4.

156. Letter, Nancy Korman to Edward M. Kennedy, 7 January 1980, Korman Papers, Box 2; Notes on speech, undated, Korman Papers, Box 2.

157. Letter, Nancy Korman to Steve Smith, 28 December 1980, Korman Papers, Box 2.

158. Letter, Joanne Howes to Nancy Korman, 21 December 1979, Korman Papers, Box 2.

159. Press Release "Women's Advisory Committee Formed for Kennedy Campaign," 9 February 1980, Korman Papers, Box 2.

160. "Liberals Find the Man; Women Reach for Clout," *Boston Herald*, 13 January 1980, 1.

161. "Minutes of the December 10 Meeting of the Women's Advisory Committee for Kennedy for President," 19 December 1979, Korman Papers, Box 2.

162. "Address of Edward M. Kennedy to AFL-CIO State Convention, Ohio," 21 May 1980, Clymer Papers, Box 9.

163. Memo, Hubert L. Harris to Jordan, 9 October 1979, Chief of Staff Files, Jimmy Carter Library, Box 142.

164. "Wurf Says Labor Should Seek Alternative to Carter," *New York Times*, 13 July 1979, A11.

165. "Many Union Heads Cautious on Endorsing '80 Candidate," *Washington Post*, 19 September 1979, in White House Press Office, Jimmy Carter Library, Box 9.

166. Memo, Butler to Jordan, 21 December 1979, White House Press Office, Jimmy Carter Library, Box 9

167. Memo, Butler to Jordan, 4 January 1980, Chief of Staff Files, Jimmy Carter Library, Box 142.

168. The secretary of labor advised Jordan that to open up support in other states he needed a strong vote in Iowa, "particularly among labor." Memo, Butler to Jordan, 21 December 1979, White House Press Office, Jimmy Carter Library, Box 9.

169. Similarly, Carter-supporting unions provided massive financial and numerical assistance. "The National Education Association . . . is spearheading our effort in Iowa. They have 12 full time local operatives working for us. NEA locals are phone banking their members." Memo, Butler to Jordan, 4 January 1980, Chief of Staff Files, Jimmy Carter Library, Box 142.

170. "State by State Report," 23 February 1980, Chief of Staff Files, Jimmy Carter Library, Box 142.

171. "Announcement of the Formation of the Kennedy for President National Labor Committee," 19 January 1980, Chief of Staff Files, Jimmy Carter Library, Box 142.

172. Statement by Brick Layers and Allied Craftsmen, 14 November 1979, Chief of Staff Files, Jimmy Carter Library, Box 142.

173. Food and Commercial Worker's election leaflet, undated, Chief of Staff Files, Jimmy Carter Library, Box 142.

174. The International Union of Operating Engineers produced a leaflet that ran with the headlines "Fair Play for All Americans," "Better Jobs for Women," and "To Raise the Minimum Wage." IUOE election leaflet, undated, Chief of Staff Files, Jimmy Carter Library, Box 142.

175. Statement by the administration to "Members of the Building and Construction Trades," undated, Chief of Staff Files, Jimmy Carter Library, Box 142.

176. Memo, John Farmer to Mondale, undated, Legal and Procedural Files, Mondale Papers, Box 154.I.5.2.F.

177. Memo, Ray Marshal to Jordan, 31 December 1980, White House Press Office, Jimmy Carter Library, Box 9.

178. Memo, Butler to Jordan, 4 January 1980, Chief of Staff Files, Jimmy Carter Library, Box 142.

179. Memo, Butler to Jordan, undated, Chief of Staff Files, Jimmy Carter Library, Box 142.

180. "The AFL-CIO Adrift," *Nation*, 8 September 1979, 167–268.

181. Carter's total union membership significantly outnumbered Kennedy's. The teachers' union was the largest in Iowa, with 34,000 members, and combined with the food and communication workers, they could boast 61,400. Kennedy's unions only had 49,100 members. Summary of union membership, 21 January 1980, Chief of Staff Files, Jimmy Carter Library, Box 142; Memo, Bernie Anorson to Butler, 16 January 1980, White House Press Office, Jimmy Carter Library, Box 9.

182. "Major Labor Unions in California Totals," undated, Chief of Staff Files, Jimmy Carter Library, Box 142.

183. Memo, Dave Jessup to Al Barkan, 29 July 1980, Meany Papers, Box 99.

184. Memo, Bernie Anorson to Phil Wise, 12 June 1980, Chief of Staff Files, Jimmy Carter Library, Box 142.

185. Arch Puddington, *Lane Kirkland: Champion of American Labor* (New York: Wiley, 2005), 108.

186. Letter, Lane Kirkland President (AFL-CIO) to all "state and local bodies," 3 January 1980, Chief of Staff Files, Jimmy Carter Library, Box 142.

187. "For Labor, No Place to Go," *Business Week*, 31 March 1980, 129.

188. Memo, Butler to Jordan, 21 January 1980, Chief of Staff Files, Jimmy Carter Library, Box 142.

189. Article in *Fresno Bee*, 1 August 1978, in Chavez Papers, Box 34. A note on the UFW: despite its conflict with the Teamsters, the UFW tried to consciously bring together what it regarded as "New Deal goals" with "New Left tactics." Thus, its identity as a union is both difficult to define and an excellent example of the cross-fertilization of liberal identities in the 1970s. Richard A. Garcia, "Dolores Huerta: Woman, Organizer and Symbol," *California History* 72, no. 1 (1993): 56–71; Ronald B. Taylor, *Chavez and the Farmworkers* (Boston: Beacon Press, 1972), 150.

190. Minutes of Executive, 18–20 January 1980, Shanker Papers, Box 7.

191. Interview with Douglas Fraser, 19 February 2007.

192. Memo, Butler to Jordan, 4 January 1980, Chief of Staff Files, Jimmy Carter Library, Box 142.

193. Press Release, "Labor for an Open Convention," 1 August 1980, Shanker Papers, Box 45.

194. "Unions' Dilemma—Support Carter or Kennedy?," *U.S. News and World Report*, 26 November 1979, 91–92.

195. Memo, Borkowski to Mondale, 26 February 1980, Mondale Papers, Box 25.A.O.10.F.

196. "Unions That Have Endorsed Senator Kennedy," undated, Leadership Files, O'Neill Papers, Box 32.

197. Minutes of Executive, 18–20 January 1980, Shanker Papers, Box 7.

198. "11 Top State UAW Leaders Go 9 for Kennedy, 2 for Carter," *Detroit News*, 15 May 1980, in White House Press Office, Jimmy Carter Library, Box 9.

199. Brick Layers and Allied Craftsmen Press Release, undated, Chief of Staff Files, Jimmy Carter Library, Box 142.

200. "The International Union of Bricklayers and Allied Craftsmen Democratic Party Platform Proposals," undated, Chief of Staff Files, Jimmy Carter Library, Box 142.

201. Resolutions to Carter from Bud Rahberger (International Vice President, IWA), 14 March 1980, Chief of Staff Files, Jimmy Carter Library, Box 142.

202. "Reprieved by Jaws," *New York Times*, 9 November 1979, A35.

203. Interview with Richard Goodwin, 17 September 1993, Clymer Papers, Box 4.

204. Interview with Robert Shrum, 24 February 1998, Clymer Papers, Box 5.

205. "CBS News Special with Roger Mudd," MR2002-11 Q, Kennedy, Edward Moore, 1932–2009: Audiovisual Archives, JFK Library.

206. A nice description from *New York Magazine* put it thus: "And then Kennedy walked into the Mudd interview like a fighter when the first bell rings, walking into the mike." "Teddy Kennedy Has No Regrets," *New York Magazine*, 14 August 1980, 25.

Chapter 5: Iran, Afghanistan, and Defeat in Iowa

1. "Kennedy Shifts Put Fire in Carter Campaign," *New York Times*, 12 October 1979, A20.

2. Interview with Peter Hart, 25 September 2006.

3. Murray B. Levin, *Edward Kennedy: The Myth of Leadership* (Boston: Houghton Mifflin, 1980), 211; "Kennedy Declares His Candidacy," *New York Times*, 8 November 1979, A1.

4. Memo, John Fee to Jordan, 9 November 1979, White House Press Office, Jimmy Carter Library, Box 9.

5. "Doubts About Kennedy Are Rising but Dominant Feeling Is Positive," Louis Harris Poll, 15 November 1979, Mondale Papers, Box 4.

6. Gallup Poll, 2–5 November 1979, Roper Center.

7. "Carter Loses Clark to Kennedy's Camp," *New York Times*, 31 October 1979, A13.

8. Interview with Robert Shrum, 24 February 1998, Clymer Papers, Box 5.

9. "Kennedy to Tap Key Aides from 3 Presidential Races in '80 Campaign; Head of Field Operations," *New York Times*, 21 October 1979, 38.

10. Memo, Bill Abers to Jordan, 8 February 1980, White House Press Office, Jimmy Carter Library, Box 9.

11. Interview with Peter Hart, 25 September 2006.

12. Interview with John Tunney, 24 March 1998, Clymer Papers, Box 5; Article in *Boston Globe*, 21 February 1980, in Clymer Papers, Box 13.

13. "Kennedy Says Leadership Not Economics Is at Issue," *New York Times*, 13 September 1979.

14. Filed report from John Walcott in *Newsweek*, undated, in Clymer Papers, Box 13.

15. "Reagan Is Striving to Protect an Image of Moderation," *New York Times*, 14 January 1980, A13.

16. Carter makes a similar point of being seen with Mohammed Ali. Memo on organization in Pennsylvania, undated, Records of the Office of Hispanic Affairs, Jimmy Carter Library, Box 14.

17. Memo, Gary Orren to Steven Smith, Phil Bakes and Paul Kirk, 6 January 1980, Clymer Papers, Box 13.

18. Memo, Peter Hart to "The Kennedy Campaign," undated, Clymer Papers, Box 13.

19. "Kennedy Assails Carter in Appeal to Women Voters," *New York Times*, 5 December 1979, A28.

20. "I am fully committed to the principle of equal opportunity . . . to the principle of progress for the poor." But while an entitlement liberal would have addressed how, Kennedy consistently hinted that his liberalism was instinctive, rather than intellectual. "Speech at Faneuil Hall," 7 November 1979, Clymer Papers, Box 9.

21. "Address of Senator Edward M. Kennedy to Investment Association of New York," 27 September 1979, Clymer Papers, Box 9.

22. "Kennedy is moving rapidly to the right in an effort to take the center away from us." Memo, Hubert L. Harris to Jordan, 9 October 1979, White House Press Office, Jimmy Carter Library, Box 9; Article in *DM Register*, 8 January 1980, in Clymer Papers, Box 13.

23. Memo, Gary Orren and Peter Hart to Steve Smith, 2 January 1980, Clymer Papers, Box 13.

24. "Speech at Faneuil Hall," 7 November 1979, Clymer Papers, Box 9.

25. "Kennedy and Defense" briefing material, undated, Records of the Speech Writer's Office, Jimmy Carter Library, Box 19.

26. Article in *Business Week*, 22 October 1979, in Clymer Papers, Box 13.

27. "Address of Senator Edward M. Kennedy to the Investment Association of New York," 27 September 1980, Clymer Papers, Box 9.

28. "Transcript of Kennedy Iowa Radio Commercials," undated, Speechwriter's Office, Jimmy Carter Library, Box 19.

29. Letter, Roger Hilsman to Edward M. Kennedy, 24 December 1979, Sorensen Papers, JFK Library.

30. Notes by Powell entitled "Themes," undated, White House Press Office, Jimmy Carter Library, Box 9.

31. "A Disappointing Start," *Boston Globe*, 12 January 1980, 4.

32. Memo, Borkowski to Mondale, 18 January 1980, Mondale Papers, Box 25.A.O.10.F.

33. "Away from the prepared text, the face-to-face encounter, Kennedy is halting, rambling and uncertain." Article in *Boston Globe*, 5 November 1979, in Clymer Papers, Box 13; Interview with Adam Clymer, 19 September 2006.

34. "On television he comes across as a screamer . . . as a frantic wild man, ranting and raving like—to use a commonly heard phrase—a bruising Irish brawler." Article in *Boston Globe*, 2 May 1980, in Clymer Papers, Box 13.

35. Elizabeth Drew, *Portrait of an Election: The 1980 Presidential Campaign* (New York: Routledge and Kegan Paul, 1981), 62; "Kennedy the Campaigner: A Private Man's Approach," *New York Times*, 7 April 1980, D9.

36. "National Affairs," *Newsweek*, 26 November 1979, 58.

37. "ABC/Harris Poll: Public Disappointment with Kennedy as a Campaigner," 14 January 1980, Clymer Papers, Box 18.

38. "Ted Kennedy Puts His Show on the Road," *Newsweek*, 19 November 1980, 39.

39. Memo, Frank Mankiewicz to Robert Shrum, undated, Clymer Papers, Box 13.

40. Letter, Roger Hilsman to Edward M. Kennedy, 24 December 1979, Sorensen Papers, JFK Library.

41. Memo, Frank Mankiewicz to Robert Shrum, undated, Clymer Papers, Box 13.

42. "Candidates Spending a Total of $2.8 million in Iowa," *New York Times*, 21 January 1980, A13.

43. "Kennedy Campaign Ad Collection," undated, Kennedy, Edward Moore, 1932–2009: Audiovisual Archives, JFK Library.

44. Peter Collier and David Horowitz, *The Kennedys* (Ontario: Summit Books, 1984), 436.

45. Hamilton Jordan, *Crisis: The Last Year of the Carter Presidency* (New York: Putnam Adult, 1982), 20–21.

46. Jimmy Carter, *Keeping Faith: Memoirs of a President* (New York: Bantam, 1983), 473.

47. Memo, Jordan to Carter, 17 January 1979, Chief of Staff Files, Jimmy Carter Library, Box 142.

48. He also used the White House staff, acknowledging that this violated the Hatch Act passed to prevent such an abuse of federal workers: Memo, "Political Activity Guidelines," 14 December 1979, Legal and Procedural Files, Mondale Papers, Box 203.

49. Memo, Jordan to Carter, 17 January 1979, Chief of Staff Files, Jimmy Carter Library, Box 142; but this point is controversial, and Carter may not have been as unique as Jordan thought: Reagan compared Ford to Santa Claus in 1976 on the grounds of his profligate federal spending in primary states. Craig Shirley, *Reagan's Revolution: The Untold Story of the Campaign That Started It All* (Nashville: Thomas Nelson, 2005), 170.

50. Twenty governors declared for him at the Governor's Conference in 1979. One of them, Bill Clinton, added that he thought Carter had shown "a lack of leadership." Article in *Washington Post*, 8 July 1979, in Clymer Papers, Box 13.

51. Kennedy's campaign tried to sue him for it. UPI article in 28 December 1979, Records of the White House Office of Counsel to the President, Jimmy Carter Library, Box 54.

52. Memo, Watson to Carter, 7 December 1979, PL-2: Political Affairs Files, Jimmy Carter Library.

53. Letter, Mayor Maurice A. Ferre to Jordan, 22 May 1979, White House Press Office, Jimmy Carter Library, Box 9.

54. Letter, Representative Richard Stone to Jordan, 13 September 1979, White House Press Office, Jimmy Carter Library, Box 9.

55. Memo, transcript of visit to New York and press complaints regarding federal projects, 28 November 1979, Bill Smith Files, Mondale Papers, Box 2.

56. Article in *Washington Post*, 13 October 1979, in Clymer Papers, Box 13.

57. Article in *Miami Herald*, 14 October 1979, in Clymer Papers, Box 13; Article in *Miami Herald*, 10 October 1979, in Clymer Papers, Box 13.

58. Article by Roger Simon, source unknown, reprinted with attached memo and comments, Jack Watson to Carter, 9 November 1979, PL-5: Political Affairs Files, Jimmy Carter Library; Memo, Jim Copeland to Carter, 7 December 1979, PL-5: Political Affairs Files, Jimmy Carter Library.

59. Memo, "Des Moines Rail Announcement," undated, Bill Smith Files, Mondale Papers, Box 2.

60. Letter, Sidney Lee to Carter, 3 December 1979, Cabinet Secretary and Intergovernmental Affairs, Jimmy Carter Library, Box 32.

61. Memo, Jim Copeland to Carter, 7 December 1979, PL-5: Political Affairs Files, Jimmy Carter Library.

62. "Political Announcements," *New York Times*, 14 October 1979, E18.

63. *Boston Herald* article, undated, in White House Press Office, Jimmy Carter Library, Box 9.

64. "The Wooing of Labor by the White House; News Analysis Accord on Economic Policy Hopes to 'Sit on My Hands,'" *New York Times*, 22 October 1979, A19.

65. Letter, Joseph Vatlentich (president, Local 2055, UAW) to Carter, 14 February 1980, Chief of Staff Files, Jimmy Carter Library, Box 32.

66. Letter, George M. Parker (president, AFGWU) to Jordan, 29 April 1980, Chief of Staff Files, Jimmy Carter Library, Box 142.

67. Letter, Frank Ivancie to Carter, 17 April 1980, Cabinet Secretary, Jimmy Carter Library, Box 32.

68. Letter, J. Munford Scott Jr. to Carter, 11 December 1979, Cabinet Secretary, Jimmy Carter Library, Box 32; Letter, Erman L. Forde to Carter, 30 September 1979, Records of the Office of Hispanic Affairs, Jimmy Carter Library, Box 2.

69. Letter, Congressman Frank Annunzio to Jordan, 8 September 1979, White House Press Office, Jimmy Carter Library, Box 9.

70. Memo, Sarah Weddington to Jordan, 17 December 1979, White House Press Office, Jimmy Carter Library, Box 9.

71. All stored in the White House Press Office, Jimmy Carter Library, Box 9.

72. Card dated 7 January 1980, White House Press Office, Jimmy Carter Library, Box 9.

73. Jordan sent a telegram to the chair of Cumberland County Democrats

who was hospitalized for tests: Memo, Bob Thornton to Jordan, 18 January 1980, White House Press Office, Jimmy Carter Library, Box 9.

74. "A Small Town in Iowa," *New York Magazine*, 21 January 1980, 11.

75. In one call to a county attorney, Carter was warned that the activist thought that the administration's policies were "Republican economics" and that he should be "assured that the President is a 'Fundamental Democrat.'" 15 December 1979, White House Press Office, Jimmy Carter Library, Box 9.

76. Memo, Moore to Carter, 1 August 1979, PL-10: Political Affairs Files, Jimmy Carter Library.

77. Letter, Norman Kill to Louis Martin, 25 October 1978, PL-2: Political Affairs Files, Jimmy Carter Library.

78. "Jimmy Strikes Back," *Newsweek*, 8 October 1980, 26–27.

79. "TV Ads: An Aid to Some Candidates but Not to Others," *Washington Post*, 12 May 1980, A2.

80. In Montgomery, Alabama, Carter activists picketed an address by Kennedy to a church with placards that read, "How can you save the country if you couldn't save Mary Jo?," "In Nation," *Boston Globe*, 2 March 1980, 6.

81. "Reporter's Notebook: Georgians Adjust to Iowa's Politics," *New York Times*, 19 January 1980, 11.

82. Press Release, "NCPAC's Ties to National Alliance of Senior Citizens Revealed," 30 October 1980, McGovern Papers, Box 412. The group was formed in early 1978 initially as an anti–Panama Canal organization. Its ability to evolve so rapidly demonstrated the remarkable agility of the New Right movement: Democratic Congressional Campaign Committee Report, February 1978, NOW Papers, Box 194.

83. Robert Freeman, *American Populist Conservatism, 1977–88* (PhD thesis, University of Cambridge, 2006), 81–96.

84. Robert Shrum, *No Excuses: Concessions of a Serial Campaigner* (New York: Simon and Schuster, 2007), 95.

85. Garland A. Haas, *Jimmy Carter and the Politics of Frustration* (Jefferson, N.C.: McFarland, 1992), 109–111.

86. Carter, *Keeping Faith*, 448.

87. "Death Behind a Keyhole," *Time*, 26 February 1979, 34.

88. Jordan, *Crisis*, 32.

89. "Teheran Students Seize U.S. Embassy and Hold Hostages; Ask Shah's Return and Trial," *New York Times*, 5 November 1979, A1.

90. "U.S. Reports Soviet Flying Many Troops to Afghan Conflict; World Condemnation Asked," *New York Times*, 26 December 1979, A1.

91. "Poll Shows Carter Gaining Support on Afghan Moves," *New York Times*, 16 January 1980, A1.

92. "CBS/*New York Times* Poll: April 1980," April 1980, Clymer Papers, Box 18.

93. "Stocks Rise on U.S. Bar to Iran," *New York Times*, 13 November 1979, D1.

94. "President Defends Mobile Missile Plan," *New York Times*, 30 May 1979, A1.

95. Haas, *Politics of Frustration*, 112–113.

96. "The Campaign Pendulum," *New York Times*, 18 January 1980, A12.

97. It lost him the key endorsement of Senator Moynihan of New York, who had been a key neoconservative supporter in 1979: "Moynihan Prefers the Role of a Neutral," *New York Times*, 17 March 1980, B1.

98. Hart December 1979 Polls, Clymer Papers, Box 15.

99. CBS/*New York Times* Poll, April 1980, Clymer Polls, Box 15.

100. Memo Jordan to Carter, undated, Chief of Staff Files, Jimmy Carter Library, Box 78.

101. Yankelovich Poll, 10–12 December 1979, Roper Center.

102. "Poll Shows Carter Gaining Support on Afghan Moves, Slipping on Iran," *New York Times*, 16 January 1980, A1.

103. *New York Times* collated survey polls, Clymer Papers, Box 15.

104. AIPO Poll, No. 144G, 27 November 1979, Roper Center.

105. Gallup Poll, 14–16 November 1979, Roper Center.

106. Gallup Poll, 30 November–3 December 1979, Roper Center.

107. Gallup Poll, 4–7 January 1980, Roper Center.

108. Yankelovich Poll, 23–24 July 1980, Roper Center.

109. Gallup Poll, 7–10 December 1979, Roper Center.

110. Gallup Poll, 4–7 January 1980, Roper Center.

111. "Prospect of the Draft Gets Mixed Response from Feminists," *New York Times*, 25 January 1980, FS1.

112. Letter, Edward J. Carlough to Carter, 22 January 1980, Chief of Staff Files, Jimmy Carter Library, Box 142.

113. Resolution, Raymond C. Lith (president, SMW International Association) to Carter, 3 January 1980, Chief of Staff Files, Jimmy Carter Library, Box 142.

114. "Labor Bides Its Time on 1980 Endorsements," *New York Times*, 6 January 1980, NE6.

115. Telegram, Vito J. Pitta to Carter and notes attached, 14 January 1980, Chief of Staff Files, Jimmy Carter Library, Box 142.

116. "Press Release," 9 April 1980, White House Press Office, Jimmy Carter Library, Box 89.

117. Press Release, "Former Congressman Austin Murphy Endorses President Carter," 14 April 1980, White House Press Office, Jimmy Carter Library, Box 89.

118. Card dated 13 January 1980, White House Press Office, Jimmy Carter Library, Box 9.

119. Interview with Tom Harkin, undated, Clymer Papers, Box 3.

120. Letter, James B. Longley to Carter, 10 March 1980, Cabinet Secretary, Jimmy Carter Library, Box 32.

121. "Iran Crimping Race," *New York Times*, 2 December 1979, NJ23.

122. "Former Congressman Thomas Morgan of Pennsylvania Endorses Pres. Carter," 26 March 1980, White House Press Office, Jimmy Carter Library, Box 89.

123. Miller told reporters that the administration "had not done enough for the coal miner." In contrast, Kennedy was attractive "because of his health insurance program." Article in *Washington Post*, 2 September 1979, in Chief of Staff Files, Jimmy Carter Library, Box 139.

124. "Statement of Edward M. Kennedy to the Annual Convention of the UMW," 13 December 1979, Clymer Papers, Box 19.

125. "Carter's Coal Conundrum," *New Republic*, 4 March 1978, 19.

126. Memo, Harry Huge to Carter, 14 June 1977, Chief of Staff Files, Jimmy Carter Library, Box 139: "Strikes have cost at least 11 percent of estimated total production or a loss of at least 15 million tons of coal. That is a severe impact upon economic growth." Memo, Harry Huge to Carter, 11 May 1977, Chief of Staff Files, Jimmy Carter Library, Box 139: Letter, Watson to Thomas O. Harris, 11 October 1978, Cabinet Secretary, Jimmy Carter Library, Box 37.

127. Interview with Don Stillman, 25 September 2006; "Confusion in the Coalfields," *New Republic*, 18 July 1970, 17; "Mine Workers United Against the United Mine Workers," *New Republic*, 6 March 1971, 14–16.

128. "This Week We Report on the Coal Strike," *John Herling Labor Letter*, 18 February 1978.

129. "Arnold Miller, Victor in UMW Election," *John Herling Labor Letter*, 20 June 1977.

130. Memo, Marshal to Carter, 17 June 1977, White House Central File: LA-7, Jimmy Carter Library.

131. "The membership of the UMWA are for the most part very conservative and patriotic and they will respond to a public statement." Memo, Harry Huge to Carter, 14 June 1977, Chief of Staff Files, Jimmy Carter Library, Box 139.

132. Memo, Carter to Milton Shapp, undated, White House Central File: LA-7, Jimmy Carter Library; Letter, Eizenstat to Representative Chalmers P. Wylie, 24 April 1978, White House Central File: LA-7, Jimmy Carter Library.

133. Memo, Ray Andrus to Leo Perlis, 10 March 1978, Meany Papers, Box 45; Letter, Fred Richmond to Meany, 10 March 1978, Meany Papers, Box 45; Minutes of press conference, 20 February 1978, Meany Papers, Box 100; Letter, Fraser to Dick Moore, undated, Fraser Papers, Box 75; "Start from Scratch," *New Republic*, 18 March 1978, 5; Letter, Catherine Ames, president, Local 140 AFSCME, to Carter, 23 March 1978, Meany Papers, Box 45.

134. Letter, Miller to Meany, 8 March 1978, Meany Papers, Box 45; Letter, Henry A. Gryn to Fraser, undated, Fraser Papers, Box 75.

135. Memo, Schultze to Carter, 29 September 1978, CEA, Jimmy Carter Library, Box 72; Memo, Marshal to Carter, 5 October 1978, Papers of the Council of Economic Affairs, Jimmy Carter Library, Box 78; Memo, David Wyss to William Nordhaus, 29 September 1978, CEA, Jimmy Carter Library, Box 78.

136. Memo, Marshal to Carter, 26 September 1978, CEA, Jimmy Carter Library, Box 72.

137. "Strikes Winding Down," *John Herling Labor Letter*, 26 November 1977; "Struggle in Steel," *New Republic*, 5 February 1977, 12.

138. "UMW in the Pits," *New Republic*, 1 April 1978, 5; "Carter's Coal Conundrum," *New Republic*, 4 March 1978, 19.

139. Gannet News Service piece, undated, in Chief of Staff Files, Jimmy Carter Library, Box 139.

140. Letter, Sam Church Jr. to Carter, 19 November 1979, Chief of Staff Files, Jimmy Carter Library, Box 139.

141. Washington UPI news release, undated, in Chief of Staff Files, Jimmy Carter Library, Box 140.

142. Letter, Sam Church to Carter, 16 May 1980, Chief of Staff Files, Jimmy Carter Library, Box 140.

143. Resolution, undated, in Chief of Staff Files, Jimmy Carter Library, Box 140; "Statement by Sen. Edward M. Kennedy on Behalf of Campaign for Safe Energy '80," 15 February 1980, Chief of Staff Files, Jimmy Carter Library, Box 139; The building tradesmen organized Carter's campaign in New Hampshire largely because of Kennedy's commitment to stop the building of the Seabrook nuclear power plant: "State by State Report," 25 February 1980, Chief of Staff Files, Jimmy Carter Library, Box 139.

144. Miller denounced the decision from retirement: *Washington Post* article, undated, in Chief of Staff Files, Jimmy Carter Library, Box 140. A bad mood was reported at the UMWA Convention in Gannett News Service transcript. Undated, in Chief of Staff Files, Jimmy Carter Library, Box 139; Memo, Borkowski to Mondale, 26 May 1980, Legal and Procedural Files, Mondale Papers, Box 219.

145. Transcript of Iowa spot, undated, in Chief of Staff Files, Jimmy Carter Library, Box 140.

146. "Surprise Harvest," *Time*, 4 February 1980, 24.

147. Bruce Miroff, *The Liberals' Moment: The McGovern Insurgency and the Identity Crisis of the Democratic Party* (Lawrence: University Press of Kansas, 2007), 59–63.

148. "How Carter Can Win," *New York Times*, 25 November 1979, SM9.

149. Letter, William Rodgers to Carter, 24 August 1979, Cabinet Secretary, Jimmy Carter Library, Box 32.

150. Andrew E. Busch and William G. Mayer, *The Front Loading Problem in Presidential Nominations* (Washington, D.C.: Brookings Institution Press, 2003), 11–12.

Chapter 6: "We Gotta Fight Back!"

1. Press Release, "Why Not Wage and Price Controls?," 10 March 1980, Legislative Files, O'Neill Papers, Box 41; Letter, Kennedy to O'Neill, 15 April 1980, Legislative Files, O'Neill Papers, Box 41.

2. "Speech to Georgetown University," 28 January 1980, Clymer Papers, Box 9; Memo, Frank Mankiewicz to Robert Shrum, undated, Clymer Papers, Box 13.

3. "To Sail Against the Wind," *Time*, 11 February 1980.

4. Interview with Peter Hart, 25 September 2006.

5. "Kennedy seems actually to believe what he's saying—a phenomenon that should not be noteworthy." Elizabeth Drew, *Portrait of an Election: The 1980 Presidential Campaign* (New York: Routledge and Kegan Paul, 1981), 250.

6. "Voice of the People: Voters Evaluate the Illinois Presidential Primary Candidates," 12 March 1980, *Chicago Tribune*, D2.

7. Article in *Boston Herald*, 31 January 1980, in Clymer Papers, Box 24.

8. "Why Ted's Still in the Race," *Boston Globe*, 31 July 1980, in Clymer Papers, Box 24.

9. Letter, Rabbi Alexander M. Schindler to residents of New York, undated, White House Press Office, Jimmy Carter Library, Box 89.

10. "Kennedy Camp Starts to Lay Off Some of Its Staff, but Many Will Continue Working Without Pay," *New York Times*, 24 January 1980, B8.

11. Connecticut Women's Advisory Committee for Kennedy Press Release, 1 February 1980, Korman Papers.

12. Press Release, "Connecticut: The Kennedy Campaign," 9 February 1980, Korman Papers.

13. Kennedy ad, 9 April 1980, Audiovisual Archives, JFK Library.

14. "Address of Senator Edward M. Kennedy to the Association for the Betterment of New York City," 5 March 1980, Clymer Papers, Box 19.

15. Both shown on 27 March 1980, "Ted Kennedy Spots, 1980," Audiovisual Archives, JFK Library.

16. Kennedy ad, 6 July 1980, Audiovisual Archives, JFK Library; Kennedy ad, 9 April 1980, Audiovisual Archives, JFK Library.

17. "Democrats See Maine Vote as Kennedy Resurgence," *New York Times*, 12 February 1980, A19.

18. "Carter Wins in Vermont; Anderson and Reagan Close," *New York Times*, 5 March 1980, A23.

19. "Kennedy: We're in It to Stay," *Time*, 10 March 1980, 10.

20. "Kennedy Wins by 2–1 in Massachusetts; G.O.P. in 3-Way Race," *New York Times*, 5 March 1980, A1.

21. "Carter Defeats Kennedy at Caucuses in 4 of 5 States," *New York Times*, 13 March 1980, B11. This came as a surprise to the administration, who had expected an easy victory in the state: Memo, Powell to Jordan, 12 March 1980, White House Press Office, Jimmy Carter Library, Box 9.

22. "Carter Wins Strong Victory in Iowa," *New York Times*, 22 January 1980, A1; "Clear Cut Triumphs," *New York Times*, 12 March 1980, A1.

23. As a result, Kennedy effectively withdrew from some primaries, which the administration understood meant that some of its victories were morally hollow: Memo, Borkowski to Mondale, 14 May 1980, Legal and Procedural Files, Mondale Papers, Box 219. This affected the outcome in some key primaries that otherwise Kennedy might have performed well in, including Maryland: Memo, Borkowski to Mondale, 29 April 1980, Legal and Procedural Files, Mondale Papers, Box 219.

24. "Last Chance for Kennedy," *Newsweek*, 10 March 1980, 36.

25. Carter outspent Kennedy 2–1 in the Vermont primary: Herbert E. Alexander, *Financing the 1980 Election* (Lexington, Mass.: Lexington Books, 1983), 222.

26. "Kennedy Trims and Recasts Drive in Move to Rescue Presidential Bid," *New York Times*, 1 March 1980, 1.

27. "Kennedy Under Stress," *New York Times*, 17 March, A19; it was predicted

to be an easy win in late 1979: "Carter Not Willing to Give Up Chicago Without a Fight," *Washington Star*, 2 November 1979, A5.

28. "Mayor Byrne, Endorsing Kennedy, Favors a Slate Committed to Him; Says Chairman Will Decide," *New York Times*, 31 October 1979, A11.

29. "Chicago Mayor to Back Kennedy; She Feels Carter Can't Win Illinois," *New York Times*, 18 October 1979, 1.

30. The endorsement of Mayor Bill Green of Philadelphia was similarly complicated for Kennedy. Green, like Byrne, ran against the city machine on an anticorruption, socially liberal ticket. Like Byrne's, Green's endorsement caused many city officeholders to support Carter. However, Green's endorsement had less of a negative impact in Philadelphia than Byrne's did in Chicago—Kennedy swept the city: Memo, Borkowski to Mondale, 12 March 1980, Mondale Papers, Box 25.A.O.10.F.

31. "In Chicago," *New Republic*, 27 October 1979, 8.

32. "Machine Woman," *New Republic*, 17 March 1979, 16; "Hard Times in Chicago," *New York Times*, 9 March 1980, SM5.

33. Memo, Tim Kraft to Jordan, 22 October 1979, White House Press Office, Jimmy Carter Library, Box 9.

34. "Assessor Hynes Gives Carter Endorsement," *Chicago Sun Times*, 19 November 1979, in White House Press Office; "Local Support for Carter Grows," *Chicago Tribune*, 13 November 1979, 2.

35. "Byrne Move to Kennedy Splits Chicago Votes," *Washington Post*, 15 November 1980, 2.

36. "Kennedy Hails the Irish: Mayor Byrne Is Booed," *New York Times*, 18 March 1980, B6.

37. "Key Victories for Favorites; Carter and Reagan Gain Formidable Advantages," *New York Times*, 19 March 1980, 1.

38. "Kennedy: We're in It to Stay," *Time*, 10 March 1980, 10.

39. "In Iowa and Elsewhere, the Kennedy Campaign Is Getting into Shape for Battle," *New York Times*, 3 December 1979, D10.

40. "Byrne Gives Mixed Report on Kennedy's Chances Next Tuesday," *Chicago Tribune*, 13 March 1980, 12.

41. "Campaigns Wind Down," *Chicago Tribune*, 16 March 1980, 16.

42. CBS/*New York Times* Illinois Primary Poll, 18 March 1980, Clymer Papers, Box 15.

43. "Chicago Chill Dims Kennedy's Chances," *Chicago Tribune*, 20 March 1980, 13.

44. CBS/*New York Times* Poll, March 1980, Clymer Papers, Box 15.

45. "Carter Deals Severe Blow to Kennedy," *Chicago Tribune*, 19 March 1980, 4.

46. CBS/*New York Times* Illinois Primary Poll, 18 March 1980, Clymer Papers, Box 15.

47. "Kennedy Wins Poll of Urban Panels," *Chicago Tribune*, 14 March 1980, 14.

48. CBS/*New York Times* Illinois Primary Poll, 18 March 1980, Clymer Papers, Box 15.

49. "Polls Show Big Party Crossover," *Chicago Tribune*, 17 March 1980, 1.

50. "Carter Deals Severe Blow to Kennedy," *Chicago Tribune*, 19 March 1980, 4.

51. "Carter Seeks Aid for Chicago," *Chicago Tribune*, 21 March 1980, 1.

52. Hamilton Jordan, *Crisis: The Last Year of the Carter Presidency* (New York: Putnam Adult, 1982), 23.

53. Memo to Carter/Mondale Presidential Committee, 25 February 1980, White House Press Office, Jimmy Carter Library, Box 9.

54. "Chicago Chill Dims Kennedy's Chances," *Chicago Tribune*, 20 March 1980, 13.

55. "Kennedy's New York Campaign in Severe Disarray," *New York Times*, 18 March 1980, B7.

56. "Carter Vows to Press for Urban Aid," *New York Times*, 22 March 1980, 1.

57. "New York Thinks Liberal but May Vote Conservative," *New York Times*, 23 March 1980, E2.

58. "Kennedy Wins Upset in New York," *New York Times*, 26 March 1980, 1.

59. "Predicting Outcome of Primaries Proves Elusive Goal for Pollsters," *New York Times*, 27 March 1980, B7.

60. ABC New York Primary Poll, 25 March 1980, Roper Center.

61. "In Midwood Strong Support for Kennedy over U.N. Vote," *New York Times*, 26 March 1980, B4; he was not alone in doubting Kennedy's actual electoral strength. "Kennedy Wins but Carter Worries About Reagan," *L.A. Times*, 26 March 1980, 1.

62. CBS/*New York Times* New York Primary Poll, 25 March 1980, Clymer Papers, Box 15; Jews were also consistent supporters of Kennedy throughout the primaries: "The New York Poll," Winter 1979, Mondale Papers, Box 24.L.O.5.B.

63. ABC New York Primary Poll, 25 March 1980, Roper Center.

64. CBS/*New York Times* New York Primary Poll, 25 March 1980, Clymer Papers, Box 15.

65. Contrasted with 61 percent to 30 percent in Illinois: CBS/*New York Times* Illinois Primary Poll, 18 March 1980, Clymer Papers, Box 15.

66. "Inflation, Israel and Aid to City the Main Issues," *New York Times*, 26 March 1980, A1.

67. "Wide Margin in City; Democrats Award Senator 192–146 Delegate Edge in the 2 Primaries," *New York Times*, 26 March 1980, A1.

68. "Two Victories for Senator Mean He's Still in the Race," *New York Times*, 26 March 1980, A1.

69. "Kennedy's Startling Win," *Time*, 7 April 1980, 14.

70. Speech, Sarange Lake, New York, 10 April 1980, Moynihan Papers, Box 4750.

71. "The New Elite and an Urban Renaissance: The Exodus from the City a New Kind of Industry," *New York Times*, 14 January 1979, SM4.

72. "Wins First Victory in Northern Vote," *New York Times*, 17 May 1972, 30.

73. Jody Carlson, *George C. Wallace and the Politics of Powerlessness: The Wallace Campaigns for the Presidency, 1964–76* (New Brunswick, N.J.: Transaction Books, 1981), 225.

74. "Anti-busing, Pro-gun, Pro-life Forces Haunting Kennedy," *Boston Herald*, 2 March 1980; "Muskie Far Back in 3-Man Battle," *New York Times*, 3 May 1972, 32.

75. Memo, Borkowski to Mondale, 1 March 1980, Mondale Papers, Box 25. A.O.10.F.

76. Comparison of results printed in *New York Times*, 17 May 1972, and *New York Times*, 14 May 1980.

77. "McGovern Nears Nomination Total," *New York Times*, 7 June 1972, 28.

78. "Maine Results Hint Impact of Students; Close New Hampshire Battle Seen After Kennedy Resurgence Further Impact Held Possible," *New York Times*, 12 February 1980, A1; Memo, Borkowski to Mondale, 18 January 1980, Mondale Papers, Box 25.A.O.10.F.

79. "Dakotan Beats Humphrey by a Big Margin in Jersey," *New York Times*, 7 June 1972, 1.

80. "Humphrey Loss," *New York Times*, 7 June 1972, 1.

81. "Dakotan Strong," *New York Times*, 21 June 1972, 1.

82. "Reagan and Carter Near Presidential Nominations; Dwindling Hopes How the Vote Went," *New York Times*, 15 May 1980, B14.

83. "The Kennedy Coalition," *New York Times*, 25 April 1980, A18. For a rendering of the standard myth of Robert Kennedy's 1968 Democratic primary electoral coalition, see Lester David and Irene David, *Bobby Kennedy: The Making of a Folk Hero* (London: Sidgwick and Jackson, 1986), 300–316; and for a key reappraisal, see Brian Dooley, *Robert Kennedy: The Final Years* (Keele: Ryburn, 1995), 19.

84. "Pattern in State; Senator and Arizonan Are Strong in City," *New York Times*, 7 April 1976, 85.

85. Comparison of results printed in *New York Times*, 8 April 1976, and *New York Times*, 27 March 1980.

86. "Reagan Gets Democratic Support," *L.A. Times*, 5 June 1980, 13.

87. "Wisconsin Poll Shows Protest Fading," *New York Times*, 2 April 1980, A20.

88. CBS/*New York Times* Wisconsin Primary Poll, 1 April 1980, Clymer Papers, Box 15.

89. Interview with Walter Mondale, 7 June 2007.

90. Private notes on "Program," undated; private notes on "Arizona Primary Project," undated, United Farm Workers: Office of the President Files, Walter Reuther Library, Wayne State University, Detroit, Michigan, Box 34.

91. "Kennedy Defeats Carter in Arizona Caucus Votes," *New York Times*, 14 April 1980, B10; "Kennedy Wins Arizona Primary," *Tucson Citizen*, 14 April 1980, 1.

92. "Kennedy Overtakes Carter," *Arizona Daily Star*, 13 April 1980, 1.

93. Private notes on "Results," undated, Chavez Papers, Box 34.

94. "Kennedy and Carter End Efforts in a Close Race in Pennsylvania," *New York Times*, 22 April 1980, A1.

95. "Carter Victor in Ohio Voting, Exceeds 1,666 Delegate Goal; Kennedy Wins Jersey Contest," *New York Times*, 4 June 1980, A1.

96. "Pennsylvania Results Give Kennedy 9,800-Vote Edge," *New York Times*, 24 April 1980, A22.

97. "Kennedy's Startling Win," *Time*, 7 April 1980, 14.

98. CBS/*New York Times* Pennsylvania Primary Poll, 22 April 1980, Clymer Papers, Box 15.

99. "Who Votes for Whom and Why," *Philadelphia Inquirer*, 23 April 1980, 1.

100. CBS/*New York Times* Pennsylvania Primary Poll, 22 April 1980, Clymer Papers, Box 15; Memo, Borkowski to Mondale, 11 March 1980, Mondale Papers, Box 25.A.O.10.F.

101. "Kennedy: Why He Lost W. Penna," *Philadelphia Inquirer*, 24 April 1980, 6A.

102. "Why the Voters Chose the Candidates They Did," *Philadelphia Inquirer*, 23 April 1980, 4A.

103. "Late Surge for Underdogs," *New York Times*, 23 April 1980, A1.

104. "Presidential Primary Vote by Counties," *Philadelphia Inquirer*, 29 April 1976, 10A.

105. "Carter Scores Solid Victory, Jackson Runs 2, Udall 3," *Philadelphia Inquirer*, 28 April 1976, 4A.

106. "Clinton Clearly Outduels Obama in Pennsylvania," *New York Times*, 23 April 2008.

107. "It's a Mistake to Say Democratic Race Over," ABC News Harris Poll, 7 April 1980, United Farm Workers: Office of the President Files, Walter Reuther Library, Wayne State University, Detroit, Michigan, Box 34.

108. "Kennedy Is Winner by Narrow Margin in Michigan Voting," *New York Times*, 27 April 1980, 1; *DSOC Michigan News*, March 1980, UAW Region 1, Box 232.

109. "Kennedy Scores Upset in Vermont," *L.A. Times*, 25 May 1980, A21.

110. Memo, Borkowski to Mondale, 30 March 1980, Mondale Papers, Box 25.A.O.10.F.

111. "Who's Supporting Who and Other Stats from the Democrats," *Colorado Statesman*, 24 May 1980, 8.

112. Memo, Borkowski to Mondale, 2 April 1980, Legal and Procedural Files, Mondale Papers, Box 219.

113. "Kennedy Wins Denver Caucuses; but Convention Race a Toss-up," *New York Times*, 31 May 1980, 12.

114. "Carter Edges Kennedy for Delegate," *New York Times*, 14 June 1980, 12.

115. "Kennedy Won Popular Vote," *New York Times*, 5 June 1980, B8.

116. "Release from the Office of the Senator: Comments of Edward M. Kennedy," 3 June 1980, Clymer Papers, Box 9.

117. "News on Hispanic Affairs #3," published by the White House, March/April 1980, Weddington Papers, Jimmy Carter Library, Box 69.

118. This was an expressly political move related to the primaries: Memo, Harrison to Richard Moe, 12 November 1979, Bill Smith Files, Mondale Papers, Box 2.

119. "What Has the Carter Administration Done for Hispanics?," undated, Office of Hispanic Affairs, Jimmy Carter Library, Box 14.

120. "Most Hispanics Support Kennedy," *Rocky Mountain News*, 10 December 1979, 3; Memo, Harrison to Richard Moe, 16 November 1979, Bill Smith Files, Mondale Papers, Box 2.

121. Memo, Joseph M. Gomez to Tim Kraft, 4 March 1980, Office of Hispanic Affairs, Jimmy Carter Library, Box 14.

122. Memo, Franklin D. Lopez to Robert Strauss, 8 July 1980; Memo, "The 1980 Democratic Primary Mexican American Presidential Preference Vote," undated,

Office of Hispanic Affairs, Jimmy Carter Library, Box 1; "Reagan Heads for Narrow Victory over Bush in Texas Primary Vote," *New York Times*, 4 May 1980, 1.

123. "Kennedy Victory a Surprise," *Albuquerque Journal*, 5 June 1980, 5.

124. "Carter, Kennedy Divide Delegates in State's Primary," *Albuquerque Journal*, 4 June 1980, 1.

125. "Presidential Primary Totals," *Albuquerque Journal*, 5 June 1980, 5; "Chavez Ends Fast at Kennedy Rites," *New York Times*, 5 June 1972, 65; "Chavez Boosts Kennedy Here," *Arizona Daily Star*, 10 April 1980, 1.

126. Interview with Fred Harris, 8 August 2006.

127. "Presidential Primary Totals," *Albuquerque Journal*, 5 June 1980, 5.

128. "Tuesday's Vote Ends First Round of 1980 Campaigning," *Aberdeen American News*, 1 June 1980, 2.

129. "Indians Help Kennedy's Narrow Win," *Argus*, 5 June 1980.

130. "Late Push in S.D. Worked for Kennedy," *Aberdeen News*, 4 June 1980, 1; "Democratic Presidential Primary," *Daily Capital Journal*, 4 June 1980, 4.

131. As with Hispanics, the Carter administration made a concerted effort to court Indian votes in the run-up to the primaries, to no avail: Memo, Maryline to Maxine, 5 January 1978, Deputy Chief of Staff Files, Mondale Papers, Box 244.

132. "Carter, Reagan Win Big in State Caucuses," *Chicago Tribune*, 13 March 1980, 5.

133. Betty Glad, *Jimmy Carter: In Search of the Great White House* (New York: Norton, 1980), 323–330.

134. Reagan March/April Poll, Clymer Papers, Box 15; "Despite Memories of the '60's Blacks Lean Toward Carter," *New York Times*, 11 May 1980, 58.

135. "Carter and Reagan Win Easy Victories in 3 State Primaries," *New York Times*, 7 May 1980, A1.

136. "New Show Me Stance of Black Voters," *U.S. News and World Report*, 10 April 1978, 64.

137. Memo, Borkowski to Mondale, 11 March 1980, Mondale Papers, Box 25.A.O.10.F.

138. CBS/*New York Times* Florida Primary Day Poll, 11 March 1980, Clymer Papers, Box 15.

139. "Displeasure with Carter Turned Many to Reagan," *New York Times*, 9 November 1980, 28. The administration knew it had lost the Jewish vote in the course of the primaries. It privately recognized the damage inflicted by its equivocal stance on Israel and predicted, correctly, that Anderson would gain significantly from defecting liberal Jews. Memo, "Florida," unsigned and undated, White House Press Office, Jimmy Carter Library, Box 9.

140. Alan M. Fisher, "Jewish Political Shift? Erosion, Yes; Conversion, No," in Seymour Martin Lipset, "Party Coalitions and the 1980 Election," in *Party Coalitions in the 1980s*, ed. Seymour Martin Lipset (New Brunswick, N.J.: Transaction Books, 1981).

141. "An Uneasy Electorate," *New York Times*, 4 June 1980, A1.

142. "Kennedy's Jersey Victory Indicates Trouble for Carter," *New York Times*, 5 June 1980, B10.

143. "President and Kennedy to Meet Today," *New York Times*, 6 June 1980, A1.

144. CBS/*New York Times* New Jersey Primary Poll, 3 June 1980, Roper Center.

145. "Last Primaries Held," *New York Times*, 4 June 1980, A1.

146. "Kennedy's Jersey Victory Indicates Trouble for Carter," *New York Times*, 5 June 1980, B10.

147. "Kennedy Continues Drive for Minority Group Support," *L.A. Times*, 25 May 1980, A23.

148. "Democrats in Poll Back Carter over Kennedy 2–1," *L.A. Times*, 1 June 1980, A6.

149. "Latino Leader Stresses Ties with Blacks," *L.A. Times*, 25 May 1980, A3.

150. "6 California Congressmen Back Kennedy," *New York Times*, 28 May 1980, B16.

151. "Kennedy Cites Failed Economic Policies," *New York Times*, 29 May 1980, B1.

152. Drew, *Portrait of an Election*, 170–171; "Reagan, Kennedy Wind Up Campaigns in California," *L.A. Times*, 3 June 1980, 1.

153. ABC California Primary Poll, 3 June 1980, Roper Center.

154. "Kennedy, Reagan Victors in State," *L.A. Times*, 4 June 1980, B1.

155. "Reagan Gets Democrat Support," *L.A. Times*, 5 June 1980, 18.

156. "Ford Victor in Jersey and Ohio; Carter Is Set Back in Jersey; Reagan, Brown Lead California," *New York Times*, 9 June 1976, 1.

157. "Tax Cut Is Rejected, 3–2, on Coast; Defeats Former Mayor," *New York Times*, 5 June 1980, B9.

158. "Ballot Measures Spark Voter Interest," *L.A. Times*, 1 June 1980, A1.

159. "The Case for Controls," *New Republic*, 14 October 1978, 18; "The Case for Wage-Price Controls," *Wall Street Journal*, 27 February 1980, 26.

160. "Economic Scene: Price Controls Gaining Friends," *New York Times*, 27 February 1980, D2.

161. "The People Want Controls," *New York Times*, 3 February 1980, F18.

162. "Polls Find Protectionism Trend," *New York Times*, 27 June 1980.

163. "What Is a Conservative?," *New York Times*, 31 August 1980, SM4.

164. CBS/*New York Times* New Hampshire Primary Poll, 26 February 1980, Clymer Papers, Box 15.

165. CBS/*New York Times* Massachusetts Primary Poll, 4 March 1980, White House Press Office, Jimmy Carter Library, Box 2.

166. CBS/*New York Times* Florida Primary Poll, 11 March 1980 and CBS/*New York Times* New Hampshire Primary Poll, 26 February 1980, Clymer Papers, Box 15.

167. Some voices in the administration recognized this and urged Carter to consider restraining defense expenditure while increasing social spending: Memo, Mondale to Carter, 5 February 1979, Legal and Procedural Files, Mondale Papers, Box 204.

168. The policy drew support because it built on popular antipathy toward big business and awareness of the growing need for conservation. See Al Richman,

"The Polls: Public Attitudes Toward the Energy Crisis," *Public Opinion Quarterly* 43 (1979): 576–585.

169. "Most Americans No Longer Favor Tax Cuts, Due to Inflation and Recession Fears," Louis Harris Poll, 24 September 1979, Mondale Papers, Box 4; "The Election Year Climate: A Centrist Trend?," American Political Report, 20 June 1980, Leadership Files, O'Neill Papers, Box 30.

170. Baron Report, 13 October 1978, Leadership Files, O'Neill Papers, Box 2.

171. Memo, Richard Moe to White House Staff, 20 June 1978, Richard Moe Files, Mondale Papers, Box 2.

172. "Candidates Economic Stances Defy Tradition," *L.A. Times*, 27 May 1980, OC1.

173. Walter Dean Burnham, "The 1980 Earthquake: Realignment, Reaction or What?" in *The Hidden Election: Politics and Economics in the 1980 Presidential Election*, ed. Thomas Ferguson and Joel Rogers (New York: Pantheon Books, 1981), 127.

174. Everett Carll Ladd Jr., "The Polls: Taxing and Spending," *Public Opinion Quarterly* 43 (1979): 126–135.

175. "Americans Believe a President Can Make Decisive Difference in Solving Nation's Problems," Louis Harris Poll, 3 July 1980, Mondale Papers, Box 4.

176. National Congressional Districts Survey, 6 March 1980, Legislative Files, O'Neill Papers, Box 30.

177. A comparison of data from Hart December 1979 Polls, Clymer Papers, Box 15, and "National Survey of Voter Attitudes: Reagan for President for Committee," April 1979, Clymer Papers, Box 15.

178. Letter, Douglas E. Schoen to Smeal, 25 August 1979, NOW Papers, Box 200; "ERA Campaign Paying Off," Louis Harris Poll, 17 July 1978, NOW Papers, Box 87.

179. "Charts and Graphs Study of Nat. Attitudes Towards the ERA," undated, NOW Papers, Box 200.

180. CBS/*New York Times* Poll, June 1978, Part III "ERA," NOW Papers, Box 194.

181. Louis Harris Poll, 6 July 1978, NOW Papers, Box 194; Press Release, Louis Harris's remarks on polls, 30 January 1980, NOW Papers, Box 200.

182. *Chicago Tribune* article and notes, undated, in NOW Papers, Box 200.

183. "Campaign Issues," ABC/Harris Poll, 15 July 1980, NOW Papers, Box 194.

184. CBS/*New York Times* Poll, June 1978, part 3, "ERA," NOW Papers, Box 194.

185. "Profile of the 1980 Electorate," ABC/Harris Poll, 29 May 1980, NOW Papers, Box 194.

186. "The Evangelical Vote," ABC/Harris Poll, 6 October 1980, NOW Papers, Box 194.

187. Memo, Louis Harris to file, 4 November 1976, NOW Papers, Box 200.

188. "It's Rightward On," *Time*, 1 June 1980, 12.

189. Garry Wills, *Under God: Religion and American Politics* (New York: Simon and Schuster, 1990), 272.

190. Interview with Eleanor Smeal, 25 February 2007.

191. Austin Ranney, *The American Elections of 1984* (Durham, N.C.: Duke University Press, 1985), 51.

192. "The Catholic Issue," ABC/Harris Poll, 24 April 1980, Clymer Papers, Box 15; "*L.A. Times* Poll: Chappaquiddick a Factor in Times Survey—Kennedy Rating Drops 34 Percent," undated, White House Press Office, Jimmy Carter Library, Box 9.

193. CBS/*New York Times* Pennsylvania Primary Poll, 22 April 1980, Clymer Papers, Box 15 .

194. "Carter Taking Support from Kennedy in the Challenger's Own Strongholds," *L.A. Times*, 17 January 1980, 19.

195. Memo, "Milwaukee Sentinel Survey," undated, White House Press Office, Jimmy Carter Library, Box 9.

196. CBS/*New York Times* Massachusetts Primary Day Poll, 4 March 1980, White House Press Office, Jimmy Carter Library, Box 9.

197. Interview with Richard Goodwin, 17 September 1993, Clymer Papers, Box 4.

Chapter 7: Letting the Dream Die

1. "Carter and Kennedy to Meet Today to Cope with Democratic Breach," *New York Times*, 5 June 1980, A1.

2. Interview with Carter, Clymer Papers, Box 4.

3. Interview with Peter Hart, 25 September 2006.

4. "Kennedy Supports New Move for an Open Convention," *New York Times*, 28 July 1980, A18.

5. Interview with Mondale, 27 March 1997, Clymer Papers, Box 4.

6. "Kennedy Meets with the President and Declares He Is Still Candidate," *New York Times*, 6 June 1980, A1.

7. Interview with Adam Clymer, 19 September 2006.

8. "Democratic Platform Battle: Context Is Key," *New York Times*, 26 June 1980, B9.

9. Byron E. Shafer, *Bifurcated Politics: Evolution and Reform in the National Party Convention* (Cambridge, Mass.: Harvard University Press, 1988), 331.

10. Workbook on the 1980 Democratic Convention, July 1980, Leadership Files, O'Neill Papers, Box 31; Memo, delegate selection rules for the 1980 Democratic Convention, 4 June 1978, Leadership Files, O'Neill Papers, Box 31.

11. "Democrats Endorse Rules Change," *Baltimore Sun*, 11 May 1978, A-9; Booklet, "Openness, Participation and Party Building," by the Winograd Commission, 1978, Leadership Files, O'Neill Papers, Box 28.

12. "Delegate Revolt Tactic Defended by Kennedy," *Washington Star*, 17 April 1980.

13. "Scenario for an Open Rebellion at the 1980 Democratic Convention," *Washington Star*, 25 May 1980, A4.

14. "Carey Supports 'Open Convention' and Koch Trims His Backing for Carter; Talk of Jackson as Nominee," *New York Times*, 29 July 1980, A1; Interview

with Byrd, 11 April 1998, Clymer Papers, Box 3; Adam Clymer speculates that Byrd would have accepted: "Byrd certainly supported Kennedy . . . he understood poverty." His silence during the campaign was probably influenced, like O'Neill's, by his position within the party leadership. Interview with Adam Clymer, 19 September 2006.

15. Memo to file on delegate rules challenge, undated, Staff Files, O'Neill Papers, Box 3.

16. Press Release, "House Democrats Overwhelmingly Support Open Convention Proposal," 1 August 1980, Staff Files, O'Neill Papers, Box 4.

17. "Disgruntled Democrats in Congress Weigh Bid for New Party Nominee," *New York Times*, 26 July 1980, 1.

18. "Carter Battles a Revolt," *Time*, 11 August 1980, 14.

19. "Disgruntled Democrats in Congress Weigh Bid for New Party Nominee," *New York Times*, 26 July 1980, 1.

20. "Campaign Report; Democrats to Begin Fight over Carter Loyalty Rule," *New York Times*, 8 July 1980, B6.

21. Memo, Steven Ross to Kevin Peterson, 21 July 1980, Legislative Files, O'Neill Papers, Box 60.

22. John A. Farrell, *Tip O'Neill and the Democratic Century* (London: Little, Brown, 2001), 526–534.

23. Letter, Kennedy to White, 5 May 1980, Leadership Files, O'Neill Papers, Box 31.

24. Countering Carter's offensive, the leaders of some state delegations began to countenance voting with Kennedy against F(3)(c). In the Illinois delegation, Mayor Byrne attempted to regain her authority after Kennedy's defeat in the state in March by claiming she could deliver 50 to 60 votes for the challenge. "She then tried to get those votes with a lobbying effort that made Dick Daley look timid." Despite the attraction of lucrative job offers, only 10 Carter delegates voted against F(3)(c). "A Veneer of Unity," *Newsweek*, 25 August 1980, 24–30.

25. Letter, Fraser to delegates, 12 August 1980, Fraser Papers, Box 68.

26. Statement to Platform Committee by Thomas R. Donahue, on Behalf of the AFL-CIO, 14 June 1980, Leadership Files, O'Neill Papers, Box 32.

27. Press Release, "Jerry Wurf's Presentation to the Democratic Platform Committee," undated, Leadership Files, O'Neill Papers, Box 32.

28. Press Release, Building and Construction Trades, Department of the AFL-CIO, testimony before the Platform Committee, undated, Leadership Files, O'Neill Papers, Box 32.

29. Testimony of the NEA before the Platform Committee, undated, Legislative Files, O'Neill Papers, Box 60.

30. Testimony of Garment Workers before Platform Committee, undated, Legislative Files, O'Neill Papers, Box 60.

31. Press Release, "From Abe Ribicoff," 13 June 1980, Legislative Files, O'Neill Papers, Box 58.

32. Memo, Stephen C. Duffy to Kevin Peterson, 21 July 1980, Legislative Files, O'Neill Papers, Box 60.

33. Memo, Paul Kirk to O'Neill, 23 July 1980, Staff Files, O'Neill Papers, Box 4.

34. Memo, Jack Lew to O'Neill, 17 July 1980, Staff Files, O'Neill Papers, Box 3.

35. Memo, Paul Kirk to O'Neill, 23 July 1980, Staff Files, O'Neill Papers, Box 4.

36. "Billy Carter Is Not a Buffoon," *Time*, 1 September 1980, 24.

37. "Carter's Democratic Base Eroding," Louis Harris Poll, 4 August 1980, Mondale Papers, Box 4.

38. "Democratic Voters Favor an Open Convention," Louis Harris Poll, 8 August 1980, Mondale Papers, Box 4.

39. "Poll Shows Carter Gaining After New Conference on Brother," *New York Times*, 10 August 1980, 1.

40. "Kennedy had come to believe that his was not simply a candidacy but also a cause—an instrument for moving the Democratic Party closer to what he saw as its proper ideological home. If Kennedy did lose, Carter would need his following, and there remained the platform and even Carter's policies to be affected." "A Reporter at Large: 1980—The Democratic Convention," article in Kirkland Papers, Box 52.

41. "Carter Campaign Giving Delegates the Treatment," *Washington Post*, 13 May 1980, 4.

42. "A Reporter at Large: 1980—The Democratic Convention," article in Kirkland Papers, Box 52.

43. "Kennedy Decries Party's Platform as Union Cheer," *New York Times*, 26 June 1980, A1.

44. "Both Carter and Kennedy Appear on Same Equal Rights Podium," *New York Times*, 19 June 1980, A19.

45. "On the Floor, Carter and Kennedy Camps Deploy Foot Soldiers to Follow Delegates; Instructions to Whips Drawn into a Circle," *New York Times*, 12 August 1980, B10.

46. "All That Unifies the Democrats Is November; For Carter, an Opportunity Missed," *New York Times*, 17 August 1980, E1.

47. "A Veneer of Unity," *Newsweek*, 25 August 1980, 24.

48. "Loser in Showdown; 1,936-to-1,390 Vote Easily Assures the President of Renomination," *New York Times*, 12 August 1980, A1.

49. Letter, Kennedy to O'Neill, 13 August 1980, Staff Files, O'Neill Papers, Box 3; "A Veneer of Unity," *Newsweek*, 25 August 1980, 24.

50. Statement of Peter Edelman to Platform Committee, 12 June 1980, Legislative Files, O'Neill Papers, Box 60.

51. "A Rededication to Democratic Principles," undated, Legislative Files, O'Neill Papers, Box 39.

52. Memo, Kennedy to O'Neill, 27 August 1980, Legislative Files, O'Neill Papers, Box 59.

53. Memo, Jack Lew to O'Neill, undated, Legislative Files, O'Neill Papers, Box 60.

54. Minority Planks #10 and #11, undated, Legislative Files, O'Neill Papers, Box 60.

55. "Democratic Voters Agree with Kennedy, Not Carter, on Platform Issues," Louis Harris Poll, 11 August 1980, Mondale Papers, Box 4.

56. "Voters Support Democratic Platform Plank Calling for $12 Billion Jobs Program," Louis Harris Poll, 28 August 1980, Mondale Papers, Box 4.

57. "Americans More Concerned with the Recession Than with Inflation," Louis Harris Poll, 21 July 1980, Mondale Papers, Box 4.

58. Memo, Jack Lew to O'Neill, 8 August 1980, Legislative Files, O'Neill Papers, Box 60.

59. For issues of authorship and reception see Adam Clymer, *Edward M. Kennedy: A Biography* (New York: William Morrow, 1999), 316–318.

60. Interview with Adam Clymer, 19 September 2006.

61. Letter, Kennedy to Delegates, 18 July 1980, White House Press Office, Jimmy Carter Library, Box 9.

62. "Democrats '80 Transcript of Kennedy's Speech on Economic Issues at Democratic Convention," *New York Times*, 13 August 1980, B2.

63. "A Brief Shining Moment," *New York Times Magazine*, 25 August 1980, 26.

64. "Backers Roar for Kennedy as He Hails Party's Cause," *New York Times*, 13 August 1980, A1.

65. Hamilton Jordan, *Crisis: The Last Year of the Carter Presidency* (New York: Putnam Adult, 1982), 329.

66. "Kennedy's Performance at Convention Met with Widespread Approval," Louis Harris Poll, 25 August 1980, Mondale Papers, Box 4.

67. Interview with Eleanor Smeal, 25 February 2007.

68. Interview with Douglas Fraser, 19 February 2007.

69. Memo, Douglas Fraser and Don Stillman to Steve Sclossberg, 2 September 1980, Fraser Papers, Box 68.

70. Letter, Bill Dodds and Bob Carolla to Douglas Fraser and Jerry Wurf, 26 June 1980, Fraser Papers, Box 68.

71. "Now for the Hard Part," *Newsweek*, 25 August 1980, 18–19.

72. "Some Doubt Kennedy Enthusiasm After Podium Finale with Carter," *New York Times*, 16 August 1980, 1.

73. Austin Ranney, *The American Elections of 1984* (Durham, N.C.: Duke University Press, 1985), 333.

74. "Democrats Seek Election Reform," *New York Times*, 3 July 1981, A10; "Workshops at Democratic Mini-Convention Mix Hoopla and Cynicism," *New York Times*, 26 June 1982, 12.

Chapter 8: Giving It to the Gipper

1. "Carter, Joined by His Wife and Kennedy, Signs Law," *New York Times*, 8 October 1980, B6.

2. "Kennedy to Film Ads Praising President," *New York Times*, 7 October 1980, D21.

3. "Kennedy Rouses Mexican-Americans to Aid Carter's Drive to Win Texas," *New York Times*, 23 October 1980, B12.

4. "Carter Intensifies Criticisms of Reagan," *New York Times*, 30 October 1980, 16.

5. "Right Now, a Dead Heat," *Time*, 3 November 1980, 26.

6. "Post-Convention Polls: Quick Turnabout, as Usual," *New York Times*, 20 August 1980, A1.

7. "The Campaign's Final Week," *New York Times*, 2 November 1980, 40.

8. "Democratic Party Comeback Aids Carter's Race Against Reagan," Louis Harris Poll, 20 August 1980, Mondale Papers, Box 4.

9. "Poll Shows President Has Pulled to Even Position with Reagan," *New York Times*, 23 October 1980, A1.

10. "Where the Polls Went Wrong," *Time*, 1 December 1980, 21.

11. *Time*/Yankelovich Poll, 14–16 October 1980, Roper Center.

12. Gallup Poll, 10–13 October 1980, Roper Center.

13. "Carter's Camp Is Optimistic as It Discerns a Voter Shift," *New York Times*, 19 October 1980, 38.

14. "Controversial Remarks Have Potential to Hurt Reagan's Campaign," Louis Harris Poll, 15 September 1980, Mondale Papers, Box 4.

15. "Reagan Denies Plan to Answer Carter; Says He Will Not Defend Himself Against 'Distorted Charges,'" *New York Times*, 17 August 1980, 1.

16. Baron Report, 23 May 1980, McGovern Papers, Box 1008; Interview with Anne Wexler, 22 September 2006; Interview with Walter Mondale, 7 June 2007.

17. "Carter's Integrity Rating Sliding," Louis Harris Poll, 13 October 1980, Mondale Papers, Box 4.

18. Memo, Al Eisele to Mondale, 7 July 1980, Mondale Papers, Box 4.

19. Interview with Eleanor Smeal, 25 February 2007.

20. Interview with Douglas Fraser, 19 February 2007.

21. Gallup Poll, 12–15 October 1979, Roper Center.

22. In trial polling heats in 1978, Louis Harris ran Ford and Reagan against Kennedy and found Ford to be the stronger candidate. Among independents Kennedy led Reagan by 51 percent to 44 percent, but Ford by only 48 percent to 46 percent. Reagan trailed Ford among the well educated, the wealthy, and small-business men. "Republicans Need More Than Conservative Votes to Regain the White House," Louis Harris Poll, 22 June 1978, Leadership Files, O'Neill Papers, Box 2.

23. Memo, G. H. Ochenrider to S. M. Skurla and O'Neill, 17 April 1979, Staff Files, O'Neill Papers, Box 3.

24. "Will He or Won't He?," *New York Times*, 5 October 1979, A31.

25. "Reagan Loses Ground as Ford Edges the Former Governor Out as First Choice for Republican Nomination," Louis Harris Poll, 16 October 1980, Mondale Papers, Box 4.

26. "Ford Now Runs Much Stronger Race Against Carter Than Reagan," Louis Harris Poll, 18 October 1979, Mondale Papers, Box 4.

27. In March 1980, despite Reagan's early victories, Ford led the ex-governor 36 percent to 32 percent among Republicans and 54 percent to 44 percent among all voters: "Ford Leads Both Carter and Reagan, Although Still Undeclared Candidate," Louis Harris Poll, 10 March 1980, Mondale Papers, Box 4.

28. "Late Surge for the Underdogs; Bush's Moderate Image a Help," *New York Times*, 23 April 1980, A1.

29. "Bush a Major Contender for GOP Nomination," Louis Harris Poll, 24 January 1980, Mondale Papers, Box 4.

30. "Bush Now First Choice for Nomination," Louis Harris Poll, 12 February 1980, Mondale Papers, Box 4.

31. "Race for Presidency Has Narrowed Again," Louis Harris Poll, 10 September 1980, Mondale Papers, Box 4.

32. "April National Poll," NBC, 1 May 1980, White House Press Office, Box 2.

33. "Key Barometers Point to Close Race in November," Gallup Polling Report, August 1980, Mondale Papers, Box 4.

34. "Personality and Leadership Qualities of Candidates Dimly Perceived," Louis Harris Poll, 1 October 1980, Mondale Papers, Box 4.

35. "Doubts About Carter and Reagan Expressed," Louis Harris Poll, 18 September 1980, Mondale Papers, Box 4.

36. "Turn-off '80: Many Voters Are Apathetic and Hostile," *New York Times*, 26 October 1980, E1.

37. "On the Issues: John B. Anderson," *New York Times*, 29 March 1980, 9.

38. Letter, Anderson to Jim Buchfuehrer, 30 April 1980, East Papers, Box 25.

39. Article in *Fosters Daily Democrat*, 28 November 1979, in East Papers, Box 25.

40. "Attractive Dark Horse Might Press, Won't Win," *Lincoln Star*, 15 January 1980, 8.

41. Letter, Catherine East to the editor of the *Washington Post*, 7 February 1980, East Papers, Box 25.

42. Booklet, "The Program of the Anderson/Lucey Campaign," undated, East Papers, Box 25.

43. "The Anderson Principle," *New York Times*, 17 February 1980, SM9.

44. "Anderson Strategy Helped by Baker," *Lincoln Star*, 6 March 1980, 7.

45. "Reagan, Daley, Dixon Win—Kennedy and Scott Lose," *Chicago Tribune*, 19 March 1980, 1.

46. "Carter Wins Easily in Illinois Primary; GOP Backs Reagan," *New York Times*, 19 March 1980, 1.

47. Mark Bisnow, *The Diary of a Dark Horse: The 1980 Anderson Presidential Campaign* (Chicago: Southern Illinois University Press, 1983), 214; "This Year the Independents Are a Hard-to-Peg Elite," *New York Times*, 6 April 1980, E4.

48. Memo, "How John Anderson Can Win," undated, East Papers, Box 25.

49. Memo, David L. Walsh to O'Donnell, Legislative Files, O'Neill Papers, Box 21.

50. Letter, Anderson to voters, undated, White House Press Office, Box 7.

51. "National Politics," American Political Report, 20 June 1980, Leadership Files, O'Neill Papers, Box 4.

52. "How Anderson Changes the Race," Time, 2 June 1980, 22.

53. Memo, Rick Hertzberg to Powell, 6 June 1980, Records of the White House Press Office, Box 7.

54. Press Release, "Litigation Summary," undated, East Papers, Box 25; Memo, John Wade to Dennis Giles, state desk summary, 31 July 1980, East Papers, Box 25.

55. Press Release, "Litigation Summary," 6 August 1980, East Papers, Box 25.

56. Press Release, "Anderson Files in South Dakota," 5 August 1980, East Papers, Box 25.

57. Press Release, 6 August 1980, East Papers, Box 25.

58. Letter, Chuck Hilty to McCleod, 30 April 1980, East Papers, Box 25.

59. "Reagan vs. Anderson," Washington Star, 22 September 1980, 1.

60. Press Release, "Hollywood's Hero," undated, White House Press Office, Box 75.

61. Marianne Means's Washington Column, King Features News Syndicate, undated, in Records of the White House Press Office, Box 1.

62. "Looking at Anderson's Record," Baltimore Sun, 21 September 1980, K2.

63. "Anderson Discussing Western Issues," Rocky Mountain News, 17 September 1980, P-5.

64. Clifford W. Brown Jr. and Robert J. Walker, A Campaign of Ideas: The 1980 Anderson/Lucey Platform (Westport, Conn.: Greenwood Press, 1984), 8–9.

65. Press Release, "Questions to Reagan/Meece," undated, East Papers, Box 25.

66. Press Release, "Advocate Questions," undated, East Papers, Box 25.

67. Press Release, "The Response to the Real John Anderson," undated, East Papers, Box 25.

68. "The Independent," Wall Street Journal, 29 May 1980, 29.

69. "Casting a Vote for Anderson," article unsourced, undated, in East Papers, Box 26.

70. Letter, Macleod to Iris Mitang, 27 May 1980, East Papers, Box 26; Kennedy said in March 1980 that the administration was "trying to achieve a precarious budgetary balance on the backs of the cities, the poor, working families"; "Kennedy Stumps on L.I. and in Manhattan," New York Times, 6 March 1980, D17.

71. Press Release of Lucey speech, 18 October 1980, East Papers, Box 25.

72. Memo, Macleod to all staff, undated, East Papers, Box 25.

73. Position Paper on Women's Rights, undated, East Papers, Box 25; Press Release on nuclear power, August 1981, East Papers, Box 25.

74. Letter to Charles Lee Morris, 25 September 1980, East Papers, Box 25.

75. Press Release, "Anderson on Major Legislation Issues Concerning Israel and Soviet Jewry Since 1960," undated, East Papers, Box 25.

76. Transcript, Meet the Press with Lucey, 14 September 1980, East Papers, Box 25.

77. Memo, Chuck Hilty-McCleod to East, 30 April 1980, East Papers, Box 25; Memo, East to Ed Doyle, 19 June 1980, East Papers, Box 25.

78. "Anderson Says He Will Reconsider Candidacy If Carter Is Not Nominee," *New York Times*, 1 August 1980, A1.

79. Letter, Nan Coleman to East, 1 September 1980, East Papers, Box 25.

80. *National Unity Newsletter*, 16 October 1980, East Papers, Box 25.

81. Press Release, "Hollywood's Hero," undated, White House Press Office, Box 75.

82. *National Unity Newsletter*, 9 October 1980, East Papers, Box 25.

83. Press Release, undated, East Papers, Box 25.

84. Letter, Steinem to Anderson, 21 February 1980, East Papers, Box 25; Letter, East to Macleod, 5 March 1980, East Papers, Box 25.

85. Bisnow, *Diary of a Dark Horse*, 247. The anecdote that Bisnow recounts as evidence of this assertion is supported by McGovern's private and public support for Anderson's candidacy and qualities as a representative: Letter, McGovern to Brad Hart, 29 July 1980, McGovern Papers, Box 401. He lobbied the DNC to stop trying to prevent Anderson from appearing on the ballot: Letter, McGovern to John White, 14 June 1980, McGovern Papers, Box 401.

86. "How Will Anderson Affect Race?," *Denver Post*, 12 May 1980, 11.

87. "A Chance to Follow the Idealistic Path," *Washington Star*, 26 October 1980, F1; "Liberals and Carter," *New Republic*, 27 September 1980, 8.

88. Press Release, "ADACC Charges Carter as President Has Abandoned Major 1976 Campaign Pledges," 19 January 1980, White House Press Office, Jimmy Carter Library, Box 89; Press Release, "Introduction," undated, East Papers, Box 26; "Anderson for President," *New Republic*, 4 October 1980, 5.

89. Letter, Donald Szantho Harrington to Carter, 17 June 1980, Handwriting Files, Jimmy Carter Library; Memo, Keit Martin, Tom Melia to Moynihan, 20 June 1980, Moynihan Papers, Box 86.

90. "Estranged Friends' Pivotal Jewish Voters Are Down on Carter," *Wall Street Journal*, 22 September 1980, 21.

91. Letter, "Sue" to East, 14 April 1980, East Papers, Box 25.

92. Letter, Joan Sullivan to Anderson, 30 April 1980, East Papers, Box 25.

93. Letter, Helen Miliken to "dear friend," undated, East Papers, Box 25.

94. Letter, Mary Stanley to Mike Macleod, 16 April 1980, East Papers, Box 25.

95. "Executives Sign Up to Aid John Anderson," *Business Week*, 7 July 1980, 3.

96. Press Release, 14 August 1980, East Papers, Box 25.

97. Press Release, "Why Women Should Vote for John Anderson," Mary Crisp, undated, East Papers, Box 25.

98. "The Dilemma of Republican Women," *San Francisco Chronicle*, 4 September 1980, 45.

99. Press Release, "Women's Rights," undated, East Papers, Box 25; Press Release, "Feminists Believe in the Anderson Difference," 17 March 1980, East Papers, Box 25.

100. Letter, Robbin Setzer to Anderson, 5 March 1980, East Papers, Box 25.

101. Sonia Pressman Fuentes, "Three United States Feminists—A Personal Tribute," *Jewish Affairs* 53, no. 1 (1998): 37.

102. Letter, East to Lois Hayweiser, 22 January 1980, East Papers, Box 25.

103. Draft speech, "Justice for American Women," 13 September 1980, East Papers, Box 25.

104. "Arkansas Notes," undated, East Papers, Box 25; Letter, Macleod to Kansas NOW members, undated, East Papers, Box 25.

105. "NOW Parley Dominated by Politics," *New York Times*, 4 October 1980, 11.

106. Interview with Eleanor Smeal, 25 February 2007.

107. Memo, East to Cliff Brown, 9 October 1980, East Papers, Box 25.

108. Gloria Steinem wrote to Anderson to regretfully warn him that his presence on the ballot would offer "a dangerous boost to the Reagan candidacy. . . . I cannot believe that you as a third alternative would not hurt Carter much more than Reagan." Letter, Steinem to Anderson, 18 April 1980, East Papers, Box 25.

109. Talmadge was undermined by both financial scandal and the candidacy for the nomination of the more "liberal" Zell Miller. Memo, "Update: Election 1980," undated, Mondale Papers, Box 24.L.O.5.B.

110. Mike Gravel and Joe Lauria, *A Political Odyssey: The Rise of American Militarism and One Man's Fight to Stop It* (New York: Seven Stories Press, 2008), 261.

111. "Disaffected Democrat Who Is Now a GOP Dream," *New York Times*, 1 September 2004, A21.

112. "The New Right Brigade," *Washington Post*, 10 August 1980, 12; Memo, Jesse Helms to RNC, 22 June 1979, McGovern Papers, Box 1008.

113. Andrew E. Busch, *Reagan's Victory: The Presidential Election of 1980 and the Rise of the Right* (Lawrence: University Press of Kansas, 2005), 145–163. Cranston's reelection seemed highly likely, and the Republicans' targeting of him was probably a fund-raising ploy.

114. "Some of 1980's potentially vulnerable liberal Democrats, having been frightened by the 1978 elections, are trimming their ideological sails and won't be caught napping." Memo, "Update: Election 1980," undated, Mondale Papers, Box 24.L.O.5.B.

115. Press Release, remarks by McGovern before South Dakota State Democratic Convention, 28 June 1980, McGovern Papers, Box 504; LeRoy Ashby, *Fighting the Odds: The Life of Senator Frank Church* (Pullman: Washington State University Press, 1994), 599–604.

116. *Re-elect McGovern Newsletter*, undated, McGovern Papers, Box 323; Memo, Ted Nist to canvassers, 12 January 1980, McGovern Papers, Box 486.

117. "Culver Theme Is Contact," *Chicago Tribune*, 15 February 1979, in Mondale Papers, Box 204.

118. "The Feisty Culver Campaign," *Wall Street Journal*, undated, in McGovern Papers, Box 373.

119. Text of speech, Culver to Iowa Democratic Party Convention, 14 June 1980, McGovern Papers, Box 401.

120. Letter, McGovern to John Denver, 24 July 1979, McGovern Papers, Box 323; Article in *Sioux Falls Gazette*, 21 January 1979, in McGovern Papers, Box 486; "McGovern's Campaign Fund Boosted by 1972 Leftovers," *Rapid City Gazette*, 13 August 1980, in McGovern Papers, Box 1008.

121. "Vote Abdnor," *Daily Republic*, 1 November 1980, 6.

122. Form Letter, Hal Wick to Target members, undated, McGovern Papers, Box 1008.

123. "Voting Records Reflect Political Philosophies," *Rapid City Journal*, 15 June 1980, 14.

124. "Abdnor Says People Fed Up with Congress," *Brookings Gazette*, 18 February 1980, in McGovern Papers, Box 486; "McGovern Seeks Last Senate Term," *New York Times*, 14 February 1980, 23.

125. "Democratic Platform Ignores Abortion Plank," *Argus*, 29 June 1980, C1.

126. "McGovern: Abortion May Decide Race," *Argus*, 25 June 1980, C1.

127. "Conservative and Antiabortion Groups Press Attack Against McGovern," *New York Times*, 2 June 1980, B11.

128. Form Letter from NCPAC to members, undated, McGovern Papers, Box 323.

129. Memo, "Strategy," 1979, McGovern Papers, Box 323.

130. "National GOP Frustrated by Lack of Political Foe," article in the *Mitchell Gazette*, 20 November 1979, in McGovern Papers, Box 486.

131. "Where Abortion Fight Goes from Here," *U.S. News and World Report*, 14 July 1980, 42.

132. Letter, Ellen Dempsey to members of LAPAC, undated, McGovern Papers, Box 486.

133. Memo, Harriet Matthews to NARAL Executive Board, undated, McGovern Papers, Box 486.

134. Memo to file, undated, McGovern Papers, Box 486.

135. Letter, Karen Mulhauser to NARAL members, undated, McGovern Papers, Box 486.

136. Letter, Steinem to supporters, undated, McGovern Papers, Box 486; Poster, "Peter, Paul, and Mary in Concert," undated, McGovern Papers, Box 487.

137. Memo to file, undated, McGovern Papers, Box 323.

138. Letter, McGovern to Jackson, 15 October 1980, McGovern Papers, Box 504.

139. "Poll Takers Defend Survey Differences," *New York Times*, 6 November 1980, A33.

140. "Carter and Reagan Dispute Views on Arms Policy, Economy and Iran in a Broad Debate Before Nation," *New York Times*, 29 October 1980, A1.

141. "Poll Shows Iran and Economy Hurt Carter Among Late-Shifting Voters," *New York Times*, 16 November 1980, 1.

142. Hamilton Jordan, *Crisis: The Last Year of the Carter Presidency* (New York: Putnam Adult, 1982), 371–372.

143. Leo P. Ribuffo, "Jimmy Carter and the Selling of the Presidency, 1978–1980," in *The Presidency and Domestic Policies of Jimmy Carter*, ed. Herbert D. Rosenbaum and Alexej Ugrinsky (London: Greenwood Press, 1994).

144. Jordan, *Crisis*, 374–375.

145. Patricia A. Hurley, "Partisan Representation, Realignment and the Senate in the 1980s," *Journal of Politics* 53 (1989): 3–33.

146. Letter, McGovern to Walter B. Smalley, 21 October 1980, McGovern Papers, Box 373.

147. "Undecided Vote Could Swing Close Local Races," *Daily Report*, 1 November 1980, in McGovern Papers, Box 504.

148. Interview with George McGovern, 27 July 2006.

149. Advertisement, "The Only 2 Politicians to Ever Refuse to Debate George McGovern Are Richard Nixon and Jim Abdnor," undated, McGovern Papers, Box 504.

150. "McGovern Splattered by Out of State Mud," *Argus*, 14 August 1980, C1.

151. "Backlash in South Dakota?," *New York Times*, 13 October 1980, A23.

152. In particular, McGovern found that federal funding for abortion was opposed by 75 percent of Dakotans. Memo, GVC to McGovern, "Results of December 1978 Questionnaire," 20 December 1978, McGovern Papers, Box 981.

153. "The Collapse of a Coalition: Carter Failed in Groups That Backed Him in '76," *New York Times*, 5 November 1980, A1.

154. Memo, "The 1980 Democratic Primary Mexican American Presidential Preference Vote," undated, Records of the Office of Hispanic Affairs, Maria Cruz Files, Jimmy Carter Library, Box 1.

155. "Displeasure with Carter Turned Many to Reagan," *New York Times*, 9 November 1980, 28.

156. "The Collapse of a Coalition: Carter Failed in Groups That Backed Him in '76," *New York Times*, 5 November 1980, A1.

157. "Now for the Hard Part," *Newsweek*, 25 August 1980, 23; "The Shifting Labor Vote," *New York Times*, 11 November 1980, B8; "Blue-Collar Democrats Slipping to Reagan," *New York Times*, 20 April 1980, 30; Interview with Peter Hart, 25 September 2006.

158. "How Americans Swung to Reagan," *U.S. News and World Report*, 17 November 1980, 29.

159. This was certainly the contemporary consensus: "The strongest asset going for Reagan in this fall's election now appears to be the incumbent President . . . rather than the inherent strengths within the Reagan candidacy itself." "ABC/Harris Poll: Campaign Issues," 15 July 1980, Papers of NOW, Box 194.

160. "Displeasure with Carter Turned Many to Reagan," *New York Times*, 9 November 1980, 28.

161. Anderson's percentage vote was large enough to also be blamed for Carter losing the South. It was arguably high enough to have denied Carter Arkansas, Mississippi, Alabama, Tennessee, North Carolina, and South Carolina—fifty-three electoral votes in total. However, whether or not Anderson's votes, which were far smaller than in the North, would have gone to Carter is a more contentious issue.

162. "Displeasure with Carter Turned Many to Reagan," *New York Times*, 9 November 1980, 28.

163. "Anderson Says Goals of Campaign 'Must Not and Will Not End for Me,'" *New York Times*, 5 November 1980, A21.

164. "Odd Alliances Form in Order to Put Nader on the Ballot," *New York Times*, 1 July 2004, 1.

165. "Results in Races for U.S. Senate and the Makeup of the Newly Elected Congress," *New York Times*, 6 November 1980, A28.

166. Tip O'Neill's staff members were happy to note that "of the 12 senate seats we lost, our candidate ran substantially ahead of Carter in 10 states. . . . And except for McGovern's 39 percent, all of the other Democratic candidates whose seats switched won at least 45 percent, while Carter's vote was under 40 percent in every state except Wisconsin (44) and North Carolina (47)." Memo, Burt Hoffman to O'Neill, 10 November 1980, Staff Files, O'Neill Papers, Box 4.

167. Memo, "1980 Senate Race Update," 1 July 1980, Mondale Papers, Box 6.

168. "Can GOP Win Senate in '80? The Odds Now," *U.S. News and World Report*, 20 August 1979, 49.

169. It should also be noted that the Democratic Party would have won New York (Jacob Javits Republican/Liberal Party incumbent) had Javits, who lost the Republican primary, not run as the Liberal Party candidate. This split liberal and moderate voters and allowed a narrow victory for Republican D'Amato. Memo, "1980 Senate Race Update," 1 July 1980, Mondale Papers, Box 6.

170. "51 percent of Iowans 'Uncertain' on Culver: Poll," *Des Moines Register*, 25 March 1979, in Mondale Papers, Box 24.L.6.3.B.

171. Memo, "Scheduling Criteria—1980," Hart Papers, Box 67.

172. Memo, GVC to Staff, 12 February 1979, McGovern Papers, Box 981.

173. "Culver: Judge SALT II on Its Individual Merits," *Cedar Rapids Gazette*, 29 March 1979, in Mondale Papers, Box 204; Press Release, "Frank Church's Record of Shame: Frank Church Opposes a Strong National Defense," undated, McGovern Papers, Box 504.

174. "Born Again at the Ballot Box," *Time*, 14 April 1980, 94.

175. Letter, Ron Paul to Mr Zimmermann, undated, McGovern Papers, Box 323; Form Letter from Stop the Baby Killers, undated, McGovern Papers, Box 323; Form Letter from Restore School Prayer, undated, McGovern Papers, Box 323.

176. Memo, Cambridge Survey Research to the McGovern Campaign, 31 October 1979, McGovern Papers, Box 504.

177. Memo, "Winning in 1982: Lessons from the Democratic Defeat of 1980," February 1981, Legislative Files, O'Neill Papers, Box 36.

178. "Presidential Election Overview," Louis Harris Poll, 20 October 1980, Mondale Papers, Box 4.

179. "The Conservative Vote," Louis Harris Poll, 11 November 1980, Mondale Papers, Box 4.

180. "The Regeneration of the Democrats," undated, Staff Files, O'Neill Papers, Box 5.

181. DNC "General Overview" of congressional results, December 1980, Staff Files, O'Neill Papers, Box 5.

182. Memo, Burt Hoffman to O'Neill, 10 November 1980, Staff Files, O'Neill Papers, Box 4.

183. Speech on receiving the Speaker nomination, 8 December 1980, Speech Files, O'Neill Papers, Box 5.

184. Remarks before DNC, 26 February 1981, Speech Files, O'Neill Papers, Box 6.

185. Jordan, *Crisis*, 306–309; Jimmy Carter, *Keeping Faith: Memoirs of a President* (New York: Bantam, 1983), 586.

186. Memo, Cuomo to DNC, 24 November 1980, Staff Files, O'Neill Papers, Box 4.

187. Newsletter, "Democrat's Report," December 1980, Staff Files, O'Neill Papers, Box 4.

188. "Voter Shifts: Economic Worry Emerges," *New York Times*, 3 November 1982, A1.

Conclusion

1. Lou Cannon, *Ronald Reagan: The Role of a Lifetime* (Chicago: Public Affairs, 2000), 883.

2. Gil Troy, *Morning in America: How Ronald Reagan Invented the 1980s* (Princeton, N.J.: Princeton University Press, 2005), 161.

3. Haynes Johnson, *Sleepwalking Through History: America in the Reagan Years* (New York: Norton, 2003), 242.

4. Gregory Paul Domin, *Jimmy Carter, Public Opinion, and the Search for Values, 1977–1981* (Macon, Ga.: Mercer University Press, 2003), 87.

5. Mark K. Updegrove, *Second Acts: Presidential Lives and Legacies After the White House* (Guilford, Conn.: Lyons Press, 2006), 23.

6. Rod Troester, *Jimmy Carter as Peacemaker* (Westport, Conn.: Praeger, 1996), 1–4.

7. "Kennedy Reported Declining to Seek Presidency in 1982," *New York Times*, 1 December 1982, 1.

8. Garry Wills, *The Kennedys: A Shattered Illusion* (London: Orbis Books, 1980), 196–198.

9. "Kennedys in Court for Divorce," *New York Times*, 7 December 1982, A18.

10. J. David Woodward, *The America That Reagan Built* (Westport, Conn.: Greenwood Publishing, 2006), 85.

11. "Farewell," *New Yorker*, 25 August 2008, 23.

12. "Health Legislation Advances in Senate," *New York Times*, 10 June 1994.

13. "Kennedy Chooses Obama, Spurning Plea by Clintons," *New York Times*, 28 January 2008, A1.

14. "Determined to Give Speech, Kennedy Left Hospital Bed," *New York Times*, 25 August 2008, A18.

15. Byron E. Shafer, *Quiet Revolution: The Struggle for the Democratic Party and the Shaping of Post Reform Politics* (New York: Russell Sage, 1983), 523–539.

16. Arch Puddington, *Lane Kikland: Champion of American Labor* (New York: Wiley, 2005), 136–163; "A Man for All Unions," *National Journal*, 27 September 1980, 1623.

17. "Solidarity Day's Enigmatic Organizer," *New York Times*, 19 September 1981, 11.

18. "AFL-CIO Urged to Pick Presidential Candidate," *Baltimore Sun*, 12 April 1982, A1; "Democrats Beware of the AFL-CIO," *Washington Post*, 8 December 1982, C4.

19. Peter Goldman, Thomas M. DeFrank, Mark Miller, Andrew Murr, and Tom Matthews, *The Quest for the Presidency: 1992* (College Station: Texas A&M University Press, 1994), 402–405.

20. Alan Brinkley, *The End of Reform: New Deal Liberalism in Recession and War* (New York: Knopf, 1995), 3.

21. "Democrats Seek Election Reform," *New York Times*, 3 July 1981, A10; "Workshops at Democratic Mini-Convention Mix Hoopla and Cynicism," *New York Times*, 26 June 1982, 12.

22. Bernard Donoughue, *Prime Minister: The Conduct of Policy Under Harold Wilson and James Callaghan* (London: Cape, 1987), 54.

23. Peter Kerr, *Postwar British Politics: From Conflict to Consensus* (London: Routledge, 2001), 116–121.

24. David Kogan and Maurice Kogan, *The Battle for the Labour Party* (London: Fontana, 1982), 26–27.

25. David Coates, *Labour in Power? A Study of the Labour Governments, 1974–1979* (London: Longman, 1980), 2–3; Kenneth O. Morgan, *Labor People: Leaders and Lieutenants, Hardie to Kinnock* (Oxford: Oxford University Press, 1989), 305–306.

26. David Butler and Dennis Kavanah, *The British General Election of 1983* (London: Macmillan, 1999), 52.

27. Interview with Anne Wexler, 22 September 2006; Interview with Stuart Eizenstat, 21 September 2006.

28. Interview with Walter Mondale, 7 June 2007.

29. Interview with George McGovern, 27 July 2006.

30. Letter, McGovern to Gary Crossman, 5 December 1979, McGovern Papers, Box 323.

31. Interview with Douglas Fraser, 19 February 2007.

32. Interview with Eleanor Smeal, 25 February 2007.

33. Interview with Heather Booth, 19 September 2006.

34. Interview with Gary Hart, 29 August 2006.

35. Interview with Mike Dukakis, 14 September 2006.

36. Interview with Fred Harris, 8 August 2006.

37. Interview with Peter Hart, 25 September 2006.

38. Introduction to Nancy Lieber, ed., *Eurosocialism and America: Political Economy for the 1980s* (Philadelphia: Temple University Press, 1982).

39. Interview with Harold Meyerson, 22 September 2006.

40. Tony Benn, *The End of an Era: 1980–1990* (London: Hutchinson, 1992), 54–57.

41. "Reagan Draws Support of Democrats, Independents," *L.A. Times*, 5 June 1980, B1.

42. "Of Kennedy, Carter, the U.N. and the Money Gap," *Newsweek*, 24 March 1980, 9.

Bibliography

Newspapers and Periodicals

Aberdeen News
AFL-CIO News
Albuquerque News
Argus Leader
Arizona Faily Star
The Atlantic Magazine
Aubern Citizen
Baltimore Sun
Boston Globe
Boston Herald
Boston Phoenix
Business Week
Chicago Sun Times
Chicago Tribune
Colorado Camera
Colorado Gazette
Colorado Springs Gazette (CSGT)
Colorado Statesman
Commentary Magazine
Commonweal Magazine
Congressional Quarterly
Congressional Quarterly Almanac
Daily Capital Journal
The Daily Item
Daily News
Daily Republic
Denver Post
Des Moines Register
Fort Lauderdale News
Gloversville Herald
Greeley Tribune
Harpers and Queen

Herling Labor Letter
Jet Magazine
Life Magazine
Lincoln Star
Los Angeles Times
Miami Herald
The Nation
National Journal
New Left Review
The New Republic
Newsweek
The New Yorker
New York Magazine
New York Times
New York Times Magazine
Philadelphia Inquirer
The Progressive
Public Opinion
Rapid City Journal
Rocky Mountain News
San Francisco Chronicle
The Saratogan
St. Louis Post Dispatch
Staten Island Advance
Sunday Star
Time Magazine
Tucson Citizen
U.S. News and World Report
The Village Voice
Wall Street Journal
Washington Post
Washington Star

Archival Collections

Archives of the University of Boulder, Boulder, Colorado
Papers of Gary Hart

Archives of the John Fitzgerald Kennedy Library, Boston, Massachusetts
Papers of Edward Moore Kennedy, 1932–2009: Audiovisual Archives
Papers of Adam Clymer
Papers of Nancy Korman
Papers of Theodore Chaikin Sorenson

Department of Special Collections, University of California, Los Angeles, California
Papers of Augustus F. Hawkins

John J. Burns Library, Boston College, Boston, Massachusetts
Papers of Thomas (Tip) Philip O'Neill Jr.

Seeley G. Mudd Library, Princeton University, Princeton, New Jersey
Papers of George Stanley McGovern

Minnesota Historical Society, St. Paul, Minnesota
Papers of Walter Fitzgerald Mondale
Papers of Hubert Horatio Humphrey

Walter P. Reuther Library, Wayne State University, Detroit, Michigan
Papers of UAW President, Douglas Fraser
Papers of AFT President, Albert Shanker
Papers of UFW President, Cesar Chavez
Papers of Mildred Jeffrey
Papers of the UAW Social Security Department
Papers of UAW Local Region 1 (Detroit)

Arthur Schlesinger Jr. Library, Radcliffe Institute, Harvard University, Cambridge, Massachusetts
Papers of Patricia Gold
Papers of Martha Ragland
Papers of Betty Friedan
Papers of Catherine East
Papers of Charlotte Bunch, 1950–1988
Records of the National Organization for Women

Roper Center for Public Opinion Research, Connecticut
Assorted polls

Jimmy Carter Library, Atlanta, Georgia

Office of the Assistant to the President for Communication Files (including)
    Papers of Gerald Rafshoon
Office of the Chief of Staff Files
Office of the Deputy Chief of Staff
Office of Management and Budget
Office of Staff Secretary, Handwriting Files
Office of Staff Secretary Files
Papers of the Assistant to the President for Women's Affairs (including)
    Papers of Sarah Weddington
    Papers of Midge Costanza
Papers of the Cabinet Secretary
Papers of the Congressional Liaison
Papers of the Council of Economic Advisers
Papers of the Counsel to Landon Butler
Papers of the Counsel to the President (including)
    Papers of Lipschutz
Papers of the Domestic Policy Staff
Papers of Martha "Bunny" Mitchell
Papers of the Office of Administration
Papers of the Office of Hispanic Affairs (including)
    Papers of Steve Arello
    Papers of Maria Cruz
Papers of the Special Adviser to the President on Inflation
Papers of the Speech Writers Office
Papers of the White House Office of Counsel to the President
Papers of the White House Press Office
Political Affairs Files (including)
    LA-2   PL-2   PL-10
    LA-7   PL-5
Presidential Cabinet Minutes
White House Central Files

Jefferson Library, National Archives, Washington, D.C.

Papers of Daniel Patrick Moynihan

George Meany Memorial Archives, National Labor College, Washington, D.C.

Papers of the AFL-CIO President, George Meany
Papers of the AFL-CIO President, Lane Kirkland
Vertical Files
AFL-CIO Executive Minutes

Miller Center, University of Virginia, Jimmy Carter Presidential Oral History Project

Assorted interviews

Private Collections
Papers of Peter Mandler
Papers of Maxine Phillips
Papers of Ruth Jordan

Interviews
Unless conducted by e-mail, all interviews were recorded on to cassette tape.
Ed Berkowitz, 26 September 2006
Heather Booth, 19 September 2006
Jack Clark, 25 September 2006
Adam Clymer, 19 September 2006
John C. Culver, 17 February 2005 (e-mail)
Mike Dukakis, 14 September 2006
Stuart Eizenstat, 21 September 2006
Douglas Fraser, 19 February 2007 (telephone)
Fred Harris, 8 August 2006 (telephone)
Gary Hart, 29 August 2006
Peter Hart, 25 September 2006
Tom Hayden, 16 April 2007 (e-mail)
Ruth Jordan, 26 February 2007
Don Lippincott, 16 September 2006
Peter Mandler, 14 September 2006
George McGovern, 27 July 2006
Harold Meyerson, 22 September 2006
Walter Mondale, 7 June 2007
Maxine Phillips, 24 September 2006 (telephone)
Mark Segal, 27 September 2006
Eleanor Smeal, 25 February 2007
Don Stillman, 25 September 2006
Jim Wallace, 27 September 2006
Ben Wattenberg, 26 September 2006
Anne Wexler, 22 September 2006

Published Materials

Alexander, Herbert E. *Financing the 1980 Election*. Lexington, Mass.: Lexington Books, 1983.
Allswang, John M. *The New Deal and American Politics: A Study in Political Change*. New York: Wiley, 1978.
Ambrose, Stephen E. *Nixon: The Triumph of a Politician*. New York: Simon and Schuster, 1989.
Anderson, Patrick. *Electing Jimmy Carter: The Campaign of 1976*. Baton Rouge: Louisiana State University Press, 1994.

Anson, Robert Sam. *George McGovern: A Biography*. New York: Holt, Rinehart and Winston, 1972.

Ashby, LeRoy. *Fighting the Odds: The Life of Senator Frank Church*. Pullman: Washington State University Press, 1994.

Ayton, Mel. *Questions of Controversy: The Kennedy Brothers*. Sunderland, U.K.: University of Sunderland Press, 2001.

Baer, Kenneth S. *Reinventing Democrats: The Politics of Liberalism from Reagan to Clinton*. Lawrence: University Press of Kansas, 2000.

Baestrup, Peter. *How the American Press and Television Reported and Interpreted the Crisis of Tet 1968 in Vietnam and Washington*. New York: Presidio, 1977.

Bailey, Christopher J. *The Republican Party in the U.S. Senate*. Manchester: Manchester University Press, 1988.

Barone, Michael. *Our Country: The Shaping of America from Roosevelt to Reagan*. London: Collier Macmillan, 1990.

Bartels, Larry M. *Presidential Primaries and the Dynamics of Public Choice*. Princeton, N.J.: Princeton University Press, 1988.

Bell, Jonathan. *The Liberal State on Trial: The Cold War and American Politics in the Truman Years*. New York: Columbia University Press, 2004.

Benn, Tony. *The End of an Era: 1980–1990*. London: Hutchinson, 1992.

Berkowitz, Edward D. *Something Happened: A Political and Cultural Overview of the Seventies*. New York: Columbia University Press, 2006.

Berman, Larry. *Lyndon Johnson's War: The Road to Stalemate in Vietnam*. New York: Norton, 1989.

Berman, William C. *America's Right Turn: From Nixon to Bush*. Baltimore, Md.: Johns Hopkins University Press, 1994.

Bisnow, Mark. *The Diary of a Dark Horse: The 1980 Anderson Presidential Campaign*. Chicago: Southern Illinois University Press, 1983.

Biven, W. Carl. *Jimmy Carter's Economy: Policy in an Age of Limits*. Chapel Hill: University of North Carolina Press, 2002.

Bourne, Peter G. *Jimmy Carter: A Comprehensive Biography from Plains to Post-Presidency*. New York: Scribner, 1997.

Braun, Alan G., and Lawrence D. Longley. *The Politics of Electoral Reform*. New Haven, Conn.: Yale University Press, 1972.

Brazelton, Robert. *Designing U.S. Economic Policy: An Analytical Biography of Leon H. Keyserling*. New York: Palgrave, 2001.

Brinkley, Alan. *The End of Reform: New Deal Liberalism in Recession and War*. New York: Knopf, 1995.

———. *Liberalism and Its Discontents*. Cambridge, Mass.: Harvard University Press, 1998.

———. "The New Deal and the Idea of the State." In *The Rise and Fall of the New Deal Order, 1930–1980*. Edited by Steve Fraser and Gary Gerstle. Princeton, N.J.: Princeton University Press, 1989.

Brown. Clifford W., Jr., and Robert J. Walker. *A Campaign of Ideas: The 1980 Anderson/Lucey Platform*. Westport, Conn.: Greenwood Press, 1984.

Burke, Richard E., William Hoffer, and Marilyn Hoffer. *The Senator: My Ten Years with Ted* Kennedy. New York: St. Martin's Press, 1992.

Burner, Thomas R., and David West. *The Torch Is Passed: The Kennedy Brothers and American Liberalism.* New York: Atheneum, 1984.

Burnham, Walter Dean. "The 1980 Earthquake: Realignment, Reaction or What?" In *The Hidden Election: Politics and Economics in the 1980 Presidential Election.* Edited by Thomas Ferguson and Joel Rogers. New York: Pantheon Books, 1981.

———. *Critical Elections and the Mainsprings of American Politics.* New York: Norton, 1970.

Busch, Andrew E. *Reagan's Victory: The Presidential Election of 1980 and the Rise of the Right.* Lawrence: University Press of Kansas, 2005.

Busch, Andrew E., and William G. Mayer. *The Front Loading Problem in Presidential Nominations.* Washington, D.C.: Brookings Institution Press, 2003.

Butler, David, and Dennis Kavanah. *The British General Election of 1983.* London: Macmillan, 1999.

Byrd, Robert C. *Robert C. Byrd: Child of the Appalchian Coalfields.* Morgantown: West Virginia University Press, 2005.

Califano, Joseph A. *Governing America.* New York: Simon and Schuster, 1981.

Cannon, Lou. *Ronald Reagan: The Role of a Lifetime.* Chicago: Public Affairs, 2000.

Carlson, Jody. *George C. Wallace and the Politics of Powerlessness: The Wallace Campaigns for the Presidency, 1964–76.* New Brunswick, N.J.: Transaction Books, 1981.

Carroll, Peter N. *It Seemed Like Nothing Happened: America in the 1970s.* Piscataway, N.J.: Rutgers University Press, 1990.

Carter, Dan T. *From George Wallace to Newt Gingrich: Race in the Conservative Counter Revolution, 1963–1994.* Baton Rouge: Louisiana State University Press, 1996.

Carter, Jimmy. *Keeping Faith: Memoirs of a President.* New York: Bantam, 1983.

———. *Why Not the Best?* New York: Bantam Books, 1976.

Carter, Rosalynn. *First Lady from Plains.* Boston: Houghton Mifflin, 1984.

Chellis, Marcia. *The Joan Story: One Woman's Victory over Infidelity, Politics and Privilege.* New York: Simon and Schuster, 1995.

Cieri, Marie, and Claire Peeps, eds. *Activists Speak Out: Reflections on the Pursuit of Change in America.* Basingstoke: Palgrave, 2000.

Clymer, Adam. *Drawing the Line at the Big Ditch: The Panama Canal Treaties and the Rise of the Right.* Lawrence: University Press of Kansas, 2008.

———. *Edward M. Kennedy: A Biography.* New York: William Morrow, 1999.

Coates, David. *Labour in Power? A Study of the Labour Governments, 1974–1979.* London: Longman, 1980.

Collier, Peter, and David Horowitz. *The Kennedys.* New York: Encounter Books, 1984.

Collins, Robert B. *More: The Politics of Economic Growth in Post War America.* Oxford: Oxford University Press, 2002.

Covington, Howard E. *Terry Sanford: Politics, Progress, and Outrageous Ambitions.* Durham, N.C.: Duke University Press, 1999.

Cox, Patrick. *Ralph W. Yarborough, the People's Senator.* Austin: University of Texas Press, 2001.

Critchlow, Donald T. "Mobilizing Women: The 'Social Issues.'" In *The Reagan Presidency: Pragmatic Conservatism and Its Legacies*. Edited by W. Elliot Brownlee and Hugh Davis Graham. Lawrence: University Press of Kansas, 2003.

———. *Phyllis Schlafly and Grassroots Conservatism: A Woman's Crusade*. Princeton, N.J.: Princeton University Press, 2005.

Dallek, Robert. *An Unfinished Life: John F. Kennedy, 1917–1963*. Boston: Little, Brown, 2003.

Damore, Leo. *Senatorial Privilege: The Chappaquiddick Cover-up*. Washington, D.C.: Regnery Gateway, 1988.

Dark, Taylor. "Organized Labor and the Carter Administration: The Origins of Conflict." In *The Presidency and Domestic Policies of Jimmy Carter*. Edited by Herbert D. Rosenbaum and Alexej Ugrinsky. London: Greenwood Press, 1994.

David, Lester. *Good Ted, Bad Ted: The Two Faces of Edward Kennedy*. New York: Carol Publishing Group, 1993.

David, Lester, and Irene David. *Bobby Kennedy: The Making of a Folk Hero*. London: Sidgwick and Jackson, 1986.

Davies, Gareth. *From Opportunity to Entitlement: The Transformation and Decline of Great Society Liberalism*. Lawrence: University Press of Kansas, 1996.

Deitcher, David, ed. *The Question of Equality: Lesbian and Gay Politics in America Since Stonewall*. New York: Scribner, 1995.

Domin, Gregory Paul. *Jimmy Carter, Public Opinion, and the Search for Values, 1977–1981*. Macon, Ga.: Mercer University Press, 2003.

Dooley, Brian. *Robert Kennedy: The Final Years*. Keele, U.K.: Ryburn, 1995.

Douglas, Susan. *The Mommy Myth: The Idealization of Motherhood and How It Has Undermined All Women*. New York: Free Press, 2004.

Drew, Elizabeth. *Portrait of an Election: The 1980 Presidential Campaign*. New York: Routledge and Kegan Paul, 1981.

Dumbrell, John. *The Carter Presidency: A Re-evaluation*. Manchester: Manchester University Press, 1995.

Eckes, Alfred E., Jr., and Eugene H. Rosenboom. *A History of Presidential Elections, from George Washington to Jimmy Carter*. New York: Macmillan, 1979.

Edsall, Mary, and Thomas Edsall. *Chain Reaction: The Impact of Race, Rights and Taxes upon American Politics*. New York: Norton, 1991.

Edsforth, Ronald. *The New Deal: America's Response to the Great Depression*. Oxford: Blackwell, 2000.

Eizenstat, Stuart E. "President Carter, the Democratic Party and the Making of the Democratic Policy." In *The Presidency and Domestic Policies of Jimmy Carter*. Edited by Herbert D. Rosenbaum and Alexej Ugrinsky. London: Greenwood Press, 1994.

Emery, Fred. *Watergate: The Corruption and Fall of Richard Nixon*. New York: Touchstone, 1995.

Farrell, John A. *Tip O'Neill and the Democratic Century*. London: Little, Brown, 2001.

Fink, Gary M. "Fragile Alliance: Jimmy Carter and the American Labor Movement."

In *The Presidency and Domestic Policies of Jimmy Carter*. Edited by Herbert D. Rosenbaum and Alexej Ugrinsky. London: Greenwood Press, 1994.

Fink, Gary M., and Hugh David Graham. *The Carter Presidency: Policy Choices in the Post–New Deal Era*. Chapel Hill: University of North Carolina Press, 2001.

Foner, Philip S. *American Labor and the Indochina War: The Growth of Union Opposition*. New York: International Publishers, 1971.

Formisano, Ronald P. *Boston Against Busing: Race, Class, and Ethnicity in the 1960s and 1970s*. Chapel Hill: University of North Carolina Press, 1991.

Fraser, Steve, and Gary Gerstle, eds. Introduction to *The Rise and Fall of the New Deal Order, 1930–1980*. Princeton, N.J.: Princeton University Press, 1989.

Freedman, Estelle B. *No Turning Back: The History of Feminism and the Future of Women*. New York: Ballantine Books, 2002.

Freeman, Robert. *American Populist Conservatism, 1977–88*. PhD thesis, University of Cambridge, 2006.

Frum, David. *How We Got Here: The Decade That Brought You Modern Life—For Better or Worse*. New York: Basic Books, 2000.

Fuentes, Sonia Pressman. "Three United States Feminists—A Personal Tribute." *Jewish Affairs* 53, no. 1 (1998): 37.

Garcia, Ignacio M. *Viva Kennedy: Mexican Americans in Search of Camelot*. College Station: Texas A&M University Press, 2000.

Garcia, Richard A. "Dolores Huerta: Woman, Organizer and Symbol." *California History* 72, no. 1 (1993): 56–71.

Garrow, David. *Privacy and Sexuality: The Right to Privacy in* Roe vs. Wade. New York: Macmillan, 1994.

Gillmore, Robert. *Liberalism and the Politics of Plunder: The Conscience of a Neo-Liberal*. Dublin, N.H.: W. L. Bauhan, 1987.

Gillon, Steven M. *The Democrats' Dilemma: Walter F. Mondale and the Liberal Legacy*. New York: Columbia University Press, 1994.

———. *Politics and Vision: The ADA and American Liberalism, 1945–85*. Oxford: Oxford University Press, 1987.

Glad, Betty. *Jimmy Carter: In Search of the Great White House*. New York: Norton, 1980.

Glenn, Norval D. "Class and Party Support in 1972." *Public Opinion Quarterly* 39 (1975): 1–20.

Goldman, Peter, Thomas M. DeFrank, Mark Miller, Andrew Murr, and Tom Matthews. *The Quest for the Presidency: 1992*. College Station: Texas A&M University Press, 1994.

Gopian, David, Derek J. Hackett, Daniel Parelman, and Leo Perotta. "Coalitions in the Eighties: A Reassessment of Ladd's Old Class/New Class Explanation of Intra-Party Conflict." *Western Political Quarterly* 40 (1986): 247–264.

Gravel, Mike, and Joe Lauria. *A Political Odyssey: The Rise of American Militarism and One Man's Fight to Stop It*. New York: Seven Stories Press, 2008.

Greenberg, Stanley B. *Middle Class Dreams: The Politics and Power of the New American Majority*. New York: Random House, 1997.

Greenberg, Stanley B., and Theda Skocpol, eds. *The Real Majority: Toward a Popular Progressive Politics*. New Haven, Conn.: Yale University Press, 1998.

Greene, John Robert. "A Nice Person Who Worked at the Job: The Dilemma of the Ford Image." In *Gerald R. Ford and the Politics of Post-Watergate America*. Edited by Bernard J. Firestone and Alexej Ugrinsky. Westport, Conn.: Greenwood Press, 1993.

———. *The Presidency of Gerald R. Ford*. Lawrence: University Press of Kansas, 1995.

Grover, William F. *The President as Prisoner: A Structural Critique of the Carter and Reagan Years*. Albany: State University of New York Press, 1989.

Haas, Garland A. *Jimmy Carter and the Politics of Frustration*. Jefferson, N.C.: McFarland, 1992.

Hacker, Jacob S. *The Divided Welfare State: The Battle over Public and Private Social Benefits in the United States*. Cambridge: Cambridge University Press, 2002.

Hamby, Alonzo. *Beyond the New Deal: Harry S. Truman and American Liberalism*. New York: Columbia University Press, 1973.

Hammon, Thomas H. "Another Look at the Rules in the 1972 Democratic Presidential Primaries." *Western Political Quarterly* 33 (1980): 50–72.

Hargrove, Erwin C., and James Sterling Young. *Jimmy Carter as President: Leadership and the Politics of Public Good*. Baton Rouge: Louisiana State University Press, 1988.

Hartman, Susan M. *From Margin to Mainstream: American Women and Politics Since 1960*. New York: Knopf, 1989.

Hendershot, Cynthia. *Anticommunism and Popular Culture in Mid-Century America*. Jefferson, N.C.: McFarland, 2003.

Hersch, Burton. *The Education of Edward Kennedy: A Family Biography*. New York: William Morrow, 1972.

———. *The Shadow President: Ted Kennedy in Opposition*. New York: Steerforth Press, 1997.

Hodgson, Geoffrey. *The Gentleman from New York: Daniel Patrick Moynihan*. Boston: Houghton Mifflin, 2000.

Honan, William Homes. *Ted Kennedy, Profile of a Survivor: Edward M. Kennedy After Bobby, After Chappaquiddick, and After Three Years of Nixon*. New York: Quadrangle Books, 1972.

Horne, Gerald. *Fire This Time: The Watts Uprising and the 1960s*. Charlottesville: University Press of Virginia, 1995.

Hurley, Patricia A. "Partisan Representation, Realignment and the Senate in the 1980s." *Journal of Politics* 53 (1989): 3–33.

Isserman, Maurice. *The Other American: The Life of Michael Harrington*. New York: Public Affairs, 2000.

Isserman, Maurice, and Michael Kazin. *America Divided: The Civil War of the 1960s*. New York: Oxford University Press, 2003.

Johnson, Haynes. *Sleepwalking Through History: America in the Reagan Years*. New York: Norton, 2003.

Jones, Charles O. *The Presidency in a Separated System*. Washington, D.C.: Brookings Institution Press, 2005.

———. *The Trusteeship Presidency: Jimmy Carter and the United States Congress.* Baton Rouge: Louisiana State University Press, 1988.

Jordan, Hamilton. *Crisis: The Last Year of the Carter Presidency.* New York: Putnam Adult, 1982.

Joseph, Peter. *Good Times: An Oral History of America in the 1960s.* New York: Charterhouse, 1973.

Kaufman, Burton I. *The Presidency of James Earl Carter Jr.* Lawrence: University Press of Kansas, 1993.

Kaufman, Robert Gordon. *Henry M. Jackson: A Life in Politics.* Seattle: University of Washington Press, 2000.

Kaus, Mickey. *The End of Equality.* New York: HarperCollins, 1992.

Kennedy, Rose Fitzgerald. *Times to Remember.* New York: Doubleday, 1974.

Kerr, Peter. *Postwar British Politics: From Conflict to Consensus.* London: Routledge, 2001.

Kettl, Donald F. "The Economic Education of Lyndon Johnson: Guns, Butter, and Taxes." In *The Johnson Years,* Volume 2. Edited by Robert A. Divine. Austin: University of Texas Press, 1988.

Kogan, David, and Maurice Kogan. *The Battle for the Labour Party.* London: Fontana, 1982.

Kruse, Kevin M. *White Flight: Atlanta and the Making of Modern Conservatism.* Princeton, N.J.: Princeton University Press, 2005.

Kusch, Frank. *Battleground Chicago: The Police and the 1968 Democratic Convention.* Westport, Conn.: Praeger, 2004.

Ladd, Everett Carll, Jr. "The Brittle Mandate: Electoral Dealignment and the 1980 Presidential Election." *Political Science Quarterly* 96 (1981): 1–25.

———. "The Polls: Taxing and Spending." *Public Opinion Quarterly* 43 (1979): 126–135.

———. *Where Have All the Voters Gone?* New York: Norton, 1978.

Ladd, Everett Carll, Jr., and Charles D. Hadley. *Transformations of the American Party System: Political Coalitions from the New Deal to the 1970s.* New York: Norton, 1975.

Leuchtenberg, William E. *The FDR Years: On Roosevelt and His Legacy.* New York: Columbia University Press, 1995.

———. *In the Shadow of FDR: From Harry Truman to Ronald Reagan.* Ithaca, N.Y.: Cornell University Press, 1993.

Levin, Murray B. *Edward Kennedy: The Myth of Leadership.* Boston: Houghton Mifflin, 1980.

Lichtenstein, Nelson. *Labor's War at Home: The CIO in World War II.* New York: Temple Press, 1982.

Lieber, Nancy, ed. *Eurosocialism and America: Political Economy for the 1980s.* Philadelphia: Temple University Press, 1982.

Lipset, Seymour Martin. "Party Coalitions and the 1980 Election." In *Party Coalitions in the 1980s.* Edited by Seymour Martin Lipset. New Brunswick, N.J.: Transaction Books, 1981.

Lipset, Seymour Martin, ed. *Party Coalitions in the 1980s*. New Brunswick, N.J.: Transaction Books, 1981.

Lowi, Theodore J. *The End of Liberalism: Ideology, Policy and the Crisis of Public Authority*. New York: Norton, 1969.

Lubell, Samual. "The Roosevelt Coalition." In *New Deal: Analysis and Interpretation*. Edited by Alonzo Hamby. New York: Longman, 1981.

Lubell, Stephen. *The Future of American Politics*. New York: Harper and Row, 1965.

Maier, Thomas. *The Kennedys: America's Emerald Kings*. New York: Basic Books, 2003.

Mailer, Norman. *Miami and the Siege of Chicago: An Informal History of the American Political Conventions of 1968*. London: Weidenfeld and Nicolson, 1969.

———. *St. George and the Godfather*. New York: Arbor House, 1972.

Mansbridge, Jane J. *Why We Lost the ERA*. Chicago: University of Chicago Press, 1986.

Marable, Manning. *Race, Reform and Rebellion: The Second Reconstruction in Black America, 1945–1990*. Jackson: University Press of Mississippi, 1991.

Mason, Robert. *Richard Nixon and the Quest for a New Majority*. Chapel Hill: University of North Carolina Press, 2004.

Matusow, Allen. *Nixon's Economy Booms, Busts, Dollars and Votes*. Lawrence: University Press of Kansas, 1998.

Mayer, William G. *Divided Democrats: Ideological Unity, Party Reform and Presidential Election*. Boulder, Colo.: Westview, 1996.

McCarthy, Eugene. *Up 'til Now: A Memoir*. San Diego: Harcourt Brace Jovanovich, 1987.

McGinniss, Joe. *The Last Brother*. New York: Simon and Schuster, 1994.

McGirr, Lisa. *Suburban Warriors: The Origins of the American New Right*. Princeton, N.J.: Princeton University Press, 2002.

McGlen, Nancy E. *Women's Rights: The Struggle for Equality in the Nineteenth and Twentieth Centuries*. New York: Praeger, 1983.

Mcleod, Jack M., Jane D. Brown, and Lee B. Becker. "Watergate and the 1974 Congressional Elections." *Public Opinion Quarterly* 41 (1977): 181–195.

Miller, Arthur H. "Partisanship Re-instated? A Comparison of the 1972 and 1976 U.S. Presidential Elections." *British Journal of Political Science* 8 (1978): 129–152.

Miller, Arthur H., Warren E. Miller, Alden S. Raine, and Thad A. Brown. "A Majority Party in Disarray: Policy Polarization in the 1972 Election." *American Political Science Review* 70 (1976): 753–758.

Miroff, Bruce. *The Liberals' Moment: The McGovern Insurgency and the Identity Crisis of the Democratic Party*. Lawrence: University Press of Kansas, 2007.

Morgan, Iwan. *Beyond the Liberal Consensus: A Political History of the United States Since 1965*. London: Hurst, 1994.

———. *Deficit Government: Taxing and Spending in Modern America*. Chicago: Ivan R. Dee, 1995.

————. *Nixon*. London: Arnold, 2002.

Morgan, Kenneth O. *Labour People: Leaders and Lieutenants, Hardie to Kinnock*. Oxford: Oxford University Press, 1989.

Morris, Kenneth E. *Jimmy Carter, American Moralist*. Athens: University of Georgia Press, 1996.

Moynihan, Daniel Patrick. *Maximum Feasible Misunderstanding: Community Action in the War on Poverty*. New York: Free Press, 1969.

————. *Politics of a Guaranteed Minimum Income: The Nixon Administration and the Family Assistance Plan*. New York: Random House, 1973.

Nader, Ralph, and Mark J. Green. *Corporate Power in America*. Harmondsworth, U.K.: Penguin, 1977.

Nie, Norman, Sidney Verba, and John Petrocik. *The Changing American Voter*. Cambridge, Mass.: Harvard University Press, 1979.

O'Neill, Tip, with William Novak. *Man of the House: The Life and Political Memoirs of Speaker Tip O'Neill*. New York: Random House, 1987.

O'Sullivan, Arthur, Terri A. Sexton, and Steven M. Sheffrin. *Property Taxes and Tax Revolts: The Legacy of Proposition 13*. Cambridge: Cambridge University Press, 1995.

Olson, James S. *Saving Capitalism: The Reconstruction Finance Corporation and the New Deal, 1933–1940*. Princeton, N.J.: Princeton University Press, 1988.

Paddock, Joel. "Beyond the New Deal: Ideological Differences Between Eleven State Democratic Parties, 1956–1980." *Western Political Quarterly* 43 (1990): 181–190.

Patel, Kant, and Mark E. Rushefsky. *Politics, Power and Policy Making: The Case of Health Care Reform in the 1990s*. New York: M. E. Sharpe, 1997.

Phillips, Kevin. *The Emerging Republican Majority*. New York: Doubleday, 1970.

————. *Post-Conservative America: People, Politics and Idelogy in a Time of Crisis*. New York: Random House, 1982.

Pierce, John C., and John L. Sullivan, eds. *The Election Reconsidered*. Beverly Hills, Calif.: Sage, 1980.

Podheretz, Norman. "The New American Majority." In *Party Coalitions in the 1980s*. Edited by Seymour Martin Lipset. New Brunswick, N.J.: Transaction Books, 1981.

Pomper, Marlene M., ed. *The Election of 1976: Reports and Interpretations*. D. McKay, 1977.

Powell, Jody. *The Other Side of the Story*. New York: William Morrow, 1984.

Puddington, Arch. *Lane Kikland: Champion of American Labor*. New York: Wiley, 2005.

Quadagno, Jill S. *One Nation Uninsured: Why the U.S. Has No National Health Insurance*. New York: Oxford University Press, 2005.

Quandt, William B. *Camp David: Peacemaking and Politics*. Washington, D.C.: Brookings Institution Press, 1986.

Radosh, Ronald. *Divided They Fell: The Demise of the Democratic Party, 1964–1996*. New York: Free Press, 1998.

Ranney, Austin. *The American Elections of 1984*. Durham, N.C.: Duke University Press, 1985.

Raskin, Jonah. *For the Hell of It: The Life and Times of Abbie Hoffman.* Berkeley: University of California Press, 1996.

Ribuffo, Leo P. "Jimmy Carter and the Selling of the Presidency, 1978–1980." In *The Presidency and Domestic Policies of Jimmy Carter.* Edited by Herbert D. Rosenbaum and Alexej Ugrinsky. London: Greenwood Press, 1994.

———. *The Old Christian Right: The Protestant Far Right from the Great Depression to the Cold War.* Philadelphia: Temple University Press, 1983.

Richman, Al. "The Polls: Public Attitudes Toward the Energy Crisis." *Public Opinion Quarterly* 43 (1979): 576–585.

Robertson, David Brian. *Loss of Confidence: Politics and Policy in the 1970s.* University Park: Pennsylvania State University Press, 1998.

Rozell, Mark J. *The Press and the Carter Presidency.* Boulder, Colo.: Westview, 1989.

Rozell, Mark J., and William D. Pederson, eds. *FDR and the Modern Presidency: Leadership and Legacy.* Westport, Conn.: Praeger, 1997.

Sandbrook, Dominic. *Eugene McCarthy: The Rise and Fall of Postwar Liberalism.* New York: Knopf, 2004.

Scammon, Richard, and Ben Wattenberg. *The Real Majority.* New York: Coward-McCann, 1970.

Schlesinger, Arthur M., Jr. *The Imperial Presidency.* Boston: Houghton Mifflin, 1973.

———. *Robert Kennedy and His Times.* Boston: Houghton Mifflin Harcourt, 2002.

Schneider, William. "Democrats and Republicans, Liberals and Conservatives." In *Party Coalitions in the 1980s.* Edited by Seymour Martin Lipset. New Brunswick, N.J.: Transaction Books, 1981.

Schulman, Bruce J. *The Seventies: The Great Shift in American Culture, Society and Politics.* Cambridge, Mass.: Da Capo Press, 2002.

Shafer, Byron E. *Bifurcated Politics: Evolution and Reform in the National Party Convention.* Cambridge, Mass.: Harvard University Press, 1988.

———. *Partisan Approaches to American Politics.* London: Chatham House, 1998.

———. *Quiet Revolution: The Struggle for the Democratic Party and the Shaping of Post Reform Politics.* New York: Russell Sage, 1983.

Shirley, Craig. *Reagan's Revolution: The Untold Story of the Campaign That Started It All.* Nashville, Tenn.: Thomas Nelson, 2005.

Shrum, Robert. *No Excuses: Concessions of a Serial Campaigner.* New York: Simon and Schuster, 2007.

Silbey, Joel, ed. *The Modern American Congress 8, 1963–1989.* New York: Carlson, 1991.

Skocpol, Theda. *Diminishing Democracy.* Norman: Oklahoma University Press, 2003.

———. *Social Policy in the United States: Future Possibilities in Historical Perspective.* Princeton, N.J.: Princeton University Press, 1995.

Skocpol, Theda, and Kenneth Finegold. *State and Party in America's New Deal.* Madison: University of Wisconsin Press, 1995.

Skocpol, Theda, and John Ikenberry. "The Political Formation of the American Welfare State." *Comparative Social Research* 6 (1983): 81–148.

Skowronek, Stephen. *The Politics That Presidents Make: Leadership from John Adams to Bill Clinton.* Cambridge, Mass.: Harvard University Press, 1993.

Sloan, John W. *The Reagan Effect: Economics and Presidential Leadership*. Lawrence: University Press of Kansas, 1999.

Small, Melvin. *Antiwarriors: The Vietnam War and the Battle for America's Hearts and Minds*. New York: SR Press, 2002.

Solberg, Carl. *Hubert Humphrey: A Biography*. New York: Norton, 1994.

Stroud, Kandy. *How Jimmy Won: The Victory Campaign from Plains to the White House*. New York: William Morrow, 1977.

Sullivan, Dennis G. "Party Unity: Appearance and Reality." *Political Science Quarterly* 92 (1977): 635–646.

Sundquist, James L. *Dynamics of the Party System: Alignment and Realignment of Political Parties in the United States*. Washington, D.C.: Brookings Institution Press, 1983.

Taylor, Ronald B. *Chavez and the Farm Workers*. Boston: Beacon Press, 1972.

Thurber, Timothy Nels. *The Politics of Equality: Hubert H. Humphrey and the African American Freedom Struggle*. New York: Columbia University Press, 1999.

Troester, Rod. *Jimmy Carter as Peacemaker*. Westport, Conn.: Praeger, 1996.

Troy, Gil. *Morning in America: How Ronald Reagan Invented the 1980s*. Princeton, N.J.: Princeton University Press, 2005.

Tsongas, Paul E. *Journey of Purpose: Reflections on the Presidency, Multiculturalism, and Third Parties*. New Haven, Conn.: Yale University Press, 1995.

Updegrove, Mark K. *Second Acts: Presidential Lives and Legacies After the White House*. Guilford, Conn.: Lyons Press, 2006.

Weir, Margaret, Ann Shola Orloff, and Theda Skocpol, eds. *The Politics of Social Policy in the United States*. Princeton, N.J.: Princeton University Press, 1988.

Wells, Tom. *The War Within: America's Battle over Vietnam*. Berkeley: University of California Press, 1994.

White, John Kenneth. *New Politics of Old Values*. Lebanon, N.H.: University Press of New England, 1988.

White, Theodore. *The Making of the President, 1972*. New York: Scribner, 1985.

Wills, Gary. *The Kennedy Imprisonment: A Meditation on Power*. Boston: Houghton Mifflin, 2002.

———. *The Kennedys: A Shattered Illusion*. London: Orbis Books, 1980.

———. *Under God: Religion and American Politics*. New York: Simon and Schuster, 1990.

Wilson, William Julius. *The Truly Disadvantaged: The Inner City, the Underclass and Public Policy*. Chicago: University of Chicago Press, 1988.

Witcover, Jules. *Marathon: The Pursuit of the Presidency, 1972–1976*. New York: Viking Press, 1977.

Woods, Randall. *LBJ: Architect of American Ambition*. New York: Simon and Schuster, 2003.

Woodward, Bob. *Shadow: Five Presidents and the Legacy of Watergate*. New York: Simon and Schuster, 2001.

Woodward, J. David. *The America That Reagan Built*. Westport, Conn.: Greenwood Press, 2006.

Index